Foundations of Atlantis,
Ancient Astronauts and
Other Alternative Pasts

Foundations of Atlantis, Ancient Astronauts and Other Alternative Pasts

148 Documents Cited by Writers of Fringe History, Translated with Annotations

EDITED BY JASON COLAVITO

McFarland & Company, Inc., Publishers

Jefferson, North Carolina

LIBRARY OF CONGRESS CATALOGUING-IN-PUBLICATION DATA

Foundations of Atlantis, ancient astronauts and other
alternative pasts : 148 documents cited by writers of fringe history,
translated with annotations / edited by Jason Colavito.
p.   cm.
Includes bibliographical references and index.

ISBN 978-0-7864-9645-7 (softcover : acid free paper) ∞
ISBN 978-1-4766-1940-8 (ebook)

1. History—Errors, inventions, etc.   2. Geographical myths.
I. Colavito, Jason, editor of compilation.

D10.F678 2015   001.94—dc23   2015000182

BRITISH LIBRARY CATALOGUING DATA ARE AVAILABLE

Cover image © Dreamstime.com

Printed in the United States of America

*McFarland & Company, Inc., Publishers
Box 611, Jefferson, North Carolina 28640
www.mcfarlandpub.com*

Contents

Introduction

The Yale sociologist William Graham Sumner wrote in his 1906 book *Folkways* that learning the ultimate origins of historical claims was important because "a complete and unbiased history hardly exists. It may be a moral impossibility. Every student during his academic period ought to get up one bit of history thoroughly from the ultimate sources, in order to convince himself what history is not."[1] It is precisely this question of historiography—where do historical claims come from?—that forms the subject of the collection you are about to read. If Mark Twain was correct that "the very ink with which all history is written is merely fluid prejudice"[2] it behooves us to understand where our ideas about history come from, and how those ideas can be twisted to support extreme ideas about the past. But this is not how fringe historians—the people who hold unusual or unsupported beliefs about history—view ancient texts.

Fringe history can be difficult to define but generally refers to the writings of non-specialists that advocate supernatural, extraterrestrial, or conspiratorial explanations for history. These tend to rely on selective evidence and a broad generalizations from a narrow range of evidence to make sweeping claims. These works frequently claim that mainstream historians, archaeologists, or the government are purposely hiding particular historical truths that only the fringe historian is able to discover, usually through appeal to obsolete literature, unusual interpretations of historical documents, or wide-ranging conspiracies.[3] Ronald H. Fritze noted the challenge of defining fringe history, which he calls pseudo-history, and offered this explanation:

> Objective scholars with an honest agenda view evidence without bias or preconceptions—or at least they try hard to guard against them as far as it is humanly possible. Pseudo-historians usually approach their subjects with preconceptions or a hidden agenda. As a result, often one would find a pseudo-historian picking and choosing their evidence—to bolster their case.[4]

More specifically, fringe history can be defined by a methodology, one that centers on making claims of fact (Did Atlantis exist? Did Ezekiel see a space ship?) based upon cherry-picked evidence and dubious interpretations, and one that confuses possibilities (Did the Vikings colonize Panama?) with probabilities, assuming that if there is even a small chance of an event having happened, it must therefore be evidence toward a broad revision of history, no matter how slim the evidence to support such a possibility.

One of the most famous fringe history figures is the writer Erich von Däniken, a proponent of the ancient astronaut theory. He has provided as good an explanation as any of the methodology of fringe historians of all stripes when it comes to dealing with the texts and documents that make up the historical record: "If we take things literally, much that was once fitted into the mosaic of our past with great difficulty becomes quite plausible: not only the relevant clues in ancient texts, but also the 'hard facts' which offer themselves to our critical gaze all over the globe."[5] Unfortunately, revising one's translation of texts to include spacecraft and aliens is not taking texts literally but rather imposing a belief system tied to a conspiratorial view of history. In other words, von Däniken wishes his audience to see him as the controlling authority on the interpretation of texts through appeal to his ability to discern the "truth" hidden within. Most fringe historians similarly seek to control how the audience interprets and interacts with texts, which is one reason that such writers rarely present the original texts for the audience to examine themselves.

Such beliefs arise from continued exposure to one-sided media presentations such as *Ancient Aliens* that reinforce a conspiratorial view of history whereby a shadowy academic-government elite purposely hide or suppress the truth about exciting episodes in history in an effort to assert control over historical narratives, ultimately to control everyday people's lives. In far too many cases, the "suppressed" history conveniently supports the political or social beliefs of the audience for such theories. To that end, lost civilization theories tend to emphasize the heroism of the advocate's own culture and race; ancient astronaut theories drawn on ufology's conspiratorial view of government as well as (again) older colonialist and imperialist views of race; and everywhere fringe history attempts to find ways to give the Bible a more satisfying foundation in supposed "fact"—be it alien, Atlantean, or conspiratorial.

Extreme ideas about ancient history are extremely popular. They command untold hours of cable television coverage. For example, in a single week in May 2014, the H2 network showed more than 40 hours of conspiracy and fringe-history themed programming, including 20 hours of *Ancient Aliens* alone. And this was not an unusual occurrence. Between the History Channel, the H2 network, the American Heroes Channel, and other outlets, fringe history viewers with a digital cable package could routinely watch more than 100 hours of fringe history programming each week in 2014.[6] Similarly, surveys have found a consistently high level of belief in extreme claims about history among the public at large. Surveys routinely find that around one in five Americans believes aliens have visited the earth or that ancient secret societies like the Freemasons are secretly scheming to take over the world.[7] One recent survey found more than three-quarters of Americans say they believe there is good evidence that aliens have visited the earth in the past, and more than a third think that the Great Pyramid and Stonehenge are evidence in favor of the ancient astronaut theory.[8]

Nevertheless, despite the popularity of such theories and the hundreds of books published on such subjects since the rise of the modern fringe history movement in the 1960s, the fringe authors and speakers who present themselves as scholars and truth-tellers have never published a critical edition of the texts they claim support their points of view. The closest fringe historians have come to such a sourcebook was *Wonders in the Sky* (2009) by the famed ufologist Jacques Vallée and his co-author, Chris Aubeck, which collected what its authors claimed were excerpts from primary sources on the UFO phenomenon from ancient times down to the beginning of the modern UFO era in 1947. However, as we shall see in this volume, the two authors were no linguists and their volume was deeply flawed. Because they did not know their sources in the original, and frequently not even in scholarly translation, many of their "documents" were secondhand summaries, mistranslations, and in several instances fabrications by the secondhand sources they used. Several of their pieces of "evidence" are given in this volume in the primary sources neither author read. If Vallée and Aubeck represented the "best" of fringe history scholarship, other authors were much less careful and their work still less useful for the student of ancient mysteries.

The purpose of this book therefore is to provide a selection of documents that are the ultimate sources for many of the most popular "alternative" history claims, particularly those involving ancient astronauts, lost civilizations like Atlantis, pre–Columbian Old World contact with the New World, and the alleged descendants of Jesus Christ and Mary Magdalene. When fringe history authors claim that "ancient texts" support their views about prehistoric extraterrestrial contact, ancient conspiracies, or world-bestriding Aryan super-cultures, we are right to ask whether there is truth to these assertions. Unsurprisingly, many authors who make extreme claims for extraordinary material in ancient texts fail to show the proof of their claims by citing directly from the texts in question, often because they have never read the originals, and sometimes because the original texts have been so manipulated as to be unrecognizable. It is only by reviewing the original documents that we can evaluate fringe historians' claims about them.

Fringe historians draw from an astonishing array of material crossing the boundaries of time, space, cultures, and language in service of their exotic ideas about the past, but their lack of careful citation (or sometimes any familiarity at all with the source texts) makes it difficult if not impossible for the interested reader to trace the claims back to their sources. To give but the most extreme example: Ancient astronaut theorist David Childress cites simply to the *Mahabharata* a passage he claims records a nuclear bomb strike in prehistory. Without a clear citation, there is no way to know where in the 1.8 million words of the epic Sanskrit poem the original text can be found, which has the obvious benefit of preventing skeptical readers from discovering that his "quotation," taken from excerpts provided by earlier fringe writers, was in fact deceptively-edited and mistranslated. The original can be found in this volume as texts **62** and **63**.

This book, therefore, has several aims:

- To provide original documents in translation from historical sources related to a variety of claims typically classified as "fringe history"
- To provide bibliographic information allowing interested readers to locate the original documents, including their original authors (if known), full citation, date of composition, and original language of composition
- To provide references to specific fringe history theories that use each document for support, along with a selection of fringe history authors who have cited said documents
- To provide brief critical commentary outlining the history of each document, conventional interpretations, and its (mis)use in fringe history sources

Source Selection and Book Structure

The passages included in this volume provide English translations (and the occasional work originally in English) of a variety of texts cited by fringe historians. They cover a geographically and chronologically vast territory, from the very earliest civilizations (Egypt and Mesopotamia) to the early twentieth century, and from East Asia to South America and beyond. Because the number of languages involved is so vast—Akkadian, Arabic, Chinese, French, Greek, Latin, Quiche, Sanskrit, Spanish, and many more—it is impossible for even the most polyglot linguist to master the original text of every passage published herein.

Because it would be cost prohibitive to commission or license new translations for every text cited herein, in the interest of providing an affordable volume for the general reader, I have attempted to provide useful translations from the most accessible sources. In many cases, this involves reprinting a translation from a standard source. In every case where I have used reprinted material from earlier translations, I have corrected the translations against either the original language of the text or the most authoritative modern translations. Minor changes, such as modernizing the spelling of names, occur without special acknowledgment; major revisions are indicated in the source notes for the relevant text with details of what has been revised from the original published translation.

In other cases, I have produced original translations for documents that have never before been translated into English, whose standard translations are inaccurate, or which cannot be reprinted in standard translation due to copyright. In every case, I have attempted to provide translations from a source as close to the original as possible, usually directly from the primary source text. In a few cases, this was not possible. In those cases, I have translated from the most authoritative edition available in a language with which I am familiar. These are noted in the source notes for the relevant passages. Again, where possible, I have correlated these translations with the most authoritative modern editions in the languages familiar to me.

In organizing and sequencing the passages, certain difficulties arise. Chronology, geography, authorship, language, and the hypothesis a text is used to support could all be reasonably applied to organize passages. Instead, I have chosen to place passages together in chapters defined by a loose theme that repeats in fringe history works. Within each chapter, texts are roughly organized so that reading the chapter from beginning to end will tell a more or less coherent story about that topic. For example, the first chapter covers the mythic prehistory of the earth from the creation to the time of the Flood. While the texts themselves are not presented in their chronological order of composition, they are arranged in the (mythic) chronology of their contents so the reader would follow events from the creation of the earth to the activities of the Watchers and the Nephilim as they interact with the first generations of humans. Subsequent chapters follow this model as much as is practicable.

Chapter I looks at the primeval history of the world in ancient legend, focusing on the story of the Sons of God, a group of fallen angels who fathered a race of giants called the Nephilim in the Book of Genesis, a story that developed into a mythology known as the "Watchers," after the name given to the fallen angels in an apocryphal text called the Book of Enoch, frequently cited by fringe history writers. Their story formed the foundation for many obscure ancient legends and modern stories of the arrival of extraterrestrials from outer space who civilized ancient peoples.

Chapter II examines the mythology of the Egyptian pyramids as antediluvian constructions, particularly stories that focus on the supernatural construction of the pyramids, their great antiquity, the treasures and scientific wonders within them, and their relationship to the Watchers discussed in Chapter I.

Chapter III covers the Great Flood and its immediate aftermath with passages from Mesopotamian, Greek, and Hebrew authors outlining the development of the legend in the Ancient Near East. This will lead into a discussion of the fate of the Watchers and the Giants, which fringe historians have claimed were really aliens or Atlanteans.

Chapter IV examines ancient encounters with flying craft and sky beings, while chapters

V through VII present texts used to support claims about lost civilizations, knowledge provided by extraterrestrials, and high technology in ancient times. These chapters present classic fringe history evidence of miraculous machines, otherworldly visitations, strange lights in the sky, and assorted phenomena referenced in many fringe history texts.

Turning from the Old World to the New, Chapter VIII examines the mysteries of the Americas, including the Aztecs, the Maya, and the Inca. Passages will explore these cultures' architectural wonders, their creation myths, and the stories of "white" gods who came to civilize them from afar—passages often used to suggest alien, Old World, or Atlantean intervention in the most distant past.

Chapter IX presents textual evidence used to support claims of pre–Columbian trans–Atlantic contacts between the Old and New Worlds. Material in this section will build on previous discussion of white gods to look at evidence for trans-oceanic contact in historic times, including claimed contact with the Americas among the Chinese, Moors, Vikings, and many more.

Chapter X examines unusual claims made about Jesus Christ, Mary Magdalene, and the Holy Grail, particularly those involving the alleged marriage of Jesus and Mary Magdalene and the possibility of offspring from that union, as well as legends that Christ survived the crucifixion. The Holy Grail has been variously claimed as the womb of Mary Magdalene, a pre–Christian relic, or a rock from outer space, and the passages here will examine the foundations for such claims.

Chapter XI presents miscellaneous mysteries that do not fit into the previous categories. These include an ancient prophecy of the end of the world, the first Loch Ness Monster sighting, and other assorted adventures in the weird.

A final chapter presents modern fabrications that purport to be ancient and have been accepted as such by fringe historians (and sometimes mainstream historians) at various points in history, or otherwise describe alleged ancient material. These texts are often hoaxes, like the first newspaper account of the alleged lost Egyptian civilization of the Grand Canyon, or fraudulent discoveries, like a set of inscribed lead artifacts found in Arizona in the 1920s, designed to fool.

However, this organizational framework should not be taken as definitive; indeed, there are recurring themes and motifs, as well as intertexual connections, that cut across chapters. I have used ample cross-referencing to highlight the most important of these.

Chapters begin with an editorial overview briefly outlining the material under discussion and its role in fringe history theories. Then the ancient texts are presented without further introduction. Each passage is numbered sequentially for cross-referencing, and each begins with a formal citation of its author (if known), the title of the work from which it is drawn, referencing information for the original work, its date of composition, and the original language of composition. To assist readers in placing the text within the milieu of fringe history, the prefatory material also lists the major fringe theories the information in the text has been used to support. I have also indicated when a text is cited in one of the sample works of fringe history I have used as references in compiling this anthology. Because most fringe books have been published in varying editions, including now ebook editions, I have not provided page numbers to the specific copies of these fringe texts I consulted. Each passage ends with a note on the sources for the text. After each document (or series of related passages), I provide a critical commentary on the passage. The commentaries vary in length and are intended to explore specific scholarly issues related to each text, mainstream interpretations of the text, and how the text has been interpreted or misused by fringe historians. These commentaries, by their nature, cannot be exhaustive, but instead are intended to provide avenues for further research.

I would like to thank historical archaeologist Dr. Jeb J. Card and physicist Dr. Aaron Adair for their insightful comments and criticisms on this book while it was in manuscript form. Their contributions have improved it greatly, and it goes without saying that any remaining errors are entirely my own.

Notes

1. William Graham Sumner, *Folkways* (Boston: Ginn and Company, 1906), 636.
2. Mark Twain, *Following the Equator* (Hartford: American Publishing, 1897), 459.
3. For overviews and definitions, see Michael Barkun, *A Culture of Conspiracy: Apocalyptic Visions in Contemporary America*, 2nd ed. (Berkeley: University of California, 2013); Ronald H. Fritze, *Invented Knowledge: False History, Fake Science, and Pseudo-Religions* (London: Reaktion Books, 2009); Garrett Fagan (ed.), *Archaeological Fantasies: How Pseudoarchaeology Misrepresents the Past and Misleads the Public* (London: Routledge, 2006).
4. Fritze, *Invented Knowledge*, 12.
5. Erich von Däniken, *Chariots of the Gods? Unsolved Mysteries of the Past*, trans. Michael Heron (New York: Bantam, 1973), 65.
6. Based on published television listings for the week of May 26–June 1, 2014. The exact content of each hour could not always be determined, and for research purposes programs exploring fringe and conspiracy themes were counted even if they ultimately came to skeptical conclusions.
7. Public Policy Polling survey, March 27–30, 2013; see also discussion in Christopher Bader, Carson Mencken, and Joseph O. Baker, *Paranormal America: Ghost Encounters, UFO Sightings, Bigfoot Hunts, and Other Curiosities in Religion and Culture* (New York: New York University Press, 2010).
8. Kelton Research survey for National Geographic Channel, May 21–May 29, 2012.

Abbreviations

Types of Fringe History and Alternative Archaeology

Astro	Ancient Astronaut Theory
Atlantis	Atlantis Myth
General	General Unexplained Mystery
Holy	Holy Bloodline Conspiracy
Hyper	Hyperdiffusionism
Prehistoric	Prehistoric Advanced Civilization
Theo	Theosophy
UFO	Unidentified Flying Objects

Representative Fringe Works of Ancient History and Archaeology

AA	*Ancient Aliens*, History Channel and H2 (2009–present)
AF	Scott Wolter, *Akhenaten to the Founding Fathers* (2013)
AW	Ignatius Donnelly, *Atlantis: The Antediluvian World* (1882)
BC	Ivan Van Sertima, *They Came Before Columbus* (1976)
CG	Erich von Däniken, *Chariots of the Gods?* (1968)
EV	Jacques Bergier, *Extraterrestrial Visitation from Prehistoric Times to the Present* (1972)
FG	Graham Hancock, *Fingerprints of the Gods* (1995)
GG	Erich von Däniken, *Gold of the Gods* (1970)
MM	Jacques Bergier and Louis Pauwels, *Morning of the Magicians* (1960)
SD	Helena Blavatsky, *The Secret Doctrine* (1888)
SM	Robert Temple, *The Sirius Mystery* (1976)
TP	Zecharia Sitchin, *Twelfth Planet* (1976)
WS	Jacques Vallée and Chris Aubeck, *Wonders in the Sky* (2009)

Prologue: The Origins
of Fringe History

The modern origins of fringe history can be a bit difficult to pinpoint since mainstream ideas in the nineteenth and twentieth centuries were often, by today's standards, every bit as strange as fringe ideas. The most important early work of fringe history was likely Josiah Priest's *American Antiquities* (1833), one of the first books to make pseudohistorical arguments about ancient texts and archaeological sites through drawing dramatic conclusions about an uncritical assembly of anomalies and unusual facts. Priest's pseudohistorical arguments centered on a lost white race and its relationship to Biblical history. Other major works of the early period include Ignatius Donnelly's *Atlantis: The Antediluvian World* (1882) and Helena Blavatsky's *Secret Doctrine* (1888). Most modern fringe archaeology theories derive directly or indirectly from one of these three texts.

Donnelly laid out the methodology that would serve modern fringe history, explaining that in reading ancient texts one must understand "that the gods and goddesses of the ancient Greeks, the Phœnicians, the Hindoos, and the Scandinavians were simply the kings, queens, and heroes of Atlantis; and the acts attributed to them in mythology are a confused recollection of real historical events."[1] This hypothesis is recognizably the same as the later ancient astronaut theory, with the human actors swapped out for aliens, and also the same as every other fringe claim that asks readers to engage in a rationalized interpretation of mythology, such as the lost civilization claims of David Hatcher Childress and Graham Hancock.

But this view, which fringe historians owe to Donnelly, is not his. It originates in euhemerism, a rationalizing attempt to use reason to rid Greek mythology of the supernatural, created by and named for Euhemerus in the fourth century BCE. Little of his work survives, primarily in a summary in the extant work of Diodorus Siculus (*Historical Library* 5.41–67) and a summary of its lost section in Eusebius (*Praeparatio Evangelica* 2.45). His followers would go on to propose all manner of rationalizations to explain myth in "scientific" terms: One, for example, claimed that the Argonauts' Golden Fleece, taken from the magical Golden Ram, had really been the skin of a man named Mr. Ram (*Krios*), who had been skinned and gilded, while another called it a ram-shaped figurehead on a ship (Diodorus 4.47.9). These explanations were not based on historical investigation but rather on what sounded the most logical to writers who did not believe in the supernatural and refused to accept the concept of symbolism, much like modern fringe theorists' interpretations of ancient texts, and even some modern scientists' efforts to explain myths and legends in "scientific" terms, such as

9

claiming vampires had porphyria or that the plagues of Egypt were caused by the eruption of the volcano on Thera. Our prologue will review the euhemeristic idea as precedent for the fringe history that follows.

Note

1. Ignatius Donnelly, *Atlantis: The Antediluvian World* (New York: Harper & Brothers, 1910), 2.

1. Conflict between Faith and Euhemerism

Diodorus Siculus
Library of History
Book 6, frag. 1
c. 60–30 BCE
Greek
Preserved in Eusebius, *Praeparatio Evangelica* 2.45
c. 313 CE

With regard then to gods the men of old have handed down to their posterity two sets of notions. For some, say they, are eternal and imperishable, as the Sun and Moon and the other heavenly bodies, and besides these the winds, and the rest who partake of the like nature with them; for each of these has an eternal origin and eternal continuance. Other deities they say were of the earth; but, because of the benefits which they conferred on mankind, they have received immortal honour and glory, as Heracles, Dionysus, Aristaeus, and the others like them.

Concerning the terrestrial gods many various tales have been handed down in the historical and mythological writers. Among the historians Euhemerus, the author of the *Sacred Record*, has written a special history; and of the mythologists Homer, Hesiod, Orpheus, and such others as these, have invented very marvellous myths concerning the gods: and we shall endeavour to run over what both classes have recorded concisely and with a view to due proportion.

Source: Translated by E. H. Gifford in Eusebius, *Evangelicae Praeparationis*, vol. 3, part 1, trans. and ed. E. H. Gifford (Oxford: E Typographeo Academico, 1903), 65–66.

Commentary: *In expanding on the same theme in* On the Nature of the Gods *Cicero describes those who claimed that the gods were deified humans, including Persaeus (1.15) and Euhemerus and Ennius (1.42). He himself believed that "unlearned" common Greeks and Romans had wrongly promoted many humans to divine status, though not the immortal Olympians (3.15, 19).*

2. Euhemerus Identifies the Gods as Humans

Plutarch
Moralia 5.26.23 (Isis and Osiris 23)
1st century CE
Greek

[Atheists] convert all divine matters into human, giving also a large license to the impostures of Euhemerus the Messenian, who out of his own brain contrived certain memoirs of a most incredible and imaginary mythology, and thereby spread all manner of Atheism throughout the world. This he did by describing all the received Gods under the style of generals, sea-captains, and kings, whom he makes to have lived in the more remote and ancient times, and to be recorded in golden characters in a certain country called Panchon, with which notwithstanding never any man, either Barbarian or Grecian, had the good fortune to meet, except Euhemerus alone, who (it seems) sailed to the land of the Panchoans and Triphyllians, that neither have nor ever had a being.

Source: Translated by William Baxter in *Plutarch's Morals*, ed. William W. Goodwin (Boston: Little, Brown, and Company, 1874), 84–85.

Commentary: *Part of the account alluded to above is preserved in Eusebius (Praeparatio Evangelica 2.45), quoting Diodorus, summarizing the same passage from Euhemerus, where the mysterious (and fictional) land is called Panchaea. Plutarch, however, is more explicit about Euhemerus' specific claims about the gods as prehistoric humans.*

3. Pagan Religion Grew from Funeral Rites for Dead Kings
Cyprian
Treatise 6.1
On the Vanity of Idols
247 CE
Latin

That those are no gods whom the common people worship, is known from this: they were formerly kings, who on account of their royal memory subsequently began to be adored by their people even in death. Thence temples were founded to them; thence images were sculptured to retain the countenances of the deceased by the likeness; and men sacrificed victims, and celebrated festal days, by way of giving them honour. Thence to posterity those rites became sacred, which at first had been adopted as a consolation.

Source: Translated by Robert Ernest Wallis in *The Writings of Cyprian, Bishop of Carthage*, vol. 1, trans. Robert Ernest Wallis (Edinburgh: T. & T. Clark, 1868), 443–444.

Commentary: *Cyprian was the Christian bishop of Carthage; while some have suggested he is not the author of the above text, most scholars now believe the traditional attribution is correct. Euhemerism was useful for Christian polemicists because it provided a pagan precedent for condemning the pagan gods as false idols. Tertullian offers a parallel text in* On Idolatry *15, citing euhemeristic beliefs in the human origins of the gods ("even their worshipers agree that the gods of the nations were once men") as reason not to worship them. But, by contrast, Augustine in* City of God *7.33 said that the pagan gods were really "impure demons who wish to be thought gods," thus diabolizing the pagan supernatural, as did Commodian in* Instructiones *3, where he identified the pagan gods with the evil angels called Watchers (see* **9, 10**).[1] *The latter belief fuels ancient astronaut theories, which substitute aliens for demons, angels, and gods. The interested reader can see the process of reinterpretation at work by comparing the pagan account of Roman king Numa's dalliance with a goddess and receipt of wisdom from her in Plutarch's* Life of Numa *(4.1–2, 22.2–4) to its Christian reinvention as seduction by a demon in* City of God *7.34. A euhemeristic reinterpretation occurs in* The Gods Were Astronauts *(2002) where in a brief aside ancient astronaut theorist Erich von Däniken rationalizes the story, implying that the goddess or demon was in fact a space alien.*

Note

1. Commodian follows Jubilees in making the Watchers come as agents of God before being seduced by human women (**10**), in contradistinction to the narrative in 1 Enoch, where their lust brings them down from heaven (**9**).

I

The Watchers and the World Before the Flood

For fringe historians, the Flood of Noah is one of the defining events of world history, and the events before the Flood are therefore of pivotal importance for understanding the origins and development of the human race. Among the antediluvian figures, none holds so high a place in the fringe history pantheon as the mysterious Sons of God (*benê hā Elōhîm*) of the Bible, traditionally held to be fallen angels, and identified with the Watchers of apocryphal Jewish literature. For mainstream scholars, these beings are likely a Jewish interpretation of Near Eastern myths of gods and semi-divine heroes (as the ancients themselves suspected),[1] but when Zecharia Sitchin, in *TP*, identified the Watchers with a shadowy group of gods from Mesopotamian lore, the Anunnaki, the Watchers became the essential ingredient for fringe history's myth of the human past, appearing as aliens in ancient astronaut works by Erich von Däniken and others, and as a prehistoric cult in the works of Andrew Collins, Philip Gardiner, and others. This was all the more ironic since it was a different set of Mesopotamian figures, the *apkallu*, or sages—whose most famous member was Oannes—that many scholars believe were the real inspiration for the Watchers.

Various fringe authors like those mentioned above have identified these beings as extraterrestrials, trans-dimensional beings, survivors of a lost civilization, or a prehistoric wisdom cult. Among some Biblical literalists who call themselves Nephilim theorists, such as L. A. Marzulli, they are and remain the agents of Satan, continuing to do evil on earth through their children, the infamous Nephilim, or giants. Marzulli, for example, sees these beings as an ingredient in a Satanic conspiracy, one that mainstream science is trying to hide from the public by covering up discoveries of the bones of giants. It is for this reason that fringe theorists of all stripes seek out the bones of giants, in order to prove that biblical events were literally true.

As we shall see, the effort to provide a scientific basis for biblical stories was and remains one of the motivating forces in fringe historiography, something that fringe historians took over from Victorian scholarship, where for example writers like Jacob Bryant and John Bathurst Deane argued that all pagan mythology was a misunderstanding of Genesis by the corrupt descendants of Noah after the Flood, and even mainstream scholars like George Smith assumed that the similarities between the Bible and the Mesopotamian myths emerging from the cuneiform tablets he was among the first to translate proved the historicity of Genesis.

This chapter, therefore, looks at the beginning of things: the widespread Near Eastern myth, one of the oldest recorded in writing, of the gods and demigods who bequeathed civilization to the earliest humans.

Note

1. See Amar Annus, "On the Origin of the Watchers: A Comparative Study of the Antediluvian Wisdom in Mesopotamian and Jewish Traditions," *Journal of the Study of the Pseudepigrapha* 19 (2010): 277–320.

4. Aliens Create Humans, Build Babylon

Enûma Eliš 1.1–9, 143–162; 4.93–146; 5.1–8; 6:1–65
c. 1500 BCE (extant text c. 7th c. BCE)
Old Babylonian
Astro, Prehistoric, Theo
Discussion in AA, CG, MM, SM, TP

TABLET ONE

When the heavens above were yet unnamed,
And the name of the earth beneath had not been recorded,
Apsu, the oldest of beings, their progenitor,
"Mummu" Tiâmat, who bare each and all of them—
Their waters were merged into a single mass.
A field had not been measured, a marsh had not been searched out,
When of the gods none was shining,
A name had not been recorded, a fate had not been fixed,
The gods came into being in the midst of them.
[...]
Mother Hubur,[1] who fashioned all things,
Set up the unrivalled weapon, she spawned huge serpents,
Sharp of tooth, pitiless in attack.
She filled their bodies with venom instead of blood,
Grim, monstrous serpents, arrayed in terror,
She decked them with brightness, she fashioned them in exalted forms,
So that fright and horror might overcome him that looked upon them,
So that their bodies might rear up, and no man resist their attack,
She set up the Viper, and the Snake, and the monster Lahamu,
The Whirlwind, the ravening Lion, the Scorpion-Man,
The mighty Weather-Beast, the Fish-Man, the Bull-Man
They carried the Weapon which spared not, nor flinched from the battle.
Most mighty were Tiâmat's decrees, they could not be resisted,
Thus she caused eleven monsters of this kind to come into being,
Among the gods, her first-born son who had collected her company,
That is to say, Kingu, she set on high, she made him the great one amongst them,
Leader of the hosts in battle, disposer of the troops,
Bearer of the firmly grasped weapon, attacker in the fight,
He who in the battle is the master of the weapon,
She appointed, she made him to sit down on a throne, (saying,)

"I have uttered the incantation for thee. I have magnified thee in the assembly of the gods.

"I have filled his [*sic*, read 'thy'] hand with the sovereignty of the whole company of the gods.

"Mayest thou be magnified, thou who art my only spouse,

"May the Anunnaki make great thy renown over all of them."

She gave him the TABLET OF DESTINIES, she fastened it on his breast, (saying,)

"As for thee, thy command shall not fall empty, whatsoever goeth forth from thy mouth shall be established."

When Kingu was raised on high and had taken to the level of Anu

He fixed the destinies for the gods his sons,

"Open your mouths, let the Fire-god be quenched,

"He who is glorious in battle and is most mighty, shall do great deeds."

TABLET FOUR

[...]

Tiâmat and Marduk, the envoy of the gods, roused themselves,

They advanced to fight each other, they drew nigh in battle.

The Lord cast his net and made it to enclose her,

The evil wind that had its place behind him he let out in her face.

Tiâmat opened her mouth to its greatest extent,

Marduk made the evil wind to enter whilst her lips were unclosed.

The raging winds filled out her belly,

Her heart was gripped, her mouth opened wide.

Marduk grasped the spear, he split up her belly,

He clave open her bowels, he pierced the heart,

He brought her to nought, he destroyed her life.

He cast down her carcase, he took up his stand upon it,

After Marduk had slain Tiâmat the chief,

Her host was scattered, her levies became fugitive,

And the gods, her allies, who had marched at her side,

Quaked with terror, and broke and ran

And betook themselves to flight to save their lives.

But they found themselves hemmed in, they could not escape,

Marduk tied them up, he smashed their weapons.

They were cast into the net, and they were caught in the snare,

Concealed in corners, they filled the world with cries of grief.

They received [Marduk's] chastisement, they were confined in restraint,

And the Eleven Creatures which Tiâmat had filled with awfulness,

The company of the devils that marched at her right hand,

He threw in fetters, he bound their arms.

They and their resistance he trod under his feet.

The god Kingu who had been magnified over them

He crushed, bound, and reckoned him as among the Dead Gods.

Marduk took from him the TABLET OF DESTINIES, which should never have been his,

He sealed it with a seal and fastened it on his breast

After he had crushed and overthrown his enemies,
He made the haughty enemy to be like the dust underfoot.
He established completely Anshar's victory over the enemy,
The valiant Marduk achieved the object of Nudimmud (Ea),[2]
He imposed strict restraint on the gods whom he had made captive.
He turned back to Tiâmat whom he had defeated,
The Lord trampled on the rump of Tiâmat,
With his unsparing club he clave her skull.
He slit open the arteries of her blood.
He caused the North Wind to carry it away to a place underground.
His fathers (i.e., the gods) looked on, they rejoiced, they were glad.
They brought unto him offerings of triumph and peace,
The Lord paused, he examined Tiâmat's carcase,
To cleave the mass, he worked cunningly.
He slit Tiâmat open like a flat fish into two pieces,
The one half he raised up and shaded the heavens therewith,
He pulled the bolt, he posted a guard,
He ordered them not to let her water escape.
He crossed heaven, he contemplated the regions thereof.
He betook himself to the abode of Nudimmud (Ea) that is opposite to the Apsu,
The Lord Marduk measured the dimensions of the Deep,
He founded Ešarra, a place like unto it,
The abode Ešarra, which he made to be heaven.
He made Anu, Bel and Ea to inhabit their shrines.

Tablet Five

He appointed the Stations for the great gods,
He set in heaven the Stars of the Zodiac which are their likenesses.
He fixed the year, he appointed the limits thereof.
He set up for the twelve months three stars apiece.
After he had structured the days of the year,
He founded the Station of Nibir (Jupiter) to settle their boundaries,
That none might exceed or fall short.
He set the Station of Enlil and Ea thereby.
[...]

Tablet Six

On hearing the words of the gods,
The heart of Marduk moved him to carry out the works of a craftsman.
He opened his mouth, he spake to Ea that which he had planned in his heart,
He gave counsel (saying):
"I will solidify blood, I will form bone.
"I will set up a savage, 'Man' shall be his name.
"Verily, I will create the savage 'Man.'
"The service of the gods shall be established, and I will set them (i.e., the gods) free.

The equation between events in space and on the ground has a long history in astrology, dating back at least to Mesopotamia if not earlier. This fifteenth century woodcut depicts a clergyman blessing a farmer while Mars beams down from above. The clergyman is labeled Jupiter and the farmer Sagittarius. Although the scene is an astrological allegory, it can easily be misread as a visitation from space men, much as fringe writers like Zecharia Sitchin did with Babylonian texts like the *Enûma Eliš* (Library of Congress).

"I will make twofold the ways of the gods, and I will beautify them.
"They are grouped together in one place, but they shall be partitioned in two."
Ea answered and spake a word unto him
For the consolation of the gods he repeated unto him a word of counsel (saying):
"Let one brother of theirs be given,
"Let him suffer destruction that men may be fashioned.
"Let the great gods be assembled,
"Let this guilty one be given in order that they (i.e., the other gods) may endure."
Marduk assembled the great gods,
Graciously, he issued a decree,
He opened his mouth, he addressed the gods;
The King spake a word unto the Anunnaki (saying):
"Verily, that which I spake unto you aforetime was true.
"Render unto me with solemnity the utter truth:
"Who was it that created the strife,
"Who caused Tiâmat to revolt, to join battle with me?

"Let him who created the strife be given up,

"I will cause him to suffer punishment, that ye shall rest undisturbed."

The great gods, the Igigi, answered him,

Unto the King of the gods of heaven and of earth, the Prince of the gods, their lord (they said):

"It was Kingu who created the strife,

"Who made Tiâmat to revolt, to join battle with thee."

They bound him in fetters and brought him before Ea,

They inflicted punishment on him, they let his blood,

From his blood he (i.e., Ea) fashioned mankind

He laid on them the service of the gods, and he set the gods free.

After Ea had fashioned man

He laid the service of the gods upon him.

For that work was beyond (human) comprehension,

Ingeniously planned by Marduk and executed skilfully by Nudimmud (Ea).

Marduk, the King of the gods, divided the gods,

He set the Anunnaki up on high and far down below.

He set them as guard for Anu to protect his decrees.

Three hundred he set in heaven to serve as guard.

After, he decreed the ways of the earth,

In heaven and in the earth six hundred gods did he assign.

After he had issued the decrees

And to the Anunnaki of the heaven and the earth given their allotments,

The Anunnaki opened their mouths,

They spake unto Marduk, their lord, (saying):

"O thou Lord who hast established our deliverance,

"What benefit have we conferred upon thee?

"Come, let us make a shrine, whose name shall be renowned;

"A chamber for our nightly rest, let us take our ease therein,

"Let us erect a shrine to serve as house for his throne.

"On the day that we finish this we will take our ease therein."

When Marduk heard these words,

The features of his face shone brightly like the day.

(He said), "Construct Babylon, the construction whereof ye desire

"Let the bricks be moulded, fashion a splendid shrine."

The Anunnaki worked the mould,

They spent one year entire in making the necessary bricks.

At the commencement of the second year

They raised up the summit of Esagila, like unto the Apsu.

They made the ziggurat of the Apsu;

Unto Marduk, Enlil, Ea [shrines] they appointed as a dwelling.

Before them he (Marduk) was seated majestically.[3]

[...]

Source: Adapted and corrected from the translation of Sir E.A. Wallis Budge in *The Babylonian Legends of the Creation* (London: Harrison & Sons, 1921), 31–66.

According to the *Enûma Eliš*, some of the mud bricks used to build the city of Babylon were hand crafted by the Anunnaki gods in the most primordial of days. Ancient astronaut theorists identify these gods with space aliens. If true, these bricks would be the only genuine extraterrestrial artifacts known to exist, but sadly alien architecture wasn't built to last. Babylon fell to ruin, and its mud bricks are little more than hard-packed earth (Library of Congress).

Commentary: *The Babylonian creation myth has often been compared to the opening passages of Genesis, to which it bears a formal resemblance. For fringe historians, the value of the* Enûma Eliš *lies in what can be mined from it. Zecharia Sitchin famously used the text to help develop his idea that the Anunnaki traveled to earth on a wandering planet called Nibiru and created humans as a slave race. He most likely derived the idea from George Smith's early translation in* The Chaldean Account of Genesis *(1876), where Smith writes that "I have translated one of these names* nibir, *'wandering stars' or 'planets,' but this is not the usual word for planet, and there is a star called* Nibir *near the place where the sun crossed the boundary between the old and new years, and this star was one of twelve supposed to be favourable to Babylonia."[4] Typically, Nibir or Nibiru was Jupiter. In* TP *Sitchin transformed this into a wandering planet: "The Sumerians called the planet NIBIRU, the 'planet of crossing,' and the Babylonian version of the epic retained ... astronomical information."[5]*

The Babylonian account of the creation of humans is often read by fringe historians as a conclave of aliens planning a genetic engineering experiment. Further, a literal reading of 4.137–138 would preclude prehistoric knowledge of space aliens since it suggests that that Mesopotamians believed that the earth was encased in a solid sphere of the sky, not surrounded by endless space. The Near Eastern idea that there is a dome or shell encasing the earth can also be found among the Hebrews in Genesis 1:6–8 and 7:11 and 3 Baruch 3:7, and among the Greeks in Iliad *17.425 and Odyssey 15.329, among many references. The creation of humanity from the body of a god who rebelled against the ruler of heaven (6.29–34) prefigures the later story of the Watchers (9) who rebel against god and are the benefactors of sinful humanity, as well as the Greek Titans and Giants, who rebel against the Olympian gods and were often considered the creators of humankind. Scholars like Jan N. Bremmer believe that the Jewish and Greek myths share a close relationship with the Mesopotamian.[6]*

Notes

1. A title of Tiâmat. (E.A.W.-B.)
2. This is an oblique way of saying that Marduk succeeded where Ea failed. (E.A.W.-B.)
3. Interestingly, if read literally, the passage at 6.51–65 would indicate that the space alien Anunnaki physically constructed the ziggurats of Babylon with their bare hands, which ought to be a testable hypothesis, yet no ancient astronaut theorist has attempted to prove the story true.
4. George Smith, *The Chaldean Account of Genesis* (London: Sampson Low, Marston, Searle, and Rivington, 1876), 73–74.
5. Zecharia Sitchin, *Twelfth Planet* (New York: Avon, 1978), 237.
6. See, for example, Jan N. Bremmer, *Greek Religion and Culture, the Bible, and the Ancient Near East* (Leiden: Brill, 2008).

5. Bilingual Babylonian Creation Myth

Tablet from Abû Habbah
c. 6th c. BCE
Sumerian and Babylonian
Astro, Prehistoric, Theo
Discussion in TP

The holy house, the house of the gods in the holy place had not yet been made.
No reed had sprung up, no tree had been made.
No brick had been laid, no structure of brick had been erected.
No house had been made, no city had been built.
No city had been made, no creature had been constituted.
Enlil's city, (i.e., Nippur) had not been made, Ekur had not been built,
Uruk had not been made, Eanna had not been built,
The Deep (or Apsu) had not been made, Eridu had not been built.
Of the holy house, the house of the gods, the dwelling-place had not been made.
All the lands were sea
At the time that the mid-most sea was [shaped like] a trough,
At that time Eridu was made, and Esagila was built,
The Ésagila where in the midst of the Deep the god Lugal-dul-azaga (i.e. Marduk) dwelleth,
Babylon was made, Esagila was completed.
The gods the Anunnaki he created at one time.
They proclaimed supreme the holy city, the dwelling of their heart's happiness.
Marduk laid a rush mat upon the face of the waters,
He mixed up earth and moulded it upon the rush mat,
To enable the gods to dwell in the place where they fain would be.
He fashioned man.
The goddess Aruru with him created the seed of mankind.
He created the beasts of the field and [all] the living things in the field.

He created the river Idiglat (Tigris) and the river Purattu (Euphrates), and he set them in their places,

He proclaimed their names rightly.

He created grass, the vegetation of the marsh, seed and shrub;

He created the green plants of the plain,

Lands, marshes, swamps,

The wild cow and the calf she carried, the wild calf, the sheep and the young she carried, the lamb of the fold,

Plantations and shrub land,

The he-goat and the mountain goat....

The lord Marduk piled up a dam in the region of the sea (i.e., he reclaimed land)

He ... a swamp, he founded a marsh.

... he made to be

Reeds he created, trees he created,

... in place he created

He laid bricks, he built a brick-work,

He constructed houses, he formed cities.

He constructed cities, creatures he set [therein].

Nippur he made, Ekur he built.

[Uruk he made, Eanna] he built.

(*The rest is fragmentary*)

Source: Translated by Sir E. A. Wallis Budge in *The Babylonian Legends of the Creation* (London: Harrison & Sons, 1921), 5–8.

Commentary: *This alternative version of the creation myth differs in some details and demonstrates that the Babylonians did not have a single creation myth. In this version, the Anunnaki are specifically not from the sky but are created on earth by Marduk. Therefore, they cannot be space aliens in this telling. Both this version and the* Enuma Eliš *postdate the* Atrahasis Epic *(c. 1900 BCE), a fragmentary text which tells how Enlil, Enki, and Anu divided earth, water, and sky among themselves and created lesser gods to do the work. These rebelled, and as in the later versions, the gods create humanity to toil on earth as the gods idle above.*

6. Oannes and the Babylonian Creation of Humanity

Berossus

Babyloniaca

c. 290–278 BCE

Greek

Preserved in Eusebius,[1] *Chronicle* 17–26 and George Syncellus,[2] *Chronicle* 28–30

Astro, Prehistoric

Discussion in AA, AQ, FG, SM

Berossus, in the first book of his history of Babylonia, informs us that he lived in the age of Alexander the son of Philip. And he mentions that there were written accounts, preserved at Babylon with the greatest care, comprehending a period of above fifteen myriads (150,000) of years: and that these writings contained histories of the heaven and of the sea; of the birth of mankind; and of the kings, and of the memorable actions which they had achieved.

And in the first place he describes Babylonia as a country situated between the Tigris and the Euphrates: that it abounded with wheat, and barley, and ocrus, and sesame; and that in the lakes were produced the roots called gongre, which are fit for food, and in respect to nutriment similar to barley. That there were also palm trees and apples, and a variety of fruits; fish also and birds, both those which are merely of flight, and those which frequent the lakes. He adds, that those parts of the country which bordered upon Arabia, were without water, and barren; but that the parts which lay on the other side were both hilly and fertile.

At Babylon there was (in these times) a great resort of people of various nations, who inhabited Chaldæa, and lived in a lawless manner like the beasts of the field. In the first year there appeared, from that part of the Erythræan sea which borders upon Babylonia, an animal destitute of reason,[3] by name Oannes, whose whole body (according to the account of Apollodorus) was that of a fish; that under the fish's head he had another head, with feet also below, similar to those of a man, subjoined to the fish's tail. His voice too, and language, was articulate and human; and a representation of him is preserved even to this day.

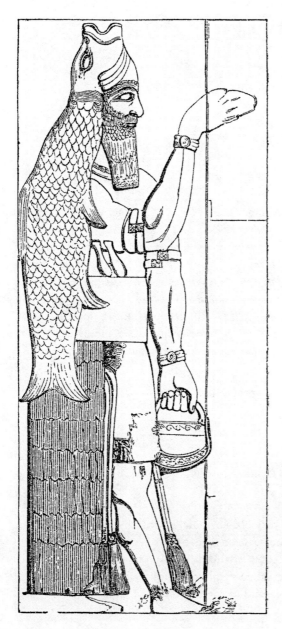

This Being was accustomed to pass the day among men; but took no food at that season; and he gave them an insight into letters and sciences, and arts of every kind. He taught them to construct cities, to found temples, to compile laws, and explained to them the principles of geometrical knowledge. He made them distinguish the seeds of the earth, and shewed them how to collect the fruits; in short,

Ancient astronaut writers call Oannes one of the best pieces of evidence for ancient astronauts. According to modern scholars, the fish-man of late Babylonian myth was a symbolic representation of a human figure, the sage Adapa, who was condemned to a subaqueous life for offending the gods. Due to a misinterpretation of 1 Samuel 5:4 and rabbinical tradition, this fish man was wrongly identified with the Phoenician god Dagon. When ancient relief carvings like this one were found in the nineteenth century they were labeled carvings of Dagon (scanned from *Illustrerad verldshistoria utgifven av E. Wallis*, volume I [1875]).

he instructed them in every thing which could tend to soften manners and humanize their lives. From that time, nothing material has been added by way of improvement to his instructions. And when the sun had set, this Being Oannes, retired again into the sea, and passed the night in the deep; for he was amphibious. After this there appeared other animals like Oannes, of which Berossus proposes to give an account when he comes to the history of the kings. Moreover Oannes wrote concerning the generation of mankind; and of their civil polity; and the following is the purport of what he said:

There was a time in which there existed nothing but darkness and an abyss of waters, wherein resided most hideous beings, which were produced of a two-fold principle. There appeared men, some of whom were furnished with two wings, others with four, and with two faces. They had one body but two heads: the one that of a man, the other of a woman: and likewise in their several organs both male and female. Other human figures were to be seen with the legs and horns of goats: some had horses' feet: while others united the hind quarters of a horse with the body of a man, resembling in shape the hippocentaurs. Bulls likewise were bred there with the heads of men; and dogs with fourfold bodies, terminated in their extremities with the tails of fishes: horses also with the heads of dogs: men too and other animals, with the heads and bodies of horses and the tails of fishes. In short, there were creatures in which were combined the limbs of every species of animals. In addition to these, fishes, reptiles, serpents, with other monstrous animals, which assumed each other's shape and countenance. Of all which were preserved delineations in the temple of Belus at Babylon.

The person, who presided over them, was a woman named Omoroca; which in the Chaldæan language is Thalatth; in Greek Thalassa, the sea; but which might equally be interpreted the Moon. All things being in this situation, Belus came, and cut the woman asunder: and of one half of her he formed the earth, and of the other half the heavens; and at the same time destroyed the animals within her. All this (he says) was an allegorical description of nature. For, the whole universe consisting of moisture, and animals being continually generated therein, the deity above-mentioned took off his own head: upon which the other gods mixed the blood, as it gushed out, with the earth; and from thence were formed men. On this account it is that they are rational, and partake of divine knowledge. This Belus, by whom they signify Zeus,[4] divided the darkness, and separated the Heavens from the Earth, and reduced universe to order. But the animals, not being able to bear the prevalence of light, died. Belus upon this, seeing a vast space unoccupied, though by nature fruitful, commanded one of the gods to take off his head, and to mix the blood with the earth; and from thence to form other men and animals, which should be capable of bearing the air. Belus formed also the stars, and the sun, and the moon, and the five planets.

Source: Translated by I. P. Cory, *Ancient Fragments,* 2nd ed. (London: William Pickering, 1832), 21–26. Cory offered a somewhat corrected but uncredited version of the translation originally made by Jacob Bryant in his *New System* (Vol. 3, 1774).

Commentary: *This late version of the Babylonian creation comes to us circuitously from Eusebius, in both Greek quotation by George Syncellus and Armenian translation, preserving fragments of Alexander Polyhistor, who in turn preserves fragments of Berossus. The translator of the above has correlated the versions preserved by the two Greek-language authors. The similarity to the earlier Babylonian material is self-evident, and Berossus, a priest of Marduk (Bel), used temple materials for his history. The material about the fish-man Oannes is one of the most* *famous in fringe history, widely cited by nearly every fringe writer on ancient history for the past two centuries, either as a space alien or a representative of a lost civilization. It derives from an earlier (non-fishy) Mesopotamian myth of Uan-Adapa, one of the Seven Sages, which in Sumerian derives from a word meaning "great water," leading to the later (but still ancient) myth he became a fish, a myth that grows out of the story that Ea banishes the human sages to the underground sea after they anger him, as described in the* Erra and Ishum *(8th c.* BCE, *reinterpreting earlier material). The Seven Sages of Mesopotamian lore heavily influenced the Jewish myth of Enoch, who plays the role of a sage and reports on the doings of diabolized beings not dissimilar to Oannes and his ilk (see* 9). *Indeed, these diabolized "Watchers" likely grew out of a Jewish reaction against the Seven Sages and Mesopotamian mythology.*[5]

Because he was not aware of this mythic development, Carl Sagan considered Oannes the best evidence for ancient astronauts in 1966 (though he changed his mind soon after),[6] *as did ancient astronaut theorist Philip Coppens four decades later. Robert Temple made it one of the most important parts of his* SM *when he asked readers to take the story literally as the tale of an amphibious alien of Sirius, despite the fact that the story said Oannes rose from the sea. Temple allowed that to be figurative, presuming a splashdown of an Apollo-style spacecraft. It was the combination of Oannes' appearance in* SM *with the apparent blessing of known skeptic Carl Sagan that vaulted him to the head of the ancient astronaut pantheon.*

Notes

1. Numbering of Eusebius's work varies by editor. I have used the page numbers of the Classical Armenian text as given in Robert Bedrosian (trans.), *Eusebius' Chronicle* (2008), <http://www.tertullian.org/fathers/eusebius_chronicon_02_intro.htm>.
2. Numbering of Syncellus's work varies by editor. My numbering follows that of William Adler and Paul Tuffin (trans.), *The Chronography of George Synkellos* (Oxford: Oxford University Press, 2002).
3. Possibly a corruption for "sensible," or else Syncellus' own opinion.
4. The Armenian translation of Eusebius reads "...by whom the Greeks signify Zeus and the Armenians Aramasdes," referring to Ahura-Mazda of Zoroastrian belief.
5. Annus, "On the Origin of the Watchers," 277–320.
6. Carl Sagan and I.S. Shklovskii, *Intelligent Life in the Universe* (San Francisco: HoldenDay, 1966), 461; but see Sagan's dismissal of alien origins for such legends seven years later in *Carl Sagan's Cosmic Connection: An Extraterrestrial Perspective* (Cambridge: Cambridge Univeristy Press, 2000 [1973]), 205.

7. Phoenician Creation Myth

Sanchuniathon
Phoenician History
Date unknown
Phoenician, preserved in Greek
Preserved in Philo of Byblos (c. 64–141 CE), quoted in Eusebius, *Praeparatio Evangelica* 1.10
Astro, Prehistoric

"The first principle of the universe he supposes to have been air dark with cloud and wind, or rather a blast of cloudy air, and a turbid chaos dark as Erebus; and these were boundless and for long ages had no limit. But when the wind, says he, became enamoured of its own parents, and a mixture took place, that connexion was called Desire. This was the beginning of the creation of all things: but the wind itself had no knowledge of its own creation. From its connexion Môt was produced, which some say is mud, and others a putrescence of watery compound; and out of this came every germ of creation, and the generation of the universe. So there were certain animals which had no sensation, and out of them grew intelligent animals, and were called 'Zophasemin,' that is 'observers of heaven'[1]; and they were formed like the shape of an egg. Also Môt burst forth into light, and sun, and moon, and stars, and the great constellations."

Such was their cosmogony, introducing downright atheism. But let us see next how he (Sanchuniathon) states the generation of animals to have arisen. He says, then: "And when the air burst into light, both the sea and the land became heated, and thence arose winds and clouds, and very great downpours and floods of the waters of heaven. So after they were separated, and removed from their proper place because of the sun's heat, and all met together again in the air dashing together one against another, thunderings and lightnings were produced, and at the rattle of the thunder the intelligent animals already described woke up, and were scared at the sound, and began to move both on land and sea, male and female."

Such is their theory of the generation of animals. Next after this the same writer adds and says: "These things were found written in the cosmogony of Taautus, and in his *Commentaries*, both from conjectures, and from evidences which his intellect discerned, and discovered, and made clear to us."

Next to this, after mentioning the names of the winds Notos and Boreas and the rest, he continues: "But these were the first who consecrated the productions of the earth, and regarded them as gods, and worshipped them as being the support of life both to themselves, and to those who were to come after them, and to all before them, and they offered to them drink-offerings and libations."

He adds also: "These were their notions of worship, corresponding to their own weakness, and timidity of soul. Then he says that from the wind Colpias and his wife Baau (which he translates 'Night') were born Aeon and Protogonus, mortal men, so called: and that Aeon discovered the food obtained from trees. That their offspring were called Genos and Genea, and inhabited Phoenicia: and that when droughts occurred, they stretched out their hands to heaven towards the sun; for him alone (he says) they regarded as god the lord of heaven, calling him Beelsamen, which is in the Phoenician language 'lord of heaven,' and in Greek 'Zeus.'"

And after this he charges the Greeks with error, saying: "For it is not without cause that we have explained these things in many ways, but in view of the later misinterpretations of the names in the history, which the Greeks in ignorance took in a wrong sense, being deceived by the ambiguity of the translation."

Afterwards he says: "From Genos, son of Aeon and Protogonus, were begotten again mortal children, whose names are Light, and Fire, and Flame. These, says he, discovered fire from rubbing pieces of wood together, and taught the use of it. And they begat sons of surpassing size and stature, whose names were applied to the mountains which they occupied: so that from them were named mount Cassius, and Libanus, and Antilibanus, and Brathy. From these, he says, were begotten Memrumus and Hypsuranius; and they got their names, he says, from their mothers, as the women in those days had free intercourse with any whom they met."

Then he says: "Hypsuranius inhabited Tyre, and contrived huts out of reeds and rushes and papyrus: and he quarrelled with his brother Ousous, who first invented a covering for the body from skins of wild beasts which he was strong enough to capture. And when furious rains and winds occurred, the trees in Tyre were rubbed against each other and caught fire, and burnt down the wood that was there. And Ousous took a tree, and, having stripped off the branches, was the first who ventured to embark on the sea; and be consecrated two pillars[2] to fire and wind, and worshipped them, and poured libations of blood upon them from the wild beasts which he took in hunting.

"But when Hypsuranius and Ousous were dead, those who were left, he says, consecrated staves to them, and year by year worshipped their pillars and kept festivals in their honour. But many years afterwards from the race of Hypsuranius were born Agreus and Halieus, the inventors of hunting and fishing, from whom were named huntsmen and fishermen: and from them were born two brethren, discoverers of iron and the mode of working it; the one of whom, Chrysor, practised oratory, and incantations, and divinations: and that he was Hephaestus, and invented the hook, and bait, and line, and raft, and was the first of all men to make a voyage: wherefore they reverenced him also as a god after his death. And he was also called Zeus Meilichios. And some say that his brothers invented walls of brick. After-wards there sprang from their race two youths, one of whom was called Technites (Artificer), and the other Geinos Autochthon (Earth-born Aboriginal). These devised the mixing of straw with the clay of bricks, and drying them in the sun, and moreover invented roofs. From them others were born, one of whom was called Agros, and the other Agrueros or Agrotes; and of the latter there is in Phoenicia a much venerated statue, and a shrine drawn by yokes of oxen; and among the people of Byblos he is named pre-eminently the greatest of the gods.

"These two devised the addition to houses of courts, and enclosures, and caves. From them came husbandmen and huntsmen. They are also called Aletae and Titans. From these were born Amynos and Magus, who established villages and sheepfolds. From them came Misor and Suduc, that is to say 'Straight' and 'Just': these discovered the use of salt.

"From Misor was born Taautus, who invented the first written alphabet; the Egyptians called him Thoyth, the Alexandrians Thoth, and the Greeks Hermes.

"From Suduc came the Dioscuri, or Cabeiri, or Corybantes, or Samothraces: these, he says, first invented a ship. From them have sprung others, who discovered herbs, and the healing of venomous bites, and charms. In their time is born a certain Elioun called 'the Most High,' and a female named Beruth, and these dwelt in the neighbourhood of Byblos.

"And from them is born Epigeius or Autochthon, whom they afterwards called Uranus; so that from him they named the element above us Uranus because of the excellence of its beauty. And he has a sister born of the aforesaid parents, who was called Ge (earth), and from her, he says, because of her beauty, they called the earth by the same name. And their father, the Most High, died in an encounter with wild beasts, and was deified, and his children offered to him libations and sacrifices.

"And Uranus, having succeeded to his father's rule, takes to himself in marriage his sister Ge, and gets by her four sons, Elus who is also Kronos, and Baetylus, and Dagon who is Siton, and Atlas. Also by other wives Uranus begat a numerous progeny; on which account Ge was angry, and from jealousy began to reproach Uranus, so that they even separated from each other.

"But Uranus, after he had left her, used to come upon her with violence, whenever he chose, and consort with her, and go away again; he used to try also to destroy his children by her; but Ge repelled him many times, having gathered to herself allies. And when Kronos had advanced to manhood, he, with the counsel and help of Hermes Trismegistus (who was his secretary), repels his father Uranus, and avenges his mother.

"To Kronos are born children, Persephone and Athena. The former died a virgin: but by the advice of Athena and Hermes Kronos made a sickle and a spear of iron. Then Hermes talked magical words to the allies of Kronos, and inspired them with a desire of fighting against Uranus on behalf of Ge. And thus Kronos engaged in war, and drove Uranus from his government, and succeeded to the kingdom. Also there was taken in the battle the beloved concubine of Uranus, being great with child, whom Kronos gave in marriage to Dagon. And in his house she gave birth to the child begotten of Uranus, which she named Demarus.

"After this Kronos builds a wall round his own dwelling, and founds the first city, Byblos in Phoenicia.

"Soon after this he became suspicious of his own brother Atlas, and, with the advice of Hermes, threw him into a deep pit and buried him. At about this time the descendants of the Dioscuri put together rafts and ships, and made voyages; and, being cast ashore near Mount Cassius, consecrated a temple there. And the allies of Elus, who is Kronos, were surnamed Eloim, as these same, who were surnamed after Kronos, would have been called Kronii.

"And Kronos, having a son Sadidus, dispatched him with his own sword, because he regarded him with suspicion, and deprived him of life, thus becoming the murderer of his son. In like manner he cut off the head of a daughter of his own; so that all the gods were dismayed at the disposition of Kronos.

"But as time went on Uranus, being in banishment, secretly sends his maiden daughter Astarte with two others her sisters, Ehea and Dione, to slay Kronos by craft. But Kronos caught them, and though they were his sisters, made them his wedded wives. And when Uranus knew it, he sent Eimarmene and Hora with other allies on an expedition against Kronos, and these Kronos won over to his side and kept with him.

"Further, he says, the god Uranus devised the Baetylia, having contrived to put life into stones. And to Kronos there were born of Astarte seven daughters, Titanides or Artemides: and again to the same there were born of Rhea seven sons, of whom the youngest was deified at his birth; and of Dione females, and of Astarte again two males, Desire and Love. And Dagon, after he discovered corn and the plough, was called Zeus Arotrios.

"And one of the Titanides united to Suduc, who is named the Just, gives birth to Asclepius.

"In Peraea also there were born to Kronos three sons, Kronos of the same name with his father, and Zeus Belus, and Apollo. In their time are born Pontus, and Typhon, and Nereus father of Pontus and son of Belus.

"And from Pontus is born Sidon (who from the exceeding sweetness of her voice was the first to invent musical song) and Poseidon. And to Demarus is born Melcathrus,[3] who is also called Hercules.

"Then again Uranus makes war against Pontus, and after revolting attaches himself to Demarus, and Demarus attacks Pontus, but Pontus puts him to flight; and Demarus vowed an offering if he should escape.

"And in the thirty-second year of his power and kingdom Elus, that is Kronos, having waylaid his father Uranus in an inland spot, and got him into his hands, emasculates him near some fountains and rivers. There Uranus was deified: and as he breathed his last, the blood from his wounds dropped into the fountains and into the waters of the rivers, and the spot is pointed out to this day."

This, then, is the story of Kronos, and such are the glories of the mode of life, so vaunted among the Greeks, of men in the days of Kronos, whom they also affirm to have been the first and "golden race of articulate speaking men,"[4] that blessed happiness of the olden time!

Again, the historian adds to this, after other matters: "But Astarte, the greatest goddess, and Zeus Demarus, and Adodus king of gods, reigned over the country with the consent of Kronos. And Astarte set the head of a bull upon her own head as a mark of royalty; and in travelling round the world she found a star that had fallen from the sky, which she took up and consecrated in the holy island Tyre. And the Phoenicians say that Astarte is Aphrodite.

"Kronos also, in going round the world, gives the kingdom of Attica to his own daughter Athena. But on the occurrence of a pestilence and mortality Kronos offers his only begotten son as a whole burnt-offering to his father Uranus, and circumcises himself, compelling his allies also to do the same. And not long after another of his sons by Rhea, named Muth, having died, he deifies him, and the Phoenicians call him Thanatos and Pluto. And after this Kronos gives the city Byblos to the goddess Baaltis, who is also called Dione, and Berytus to Poseidon and to the Cabeiri and Agrotae and Halieis, who also consecrated the remains of Pontus at Berytus.

"But before this the god Tauthus imitated the features of the gods who were his companions, Kronos, and Dagon, and the rest, and gave form to the sacred characters of the letters. He also devised for Kronos as insignia of royalty four eyes in front and behind ... but two of them quietly closed, and upon his shoulders four wings, two as spread for flying, and two as folded.

"And the symbol meant that Kronos could see when asleep, and sleep while waking: and similarly in the case of the wings, that he flew while at rest, and was at rest when flying. But to each of the other gods he gave two wings upon the shoulders, as meaning that they accompanied Kronos in his flight. And to Kronos himself again he gave two wings upon his head, one representing the all-ruling mind, and one sensation.

"And when Kronos came into the South country he gave all Egypt to the god Tauthus, that it might be his royal dwelling-place. And these things, he says, were recorded first by Suduc's seven sons the Cabeiri, and their eighth brother Asclepius, as the god Tauthus commanded them.

"All these stories Thabion, who was the very first hierophant of all the Phoenicians from the beginning, allegorized and mixed up with the physical and cosmical phenomena, and delivered to the prophets who celebrated the orgies and inaugurated the mysteries: and they, purposing to increase their vain pretensions from every source, handed them on to their successors and to their foreign visitors: one of these was Eisirius the inventor of the three letters, brother of Chna the first who had his name changed to Phoenix."

Then again afterwards he adds: "But the Greeks, surpassing all in genius, appropriated most of the earliest stories, and then variously decked them out with ornaments of tragic phrase, and adorned them in every way, with the purpose of charming by the pleasant fables. Hence Hesiod and the celebrated Cyclic poets framed theogonies of their own, and battles of the giants, and battles of Titans, and castrations; and with these fables, as they travelled about, they conquered and drove out the truth.

"But our ears having grown up in familiarity with their fictions, and being for long ages pre-occupied, guard as a trust the mythology which they received, just as I said at the beginning; and this mythology, being aided by time, has made its hold difficult for us to escape from, so that the truth is thought to be nonsense, and the spurious narrative truth."

Let these suffice as quotations from the writings of Sanchuniathon, translated by Philo of Byblos, and approved as true by the testimony of Porphyry the philosopher.

The same author, in his *History of the Jews*, further writes thus concerning Kronos: "Tauthus, whom the Egyptians call Thöyth, excelled in wisdom among the Phoenicians, and was the first to rescue the worship of the gods from the ignorance of the vulgar, and arrange it in the order of intelligent experience. Many generations after him a god Sourmoubelos and Thuro, whose name was changed to Eusarthis, brought to light the theology of Tauthus which had been hidden and overshadowed, by allegories."

And soon after he says: "It was a custom of the ancients in great crises of danger for the rulers of a city or nation, in order to avert the common ruin, to give up the most beloved of their children for sacrifice as a ransom to the avenging daemons; and those who were thus given up were sacrificed with mystic rites. Kronos then, whom the Phoenicians call Elus, who was king of the country and subsequently, after his decease, was deified as the star Saturn, had by a nymph of the country named Anobret an only begotten son, whom they on this account called Iedud,⁵ the only begotten being still so called among the Phoenicians; and when very great dangers from war had beset the country, he arrayed his son in royal apparel, and prepared an altar, and sacrificed him."

Again see what the same author, in his translation from Sanchuniathon about the Phoenician alphabet, says concerning the reptiles and venomous beasts, which contribute no good service to mankind, but work death and destruction to any in whom they inject their incurable and fatal poison. This also he describes, saying word for word as follows: "The nature then of the dragon and of serpents Tauthus himself regarded as divine, and so again after him did the Phoenicians and Egyptians: for this animal was declared by him to be of all reptiles most full of breath, and fiery. In consequence of which it also exerts an unsurpassable swiftness by means of its breath, without feet and hands or any other of the external members by which the other animals make their movements. It also exhibits forms of various shapes, and in its progress makes spiral leaps as swift as it chooses. It is also most long-lived, and its nature is to put off its old skin, and so not only to grow young again, but also to assume a larger growth; and after it has fulfilled its appointed measure of age, it is self-consumed, in like manner as Tauthus himself has set down in his sacred books: for which reason this animal has also been adopted in temples and in mystic rites.

"We have spoken more fully about it in the memoirs entitled Ethothiae, in which we prove that it is immortal, and is self-consumed, as is stated before: for this animal does not die by a natural death, but only if struck by a violent blow. The Phoenicians call it 'Good Daemon'⁶: in like manner the Egyptians also surname it Cneph; and they add to it the head of a hawk because of the hawk's activity.

"Epeïs also (who is called among them a chief hierophant and sacred scribe, and whose work was translated [into Greek] by Areius of Heracleopolis), speaks in an allegory word for word as follows: "The first and most divine being is a serpent with the form of a hawk, extremely graceful, which whenever he opened his eyes filled all with light in his original birthplace, but if he shut his eyes, darkness came on."

"Epeïs here intimates that he is also of a fiery substance, by saying 'he shone through,' for to shine through is peculiar to light. From the Phoenicians Pherecydes also took the first ideas of his theology concerning the god called by him Ophion and concerning the Ophion-idae, of whom we shall speak again.

"Moreover the Egyptians, describing the world from the same idea, engrave the circumference of a circle, of the colour of the sky and of fire, and a hawk-shaped serpent stretched across the middle of it, and the whole shape is like our Theta (θ), representing the circle as the world, and signifying by the serpent which connects it in the middle the good daemon.

"Zoroaster also the Magian, in the *Sacred Collection of Persian Records*, says in express words: 'And god has the head of a hawk. He is the first, incorruptible, eternal, uncreated, without parts, most unlike (all else), the controller of all good, who cannot be bribed, the best of all the good, the wisest of all wise; and he is also a father of good laws and justice, self-taught, natural, and perfect, and wise, and the sole author of the sacred power of nature.'

"The same also is said of him by Ostanes in the book entitled Octateuch."

From Tauthus, as is said above, all received their impulse towards physiological systems: and having built temples they consecrated in the shrines the primary elements represented by serpents, and in their honour celebrated festivals, and sacrifices, and mystic rites, regarding them as the greatest gods, and rulers of the universe. So much concerning serpents.

Source: Translated by E. H. Gifford in Eusebius, *Evangelicae Praeparationis*, vol. 3, part 1 (Oxford: E Typographio Academico, 1903), 37–47.

Commentary: *For much of the twentieth century scholars assumed that the above excerpt was not an authentic account of Phoenician beliefs. However, the material that passes under the name of Sanchuniathon the Phoenician is a Hellenistic interpretation of genuine Semitic myths dating back perhaps to the Bronze Age, confirmed only with the translation of ancient texts from Ugarit in the twentieth century. In its surviving form it is, however, heavily euhemerized and not a genuine Bronze Age text, as its author claims. Thus the original gods (described as having wings, like angels) have been given as mortals, in the style of Euhemerus, with Orphic-style deities inserted to fill the gap. The outline of the story, with its gods, giants, mating with mortal women, and culture heroes who invent civilization (including astrology and metallurgy) is very similar to that of the Enochian Watchers (see 9), suggesting to many scholars that the Watchers of 1 Enoch reflect a Jewish revision of a polytheistic Semitic culture myth. Either Brathy or Antilibanus—the mountains of Anti-Lebanon—is almost certainly Mount Hermon, where the Watchers descended from heaven. The area was considered the abode of the Anunnaki in the Old Babylonian Gilgamesh texts, which likely received the story from the ancient Syrians. All of these myths the Phoenician author said he learned from the records of Tauthus, or Thoth, who would later be identified with Hermes Trismegistus and Enoch. The text also preserves an unusual early mention of dragons as breathing fire. The passage about El (Cronus) sacrificing his only begotten son caused Jacob Bryant to speculate that it was a prefiguring of Christ.*

Notes

1. Cf. the Watchers of 1 Enoch (**9**). While these observers seem to be on the earth looking up, the text has been euhemerized and may have originally referred to beings like the Enochian Watchers.

2. The two pillars are reminiscent of those of the Enochian tradition (**12**) and reflect the Phoenician practice of consecrating pillars to the gods and inscribing divine names and wisdom on them (Eusebius, *Praep. Evan.* 1.9–10).

3. Better known as Melqart, who was indeed identified with Heracles (Herodotus, *Histories* 2.44).

4. Quoting Hesiod, *Works and Days* 109.

5. Cf. Hebrew: *Yaḥid*, the "only begotten." This refers to the only son of a particular mother, as Isaac was the "only begotten" son of Abraham and similarly offered in sacrifice despite Abraham having also fathered Ishmael by another mother. (Cf. the child sacrifices of Jephthah in Judges 11 and King Mesha in 2 Kings 3:26–27.)

6. The same figure is the Agathodaemon of medieval pyramid myths (see **15** and **17**).

8. Descent of the Sons of God
Genesis 6:1–4
c. 6th c. BCE
Hebrew
Astro, Prehistoric
Discussion in AA, CG

[1] And it came to pass, when men began to multiply on the face of the earth, and daughters were born unto them,

[2] That the sons of God saw the daughters of men that they were fair; and they took them wives of all which *they* chose.

[3] And the Lord said, My spirit shall not always strive with man, for that he also is flesh: yet his days shall be an hundred and twenty years.

[4] There were giants in the earth in those days; and also after that, when the sons of God came in unto the daughters of men, and they bare children to them, the same became mighty men which were of old, men of renown.

Source: King James Version.

Commentary: *This passage is of the very few mention of the Sons of God (benê hā Elōhîm) in the Bible, along with Job 1:6 and 2:1 and similar references in the Psalms, and one of only two to mention the giants (Nephilim, or "fallen ones," translated in Greek as "giants"), the other being Numbers 13:33 (with an allusion to them as fallen warriors in Sheol in Ezekiel 32:27). These Sons of God are parallel to Near Eastern divine councils, such as the* bn 'il, *who served El in the myths of Ugarit, a Bronze Age city in what is now Syria that spoke a Semitic language related to Hebrew and Akkadian. However, it is uncertain whether this text is the foundation for the Enochian tradition of the Watchers (see* **9**), *a summary of or reaction to it, or an independent version of a preexisting myth. The relationship between the Nephilim and the Sons of God has also been subject to dispute, and the two are frequently conflated. It is possible that the status of the Nephilim as "fallen" created or fed into the myth that the Sons of God "fell" in seducing human women. For other interpretations of the Sons of God, see the commentary for* **10**. *It is also unclear if the children of the Sons of God are the same as the giants, or some other group; the sentence's grammar is unhelpful. Mainstream scholars suggest the passage may represent a radical revision of a polytheistic pantheon and hero mythos, like that of Babylon or Greece, where it was common for heroes like Gilgamesh or Perseus to have a divine parent and superhuman size and strength.*[1] *In this reading, the editors of Genesis acknowledged popular belief in semi-divine heroes but attributed such beings to demonic forces. Support for this can be found in the much later* Book of Giants, *where various versions place Near Eastern heroes like Gilgamesh among the Nephilim-giants. (In Ugaritic texts, Gilgamesh is 11 cubits high.) Later attempts to understand and expand upon this enigmatic passage yielded the following texts, which form the foundation of the Watcher mythos. It also gave rise to the famed Cardiff Giant hoax, in which a stone carving of a "giant" in upstate New York fooled many into thinking a petrified giant had been uncovered,*[2] *as well as a wide-ranging effort by biblical literalists to find "giant" skeletons around the world in an effort to prove the passage true.*

Notes

1. See, for example, David Penchansky, *Twilight of the Gods: Polytheism in the Hebrew Bible* (Louisville: Westmninster John Knox Press, 2005), 25–26 and the older work of Hermann Gunkel, *Genesis,* trans. Mark E. Biddle III (Mercer University Press, 1997 [1910]), 56–60, among many who have made similar claims.

2. For an entertaining overview, see Scott Tribble, *A Colossal Hoax: The Giant from Cardiff that Fooled America* (New York: Rowman & Littlefield, 2009).

9. Account of the Watchers Before the Flood

Book of the Watchers
c. 300 BCE
Aramaic or Hebrew, preserved in Ge'ez[1]
1 Enoch 6:1–16:4
Astro, Prehistoric
Discussion in AA, CG, TP

The Fall of the Angels

CHAPTER 6

[1] And it came to pass when the children of men had multiplied that in those days were born unto them beautiful and comely daughters. [2] And the angels, the children of the heaven, saw and lusted after them, and said to one another: "Come, let us choose us wives from among the children of men and beget us children." [3] And Semjâzâ, who was their leader, said unto them: "I fear ye will not indeed agree to do this deed, and I alone shall have to pay the penalty of a great sin." [4] And they all answered him and said: "Let us all

Looming in the background of this photograph is the snowcapped peak of Mt. Hermon, long associated with pagan gods and fallen angels. It is one of the longest-used sacred sites in the world, and in pagan myth was once the home of Baal. Because of the mountain's association with the Watchers and Baal, today a UN observation post established atop the mountain after the Yom Kippur War is the focus of conspiracy theories that connect it to the Antichrist, Freemasonry, and an attempt to open the gates of hell (Library of Congress).

swear an oath, and all bind ourselves by mutual imprecations not to abandon this plan but to do this thing." [5] Then sware they all together and bound themselves by mutual imprecations upon it. [6] And they were in all two hundred; who descended in the days of Jared on the summit of Mount Hermon, and they called it Mount Hermon, because they had sworn and bound themselves by mutual imprecations upon it. [7] And these are the names of their leaders: Sêmîazâz, their leader, Arâkîba, Râmêêl, Kôkabîêl, Tâmîêl, Râmîêl, Dânêl, Êzêqêêl, Barâqîjâl, Asâêl, Armârôs, Batârêl, Anânêl, Zaqîêl, Samsâpêêl,[2] Satarêl, Tûrêl, Jômjâêl, Sariêl. [8] These are their chiefs of tens.

CHAPTER 7

[1] And all the others together with them took unto themselves wives, and each chose for himself one, and they began to go in unto them and to defile themselves with them, and they taught them charms and enchantments, and the cutting of roots, and made them acquainted with plants. [2] And they became pregnant, and they bare great giants, whose height was three thousand ells: [3] Who consumed all the acquisitions of men. [4] And when men could no longer sustain them, the giants turned against them and devoured mankind. [5] And they began to sin against birds, and beasts, and reptiles, and fish, and to devour one another's flesh, and drink the blood. [6] Then the earth laid accusation against the lawless ones.

CHAPTER 8

[1] And Azâzêl taught men to make swords, and knives, and shields, and breastplates, and made known to them the metals of the earth and the art of working them, and bracelets, and ornaments, and the use of antimony, and the beautifying of the eyelids, and all kinds of costly stones, and all colouring tinctures. [2] And there arose much godlessness, and they committed fornication, and they were led astray, and became corrupt in all their ways. [3] Semjâzâ taught enchantments, and root-cuttings, Armârôs the resolving of enchantments, Barâqîjâl, (taught) astrology, Kôkabêl the constellations, Ezêqêêl the knowledge of the clouds, Araqiêl the signs of the earth, Shamsiêl the signs of the sun, and Sariêl the course of the moon. [4] And as men perished, they cried, and their cry went up to heaven...

CHAPTER 9

[1] And then Michael, Uriel, Raphael, and Gabriel looked down from heaven and saw much blood being shed upon the earth, and all lawlessness being wrought upon the earth. [2] And they said one to another: "The earth made without inhabitant cries the voice of their crying up to the gates of heaven. [3] And now to you, the holy ones of heaven, the souls of men make their suit, saying, 'Bring our cause before the Most High.'" [4] And they said to the Lord of the ages: "Lord of lords, God of gods, King of kings, and God of the ages, the throne of Thy glory (standeth) unto all the generations of the ages, and Thy name holy and glorious and blessed unto all the ages! [5] Thou hast made all things, and power over all things hast Thou: and all things are naked and open in Thy sight, and Thou seest all things, and nothing can hide itself from Thee. [6] Thou seest what Azâzêl hath done, who hath taught all unrighteousness on earth and revealed the eternal secrets which were (preserved) in heaven, which men were striving to learn: [7] And Semjâzâ, to whom Thou hast given authority to bear rule over his associates. [8] And they have gone to the daughters of men

upon the earth, and have slept with the women, and have defiled themselves, and revealed to them all kinds of sins. [9] And the women have borne giants, and the whole earth has thereby been filled with blood and unrighteousness. [10] And now, behold, the souls of those who have died are crying and making their suit to the gates of heaven, and their lamentations have ascended: and cannot cease because of the lawless deeds which are wrought on the earth. [11] And Thou knowest all things before they come to pass, and Thou seest these things and Thou dost suffer them, and Thou dost not say to us what we are to do to them in regard to these."

CHAPTER 10

[1] Then said the Most High, the Holy and Great One spake, and sent Uriel to the son of Lamech, and said to him: [2] "Go to Noah and tell him in my name 'Hide thyself!' and reveal to him the end that is approaching: that the whole earth will be destroyed, and a deluge is about to come upon the whole earth, and will destroy all that is on it. [3] And now instruct him that he may escape and his seed may be preserved for all the generations of the world." [4] And again the Lord said to Raphael: "Bind Azâzêl hand and foot, and cast him into the darkness: and make an opening in the desert, which is in Dûdâêl, and cast him therein. [5] And place upon him rough and jagged rocks, and cover him with darkness, and let him abide there for ever, and cover his face that he may not see light. [6] And on the day of the great judgement he shall be cast into the fire.³ [7] And heal the earth which the angels have corrupted, and proclaim the healing of the earth, that they may heal the plague, and that all the children of men may not perish through all the secret things that the Watchers have disclosed and have taught their sons. [8] And the whole earth has been corrupted through the works that were taught by Azâzêl: to him ascribe all sin."⁴ [9] And to Gabriel said the Lord: "Proceed against the bastards and the reprobates, and against the children of fornication: and destroy the children of fornication and the children of the Watchers from amongst men and cause them to go forth: send them one against the other that they may destroy each other in battle: for length of days shall they not have. [10] And no request that they (*i.e.* their fathers) make of thee shall be granted unto their fathers on their behalf; for they hope to live an eternal life, and that each one of them will live five hundred years." [11] And the Lord said unto Michael: "Go, bind Semjâzâ and his associates who have united themselves with women so as to have defiled themselves with them in all their uncleanness. [12] And when their sons have slain one another, and they have seen the destruction of their beloved ones, bind them fast for seventy generations in the valleys of the earth, till the day of their judgement and of their consummation, till the judgement that is for ever and ever is consummated. [13] In those days they shall be led off to the abyss of fire: and to the torment and the prison in which they shall be confined for ever. [14] And whosoever shall be condemned and destroyed will from thenceforth be bound together with them to the end of all generations. [15] And destroy all the spirits of the reprobate and the children of the Watchers, because they have wronged mankind. [16] Destroy all wrong from the face of the earth and let every evil work come to an end: and let the plant of righteousness and truth appear: and it shall prove a blessing; the works of righteousness and truth shall be planted in truth and joy for evermore.

[17] And then shall all the righteous escape,
And shall live till they beget thousands of children,

The fall of the rebel angels has been one of the most popular themes in the Western occult tradition, spawning more than two millennia of discussion and explanation, and many competing explanations of who they were and why they fell. Today many fringe figures interpret fallen angels like those seen in this illustration by Gustave Doré as extraterrestrial visitors (Gustave Doré drawing from Dante Alighieri, *Inferno: The Vision of Hell* [1870]).

And all the days of their youth and their old age
Shall they complete in peace.

[18] And then shall the whole earth be tilled in righteousness, and shall all be planted with trees and be full of blessing. [19] And all desirable trees shall be planted on it, and they shall plant vines on it: and the vine which they plant thereon shall yield wine in abundance, and as for all the seed which is sown thereon each measure (of it) shall bear a thousand, and each measure of olives shall yield ten presses of oil. [20] And cleanse thou the earth from all oppression, and from all unrighteousness, and from all sin, and from all godlessness: and all the uncleanness that is wrought upon the earth destroy from off the earth. [21] And all the children of men shall become righteous, and all nations shall offer adoration and shall praise Me, and all shall worship Me. [22] And the earth shall be cleansed from all defilement, and from all sin, and from all punishment, and from all torment, and I will never again send (them) upon it from generation to generation and for ever.

CHAPTER 11

[1] And in those days I will open the store chambers of blessing which are in the heaven, so as to send them down upon the earth over the work and labour of the children of men. [2] And truth and peace shall be associated together throughout all the days of the world and throughout all the generations of men."

Dream-Vision of Enoch
CHAPTER 12

[1] Before these things Enoch was hidden, and no one of the children of men knew where he was hidden, and where he abode, and what had become of him. [2] And his activities had to do with the Watchers, and his days were with the holy ones. [3] And I, Enoch was blessing the Lord of majesty and the King of the ages, and lo! the Watchers called me—Enoch the scribe—and said to me: [4] "Enoch, thou scribe of righteousness, go, declare to the Watchers of the heaven who have left the high heaven, the holy eternal place, and have defiled themselves with women, and have done as the children of earth do, and have taken unto themselves wives: 'Ye have wrought great destruction on the earth: [5] And ye shall have no peace nor forgiveness of sin: and inasmuch as they delight themselves in their children, [6] The murder of their beloved ones shall they see, and over the destruction of their children shall they lament, and shall make supplication unto eternity, but mercy and peace shall ye not attain.'"

CHAPTER 13

[1] And Enoch went and said: "Azâzêl, thou shalt have no peace: a severe sentence has gone forth against thee to put thee in bonds: [2] And thou shalt not have toleration nor request granted to thee, because of the unrighteousness which thou hast taught, and because of all the works of godlessness and unrighteousness and sin which thou hast shown to men." [3] Then I went and spoke to them all together, and they were all afraid, and fear and trembling seized them. [4] And they besought me to draw up a petition for them that they might find forgiveness, and to read their petition in the presence of the Lord of heaven. [5] For from thenceforward they could not speak (with Him) nor lift up their eyes to heaven for shame of their sins for which they had been condemned. [6] Then I wrote out their petition,

and the prayer in regard to their spirits and their deeds individually and in regard to their requests that they should have forgiveness and length of days. [7] And I went off and sat down at the waters of Dan, in the land of Dan, to the south of the west of Hermon: I read their petition till I fell asleep. [8] And behold a dream came to me, and visions fell down upon me, and I saw visions of chastisement, and a voice came bidding (me) to tell it to the sons of heaven, and reprimand them. [9] And when I awaked, I came unto them, and they were all sitting gathered together, weeping in "Abelsjâîl, which is between Lebanon and Sênêsêr, with their faces covered. [10] And I recounted before them all the visions which I had seen in sleep, and I began to speak the words of righteousness, and to reprimand the heavenly Watchers.

Chapter 14

[1] The book of the words of righteousness, and of the reprimand of the eternal Watchers in accordance with the command of the Holy Great One in that vision. [2] I saw in my sleep what I will now say with a tongue of flesh and with the breath of my mouth: which the Great One has given to men to converse therewith and understand with the heart. [3] As He has created and given to man the power of understanding the word of wisdom, so hath He created me also and given me the power of reprimanding the Watchers, the children of heaven. [4] I wrote out your petition, and in my vision it appeared thus, that your petition will not be granted unto you throughout all the days of eternity, and that judgement has been finally passed upon you: yea (your petition) will not be granted unto you. [5] And from henceforth you shall not ascend into heaven unto all eternity, and in bonds of the earth the decree has gone forth to bind you for all the days of the world. [6] And (that) previously you shall have seen the destruction of your beloved sons and ye shall have no pleasure in them, but they shall fall before you by the sword. [7] And your petition on their behalf shall not be granted, nor yet on your own: even though you weep and pray and speak all the words contained in the writing which I have written. [8] And the vision was shown to me thus: Behold, in the vision clouds invited me and a mist summoned me, and the course of the stars and the lightnings sped and hastened me, and the winds in the vision caused me to fly and lifted me upward, and bore me into heaven. [9] And I went in till I drew nigh to a wall which is built of crystals and surrounded by tongues of fire: and it began to affright me. [10] And I went into the tongues of fire and drew nigh to a large house which was built of crystals: and the walls of the house were like a tesselated floor (made) of crystals, and its groundwork was of crystal. [11] Its ceiling was like the path of the stars and the lightnings, and between them were fiery cherubim, and their heaven was (clear as) water. [12] A flaming fire surrounded the walls, and its portals blazed with fire. [13] And I entered into that house, and it was hot as fire and cold as ice: there were no delights of life therein: fear covered me, and trembling got hold upon me. [14] And as I quaked and trembled, I fell upon my face. [15] And I beheld a vision, And lo! there was a second house, greater than the former, and the entire portal stood open before me, and it was built of flames of fire. [16] And in every respect it so excelled in splendour and magnificence and extent that I cannot describe to you its splendour and its extent. [17] And its floor was of fire, and above it were lightnings and the path of the stars, and its ceiling also was flaming fire. [18] And I looked and saw therein a lofty throne: its appearance was as crystal, and the wheels thereof as the shining sun, and there was the vision of cherubim. [19] And from underneath the throne came streams of

flaming fire so that I could not look thereon. [20] And the Great Glory sat thereon, and His raiment shone more brightly than the sun and was whiter than any snow. [21] None of the angels could enter and could behold His face by reason of the magnificence and glory and no flesh could behold Him. [22] The flaming fire was round about Him, and a great fire stood before Him, and none around could draw nigh Him: ten thousand times ten thousand (stood) before Him, yet He needed no counselor. [23] And the most holy ones who were nigh to Him did not leave by night nor depart from Him. [24] And until then I had been prostrate on my face, trembling: and the Lord called me with His own mouth, and said to me: 'Come hither, Enoch, and hear my word.' [25] And one of the holy ones came to me and waked me, and He made me rise up and approach the door: and I bowed my face downwards.

CHAPTER 15

[1] And He [God] answered and said to me [Enoch], and I heard His voice: 'Fear not, Enoch, thou righteous man and scribe of righteousness: approach hither and hear my voice. [2] And go, say to the Watchers of heaven, who have sent thee to intercede for them: "You should intercede" for men, and not men for you: [3] Wherefore have ye left the high, holy, and eternal heaven, and lain with women, and defiled yourselves with the daughters of men and taken to yourselves wives, and done like the children of earth, and begotten giants (as your) sons? [4] And though ye were holy, spiritual, living the eternal life, you have defiled yourselves with the blood of women, and have begotten (children) with the blood of flesh, and, as the children of men, have lusted after flesh and blood as those [also] do who die and perish. [5] Therefore have I given them wives also that they might impregnate them, and beget children by them, that thus nothing might be wanting to them on earth. [6] But you were formerly spiritual, living the eternal life, and immortal for all generations of the world. [7] And therefore I have not appointed wives for you; for as for the spiritual ones of the heaven, in heaven is their dwelling. [8] And now, the giants, who are produced from the spirits and flesh, shall be called evil spirits upon the earth, and on the earth shall be their dwelling. [9] Evil spirits have proceeded from their bodies; because they are born from men, and from the holy Watchers is their beginning and primal origin; they shall be evil spirits on earth, and] evil spirits shall they be called. [10] As for the spirits of heaven, in heaven shall be their dwelling, but as for the spirits of the earth which were born upon the earth, on the earth shall be their dwelling. [11] And the spirits of the giants afflict, oppress, destroy, attack, do battle, and work destruction on the earth, and cause trouble: they take no food, but nevertheless hunger and thirst, and cause offences. And these spirits shall rise up against the children of men and against the women, because they have proceeded from them.

CHAPTER 16

[1] From the days of the slaughter and destruction and death of the giants, from the souls of whose flesh the spirits, having gone forth, shall destroy without incurring judgement—thus shall they destroy until the day of the consummation, the great judgement in which the age shall be consummated, over the Watchers and the godless, yea, shall be wholly consummated.' [2] And now as to the Watchers who have sent thee to intercede for them, who had been aforetime in heaven, (say to them): [3] 'You have been in heaven, but all the

mysteries had not yet been revealed to you, and you knew worthless ones, and these in the hardness of your hearts you have made known to the women, and through these mysteries women and men work much evil on earth.' [4] Say to them therefore: 'You have no peace.'"

Source: Translated by R. H. Charles in *The Apocrypha and Pseudepigrapha of the Old Testament in English*, vol. 2: Pseudepigrapha (Oxford: Clarendon Press, 1913), 191–199.

Commentary: *One of ancient astronaut theorists' most important texts, cited by everyone from Erich von Däniken to the cast of* Ancient Aliens, *this passage from Enoch, believed to be based on an older text, expands on the Genesis 6:1–4 narrative and diabolized the Sons of God as fallen angels, or Watchers, taking their name from the messengers of God of Jewish lore (cf. Daniel 4:13) and showing traces of having been revised from a polytheistic text like 7 into which Enoch has been added as counterpoint. The text has a checkered history. It does not appear in the Jewish cannon but was accepted by some early Christian Church Fathers (e.g. Jude 14–15; Tertullian,* On the Apparel of Women *1.3, etc.) as antediluvian scripture kept safe by Noah. It was ultimately rejected as scripture by all but the Ethiopian and Eritrean churches. The text was lost to the West from Late Antiquity down to the Enlightenment, except in excerpts made by Syncellus and others. It was recovered in Ge'ez translation from Ethiopia where it had been part of that country's Old Testament canon since the early centuries CE, remaining canonical due to the country's isolation from the wider Christian world in the Middle Ages. That the author of the Book of the Watchers was reacting to pagan myths is evident from the appearance of Mount Hermon in the mythology of the Semitic city of Ugarit as the site of Baal's palace, and reference to its importance as a holy sanctuary for the gentiles in Eusebius'* Onomasticon *20:12. Known as the mountain of oath, the Enochian writer is intentionally conflating the pagan gods with the developing myth of the fallen angels, the demons now under the earth. Thus, this influential text contributed to the myth of Satan as well as Christian visions of the apocalypse. Ancient astronaut theorists like Zecharia Sitchin and Erich von Däniken read the fallen angels as space aliens who violated a* Star Trek *type prime directive, earning the ire of other groups of space aliens who promise punishment. The following text is dependent upon but differs from Enoch, testifying to the variety of opinion surrounding the expanding Watcher myth.*

Notes

1. Ge'ez is a Semitic language related to Hebrew, Aramaic, and Arabic. It is the liturgical language of the Ethiopian Orthodox Church.

2. This is probably a corruption of Shamsiêl from 8:3, reflecting the name of the Mesopotamian sun-god, Shamash.

3. Cf. Jude 6: "And the angels which kept not their first estate, but left their own habitation, he hath reserved in everlasting chains under darkness unto the judgment of the great day."

4. Azâzêl appears in Leviticus 16 in conjunction with a scapegoat, but it is unclear if a demon or a place is meant. The Dead Sea Scrolls (4Q180, 4Q530) make him into a demon, as does the *Apocalypse of Abraham* 13:4–9, 23:7. Scholars believe that 1 Enoch conflates two separate traditions, one centered on Azâzêl (Aramaic: Asael) and forbidden knowledge, and the other on Semjâzâ and sexual sin.

10. Further Testimony of the Watchers
Book of Jubilees
4:15, 5:1–20, 7:20–28, 8:1–4, 10:1, 8–12
c. 150 BCE
Hebrew, preserved in Ge'ez
Astro, Prehistoric

Chapter 4

[15] And in the second week of the tenth jubilee Mahalalel took unto him to wife Dînâh, the daughter of Barâkî'êl the daughter of his father's brother, and she bare him a son in the third week in the sixth year, and he called his name Jared; for in his days the angels of the Lord descended on the earth, those who are named the Watchers, that they should instruct the children of men, and that they should do judgment and uprightness on the earth.

Chapter 5

[1] And it came to pass when the children of men began to multiply on the face of the earth and daughters were born unto them, that the angels of God¹ saw them on a certain year of this jubilee, that they were beautiful to look upon; and they took themselves wives of all whom they chose, and they bare unto them sons and they were giants. [2] And lawlessness increased on the earth and all flesh corrupted its way, alike men and cattle and beasts and birds and everything that walketh on the earth—all of them corrupted their ways and their orders, and they began to devour each other, and lawlessness increased on the earth and every imagination of the thoughts of all men (was) thus evil continually. [3] And God looked upon the earth, and behold it was corrupt, and all flesh had corrupted its orders, and all that were upon the earth had wrought all manner of evil before His eyes. [4] And He said: "I shall destroy man and all flesh upon the face of the earth which I have created." [5] But Noah found grace before the eyes of the Lord. [6] And against the angels whom He had sent upon the earth, He was exceedingly wroth, and He gave commandment to root them out of all their dominion, and He bade us to bind them in the depths of the earth, and behold they are bound in the midst of them, and are (kept) separate. [7] And against their sons went forth a command from before His face that they should be smitten with the sword, and be removed from under heaven. [8] And He said "Thy spirit will not always abide on man; for they also are flesh and their days shall be one hundred and twenty years." [9] And He sent His sword into their midst that each should slay his neighbour, and they began to slay each other till they all fell by the sword and were destroyed from the earth. [10] And their fathers were witnesses (of their destruction), and after this they were bound in the depths of the earth for ever, until the day of the great condemnation when judgment is executed on all those who have corrupted their ways and their works before the Lord. [11] And He destroyed all from their places, and there was not left one of them whom He judged not according to all their wickedness. [12] And He made for all His works a new and righteous nature, so that they should not sin in their whole nature for ever, but should be all righteous each in his kind alway. [13] And the judgment of all is ordained and written on the heavenly tables in righteousness—even (the judgment of) all who depart from the path which is ordained for them to walk in; and if they walk not therein judgment is written down for every creature and for every kind. [14] And there is nothing in heaven or on earth, or in light or in darkness, or in Sheol or in the depth, or in the place of darkness (which is not judged); and all their judgments are ordained and written and engraved. [15] In regard to all He will judge, the great according to his greatness, and the small according to his smallness, and each according to his way. [16] And He is not one who will regard the person (of any), nor is He one who will receive gifts, if He saith that He will execute judgment on each: if one gave everything that is on the earth, He will not regard the gifts or the person (of any), nor accept

anything at his hands, for He is a righteous judge. [17] And of the children of Israel it hath been written and ordained: If they turn to Him in righteousness, He will forgive all their transgressions and pardon all their sins. [18] It is written and ordained that He will show mercy to all who turn from all their guilt once each year. [19] And as for all those who corrupted their ways and their thoughts before the flood, no man's person was accepted save that of Noah alone; for his person was accepted in behalf of his sons, whom (God) saved from the waters of the flood on his account; for his heart was righteous in all his ways, according as it was commanded regarding him, and he had not departed from aught that was ordained for him. [20] And the Lord said that He would destroy everything which was upon the earth, both men and cattle, and beasts, and fowls of the air, and that which moveth on the earth.

CHAPTER 7

[20] And in the twenty-eighth jubilee Noah began to enjoin upon his sons' sons the ordinances and commandments, and all the judgments that he knew, and he exhorted his sons to observe righteousness, and to cover the shame of their flesh, and to bless their Creator, and honour father and mother, and love their neighbour, and guard their souls from fornication and uncleanness and all iniquity. [21] For owing to these three things came the flood upon the earth, namely, owing to the fornication wherein the Watchers against the law of their ordinances went a whoring after the daughters of men, and took themselves wives of all which they chose: and they made the beginning of uncleanness. [22] And they begat sons the Nâphîdîm, and they were all unlike, and they devoured one another: and the Giants slew the Nâphîl, and the Nâphîl slew the Eljô, and the Eljô mankind, and one man another. [23] And every one sold himself to work iniquity and to shed much blood, and the earth was filled with iniquity. [24] And after this they sinned against the beasts and birds, and all that moveth and walketh on the earth: and much blood was shed on the earth, and every imagination and desire of men imagined vanity and evil continually. [25] And the Lord destroyed everything from off the face of the earth; because of the wickedness of their deeds, and because of the blood which they had shed in the midst of the earth He destroyed everything. [26] "And we were left, I and you, my sons, and everything that entered with us into the ark, and behold I see your works before me that ye do not walk in righteousness; for in the path of destruction ye have begun to walk, and ye are parting one from another, and are envious one of another, and (so it cometh) that ye are not in harmony, my sons, each with his brother. [27] For I see, and behold the demons have begun (their) seductions against you and against your children, and now I fear on your behalf, that after my death ye will shed the blood of men upon the earth, and that ye, too, will be destroyed from the face of the earth. [28] For whoso sheddeth man's blood, and whoso eateth the blood of any flesh, will all be destroyed from the earth...."

CHAPTER 8

[1] In the twenty-ninth jubilee, in the first week, in the beginning thereof Arpachshad took to himself a wife and her name was Râsû'ĕjâ, the daughter of Sûsân, the daughter of Elam, and she bare him a son in the third year in this week, and he called his name Kâinâm.[2] [2] And the son grew, and his father taught him writing, and he went to seek for himself a place where he might seize for himself a city. [3] And he found a writing which former (generations) had carved on the rock, and he read what was thereon, and he transcribed it and sinned owing to it; for it contained the teaching of the Watchers in accordance with which

they used to observe the omens of the sun and moon and stars in all the signs of heaven.[3] [4] And he wrote it down and said nothing regarding it; for he was afraid to speak to Noah about it lest he should be angry with him on account of it. [...]

CHAPTER 10

[1] And in the third week of this [thirty-third] jubilee the unclean demons began to lead astray the children of the sons of Noah; and to make to err and destroy them. [...] [8] And the chief of the spirits, Mastêmâ [i.e. Satan], came and said: "Lord, Creator, let some of them remain before me, and let them hearken to my voice, and do all that I shall say unto them; for if some of them are not left to me, I shall not be able to execute the power of my will on the sons of men; for these are for corruption and leading astray before my judgment, for great is the wickedness of the sons of men." [9] And He said: "Let the tenth part[4] of them remain before him, and let nine parts descend into the place of condemnation." [10] And one of us He commanded that we should teach Noah all their medicines; for He knew that they would not walk in uprightness, nor strive in righteousness. [11] And we did according to all His words: all the malignant evil ones we bound in the place of condemnation, and a tenth part of them we left that they might be subject before Satan on the earth. [12] And we explained to Noah all the medicines of their diseases, together with their seductions, how he might heal them with herbs of the earth.

Source: Translated by R. H. Charles in *The Apocrypha and Pseudepigrapha of the Old Testament in English*, vol. 2: Pseudepigrapha (Oxford: Clarendon Press, 1913), 18–28.

Commentary: *Slightly different than the version recorded by Enoch, in Jubilees God's angels descended for noble purpose before human women tempted them into sexual sin. In 1 Enoch 6, they descended in open rebellion against God. Jubilees, like 1 Enoch, was once held to be true and accurate by Church Fathers such as Justin Martyr as well as Jewish scholars, but both faiths excluded the book from their canons, and it survived only in Ge'ez translation in Ethiopia. Texts like Jubilees remove responsibility for inducing the Flood from human beings and to ascribe it entirely to the work of fallen angels, a heresy against the doctrine of Original Sin. In Judaism and much of Christianity, the Sons of God were henceforth to be interpreted as the children of pious Seth (see* 12 *as well as Sextus Julius Africanus in* 53*), fully human followers of God's way, but eventually corrupted, in opposition to the sons (and daughters) of man, descendants of the sinning fratricide Cain, which included Enoch and Noah and thus all the human race after the Flood (e.g., Augustine,* City of God *15.8).*

Notes

1. The Septuagint gives the sons of God from Genesis 6:2 as "angels."
2. A descendant of Shem and ancestor of Jesus (Luke 3:36).
3. Cf. the Pillars of Wisdom in **12** and buried writings of Xisuthrus in **20**.
4. Only one-tenth are permitted to act freely against mankind till the Day of Judgment; but in 1 Enoch 15–16, all the demons are allowed to do this. (R.H.C.)

II

The Pyramids Before the Flood

If there is one eternal truth about the pyramids of Egypt, it is that they are perpetually in wont of new explanations to justify the fascination they hold over the mind. In their great bulk and their seemingly superhuman construction, they call across the ages with the promise of wonder and mystery. Whether the observer's explanation for them be Biblical (see **11** for their building by the children of Seth and chapter 7 of Sir John Mandeville's *Travels* for claims for them as Joseph's Granaries), the work of a lost civilization (as per *AW* and *FG*), or the work of space aliens (*CG*), fringe writers cannot accept the pyramids as pharaohs' tombs. "Anyone who can believe that explanation," Erich von Däniken wrote in *CG*, "is welcome to it...."[1] Although von Däniken never explicitly says aliens *built* the pyramids in *CG*, he heavily implies that their design, construction, and perfection were impossible without alien help in a chapter that asked whether ancient monuments like the pyramids were "space travel centers."

The Egyptian pyramids have fascinated visitors since the age of the pharaohs, and it is hardly a surprise that by the Greek and Roman periods, when the Great Pyramid was more than two thousand years old, the pyramids had become the locus of myths and legends by people as distant in time from their construction as we today are from the Greeks and Romans. Herodotus had correctly reported that the Great Pyramid had been its builder's tomb (*Histories* 2.124), but after him the process of mythologizing really got under way. Intriguingly, the myths of the pyramids came not from the Egyptians or the Greeks or the Romans but rather from the Abrahamic faiths, who recreated the history Egypt in the image of the homegrown myth of the Watchers. These fallen angels gradually became identified with the mythical alchemist Hermes Trismegistus, a favorite figure among fringe historians and later the reputed builder of the pyramids.

The texts that follow outline the process by which older stories were reinterpreted and reapplied to the Pyramids, and in them we see a precursor of the way modern fringe theorists reinterpreted the resulting myths in light of lost civilization and alien theories, euhemerizing medieval myths for the space age. The Arabic historians had done the same thing almost a millennium earlier in remaking Hellenistic and Late Antique legends for the Islamic world of the Middle Ages.

Note

1. Erich von Däniken, *Chariots of the Gods? Unsolved Mysteries of the Past*, trans. Michael Heron (New York: Bantam, 1973), 80.

11. Khufu Builds the Great Pyramid, Writes Sacred Book

Sextus Julius Africanus
Chronography (lost)
After 221 CE
Preserved in George Syncellus, *Chronicle* 63
Greek

Suphis (reigned) for 63 years. He built the Great Pyramid, which Herodotus[1] says was constructed by Cheops. He became contemptuous toward the gods and also wrote the Sacred Book, which I acquired on my trip to Egypt because of its great renown.

Source: Translated by Jason Colavito from Karl Müller, *Fragmenta historicorum Graecorum* (Paris: Didot, 1848), 548.

Commentary: *Africanus, a Christian apologist and historian, acquired the Sacred Book during his time in Alexandria studying under Heraclas (Eusebius,* Church History 6.31.2)*, but the facts he discusses he took from a summary of the now-lost history of Egypt called the* Aegyptiaca *of the Egyptian priest Manetho (Manethōn) from the third century BCE, which drew upon now-lost Egyptian records and forms the basis for modern chronologies of Egyptian dynastic history. Another version of the same passage was recorded by Eusebius and can be found in Syncellus (64). It differs from the version above. In this version, Suphis (= Khufu, in Manetho's style of Greek transliteration) "became contemptuous of the gods and, repenting his impiety, wrote the Sacred Book, which the Egyptians hold in high esteem" (my translation).*

Note

1. *Histories* 2.124.

12. The Children of Seth Build the Pyramids Before the Flood

Flavius Josephus
Antiquities of the Jews 1.68–74
c. 93–94 CE
Greek
Astro, Atlantis, Prehistoric
Discussion in FG, SM

[68] ... Now this Seth [...] was himself of an excellent character, so did he leave children behind him who imitated his virtues. [69] All these proved to be of good dispositions. They also inhabited the same country without dissensions, and in a happy condition, without any misfortunes falling upon them, till they died. They also were the inventors of that peculiar sort of wisdom which is concerned with the heavenly bodies, and their order. [70] And that their inventions might not be lost before they were sufficiently known, upon Adam's prediction that the world was to be destroyed at one time by the force of *fire*, and at another time by the violence and quantity of *water*, they made two pillars, the one of brick, the other of stone: they inscribed their discoveries on them both, [71] that in case the pillar of brick should be destroyed by the flood, the pillar of stone might remain, and exhibit those discoveries to mankind; and also inform them that there was another pillar of brick erected by them. Now this remains in the land of Siriad [i.e., Egypt] to this day.

[72] Now this posterity of Seth continued to esteem God as the Lord of the universe, and to have an entire regard to virtue, for seven generations; but in process of time they were

One of the longest-lived myths in history is that of the inscribed pillars bearing the lost knowledge of a forgotten world. Such pillars, found in Mesopotamian, Egyptian, Phoenician, Greek, Jewish, Christian, and Islamic lore, reflect the very real practice where ancient peoples inscribed religious and dynastic material on pillars and stelae, like this Egyptian obelisk at Luxor (Francis Frith/ Library of Congress).

perverted, and forsook the practices of their forefathers; and did neither pay those honors to God which were appointed them, nor had they any concern to do justice towards men. But for what degree of zeal they had formerly shown for virtue, they now showed by their actions a double degree of wickedness, whereby they made God to be their enemy. [73] For many angels of God[1] accompanied with women, and begat sons that proved unjust, and despisers of all that was good, on account of the confidence they had in their own strength; for the tradition is, that these men did what resembled the acts of those whom the Grecians call giants. [74] But Noah was very uneasy at what they did; and being displeased at their conduct, persuaded them to change their dispositions and their acts for the better: but seeing they did not yield to him, but were slaves to their wicked pleasures, he was afraid they would kill him, together with his wife and children, and those they had married; so he departed out of that land.

Source: Translated by William Whiston in *The Genuine Works of Flavius Josephus,* vol. 1 (New York: David Huntington, 1815), 88–89.

Commentary: *Flavius Josephus was a Jewish historian whose works preserve fragments of myths and legends not found in other sources. Often used to support the idea that an advanced civilization such as Atlantis gave rise to Mesopotamia (brick pillar = ziggurats) and Egypt* *(stone pillar = pyramids), the text is very clearly an antecedent to the later myth of Sūrīd's dream (see **17**), for both have the same details of a prophecy of destruction by both flood and flame prompting the construction of monuments engraved with knowledge.*

*The children of Seth identified as the builders were the Nephilim of Genesis 6:4 in the interpretation favored at the time, which argued that the sons of God were corrupt descendants of Seth's pious line (see commentary for **10**; cf. the slightly different euhemerizing in the first book of the pseudo–Sibylline Oracles), making this another derivative of the Watchers-giants myth. This reading is confirmed by Sextus Julius Africanus (see **53**). More confirmation can be found in the scholarly observation that in other texts Enoch was the original builder of the pillars, as given in the Armenian texts* History of the Forefathers *40–44 and* Abel *4.3–6 (though sometimes with Enosh confused for Enoch). The pillars also appear in Jubilees 8:3–4 (**10**) as artifacts of the Watchers remaining after the Flood, under the authorship of Enoch's great-grandfather Kâinâm (Kenan) in the* Book of Jasher *(2:12–13) as prophecies, and in the Latin* Life of Adam and Eve *as tablets of stone and clay that Eve tells Seth to make to preserve all knowledge (50.1–2), exactly parallel to the tablets preserving all knowledge that Xisuthrus creates and buries at Sippara in Berossus (**20**). This belief had a wide currency in Mesopotamia. Around 1900 BCE, the* Epic of Gilgamesh *said that the antediluvian hero "has brought knowledge from farther back than the Deluge ... and has engraved on stone stelae all of his labors" (1.6–9). The seventh-century BCE king Ashurbanipal wrote in the colophon to his library's tablets that he could "read inscriptions on stone from before the Flood."*

The prophecy Adam gave had wide currency in apocryphal Jewish and Christian literature. It appears in the Latin Life of Adam and Eve *(49.3), though attributed to Eve, and also in the* Apocalypse of Adam *found in the Nag Hammandi corpus, as well as in **13** below, given now by Seth. In the medieval Byzantine* Palaea Historica *Enoch delivers the prophecy and writes the tablets himself. This tradition is also reflected in the destructions of fire and water alluded to in 2 Peter 3:3–7. The water is, of course the Flood, and the fire is interpreted as apocalyptic Judgment, from which theology the writers of these texts back-formed the prophecy. Perhaps unsurprisingly, it has a parallel in Babylonian astrology as given by Berossus (**111**).*

Note

1. The Septuagint renders "sons of God" in Genesis 6:2 as "angels of God."

13. Ham and Seth Create the Tablets of Wisdom
St. John Cassian
Collationes 8.21
c. 428 CE
Latin

[T]he sons of Seth who were the sons of God, [...] fell away from that true study of natural philosophy, handed down to them by their ancestors....[1] This knowledge then of all nature the seed of Seth received through successive generations, handed down from the fathers, so long as it remained separate from the wicked line [of Cain], and as it had received it in holiness, so it made use of it to promote the glory of God and the needs of everyday life. But when it had been mingled with the evil generation, it drew aside at the suggestion of devils to profane and harmful uses what it had innocently learned, and audaciously taught by it the curious arts of wizards and enchantments and magical superstitions, teaching its posterity to forsake the holy worship of the Divinity and to honour and worship either the elements or fire or the demons of the air. How it was then that this knowledge of curious arts of which we have spoken, did not perish in the deluge, but became known to the ages that followed, should, I think, be briefly explained, as the occasion of this discussion suggests, although the answer to the question raised scarcely requires it. And so, as ancient traditions tell us, Ham the son of Noah, who had been taught these superstitions and wicked and profane arts, as he knew that he could not possibly bring any handbook on these subjects into the ark, into which he was to enter with his good father and holy brothers, inscribed these nefarious arts and profane devices on plates of various metals which could not be destroyed by the flood of waters, and on hard rocks, and when the flood was over he hunted for them with the same inquisitiveness with which he had concealed them, and so transmitted to his descendants a seed-bed of profanity and perpetual sin. In this way then that common notion, according to which men believe that angels delivered to men enchantments and diverse arts, is in truth fulfilled. From these sons of Seth then and daughters of Cain, as we have said, there were born still worse children who became mighty hunters, violent and most fierce men who were termed giants by reason of the size of their bodies and their cruelty and wickedness. For these first began to harass their neighbours and to practise pillaging among men, getting their living rather by rapine than by being contented with the sweat and labour of toil, and their wickedness increased to such a pitch that the world could only be purified by the flood and deluge.

Source: Translated by C. S. Gibson in Henry Wace and Philip Schaff (eds.), *A Select Library of Nicene and Post-Nicene Fathers of the Christian Church*, second series, vol. 11 (Oxford: James Parker and Company, 1894), 383–384.

Commentary: *In this passage, our author, Cassian, is quoting his friend, the Egyptian abbot Serenus, who held that the children of Seth had been corrupted by the daughters of Cain; therefore, their divinely-inspired knowledge of the earth and the heavens had become corrupted into magic and superstition. He is, of course, referring to the Book of Enoch and parallel texts but has assigned Enoch's (or Seth's) role to Ham, probably under the influence of the popular belief that identified Ham with Zoroaster and thus with Chaldean astrology and the origins of magic (Pseudo-Clement,* Recognitions *4.27). This passage is cited in* Isis Unveiled *(1877), a book by Helena Blavatsky, the founder of Theosophy, a religion that postulated the influence of ancient beings from other planets on the earth, and an important influence on ancient astronaut writers like Jacques Bergier, Louis Pauwels, and Erich von Däniken. Blavatsky, preferring the angelic explanation, claims this passage as evidence that visitors from other planes (or planets) delivered secret science in primeval times.*

GEORGE KEDRENOS

A Concise History of the World, p. 27
c. 1050 CE
Greek
Astro, Prehistoric, Atlantis

Seth is recorded as the third son of Adam. [...] He was also called God, because of the shining of his face, which lasted all his life. [...] Seth gave names to the seven planets, and comprehended the lore of the movement of the heavens. He also prepared two pillars, one of stone and one of brick and wrote these things upon them. [...] In the 270th year of Adam Seth was caught away by an angel and instructed in what concerned the future transgression of his sons (that is to say, the Watchers, who were also called Sons of God), and concerning the Flood and the coming of the Saviour. And on the fortieth day after he had disappeared, he returned and told the protoplasts all that he had been taught by the angel. He was comely and well-formed, both he and those that were born of him, who were called Watchers and Sons of God because of the shining of the face of Seth. And they dwelt on the higher land of Eden near to Paradise, living the life of angels, until the 1000th year of the world.

Source: Translated by Montague Rhodes James in *The Lost Apocrypha of the Old Testament* (London: Society for Promoting Christian Knowledge, 1920), 9.

Commentary: *In this medieval variant (partially reproduced in Syncellus 10), Seth has taken over Enoch's role in the Watchers story, but it otherwise follows pillars story given in Josephus (12), testifying to the continued existence of two coequal variants of the same story, the angelic and the Sethite. Slightly earlier, George Syncellus gave both accounts separately but did not reconcile the discrepancies (10, 12, 19); the Byzantine historian Kedrenos has merged them into one under Seth's name, which is important for understanding how such stories eventually were transferred from Enoch and Seth to Hermes Trismegistus, as we will see below.*

Note

1. Cassian has Serenus quote Wisdom of Solomon 7:17–21 hereafter to describe this wisdom God gave to Adam, who passed it on to Seth. However, the passage purports to quote Solomon, not Adam, whom nonetheless Serenus suspects of also having received knowledge of pharmacology, astronomy, and the cycles of the earth as part of God's wisdom curriculum.

14. The Egyptians Prepare for the Flood

Ammianus Marcellinus
Roman History 22.15.30
Before 391 CE
Latin
Astro, Prehistoric, Atlantis

There are also [in Egypt] subterranean passages, and winding retreats, which, it is said, men skilful, in the ancient mysteries, by means of which they divined the coming of a flood, constructed in different places lest the memory of all their sacred ceremonies should be lost. On the walls, as they cut them out, they have sculptured several kinds of birds and beasts, and countless other figures of animals, which they call hieroglyphics.

Source: Translated by C. D. Yonge in Ammianus Marcellinus, *The Roman History* (London: George Bell & Sons, 1902), 311–312.

Commentary: *The soldier-historian Ammianus was describing the royal tombs of Egypt but interpreting them in a Judeo-Christian framework similar to that given in Josephus. His account is important for showing the transition of the story from a Jewish to an Egyptian context, all the more remarkable since Ammianus is believed to have been a pagan, albeit tolerant of Christians. He lived in the period of Julian the Apostate, the last period of pagan revival during the process of Christianization, and during this time even pagans had begun to adopt Christian beliefs and concepts as part of a wider syncretizing of ancient faiths. This passage testifies to the* *wide dissemination of the myths in question, marrying the Near East flood myth with the prover-bial wisdom of Egypt, the Tablets of Hermes already proverbial in Greek times (Iamblicus, Theurgia 1.2)*

15. Hermes Inscribes Pillars of Wisdom Before the Flood

George Syncellus
Chronicon 41
c. 800 CE
Greek
Astro, Prehistoric, Atlantis

It remains, therefore, to make certain extracts concerning the dynasties of the Egyptians, from the writings of Manetho the Sebennyte, the high priest of the idolatrous temple of Egypt in the time of Ptolemy Philadelphus. These, according to his own account, he copied from the inscriptions which were engraved in the sacred dialect, and hieroglyphic characters, upon the columns[1] set up in the Seriadic land, by Thoth, the first Hermes[2]; and after the deluge, translated from the sacred dialect into the Greek tongue in hieroglyphic characters: and committed to writing in books, and deposited by Agathodaemon, the son of the second Hermes, the father of Tat, in the temple-shrines of Egypt.

Source: Adapted from the translation of I. P. Cory in *Ancient Fragments,* 2nd ed. (London: William Pickering, 1832), 168.

Commentary: *Syncellus believed he was discussing a genuine text of the Egyptian priest-historian Manetho (see 11), but he was instead referring to an imperial-era forgery called the* Book of Sothis. *While the Flood reference in this passage suggests contamination from the Jose-phus narrative (12, known to Syncellus), its primary value is demonstrating that Hermes Tris-megistus (in one of his many forms) was associated with the pillars of wisdom before the Flood, almost certainly due to the wide association of Hermes with hieroglyphic inscriptions on Egyptian temple columns and obelisks, as in the "sacred books ... and mysterious stelae" of Hermes alluded to in pseudo–Manetho's imperial-era* Apotelesmatica 5:1–2 *and the "secret stelae" of the* Kore Kosmou *(57).*

In the Arabic-speaking world, the conflation was even more explicit. Around 1140 CE, for example, Muhammad al-Shahrastānī wrote in his Kitāb al-Milal wa al-Nihal, *"They (the Sabi-ans) say that Adsimun (Agathodaemon) and Hermes were Seth and Enoch respectively" (2.1.1, my trans.). Such texts provide the connecting link between the Judeo-Christian myth that Enoch or Seth built pillars of wisdom in Egypt and the later Arab myth that these were built by Hermes (16) or Sūrīd (17). However, other authors make Seth, Agathodaemon, and Hermes-Enoch three separate figures each associated with a pyramid. The fifteenth century historian Al-Maqrīzī, quoting an earlier author, says that at Giza "one of these pyramids is the tomb of A'adimun (Agathodaemon) and the other of Hermes" (Al-Khitat 1.40). Interestingly, this seems to be a corruption of the late Antique tradition recorded by Zosimus of Panopolis (53) that Hermes Trismegistus recorded the history of the fallen angels and attributed to them the invention of alchemy.*

Notes

1. *Stēlai*; literally, blocks of stone.
2. The Greeks identified Hermes with the Egyptian god Thoth because both were gods of writing, but

so confusing had the legends of Hermes become that the ancients proposed that several gods and demigods shared the name; Cicero recorded five (*De natura deorum* 3.22). Christians and Muslims adopted the idea of more than one Hermes to allow him to exist before the Flood and still serve as patron of alchemy after it.

16. Hermes Builds the Pyramids Before the Flood
Abū Maʿšar al-Balkhī
The Thousands
10th c. CE
Arabic
Preserved in Ṣāʿid al-Andalusī, *Al-tarif bi-tabaqat al-umm* 39.7–16
1068 CE
Arabic
Astro, Prehistoric, Atlantis

A group of scholars have reported that all the sciences known before the Flood were first taught by Hermes, who lived in Upper Egypt. This Hermes was the first to ponder celestial events[1] and the movement of the stars. This Hermes is the one the Hebrews named Enoch, son of Jared, son of Mahalalel, son of Kenan, son of Enos, son of Seth, son of Adam, peace be upon him. He is the same as the prophet Idrīs,[2] peace be upon him. He was the first to build temples to worship God the Exalted. He occupied himself with science and medicine, and he wrote well-measured poems for his contemporaries about things terrestrial and celestial. It is also said that he was the first to predict the Flood and anticipate that a celestial cataclysm would befall the earth in the form of fire or water, so, fearing the destruction of knowledge and the disappearance of the arts, he built the pyramids and temples of Upper Egypt. Within these, he included representations of the arts and instruments, including engraved explanations of science, in order to pass them on to those who would come after him, lest he see them disappear from the world.

Source: Translated by Jason Colavito from the quotation appearing in the French edition of Maqrīzī, *Description topographique et historique de l'Égypte,* part 1, trans. U. Bouriant, Mémoires de la mission archéologique française du Caire 17 (Paris: 1895), 75–76, with corrections against modern translations of the original.

Commentary: *Ṣāʿid al-Andalusī is here repeating information from the ninth-century Iranian astrologer Abū Maʿšar al-Balkhī (d. 886 CE), whose* Book of Thousands *does not survive. A parallel text, also taken from Abū Maʿšar, largely in the same words, appears in Ibn Ğuğul in his* Ṭabaqāt al-aṭibbāʾ *5–10 in the 900s CE, confirming the substance of the lost text. The group of scholars to whom Ṣāʿid refers are those who have also copied material from Abū Maʿšar. The dependence of this story on the stories represented in 12 and 14 should be obvious.*

Notes

1. The Arabic reads "substances," but here Ṣāʿid al-Andalusī has misread the word for "events" in the original of Abū Maʿšar al-Balkhī, as confirmed by the parallel text of Ibn Ğuğul (*Ṭabaqāt al-aṭibbāʾ* 5–10). Since we are interested in the older author's original thoughts, not a later author's transcription error, I have restored the original.

2. A prophet translated bodily to heaven, as was Enoch (Qurʾan 19:56–57; cf. Genesis 5:24), and said in Islamic commentaries to have been the first to study astronomy, the first to write, and the composer of scriptures. The identity of the two prophets was accepted from at least the ninth century.

17. Sūrīd Builds the Pyramids Before the Flood

Ibrāhīm ibn Waṣīf Shāh
History of Egypt and Its Wonders
Late 12th c.
Arabic
Preserved in Al-Maqrīzī, *Al-Khitat* 1.40
c. 1400 CE
Astro, Prehistoric, Atlantis
Discussion in CG

The writer Master Ibrāhīm ibn Waṣīf Shāh, in his *History of Egypt and Its Wonders*, speaking of Sūrīd bin Sahlūq bin Seriaq bin Tumidun bin Badresan bin Husal, one of the kings who ruled Egypt before the Flood and who resided in the city of Amsūs[1] (which will be discussed in the chapter of this book [i.e., *Al-Khitat* 2.2] that deals with the cities of Egypt), said: The raising of the Two Pyramids[2] in Egypt is attributed to Shaddād bin 'Ād: Copts claim that, thanks to the power of their magic, 'Ādites[3] could not enter their country. Here is what was the cause of the erection of the two pyramids: Three hundred years before the flood, Sūrīd had a dream in which it seemed that the earth overturned, and the men fled straight ahead, and the stars fell and collided against each other with a terrible crash; Sūrīd, scared, spoke to no one about this dream, but he was convinced that a major event would occur in the world. A few days later he had another dream in which he felt that the fixed stars had descended on the earth in the form of white birds and, catching men while in flight, rushed between two high mountains which closed over them; and the bright stars became dark and obscure. Full of terror when he awoke, he went to the temple of the Sun, prayed, rolled in the dust, and wept. As soon as it was day, he gathered the chief priests of all the provinces of Egypt; the number was 130. He shut himself up with them and explained what he had seen in his first and second dream. The priests explained to the King that an extraordinary event would occur in the world, and the greatest of them, named Aqlimun, said unto him, "The dreams of Kings do not happen for no reason, because of the importance of princes. I shall tell Pharaoh of a dream I had myself and that I have not spoken of to anyone. It seemed that while I was sitting with the King in the tower at Amsūs, the sky, leaving its place, fell down and approached our heads, forming above us a dome that enveloped us. The King raised his hands to the sky with the stars mingling among men in various forms. People ran, seeking refuge at the King's palace and requesting help. The King raised his hands to his head, telling me to do the same, and we were both in terrible anxiety. And now, from the tower where we were, we saw a part of the sky about to open and a bright light escaped from the breach. The Sun appeared, and we began to beg. And the Sun told us that the sky would return to its original place. I awoke full of terror, and then I fell asleep and I saw the city of Amsūs overturned with its inhabitants, the idols fallen on their heads, and men descended from heaven holding in their hands iron whips, with which they hit mortals. 'Why,' I asked them, 'do you strike at men?' They said, 'They have shown their wickedness to God.' 'Is there not,' I said, 'some way for us to redeem ourselves?' And they said: 'Yes, whoever wants to be saved must go to reach the master of the Ark.' Thereupon I awoke full of terror." The King said: "Take the elevations of the stars and see what needs to happen." After a thorough review, it was recognized that a deluge would occur after which would appear a fire out of the constellation Leo which will burn the world. "See," said the

King said, "if this disaster will reach our country." "Yes," they said, "the flood will reach us and we will be ruined for many years." "See," said the King, "if this country becomes prosperous as before or if it will remain still covered by water." "The country," said the priests, "will return to its former state and remain prosperous." "And after?" asked the King. "Our country will be attacked by a king who will raise up the inhabitants and will take hold of their wealth." "And after?" "A barbaric people, coming to the mountains of the Nile, will attack it and will be master of the largest part of the territory." "And after?" "The Nile will be cut off and the country abandoned by its inhabitants." Then the king commanded the building of the pyramids and canals where the Nile would fill up reservoirs to a specific spot, and then would flow to certain areas of the West and Saïd. He completed the pyramids with talismans, wonders, wealth, and idols, and he deposited within them the bodies of kings. According to his orders, priests engraved on these monuments all sayings of the wise.[4] They wrote on every surface of the pyramids—the ceilings, foundations, and walls—all the sciences familiar to the Egyptians. They drew the figures of the stars; they wrote the names of the drugs and their useful and harmful properties, the science of talismans, mathematics, architecture—all the sciences of the world—and it was all laid out very clearly.

Having made this decree, the king had blocks cut and polished slabs of enormous size extracted from the land of the West and the rocks of the Aswan region, and thus laid the

Fringe historians of many stripes have ideas about the true builders of the pyramids of Egypt. Although Egyptologists and historians are nearly unanimous in concluding that the structures were funerary monuments constructed by the Egyptians for their kings, most fringe historians agree that the Egyptians needed outside help to achieve these wonders. They disagree whether that help came from aliens, angels, Atlantis, or somewhere else (Library of Congress).

foundations of the three pyramids: East, West, and Colored.[5] The workers had with them sheets (papyrus) covered with writing, and as soon as a stone was cut and trimmed, they placed one of the sheets on the stone and gave it a blow, and the blow was enough to make it travel a distance of 100 *sahmes* (200 shots of the arrow), and this continued until the stone arrived at the Pyramids' plateau. In the middle of a slab was drilled a hole; in this hole was planted vertically an iron pin, and then this was placed on the preceding slab. A second hole for the iron pin penetrated the second slab, and then molten lead was run into the hole around the pin in order to secure the two slabs and make them steadfast. This continued until the completion of the pyramid. When the monuments were complete, the king dug doors 40 cubits below ground level. The door of the East pyramid turns eastward and opens 100 cubits from the face of the pyramid. The door of the West pyramid is west and at 100 cubits from the face of the pyramid. The door of the Colored pyramid turns south and is also 100 cubits from the face of the pyramid. If this distance is dug (vertically), there is (at 40 cubits deep) the door that gives access, by vaulted corridors and masonry, to enter the pyramid. The king calculated for each of the pyramids a height above ground of 100 of his cubits, which is 500 of our current cubits.[6] The length of each side was also 100 cubits, and the faces were calculated so that the pyramid's height stopped eight cubits before the geometric summit. The construction of these pyramids began under favorable constellations, all chosen by mutual agreement. When they were finished, they were covered up and down with colored silk, and a party was held which was attended by all the inhabitants of Egypt. In the Western pyramid were built thirty colored granite rooms filled with all kinds of wealth and various objects: statues of precious stones, beautiful iron tools, weapons that could not rust, malleable glass, extraordinary talismans, simple and compound drugs, and deadly poisons. In the East pyramid's rooms were executed representations of the sky and the stars, and they were crammed with statues of the ancestors of Sūrīd, perfumes which were burned for the planets, and the books that concerned the table of the fixed stars and the table of their revolution in the course of time, the list of events of past eras under their influence, and when they must be examined to know the future of everything about Egypt until the end of time. In addition, there lay basins containing magic elixirs and such things. In the Colored pyramid, they laid the bodies of priests locked in coffins of black granite, and with each priest was a book that traced the wonders of his art that he had exercised in his actions and his life, that which had been done in his time, and all that was from the beginning and will be until the end of time. On each side of the pyramids were made representations of characters performing all kinds of work and arranged according to their importance and dignity; these representations were accompanied by a description of their occupation, the tools they needed, and everything about them. No science was neglected; these were all drawn and described. Also placed in the pyramid were the treasures given to the planets, those given to the stars, and the treasures of the priests, all vast and incalculable in value.

At each of the pyramids a guardian was assigned: The Western pyramid was placed in the custody of a statue composed of granite; this statue was standing, holding in his hand something like a spear, and wore a viper wrapped around him. As soon as someone approached the statue, the viper sprang upon him, wrapped itself around his neck, killed him, and returned to his place. The guardian of the Eastern pyramid was a stone statue spotted black and white with eyes open and bright. She was seated on a throne and held a spear. If someone looked at her, he heard on the side of the statue a terrible voice that made him fall on his face and he died there without being able to get up. At the Colored pyramid was a stone statue of an eagle set on a similar stone base. Anyone who looked at it was attracted to it, stuck to it, and could not be detached until dead. With all of this completed, the pyramids were surrounded by intangible spirits; they were the victims of sacrifice, a ceremony intended to protect the pyramids against those who would like to approach them, with the exception of the initiates who complete the necessary rites to enter.

The Copts tell in their books that the sides of the pyramids were engraved with a text which in their language means: "I am Surīd, the king who raised these pyramids at such and such a time. I completed the construction in six years. If someone who comes after me claims to be my equal, let him destroy them in six hundred years, for we know that it is easier to destroy than to build. I have, after completing these, covered them with silk; let another try to cover them only with mats." And after consideration it was recognized that the most prolonged passage of time could not destroy them.

The Copts recount that the spirit attached to the pyramid of the North[7] is a naked yellow devil whose mouth is filled with long teeth. That of the Southern pyramid is a naked woman who reveals her natural parts; she is beautiful, but her mouth is filled with long teeth. She charms men who look at her, smiles at them, draws them in, and makes them lose their reason. The spirit of the Colored pyramid is an old man holding a church censer wherein burn perfumes. Many people have seen these spirits on numerous occasions around the pyramids in the middle of the day and at sunset.

After his death, Surīd was buried in the pyramid and his riches and treasures with him. Surīd, according to the Copts, is said to have built temples, filled them with treasures and engraved on their walls all the sciences, and given them spirits for guardians to protect them against those that may want to destroy them. The pyramids of Dashur were said to have been raised by Shadāt bin 'Ādim with stones once cut by his father.[8] According to some authors, this Shadāt is the same as Haddah bin 'Ād, but those who refuse to admit that the 'Ādites entered Egypt ignore the name Shadāt bin 'Ādim and instead say Shaddād bin 'Ād, a name that they have much more opportunity to say, for the other is not widely used. According to these, a single king (strange) would have entered Egypt and tamed its inhabitants; this king is Bokht-Nasr [Nebuchadnezzar]. But God is the most learned!

Source: Translated by Jason Colavito from the French in Maqrīzī, *Description topographique et historique de l'Égypte,* part 1, trans. U. Bouriant, Mémoires de la mission archéologique française du Caire 17 (Paris: 1895), 321–326.

Commentary: *Alternative historians see this myth, which bears a structural and thematic similarity to the dream of Pharaoh in Genesis 41, as evidence that the pyramids predate dynastic Egypt and thus were constructed by a prehistoric advanced civilization. The story is given in many other medieval Arabic writers, almost always in near-identical words, notably that of Murtaḍā ibn al-'Afīf and Idrīsī. The oldest full version is that of the* Akhbār al-zamān, *which Aloys Sprenger attributed to Al-Mas'ūdī in Vyse's* Operations Carried on at the Pyramid of Gizeh, *vol. 2 (1840) in partially translating the text, from which most fringe authors take their information, particularly Erich von Däniken in* CG, *who knows nothing of it beyond Vyse's book. However, the author of the* Akhbār al-zamān *is in dispute. Most scholars no longer believe it could be an abridgement of Al-Mas'ūdī, and some consider it the work of the same Ibrāhīm ibn Waṣīf Shāh quoted by Al-Maqrīzī. The legend itself probably originated in the eleventh century, derived from the earlier myth that Hermes built the pyramids (16), and more distantly* *from the Watchers. Here, however, the Arabic historians have attempted to de-mythologize the story by seeking out its presumed historical foundation, likely by correlating it with the work of Manetho (11), in the Syriac translation, and attributing their own legends about the builder of the Great Pyramid (Hermes) to the historical pharaoh Khufu, now called Sūrīd, on account of the Sacred Book he wrote, which they identified with the sacred writings of Hermes Trismegistus. Fringe historians, not recognizing these connections, treat this rationalized myth as a genuine historical account.*

Notes

1. The mythical antediluvian capital of Egypt in Islamic legend, located on the Mediterranean coast.
2. The Great Pyramid and the Pyramid of Khafre.
3. The ʿĀdites are the people of Iram, destroyed for their sins in Qurʾan 89:6–13 (see **61**). According to Al-Masʿūdī in his *Meadows of Gold, Mines of Gems* (c. 947 CE), chapter 37, the ʿĀdites were giants (cf. **8** at Genesis 6:4).
4. In the older version of the *Akhbār al-zamān*, the King ordered "the predictions of the priests to be inscribed upon columns, and upon the large stones belonging to them" within the pyramids, recalling the Pillars of Wisdom (**12**) (trans. Aloys Sprenger).
5. The Great Pyramid of Khufu, the pyramid of Khafre, and the pyramid of Menkaure, respectively.
6. The people of that age being, of course, antediluvian giants—the Nephilim.
7. Maqrīzī is now describing the Red and Bent Pyramids of Sneferu at Dashur, also called the North and South Pyramids respectively.
8. The antediluvian wizard-king ʿĀd of Iram. See **53**, **60**, and **61**.

III

The Flood, the Giants and the Ark

In Near Eastern myth, the Flood is the punishment visited on humanity and their Watcher overlords for grievous sin, whether that be impiety, rebellion, sexual libertinism, or noisiness. It is one of the most widespread of myths, found from Babylon to Greece and beyond. Historians generally agree that the oldest flood myth is that of the Sumerians, from which the Babylonian version derives. Close correspondences between these versions and those of Genesis and the Greeks suggest a transfer of motifs form the ancient Near East. Analogous myths occur in the New World as well (see **76**), though there is a question of the extent to which these stories have been influenced by contact with Old World versions, especially through missionary activity. Despite the claims of creationists and some fringe historians, there is no geological evidence of a global flood. Recent rationalizing claims have argued that the Flood myth was inspired by tales told by the survivors of the catastrophic filling of the Black Sea basin, which flooded when the Mediterranean broke through the Dardanelles around 5600 BCE.[1] Such claims, however, do not have sufficient proof to recommend the hypothesis. Instead, mythologists look at the flood myth in its Near Eastern form as a symbolic return of the waters of creation (see **1**, *Enuma Eliš* 1.5, parallel to Genesis 1:2) to remake the world.

For fringe historians, the Flood has a number of interpretations that push beyond a literal or even symbolic interpretation of biblical events. For many ancient astronaut theorists, it is, as Erich von Däniken wrote in *CG*, "a preconceived project by unknown beings with the intention of exterminating the human race."[2] For others, following astronomer Edmund Halley's statement to the Royal Society in 1694, the Flood was the work of "a *Comet,* or other transient Body" that crashed into the earth.[3] For Ignatius Donnelly in *AW*, the Flood of Noah was also the same Flood that ended the antediluvian civilization of Atlantis (see **48**), the inhabitants thereof being the same as the Sethites, or Watchers (see **12**). In *FG* Graham Hancock follows a similar line, rationalizing such stories as references to the rising sea levels at the end of the last Ice Age. For nearly all fringe historians, the appearance of Flood myths across cultures is used as evidence of diffusionism and connections between cultures separated by time and space.

This chapter examines the Flood and what followed, including the alleged survival of the antediluvian giants and the hunt for the remains of these giants as well as the Ark itself.

Notes

1. The claim was put forward by William Ryan and Walter Pitman in *Noah's Flood: The New Scientific Discoveries about the Event that Changed History* (New York: Simon and Schuster, 1998). Arguments and evidence

for and against can be found in Valentina Yanko-Hombach et al. (eds.), *The Black Sea Flood Question: Changes in Coastline, Climate and Human Settlement* (Netherlands: Springer, 2007).

2. Erich von Däniken, *Chariots of the Gods? Unsolved Mysteries of the Past*, trans. Michael Heron (New York: Bantam, 1973), 43.

3. "Considerations on the Cause of the Universal Deluge," *The Philosophical Transactions (From the Year 1719, to the Year 1733) Abridged*, vol. VI part II, eds. John Eames and John Martyn (London: 1734), 3.

18. The Egyptian Flood Myth
Book of the Dead, Chapter 175
c. 1250 BCE
Egyptian
Atlantis, Prehistoric
Discussion in FG

CHAPTER CLXXV.
Chapter of not dying a second death in the Netherworld.

[*Osiris is speaking.*] Thoth! What has become of the children of Nut? they have stirred up hostilities, they have raised storms, they have committed iniquity, they have raised rebellion, they have perpetrated murder, they have done oppression, and thus have acted, the strong against the weak, in all that they have done to me.

Grant, O Thoth, what Tmu hath decreed. Thou seest not the iniquities, thou art not pained at their attacks upon the years, and their invasions upon the months, because they have done their mischiefs in secret.

I am thy pallet, O Thoth, and I bring to thee thine inkstand; I am not one of those who do mischief in secret. Let not mischief be done unto me.

O Tmu! what is this place to which I have journeyed? for it is without water and without air! It is all abyss, utter darkness, sheer perplexity. One liveth here in peace of heart. There is no pleasure of love here. Let there be granted to me glory instead of water, air and pleasures of love; and peace of heart instead of bread and beer.

[Decree this, Tmu, that if I see thy face I shall not be pained by thy sufferings Tmu decrees; behold the great gods have given him this mission, he will reign on his throne and he will inherit his throne in the Isle of fire: and for thee I decree that the god may see him as his second self, and that my face may see thy face.

My lord Tmu, what is the duration of my life? Thou art for eternities of eternities, the duration of endless years; and behold I am going to deface all I have done: this earth will become water, an inundation as it was in the beginning. I will remain with Osiris, and I will make my form like another serpent, whom no man will know, and no god will see.

It is good what I have done to Osiris, who is exalted above all the gods. I have given him the power in the region of the Netherworld, and his son Horus will inherit his throne in the Isle of flame. I will make his throne in the boat of millions of (years). Horus is well established on his seat in order that he may take possession of his place of rest; also I send a soul to Sut in the West, who is exalted above all gods; and I have caused his soul to be guarded in the boat, so that he may feel reverential fear of the divine body (Osiris).][1]

O my father Osiris! I have done for thee what thy father Ra did for thee. Let me have increase upon earth, let me keep my dwelling place, let my heir be vigorous, let my sepulchre flourish and my dependents upon earth. Let all my adversaries be crushed to pieces with

Selk'et (the scorpion goddess) over their ruin. I am thy son, O my father Ra! thou hast been the cause of this Life,

Health and Strength. Horus is established upon his throne. Grant that my duration of Life may be that of one who attains beatitude.

Source: Translated by Sir P. Le Page Renouf in Renouf and E. Naville, *The Egyptian Book of the Dead* (London: Society for Biblical Archaeology, 1904), 356–357.

Commentary: *The book of the dead was a ritual funerary text and never intended to be taken as a historical chronicle. Nevertheless, this text is widely cited as proof that the Egyptians had a legend of the Great Flood similar to that of Noah. The passage giving this text, marked above in brackets, is wrongly attributed in alternative history literature to the famous* Papyrus of Ani. *Instead, it has been added to the text by translators from a fragmentary papyrus in the Museum of Leiden. Modern scholars interpret the passage as referring to a future event, the end of creation, rather than to a prehistoric flood event.*

Note

1. The bracketed text appears in a separate, fragmentary papyrus and was added to the rest of text by the translator. The text does not appear in the extant *Papyrus of Ani*, the source for the rest of the text.

19. The Mesopotamian Flood Myth

Epic of Gilgamesh, Tablet XI
1300 BCE or earlier
Akkadian
Astro, Prehistoric, Atlantis
Discussion in CG, SM

Gilgamesh said to him, to Utnapishtim, the distant: "I gaze upon thee (in amazement), O Utnapishtim! Thy appearance has not changed, like unto me thou art also. And thy nature itself has not changed, like unto me thou art also, though thou hast departed this life. But my heart has still to struggle against all that no longer lies upon thee. Tell me, How didst thou come to dwell (here) and obtain eternal life among the gods?"

Utnapishtim then said unto Gilgamesh: "I will reveal unto thee, O Gilgamesh, the mysterious story, and the mystery of the gods I will tell thee. The city of Shuruppak, a city which, as thou knowest, is situated on the bank of the river Euphrates. That city was very old, as were the gods within it. Even the great gods, as many as there were, decided to bring about a deluge[1]: their father, Anu; their counsellor, the warrior Enlil; their leader, Ninurta; their champion, the god Ennugi. But Ea, the lord of unfathomable wisdom, argued with them. Their plan he told to a reed-hut,[2] (saying):

"'Reed-hut, reed-hut, clay-structure, clay-structure! Reed-hut, hear; clay-structure, pay attention! Thou man of Shuruppak, son of Ubāra-Tutu, build a house, construct a ship; forsake thy possessions, take heed of the living! Abandon thy goods, save living things, and bring living seed of every kind into the ship. As for the ship, which thou shalt build, let its proportions be well measured: Its breadth and its length shall bear proportion each to each, and into the sea then launch it.'

"I took heed, and said to Ea, my lord:

"'I will do, my lord, as thou hast commanded; I will observe and will fulfil the command. But what shall I answer to (the inquiries of) the city, the people, and the elders?'

"Ea opened his mouth and spoke, and he said unto me, his servant:

"'Man, as an answer say thus unto them: "I know that Enlil hates me. No longer can I live in your city; Nor on Enlil's territory can I live securely any longer; I will go down to the Apsu; I will live with Ea, my lord. Upon you he will pour down rich blessing. He will grant you fowl in plenty and fish in abundance, herds of cattle and an abundant harvest. In the morning he will pour down upon you bread, in the evening a rain of wheat."'

"As soon as early dawn appeared, the populace assembled 'round Atra-hasīs's[3] gate, the carpenter with his hatchet, the reed-worker with his flattening-stone, the [...] men [...]. The rich men brough pitch, and the poor men collected together all that was necessary.

"On the fifth day I set in place her exterior; it was an acre in area[4]; its sides were ten *gar* high; ten *gar* also was the extent of its deck; I added a front-roof to it and closed it in. I built it in six stories, thus making seven floors in all; the interior of each I divided again into nine partitions. Beaks for water within I cut out. I selected a punting-pole and added all that was necessary. Three *šar* of pitch I smeared on its outside; three *šar* of asphalt I used for the inside (so as to make it water-tight). Three *šar* of oil the men carried, carrying it in vessels. One *šar* of oil I kept out and used it for sacrifices, while the other two *šar* the boatman stowed away. I slaughtered oxen; I killed lambs day by day. Jugs of beer, of oil, and of sweet wine, like river water (i.e., freely) I gave the workmen to make a feast like that of the New-Year's Day. To the god Shamash my hands brought oil. The ship was completed. Launching it was heavy work, and I added tackling above and below, and after all was finished, the ship sank in the water to two thirds of its height.

"With all that I possessed I filled it; with all the silver I had I filled it; with all the gold I had I filled it; with living creatures of every kind I filled it. Then I embarked also all my family and my relatives, cattle of the field, beasts of the field, and the uprighteous people—all them I embarked. A time had Shamash appointed, (namely): 'When the rulers of darkness send at eventide a destructive rain, then enter into the ship and shut its door.' This very sign came to pass, and the rulers of darkness sent a destructive rain at eventide. I saw the approach of the storm, and I was afraid to witness the storm; I entered the ship and shut the door.

"I entrusted the guidance of the ship to Puzur-Amurri, the boatman, and also the great house, and the contents thereof. As soon as early dawn appeared, there rose up from the horizon a black cloud, within which the weather god (Adad) thundered, and the heralds Shullat and Hanish went before across mountain and plain. The gods of the abyss arose. Nergal, the great, tore loose the dams of the deep. There went Ninurta and he caused the banks to overflow; the Anunnaki lifted on high (their) torches, and with the brightness thereof they illuminated the universe. The storm brought on by Adad swept even up to the heavens and all light was turned into darkness as Adad shattered the land like a pot.

"It blew with violence one whole day, submerging the mountains. Like an onslaught in battle it rushed in on the people. Nor could brother look after brother. Nor were recognised the people from heaven. The gods even were afraid of the storm; they retreated and took refuge in the heaven of Anu. There the gods crouched down like dogs; on the inclosure of heaven they sat cowering.

"Then Ishtar cried-out like a woman in travail and the lady of the gods lamented with a loud voice, (saying): 'The world of old has been turned back into clay, because I assented to this evil in the assembly of the gods. Alas! that when I assented to this evil in the council of the gods, I was for the destruction of my own people. What I have created, where is it?

Like the spawn of fish it fills the sea.' The gods wailed with her over the Anunnaki. The gods were bowed down, and sat there weeping. Their lips were pressed together (in fear and in terror).

"Six days and nights the wind blew, and storm and tempest overwhelmed the country. When the seventh day drew nigh the tempest, the storm, the battle which they had waged like a great host began to moderate. The sea quieted down; hurricane and storm ceased. I looked out upon the sea and raised loud my voice, but all mankind had turned back into clay. Likewise the surrounding sea became as flat as a roof-top.

"I opened the air-hole and light fell upon my cheek. Dumbfounded I sank backward and sat weeping, while over my cheek flowed the tears. I looked in every direction, and behold, all was sea. I looked in vain for land, but twelve leagues distant there rose (out of the water) a strip of land. To Mount Niṣir⁵ the ship drifted. On Mount Niṣir the boat stuck fast and it did not slip away. The first day, the second day, Mount Niṣir held the ship fast, and did not let it slip away. The third day, the fourth day, Mount Niṣir held the ship fast, and did not let it slip away. The fifth day, the sixth day, Mount Niṣir held the ship, fast, and did not let it slip away. When the seventh day drew nigh I sent out a dove, and let her go. The dove flew hither and thither, but as there was no resting-place for her, she returned. Then I sent out a swallow, and let her go. The swallow flew hither and thither, but as there was no resting-place for her she also returned. Then I sent out a raven, and let her go. The raven flew away and saw the abatement of the waters. She settled down to feed, went away, and returned no more.

"Then I let everything go out unto the four winds, and I offered a sacrifice. I poured out a libation upon the peak of the mountain. I placed the censers seven and seven, and poured into them calamus, cedar-wood, and sweet incense. The gods smelt the savour; yea, the gods smelt the sweet savour; the gods gathered like flies around the sacrificer. But when now the lady of the gods (Ishtar) drew nigh, she lifted up the necklace with precious jewels which Anu had made according to her wish (and said):

"'Ye gods here! by my lapis lazuli necklace, not will I forget. These days will I remember, never will I forget (them). Let the gods come to the offering; but Enlil shall not come to the offering, since rashly he caused the flood-storm, and handed over my people unto destruction.'

"Now, when Enlil drew nigh, and saw the ship, the god was wroth, and anger against the gods, the Igigi, filled his heart, (and he said): 'Who then has escaped here (with his life)? No man was to survive the universal destruction.'

"Then Ninurta opened his mouth and spoke, saying unto Enlil, the warrior: 'Who but Ea could have planned this! For does not Ea know all arts?'

"Then Ea opened his mouth and spoke, saying unto Enlil, the warrior:

"'Ay, thou wise one among the gods, thou warrior, how rash of thee to bring about a flood-storm! On the sinner visit his sin, and on the wicked his wickedness; but be merciful, forbear, let not all be destroyed! Be considerate, let not mankind perish! Instead of sending a flood-storm, let lions come and diminish mankind; instead of sending a flood-storm, let tigers come and diminish mankind; instead of sending a flood-storm, let famine come and smite the land; instead of sending a flood-storm, let pestilence come and kill off the people. I did not reveal the mystery of the great gods. I only caused Atra-hasīs to see it in a dream, and so he heard the mystery of the gods.'

"Thereupon Enlil arrived at a decision. Enlil went up into the ship, took me by the hand and led me out. He led out also my wife and made her kneel beside me; He turned us face to face, and standing between us, blessed us, (saying) 'Ere this Utnapishtim was only human; But now Utnapishtim and his wife shall be lofty like unto the gods; let Utnapishtim live far away (from men) at the mouth of the rivers.'

"Then they took me and let us dwell far away at the mouth of the rivers."

After Utnapishtim had finished this account, he turned to Gilgamesh and said: "Now as for thee, which one of the gods shall give thee strength, that the life thou desirest thou shalt obtain? Now sleep!" And for six days and seven nights Gilgamesh resembled one lying lame. Sleep came over him like a storm wind. Then Utnapishtim said to his wife: "Behold, here is the hero whose desire is everlasting life! Sleep came upon him like a storm wind." And the wife replied to Utnapishtim, the distant: "Touch him that he may waken and return to his land. Let him, restored in health, return on the road on which he came. Let him pass out through the great door unto his own country." And Utnapishtim said to his wife: "All men deceive, and this one will deceive you. Therefore, cook now for him loaves and place one at his head each day, and mark on the wall the days he has slept."

And while Gilgamesh slept, she cooked the loaves to place it at his head and marked the wall. And while he slept, the first loaf became hard; the second became leathery; the third became soggy; the fourth became white; the fifth became gray with mold; the sixth, it was fresh; the seventh—of a sudden the man awoke upon being touched.

Then spoke Gilgamesh, and said unto Utnapishtim, the distant: "I had sunk down, and sleep had befallen me. Of a sudden thou didst touch me, and I awoke! And Utnapishtim said unto Gilgamesh: 'Gilgamesh, look over yonder and count the loaves, heed the marks on the wall. The first loaf is hard; the second is leathery; the thirdly is soggy; the fourth is white; the fifth is gray with mold; the sixth, it is fresh; the seventh, while still warm I touched you and you awoke.'"

And Gilgamesh said unto Utnapishtim, the distant: "What shall I do, Utnapishtim? Whither shall I go? The demon has seized my flesh. Upon my couch death now sits. And where my foot treads, there is death."

And Utnapishtim said to Urshanabi, the ferryman: "Urshanabi, thou have become loathsome to this harbor; let the boat carry thee away; you are forever excluded from this place. The man, before whom thou goest, has his body covered with foulness, and the wild skins he wears have hidden the beauty of his body. Take him, Urshanabi, and bring him to the place of purification, where he can wash his hair in water that it may become clean as snow; let him cast off his skins and the sea will carry them away; his body shall then appear beautiful. Let the fillet also be replaced on his head, and the garment that covers his nakedness. Until he returns to his city, until he arrives at his road, the garment shall not wear with age; it shall remain entirely new."

And Urshanabi took him and brought him to the place of purification, where he washed his hair in water so that it became clean as snow; he cast off his skins and the sea carried them away; his body appeared beautiful. He replaced also the fillet on his head and the garment that covered his nakedness until he should return to his city, until he should arrive at his road; the garment would not wear with age; it remained entirely new.

Then Gilgamesh and Urshanabi embarked again, and during their journey the ship tossed to and fro. The wife of Utnapishtim spoke unto her husband, the distant, (saying):

"Gilgamesh did come here weary and exhausted. What now wilt thou give him, that he may return to his country?"

And Gilgamesh lifted up the pole, and drew the boat nearer to the shore.

Then Utnapishtim spoke unto Gilgamesh (and said): "Gilgamesh, thou didst come here weary; thou didst labour and row. What now shall I give thee, that thou mayest return to thy country? I will reveal unto thee, Gilgamesh, a mystery of the gods I will announce unto thee. There is a plant resembling buckthorn; its thorn stings like that of a bramble. When thy hands can reach that plant, then thy hands will hold that which gives life everlasting."

When Gilgamesh had heard this he opened the sluices that the sweet water might carry him into the deep; he bound heavy stones to his feet, which dragged him down to the sea floor, and thus he found the plant. Then he grasped the prickly plant. He removed from his feet the heavy stones, and the sea carried him and threw him down on the shore.

And Gilgamesh said unto Urshanabi, the ferryman: "Urshanabi, this plant is a plant of great marvel; and by it a man may attain renewed vigour. I will take it to Uruk the strong-walled, I will give it to the old men to eat. Its name shall be 'Even an old man will be rejuvenated!' I will eat of this and return (again) to the vigour of my youth."

At twenty double-leagues they then took a meal: and at thirty double-leagues they took a rest. And Gilgamesh saw a well wherein was cool water; he stepped into it and bathed in the water. A serpent smelled the sweetness of the plant and darted out; he took the plant away, and as he turned back to the well, he sloughed his skin. And after this Gilgamesh sat down and wept. Tears flowed down his cheeks, and he said unto Urshanabi, the ferryman:

"Why, Urshanabi, did my hands tremble? Why did the blood of my heart stand still? Not on myself did I bestow any benefit. On the 'ground-lion'[6] this benefit has been bestowed. Already twenty double-leagues the waters have taken the plant away. I opened the sluices and lowered my equipment into it. I saw the sign; it has become an omen to me. I am to return, leaving the ship on the shore."

Then they continued on and took a meal after twenty double-leagues, and after thirty double-leagues they took a rest. When they arrived at Uruk the strong-walled, Gilgamesh then spoke to Urshanabi, the ferryman, (and said):

"Urshanabi, ascend and walk about on the wall of Uruk, inspect the corner-stone, and examine its brick-work, whether its wall is not made of burned brick, and its foundation laid by the Seven Sages. One third for city, one third for garden, one third for field, and a precinct for the temple of Ishtar. These parts and the precinct comprise Uruk."

Source: Adapted and corrected from the translation by William Muss Arnolt in Robert Francis Harper (ed.), *Assyrian and Babylonian Literature: Selected Translations* (New York: D. Appleton and Company, 1904), 351–363. Arnolt's translation was originally presented in verse.

Commentary: *The famous eleventh tablet of the* Epic of Gilgamesh *shocked the Victorians when George Smith offered the first English translation of it in 1872. Originally, scholars such as Smith thought it represented independent confirmation of Noah's Flood, but in time scholars recognized that this text predated the Biblical account and at least some form of the Near East flood myth must have influenced the Genesis account.[7] The repetition of specific motifs is unmistakable. The version presented here derives from the* Atrahasis Epic *(c. 1900 BCE), in very close translation, but the earlier poem adds the detail that the gods had grown angry that humans had created too much noise as they labored for the gods, and therefore Enlil decides to drown them all. A Sumerian account, preserved in a fragmentary tablet called the* Eridu Genesis *tells* *of how Ziusudra survived the flood in a ship and was granted immortality. Berossus preserves his story under the Hellenized name Xisuthrus (see **20**). So ancient is this tale—the* Eridu Genesis *dates to 1600 BCE but obviously tells a much old story—that it forms the common background of flood myths across the Ancient Near East.*

Notes

1. The *Atrahasis* suggests that this is because the gods found humans were too many and too noisy, which prompted efforts to reduce their population through plague, famine, and eventually flood.

2. We learn from the *Atrahasis* that this subterfuge occurred because the gods forbade him to tell a human their plans.

3. An earlier name of the Flood hero, overlooked by the ancient editor in revising the *Atrahasis* for inclusion here. Logically, Utnapishtim should be speaking in the first person.

4. The word conventionally translated as "acre" also means "circle." According to Irving Finkel in *The Ark Before Noah* (New York: Doubleday, 2014), the earlier texts on which this was based specified that the ship was to be a round coracle.

5. One of the Zagros Mountains in the region of the Little Zab River, according to the records of Ashurnasirpal II, probably Pir Omar Gudrun. By the time of Berossus it was identified with Al-Judi (see **20**, **30**), though in Old Babylonian sources the Ark was thought to have landed on a mythic mountain at the edge of the world.

6. The "lion of the ground" is the serpent. Some have suggested that the title of the serpent here refers to a chameleon based on the Greek *khamaileon* (whence our "chameleon," via Latin and Old French), a loan word from the Semitic that also translates as "lion of the ground."

7. One important volume on the subject, which also summarizes earlier work, is Richard S. Hess, David Toshio Tsumura (eds.), *I Studied Inscriptions from Before the Flood: Ancient Near Eastern, Literary, and Linguistic Approaches to Genesis 1–11*, Sources for Biblical and Theological Study, vol. 4 (Eisenbrauns, 1994). The classic work on the subject is A. Heidel, *The Gilgamesh Epic and Old Testament Parallels* (Chicago: University of Chicago Press, 1946).

20. Berossus' Version of the Babylonian Flood Myth

Berossus
Babyloniaca
c. 290–278 BCE
Greek
Preserved in Alexander Polyhistor, as preserved in George Syncellus, *Chronicle* 30–32 and Eusebius, *Chronicle* 31–37
Astro
Discussion in SM

After the death of Otiartes[1] [= Ubāra-Tutu], his son Xisuthrus [= Ziusudra] reigned eighteen *sari*. In his time happened a great Deluge; the history of which is thus described: The Deity, Cronus [= Ea], appeared to him in a vision, and warned him that upon the fifteenth day of the month Dæsius there would be a flood, by which mankind would be destroyed. He therefore enjoined him to write a history of the beginning, procedure, and conclusion of all things; and to bury it in the city of the Sun at Sippara; and to build a vessel, and take with him into it his friends and relations; and to convey on board every thing necessary to sustain life, together with all the different animals; both birds and quadrupeds, and trust himself fearlessly to the deep. If he was asked whither he intended to sail, he should say, "To the Gods, to pray for happiness for mankind."[2] He then obeyed the divine admonition: and built a vessel five stadia[3] in length, and two in breadth. Into this he put every thing which he had prepared; and last of all conveyed into it his wife, his children, and his friends.

After the flood had been upon the earth, and was in time abated, Xisuthrus sent out birds from the vessel; which, not finding any food, nor any place whereupon they might rest their feet, returned to him again. After an interval of some days, he sent them forth a second time; and they now returned with their feet tinged with mud. He made a trial a third time with these birds; but they returned to him no more: from whence he judged that the surface of the earth had appeared above the waters. He therefore made an opening in the vessel, and upon looking out found that it was stranded upon the side of some mountain; upon which he immediately quitted it with his wife, his daughter, and the pilot. Xisuthrus then paid his adoration to the earth: and having constructed an altar, offered sacrifices to the gods, and, with those who had come out of the vessel with him, disappeared. They, who remained within, finding that their companions did not return, quitted the vessel with many lamentations, and called continually on the name of Xisuthrus. Him they saw no more; but they could distinguish his voice in the air, and could hear him admonish them to pay due regard to religion; and likewise informed them that it was upon account of his piety that he was translated to live with the gods; that his wife and daughter, and the pilot, had obtained the same honour. To this he added, that they should return to Babylonia; and, as it was ordained, search for the writings at Sippara, which they were to make known to all mankind: moreover that the place, wherein they then were, was the land of Armenia. The rest having heard these words, offered sacrifices to the gods; and taking a circuit, journeyed towards Babylonia. The vessel being thus stranded in Armenia, some part of it yet remains in the Corcyræan mountains of Armenia; and the people scrape off the bitumen, with which it had been outwardly coated, and use it to make amulets to guard against poison. And when they returned to Babylon, and had found the writings at Sippara, they built cities, and erected temples: and Babylon was thus inhabited again.

Source: Slightly adapted from the translation of I. P. Cory, *Ancient Fragments,* 2nd ed. (London: William Pickering, 1832), 26–29. Cory's translation, which is actually a partially corrected but uncredited copy of Jacob Bryant's from the *New System* (vol. 3, 1776), collates text from the Greek quotation of Eusebius preserved by Syncellus and the Armenian translation of Eusebius.

Commentary: *The Flood narrative of Berossus was long considered a derivative of the Genesis account until the translation of the cuneiform texts proved the story came direct from older Babylonian and Sumerian sources. The same fragment of Berossus, in Abydenus' telling, is given in highly abbreviated form in Eusebius,* Praeparatio Evangelica *9.12 and* Chronicle *50, where it is wood rather than bitumen used to make amulets. Another version of this Flood myth can be found in Lucian (**24**). Especially interesting is the preservation of knowledge on tablets at Sippara, the city of the sun. Enoch lives 365 years—a solar connection—and in the Watchers-derived complex of myths, the preservation of knowledge from the oncoming Flood is a major theme (**12, 13, 16, 17**). Many feel that the Mesopotamian version underlies the pillars and tablets of wisdom in the Watchers' myths. For the survival of the Ark in Armenia, see **30**. The passage on the survival of the Ark as a tourist attraction is preserved also in Flavius Josephus'* Antiquities *(1.93, see **30**) and Eusebius'* Onamasticon *(entry for Ararat), copied from Josephus.*

Notes

1. Syncellus gives "Ardates" but this appears to be a corruption. "Otiartes" is given in Eusebius, *Chronicle* 14–15 and 31; Syncellus, 40; and Cyril, *Contra Julianum* 1. Here, as elsewhere, the Armenian Eusebius appears better preserved.
2. This sentence is amended from John Jackson's translation in *Chronological Antiquities* (1752), in keeping

with modern critical readings. Cory (following Bryant) originally gave it thus: "Having asked the Deity, whither he was to sail? he was answered, 'To the Gods': upon which he offered up a prayer for the good of mankind." The Armenian Eusebius renders the prayer part of the response: "He asked where he was to sail, and (Cronus) responded: 'Make prayers to the Gods, and all will be well for mankind.'" The line, in all its forms, parallels Utnapishtim's question to Ea in the *Epic of Gilgamesh* (**19**).

3. Armenian Eusebius: 15 stadia.

21. The Biblical Flood Narrative

Genesis 6:5–9:17

c. 6th c. BCE

Hebrew

Astro

Discussion in AA, CG

CHAPTER 6

[5] And God saw that the wickedness of man was great in the earth, and that every imagination of the thoughts of his heart was only evil continually.

[6] And it repented the Lord that he had made man on the earth, and it grieved him at his heart.

[7] And the Lord said, I will destroy man whom I have created from the face of the earth; both man, and beast, and the creeping thing, and the fowls of the air; for it repenteth me that I have made them.

[8] But Noah found grace in the eyes of the Lord.

[9] These are the generations of Noah: Noah was a just man and perfect in his generations, and Noah walked with God.

[10] And Noah begat three sons, Shem, Ham, and Japheth.

[11] The earth also was corrupt before God, and the earth was filled with violence.

[12] And God looked upon the earth, and, behold, it was corrupt; for all flesh had corrupted his way upon the earth.

[13] And God said unto Noah, The end of all flesh is come before me; for the earth is filled with violence through them; and, behold, I will destroy them with the earth.

[14] Make thee an ark of gopher wood; rooms shalt thou make in the ark, and shalt pitch it within and without with pitch.

[15] And this is the fashion which thou shalt make it of: The length of the ark shall be three hundred cubits, the breadth of it fifty cubits, and the height of it thirty cubits.

[16] A window shalt thou make to the ark, and in a cubit shalt thou finish it above; and the door of the ark shalt thou set in the side thereof; with lower, second, and third stories shalt thou make it.

[17] And, behold, I, even I, do bring a flood of waters upon the earth, to destroy all flesh, wherein is the breath of life, from under heaven; and every thing that is in the earth shall die.

[18] But with thee will I establish my covenant; and thou shalt come into the ark, thou, and thy sons, and thy wife, and thy sons' wives with thee.

[19] And of every living thing of all flesh, two of every sort shalt thou bring into the ark, to keep them alive with thee; they shall be male and female.

[20] Of fowls after their kind, and of cattle after their kind, of every creeping thing of the earth after his kind, two of every sort shall come unto thee, to keep them alive.

[21] And take thou unto thee of all food that is eaten, and thou shalt gather it to thee; and it shall be for food for thee, and for them.

[22] Thus did Noah; according to all that God commanded him, so did he.

Chapter 7

[1] And the Lord said unto Noah, Come thou and all thy house into the ark; for thee have I seen righteous before me in this generation.

[2] Of every clean beast thou shalt take to thee by sevens, the male and his female: and of beasts that are not clean by two, the male and his female.

[3] Of fowls also of the air by sevens, the male and the female; to keep seed alive upon the face of all the earth.

[4] For yet seven days, and I will cause it to rain upon the earth forty days and forty nights; and every living substance that I have made will I destroy from off the face of the earth.

[5] And Noah did according unto all that the Lord commanded him.

[6] And Noah was six hundred years old when the flood of waters was upon the earth.

[7] And Noah went in, and his sons, and his wife, and his sons' wives with him, into the ark, because of the waters of the flood.

[8] Of clean beasts, and of beasts that are not clean, and of fowls, and of every thing that creepeth upon the earth,

[9] There went in two and two unto Noah into the ark, the male and the female, as God had commanded Noah.

[10] And it came to pass after seven days, that the waters of the flood were upon the earth.

[11] In the six hundredth year of Noah's life, in the second month, the seventeenth day of the month, the same day were all the fountains of the great deep broken up, and the windows of heaven were opened.

[12] And the rain was upon the earth forty days and forty nights.

[13] In the selfsame day entered Noah, and Shem, and Ham, and Japheth, the sons of Noah, and Noah's wife, and the three wives of his sons with them, into the ark;

[14] They, and every beast after his kind, and all the cattle after their kind, and every creeping thing that creepeth upon the earth after his kind, and every fowl after his kind, every bird of every sort.

[15] And they went in unto Noah into the ark, two and two of all flesh, wherein is the breath of life.

[16] And they that went in, went in male and female of all flesh, as God had commanded him: and the Lord shut him in.

[17] And the flood was forty days upon the earth; and the waters increased, and bare up the ark, and it was lift up above the earth.

[18] And the waters prevailed, and were increased greatly upon the earth; and the ark went upon the face of the waters.

[19] And the waters prevailed exceedingly upon the earth; and all the high hills, that were under the whole heaven, were covered.

[20] Fifteen cubits upward did the waters prevail; and the mountains were covered.

[21] And all flesh died that moved upon the earth, both of fowl, and of cattle, and of beast, and of every creeping thing that creepeth upon the earth, and every man:

[22] All in whose nostrils was the breath of life, of all that was in the dry land, died.

[23] And every living substance was destroyed which was upon the face of the ground, both man, and cattle, and the creeping things, and the fowl of the heaven; and they were destroyed from the earth: and Noah only remained alive, and they that were with him in the ark.

[24] And the waters prevailed upon the earth an hundred and fifty days.

CHAPTER 8

[1] And God remembered Noah, and every living thing, and all the cattle that was with him in the ark: and God made a wind to pass over the earth, and the waters assuaged;

[2] The fountains also of the deep and the windows of heaven were stopped, and the rain from heaven was restrained;

[3] And the waters returned from off the earth continually: and after the end of the hundred and fifty days the waters were abated.

[4] And the ark rested in the seventh month, on the seventeenth day of the month, upon the mountains of Ararat.[1]

[5] And the waters decreased continually until the tenth month: in the tenth month, on the first day of the month, were the tops of the mountains seen.

[6] And it came to pass at the end of forty days, that Noah opened the window of the ark which he had made:

[7] And he sent forth a raven, which went forth to and fro, until the waters were dried up from off the earth.

[8] Also he sent forth a dove from him, to see if the waters were abated from off the face of the ground;

[9] But the dove found no rest for the sole of her foot, and she returned unto him into the ark, for the waters were on the face of the whole earth: then he put forth his hand, and took her, and pulled her in unto him into the ark.

[10] And he stayed yet other seven days; and again he sent forth the dove out of the ark;

[11] And the dove came in to him in the evening; and, lo, in her mouth was an olive leaf pluckt off: so Noah knew that the waters were abated from off the earth.

[12] And he stayed yet other seven days; and sent forth the dove; which returned not again unto him any more.

[13] And it came to pass in the six hundredth and first year, in the first month, the first day of the month, the waters were dried up from off the earth: and Noah removed the covering of the ark, and looked, and, behold, the face of the ground was dry.

[14] And in the second month, on the seven and twentieth day of the month, was the earth dried.

[15] And God spake unto Noah, saying,

[16] Go forth of the ark, thou, and thy wife, and thy sons, and thy sons' wives with thee.

[17] Bring forth with thee every living thing that is with thee, of all flesh, both of fowl, and of cattle, and of every creeping thing that creepeth upon the earth; that they may breed abundantly in the earth, and be fruitful, and multiply upon the earth.

[18] And Noah went forth, and his sons, and his wife, and his sons' wives with him:

[19] Every beast, every creeping thing, and every fowl, and whatsoever creepeth upon the earth, after their kinds, went forth out of the ark.

Tales of a man who survived a great flood in a wooden ark were told all across the ancient Near East, including versions current in Sumer, Babylon, Judea, Syria, and Greece. The Biblical version, centering on the story of Noah, is the best known of these, appearing in Jewish, Christian, and Islamic lore. The Biblical landing of the Ark, seen here in Gustave Doré's atmospheric etching, is closely parallel to the account in Tablet 11 of the *Epic of Gilgamesh* (Doré's English Bible [1866]).

[20] And Noah builded an altar unto the Lord; and took of every clean beast, and of every clean fowl, and offered burnt offerings on the altar.

[21] And the Lord smelled a sweet savour; and the Lord said in his heart, I will not again curse the ground any more for man's sake; for the imagination of man's heart is evil from his youth; neither will I again smite any more every thing living, as I have done.

[22] While the earth remaineth, seedtime and harvest, and cold and heat, and summer and winter, and day and night shall not cease.

CHAPTER 9

[1] And God blessed Noah and his sons, and said unto them, Be fruitful, and multiply, and replenish the earth.

[2] And the fear of you and the dread of you shall be upon every beast of the earth, and upon every fowl of the air, upon all that moveth upon the earth, and upon all the fishes of the sea; into your hand are they delivered.

[3] Every moving thing that liveth shall be meat for you; even as the green herb have I given you all things.

[4] But flesh with the life thereof, which is the blood thereof, shall ye not eat.

[5] And surely your blood of your lives will I require; at the hand of every beast will I require it, and at the hand of man; at the hand of every man's brother will I require the life of man.

[6] Whoso sheddeth man's blood, by man shall his blood be shed: for in the image of God made he man.

[7] And you, be ye fruitful, and multiply; bring forth abundantly in the earth, and multiply therein.

[8] And God spake unto Noah, and to his sons with him, saying,

[9] And I, behold, I establish my covenant with you, and with your seed after you;

[10] And with every living creature that is with you, of the fowl, of the cattle, and of every beast of the earth with you; from all that go out of the ark, to every beast of the earth.

[11] And I will establish my covenant with you, neither shall all flesh be cut off any more by the waters of a flood; neither shall there any more be a flood to destroy the earth.

[12] And God said, This is the token of the covenant which I make between me and you and every living creature that is with you, for perpetual generations:

[13] I do set my bow in the cloud, and it shall be for a token of a covenant between me and the earth.

[14] And it shall come to pass, when I bring a cloud over the earth, that the bow shall be seen in the cloud:

[15] And I will remember my covenant, which is between me and you and every living creature of all flesh; and the waters shall no more become a flood to destroy all flesh.

[16] And the bow shall be in the cloud; and I will look upon it, that I may remember the everlasting covenant between God and every living creature of all flesh that is upon the earth.

[17] And God said unto Noah, This is the token of the covenant, which I have established between me and all flesh that is upon the earth.

Source: King James Version.

Commentary: *According to many biblical scholars, the text of the Flood story as we have it today is the result of the redactors of Genesis combining two originally separate versions of the*

story. This is why the details seem to change; for example, in Genesis 6:19 God tells Noah to bring with him two of every creature, but in 7:2 this is given as seven of clean animals and two unclean, or in 6:20 two of each bird but in 7:3 seven of each bird. Others believe that the contradictions were introduced into a single narrative at a later date.

Note

1. This ambiguous phrase gave rise to much speculation about it geographical location, centering in Antiquity on Mt. Judi in what is now Turkey (see **30**). The Syriac translation of the Bible from the second century CE known as the Peshitta replaces "mountains of Ararat" with "Mt. Qardū," another name for Mt. Judi.

22. A Parallel Persian Account

Avesta, Fargard 2.21–43.
c. 500 BCE
Avestan
Atlantis, Prehistoric
Discussion in FG

[21] The Maker, Ahura Mazda, of high renown in the Airyana Vaêgô, by the good river Dâitya, called together a meeting of the celestial gods. The fair Yima, the good shepherd, of high renown in the Airyana Vaêgô, by the good river Dâitya, called together a meeting of the excellent mortals. To that meeting came Ahura Mazda, of high renown in the Airyana Vaêgô, by the good river Dâitya; he came together with the celestial gods.To that meeting came, the fair Yima, the good shepherd, of high renown in the Airyana Vaêgô, by the good river Dâitya; he came together with the excellent mortals.

[22] And Ahura Mazda spake unto Yima, saying: "O fair Yima, son of Vîvanghat! Upon the material world the fatal winters are going to fall, that shall bring the fierce, foul frost; upon the material world the fatal winters are going to fall, that shall make snow-flakes fall thick, even an aredvî deep on the highest tops of mountains.

[23] And all the three sorts of beasts shall perish, those that live in the wilderness, and those that live on the tops of the mountains, and those that live in the bosom of the dale, under the shelter of stables.

[24] Before that winter, those fields would bear plenty of grass for cattle: now with floods that stream, with snows that melt, it will seem a happy land in the world, the land wherein footprints even of sheep may still be seen.

[25] Therefore make thee a Vara,[1] long as a riding-ground on every side of the square, and thither bring the seeds of sheep and oxen, of men, of dogs, of birds, and of red blazing fires.

Therefore make thee a Vara, long as a riding-ground on every side of the square, to be an abode for men; a Vara, long as a riding-ground on every side of the square, to be a fold for flocks.

[26] There thou shalt make waters flow in a bed a hâthra long; there thou shalt settle birds, by the ever-green banks that bear never-failing food. There thou shalt establish dwelling places, consisting of a house with a balcony, a courtyard, and a gallery.

[27] Thither thou shalt bring the seeds of men and women, of the greatest, best, and finest kinds on this earth; thither thou shalt bring the seeds of every kind of cattle, of the greatest, best, and finest kinds on this earth.

[28] Thither thou shalt bring the seeds of every kind of tree, of the greatest, best, and finest kinds on this earth; thither thou shalt bring the seeds of every kind of fruit, the fullest of food and sweetest of odour. All those seeds shalt thou bring, two of ever), kind, to be kept inexhaustible there, so long as those men shall stay in the Vara.

[29] There shall be no humpbacked, none bulged forward there; no impotent, no lunatic; no poverty, no lying; no meanness, no jealousy; no decayed tooth, no leprous to be confined, nor any of the brands wherewith Angra Mainyu stamps the bodies of mortals.

[30] In the largest part of the place thou shalt make nine streets, six in the middle part, three in the smallest. To the streets of the largest part thou shalt bring a thousand seeds of men and women; to the streets of the middle part, six hundred; to the streets of the smallest part, three hundred. That Vara thou shalt seal up with the golden ring, and thou shalt make a door, and a window self-shining within."

[31] Then Yima said within himself: "How shall I manage to make that Vara which Ahura Mazda has commanded me to make?" And Ahura Mazda said unto Yima: "O fair Yima, son of Vîvanghat! Crush the earth with a stamp of thy heel, and then knead it with thy hands, as the potter does when kneading the potter's clay."

[32] And Yima did as Ahura Mazda wished; he crushed the earth with a stamp of his heel, he kneaded it with his hands, as the potter does when kneading the potter's clay.

[33] And Yima made a Vara, long as a riding-ground on every side of the square. There he brought the seeds of sheep and oxen, of men, of dogs, of birds, and of red blazing fires. He made a Vara, long as a riding-ground on every side of the square, to be an abode for men; a Vara, long as a riding-ground on every side of the square, to be a fold for flocks.

[34] There he made waters flow in a bed a hâthra long; there he settled birds, by the evergreen banks that bear never-failing food. There he established dwelling places, consisting of a house with a balcony, a courtyard, and a gallery.

[35] There he brought the seeds of men and women, of the greatest, best, and finest kinds on this earth; there he brought the seeds of every kind of cattle, of the greatest, best, and finest kinds on this earth.

[36] There he brought the seeds of every kind of tree, of the greatest, best, and finest kinds on this earth; there he brought the seeds of every kind of fruit, the fullest of food and sweetest of odour. All those seeds he brought, two of every kind, to be kept inexhaustible there, so long as those men shall stay in the Vara.

[37] And there were no humpbacked, none bulged forward there; no impotent, no lunatic; no poverty, no lying; no meanness, no jealousy; no decayed tooth, no leprous to be confined, nor any of the brands wherewith Angra Mainyu stamps the bodies of mortals.

[38] In the largest part of the place he made nine streets, six in the middle part, three in the smallest. To the streets of the largest part he brought a thousand seeds of men and women; to the streets of the middle part, six hundred; to the streets of the smallest part, three hundred. That Vara he sealed up with the golden ring, and he made a door, and a window self-shining within.

[39] O Maker of the material world, thou Holy One! What lights are there to give light in the Vara which Yima made?

[40] Ahura Mazda answered: "There are uncreated lights and created lights. There the stars, the moon, and the sun are only once (a year) seen to rise and set, and a year seems only as a day."

[41] "Every fortieth year, to every couple two are born, a male and a female. And thus it is for every sort of cattle. And the men in the Vara which Yima made live the happiest life."

[42] O Maker of the material world, thou Holy One! Who is he who brought the law of Mazda into the Vara which Yima made? Ahura Mazda answered: "It was the bird Karshipta, O holy Zarathustra!"

[43] O Maker of the material world, thou Holy One! Who is the lord and ruler there? Ahura Mazda answered: "Urvata*d*-nara, O Zarathustra! and thyself, Zarathustra."

Source: Translated by James Darmesteter in F. Max Müller (ed.), *The Sacred Books of the East,* vol. 4 (Oxford: Clarendon, 1880), 15–21.

Commentary: *The* Zend, *the ancient commentary on the* Avesta, *attributes the "fatal winter" to Malkôsân, a demon whose name is the plural of the Hebrew word for rain, malkôs. This led the translator to conclude that it is a remnant of an attempt to rewrite the myth under the influence of the Near Eastern Flood story, with which it shares obvious similarities. In this reading, the "waters" of Genesis were misread as a proper noun and thus a demon of disaster. A fifteenth century version preserved in the* Mainyo-i-khard *is still closer to the Noachian flood, complete with rain and animals lining up for the Vard. Graham Hancock in* FG *knows the story only from a secondhand source and takes it for an independent disaster tradition.*

Note

1. A Vara is literally an enclosure.

23. The Greek Flood Myth
Pseudo-Apollodorus
Library 1.7.1–2
c. 100 BCE
Greek
Astro

Prometheus moulded men out of water and earth and gave them also fire, which, unknown to Zeus, he had hidden in a stalk of fennel. But when Zeus learned of it, he ordered Hephaestus to nail his body to Mount Caucasus, which is a Scythian mountain. On it Prometheus was nailed and kept bound for many years. Every day an eagle swooped on him and devoured the lobes of his liver, which grew by night. That was the penalty that Prometheus paid for the theft of fire until Hercules afterwards released him, as we shall show in dealing with Hercules.

And Prometheus had a son Deucalion. He, reigning in the regions about Phthia, married Pyrrha, the daughter of Epimetheus and Pandora, the first woman fashioned by the gods. And when Zeus would destroy the men of the Bronze Age, Deucalion by the advice of Prometheus constructed a chest, and having stored it with provisions he embarked in it with Pyrrha. But Zeus by pouring heavy rain from heaven flooded the greater part of Greece, so that all men were destroyed, except a few who fled to the high mountains in the neighborhood. It was then that the mountains in Thessaly parted, and that all the world outside the Isthmus and Peloponnese was overwhelmed. But Deucalion, floating in the chest over the sea for nine days and as many nights, drifted to Parnassus, and there, when the rain ceased, he landed and sacrificed to Zeus, the god of Escape. And Zeus sent Hermes to him and allowed him to choose what he would, and he chose to get men. And at the bidding of Zeus he took up stones and threw them over his head, and the stones which Deucalion threw became men, and the stones which Pyrrha threw became women. Hence people were called metaphorically people (*laos*) from *laas*, "a stone."

And Deucalion had children by Pyrrha, first Hellen, whose father some say was Zeus, and second Amphictyon, who reigned over Attica after Cranaus; and third a daughter Protogenia, who became the mother of Aethlius by Zeus.

Source: Translated by Sir James George Frazer in Apollodorus, *The Library*, vol. 1 (London: William Heinemann, 1921), 51–57.

Commentary: *The Greek version of the Flood myth derives from the Near East versions, albeit somewhat indirectly, likely through contact with the Hittites and the Near East. Other Greek flood myths, possibly from the same ultimate source, can be found in the story of Ogyges (Plato, Laws 677a; Eusebius, Praeparatio Evangelica 10.10) as well as in the flood of Samothrace (Diodorus, Library of History 5.47.3).*

24. A Conflated Greek–Babylonian Flood Myth
Lucian
De dea Syria 11–12
2nd c. CE
Greek
Astro

[11] On enquiring the number of years since the temple [of Hierapolis Bambyce in Syria] was founded, and whom they deemed the goddess to be, many tales were told to me, some of which were sacred, and some public property; some, again, were absolutely fabulous; others were mere barbarians' tales; others again tallied with the Greek accounts. All these I am ready to narrate, though I withhold my acceptance of some.

[12] The people, then, allege that it was Deukalion or Sisythus who founded the temple; I mean the Deukalion in whose time the great flood occurred. I have heard the story about Deukalion as the Greeks narrate it from the Greeks themselves. The story runs as follows: The present race of men was not the first to be created. The first generation perished to a man; the present is a second creation. This generation became a vast multitude, owing to Deukalion. Of the men of the original creation they tell this tale: they were rebellious, and wilful, and performed unholy deeds, disregarding the sanctity of oaths and hospitality, and behaving cruelly to suppliants; and it was for these misdeeds that the great destruction fell upon them. Straightway the earth discharged a vast volume of water, and the rivers of heaven came down in streams and the sea mounted high. Thus everything became water, and all men perished; Deukalion alone was saved for another generation, on the score of his wisdom and piety. The manner of his salvation was as follows: He placed his children and his wives in an ark of vast size, and he himself also entered in. Now, when he had embarked, there came to him wild boars and horses, and generations of lions and serpents, and all the other beasts which roam the earth, all in couples. He welcomed them all. Nor did they harm him; and friendship remained amongst them as Zeus himself ordained. These, one and all, floated in this ark as long as the flood remained. This is the legend of Deukalion as told by the Greeks.

Source: Translated by Herbert A. Strong in Lucian, *The Syrian Goddess,* trans. Herbert A. Strong and ed. John Garstang (London: Constable & Company, 1913), 50–51.

Commentary: *Lucian's flood myth contains Hellenized names, but the identification of Deukalion as Sisythus (Xisuthrus) marks this as a derivative of the Babylonian flood myth, and it is interesting that the detail about hospitality and sin is similar to that of the story of Sodom and Gomorrah (60). The wisdom of Deukalion here parallels the tablets of wisdom Xisuthrus carves in Berossus' account (20).*

25. Nephilim–Giants Build Babylon after the Flood

Pseudo-Eupolemus

c. 158 BCE

Greek

Preserved in Eusebius, *Praeparatio Evangelica* 9.17

c. 313 CE

Astro, Prehistoric

Eupolemus in his book *Concerning the Jews of Assyria* says that the city Babylon was first founded by those who escaped from the Deluge; and that they were giants, and built the tower renowned in history. But when this had been overthrown by the act of God, the giants were dispersed over the whole earth. And in the tenth generation, he says, in Camarina a city of Babylonia, which some call the city Uria (and which is by interpretation *the city of the Chaldees*), in the thirteenth generation Abraham was born, who surpassed all men in nobility and wisdom, who was also the inventor of astronomy and the Chaldaic art, and pleased God well by his zeal towards religion. By reason of God's commands this man came and dwelt in Phoenicia, and pleased their king by teaching the Phoenicians the changes of the sun and moon and all things of that kind.[1]

Source: Translated by E. H. Gifford in Eusebius, *Evangelicae Praeparationis*, vol. 3, part 1, trans. and ed. E. H. Gifford (Oxford: E Typographeo Academico, 1903), 450.

Commentary: *The author writing under the name of the Hellenic-Jewish historian Eupolemus (scholars differ on whether this is truly his work) seems to be recalling the Babylonian tradition that the Anunnaki built the ziggurats of Babylon (see 1, Enuma Eliš 6.46f.) and has identified the Anunnaki with the Nephilim. For an interesting but late derivative of this story, see Book 3 of the Late Antique pseudo–Sibylline Oracles, in which three Titan siblings divide and rule over the world after the collapse of the Tower of Babel, a version of the Titan story derived from Euhemerus' rationalized Sacred History with Jewish elements added (see fragments in Lactantius, Epitome of the Divine Institutes 14 and Eusebius, Praeparatio Evangelica 2.44–45 with the Abydenus fragment at 9.14). Intriguingly, the division of the earth among the three royal or divine brothers parallels the division of the earth among the three sons of Noah, the division of the cosmos among the three Olympian gods of Greece, and the division of the cosmos among Anu, Enlil, and Enki in the Atrahasis epic. Pseudo-Eupolemus goes on to say that Enoch invented astrology and was the same as the Greek Titan Atlas.*

This text, however, is also interesting for the fact that it connects the Giants with the architecture of the world after the Flood, something found in other cultures as well, where Giants of various kinds are credited with ancient buildings, as in the stories below. Modern Nephilim theorists like L. A. Marzulli see such stories as evidence for the survival of Nephilim DNA after the Flood and the Giants' continued influence on humanity.

26. The Giants Build the Mycenaean Cities
Pausanias
Description of Greece 2.16.5, 2.25.8
2nd c. CE
Greek
Astro, Prehistoric
Discussion in AW

It was jealousy which caused the Argives to destroy Mycenae. For at the time of the Persian invasion the Argives made no move, but the Mycenaeans sent eighty men to Ther-

Although archaeology knows Mycenae as the product of Bronze Age culture, the later Greeks had long forgotten the original builders and claimed that the Cyclopes or Giants had raised the fearsome walls of these ancient ruins. Because this claim is demonstrably false, it calls into question the accuracy of other texts describing the work of "giants" beloved of fringe historians (Library of Congress).

mopylae who shared in the achievement of the Lacedaemonians. This eagerness for distinction brought ruin upon them by exasperating the Argives. There still remain, however, parts of the city wall, including the gate, upon which stand lions. These, too, are said to be the work of the Cyclopes, who made for Proetus the wall at Tiryns.

[...]

Going on from here [the road to Epidauria] and turning to the right, you come to the ruins of Tiryns. The Tirynthians also were removed by the Argives, who wished to make Argos more powerful by adding to the population. The hero Tiryns, from whom the city derived its name, is said to have been a son of Argus, a son of Zeus. The wall, which is the only part of the ruins still remaining, is a work of the Cyclopes made of unwrought stones, each stone being so big that a pair of mules could not move the smallest from its place to the slightest degree. Long ago small stones were so inserted that each of them binds the large blocks firmly together.

Source: Translated by W. H. S. Jones in Pausanias, *Description of Greece,* vol. 1 (London: William Heinemann, 1918), 331, 383.

Commentary: *After the fall of Mycenaean Greece c. 1200* BCE, *civilization had so thoroughly collapsed that the Bronze Age was remembered only in shadow as a mysterious age of heroes, its works attributed to giants, gods, and monsters, including the giant Cyclopes, who were alleged to have built Mycenaean ruins, leading to the adjective "cyclopean" to describe anything large.*

27. Giants Build Stonehenge
Geoffrey of Monmouth
Historia Regum Britanniae 8.10–11
c. 1136 CE
Latin
Astro, Prehistoric
Discussion in AA

"If you are desirous," said Merlin, "to honour the burying-place of these men with an everlasting monument, send for the Giant's Dance, which is in Killaraus, a mountain in Ireland. For there is a structure of stones there, which none of this age could raise, without a profound knowledge of the mechanical arts. They are stones of a vast magnitude and wonderful quality; and if they can be placed here, as they are there, round this spot of ground, they will stand for ever."

At these words of Merlin, Aurelius burst into laughter, and said, "How is it possible to remove such vast stones from so distant a country, as if Britain was not furnished with stones fit for the work?" Merlin replied: "I entreat your majesty to forbear vain laughter; for what I say is without vanity. They are mystical stones, and of a medicinal virtue. The giants of old brought them from the farthest coasts of Africa, and placed them in Ireland, while they inhabited that country. Their design in this was to make baths in them, when they should be taken with any illness. For their method was to wash the stones, and put their sick into the water, which infallibly cured them. With the like success they cured wounds also, adding only the application of some herbs. There is not a stone there which has not some healing virtue."

Source: Translated by A. Thompson and J. A. Giles in *The British History of Geoffrey of Monmouth,* trans. A. Thompson and rev. J. A. Giles (London: James Bohn, 1842), 158–159.

Stonehenge was already so fabulously old in the Middle Ages that no one knew who had built it. This spawned many colorful legends that the monument was the work of giants, wizards, the Devil, or an early British king. It is possible, though not certain, that Diodorus Siculus records a distorted legend of Stonehenge in describing the round temple of the far northern Hyperboreans dedicated to solar Apollo (*Library of History* 2.47.2). If so, it is the oldest account to survive (Library of Congress).

Commentary: *Composed nearly four thousand years after the British monument, this mythic passage putatively about giants is notable for its confused memory that Stonehenge's stones were imported from the Celtic lands (actually Wales).*

29. Giovanni Boccaccio Reports on a Fossilized Giant

Giovanni Boccaccio
Genealogia deorum gentilium 4.68
1360–1374 CE
Latin
Astro, Prehistoric

... Many things must be said [about Greek myths of the Giants] if we wish to solve the riddle of these fictions, but before anything, we must say that it is not entirely a fiction that there existed Giants, that is, creatures with the form of men but exceeding them greatly in stature. And indeed, it appears this was the truth, and in these days [i.e., 1342] a fortuitous event in the town of Drepana (Tripani) in Sicily clearly shows this: For, in the foothills of the mountain that rises above Drepana, not far from the town, a few peasants digging the foundation for the construction of a rural house came upon the entrance to a certain cavern. When the diggers, with lit torches, entered in eagerness to see what lay within, they found a grotto of the greatest height and breadth. Continuing into the grotto, they saw opposite the entrance a seated man of immense magnitude, of whom they were much frightened. They quickly took flight and left the cave; nor did they cease their running until they reached the town, announcing to those they met what they had seen.

But the citizens were in wonder, and they wished to see what this evil was, so after lighting torches and gathering arms, they left the city together as if against an enemy; and more than three hundred entered into the grotto, and no less dumbstruck, they saw what the workers had reported. At last, they came closer, after they determined that the man was not alive, and they saw him sitting on a seat, resting with his left hand on a staff of such height and thickness that it exceeded the mast of a great ship. So, too, was he a man of a size unseen and unheard of, and neither were any of his parts gnawed at or mutilated. And when one of them stretched out his hand and touched the upright staff, the staff immediately collapsed into ashes, but there remained, as if stripped of its clothing, another staff of lead rising toward the hand of him holding it. Examining the staff to their satisfaction, they determined the lead had been poured into the staff in order to increase its weight, with respect to which, after they had weighed it, those who saw it said it weighed fifteen of Drepana's hundredweights, of which one of these weights is equal to a hundred common pounds. The body of the man also fell apart upon being touched, and it turned almost completely to dust. When this dust was handled with some of their hands, three teeth of monstrous size were discovered still intact, with a weight of three *rotuli*, that is, one hundred common ounces.

To preserve evidence of the giant they had found and to create an everlasting memory for future generations, the Drepanites bound up the remains in an iron net and hung them in a church within the city dedicated to the Annunciation of the Virgin and known by that name.

And moreover, a part of the front of the skull was found still solid and capable of holding several bushels of corn. So, too, was found one of the leg bones, of which the fullness of age had caused to reach a state of absolute rottenness; however, those who can determine the total height of a man from the size of even the smallest of his bones calculated from this remnant that his size was two hundred cubits or more.[1]

It was suspected by some of the most prudent that this was Eryx, an extremely powerful king from the area, the son of Butes and Venus, who was killed by Hercules and afterward hidden in this mountain. But he was thought by some to be Entellus, who in the funeral games given by Aeneas long ago for his father Anchises had killed a bull with his fist. Still others thought him one of the Cyclopes, and quite possibly Polyphemus, of whom Homer says much.[2] Vergil[3] wrote of him thus:

> Scarcely had he spoken when we saw on the mountaintop
> Polyphemus himself moving with his enormous bulk amidst the cattle
> And reaching for the well-known shore—
> A huge, dread monster whose eye had been put out,
> And a pine cut down by his own hand guides and steadies his footsteps.

And a little bit later he continues:

> Gnashing his teeth with a groan, he steps through the sea,
> Now at full height, while the towering waves failed to wet his tall sides.

And he says many other things that go to show the magnitude of the Cyclopes, suggesting they belong more toward the truth rather than the hyperbole which many decide to use in this matter.

Source: Translated by Jason Colavito from the Latin edition published as Ioannis Boccatii, *De Genealogia Deorum*, ed. Iacobus Micyllus (Basel: 1532), 114–115.

Commentary: *Mainstream scholars since the 1800s have held that Boccaccio is recording the discovery of the remains of a fossilized extinct elephant, the bones of which have been mistaken for humanoid giants down to the modern era. Nevertheless, writers, particularly in the nineteenth century, like the journalist John D. Champlin, Jr.,[4] used this as an example of the remains of an antediluvian giant and an example of their fate in the Flood.*

Notes

1. 300 feet or 91 meters.
2. *Odyssey* 9.105ff. Heroes and monsters of myth were thought giants from ancient times to today.
3. Vergil, *Aeneid* 3.655f.
4. John D. Champlin, Jr., "Concerning Giants," *Appleton's Journal*, December 7, 1872, 633–635.

30. The Hunt for Noah's Ark

FLAVIUS JOSEPHUS

Antiquities of the Jews 1.93–95
c. 93–94 CE
Greek
General

[93] Now all the writers of barbarian histories make mention of this flood, and of this ark; among whom is Berossus the Chaldean. For when he is describing the circumstances of the flood, he goes on thus: "It is said there is still some part of this ship in Armenia, at the mountain of the Cordyaeans; and that some people carry off pieces of the bitumen, which they take away, and use chiefly as amulets for the averting of mischiefs."[1] [94] Hieronymus the Egyptian also, who wrote the *Phoenician Antiquities*, and Mnaseas, and a great many more, make mention of the same. Nay, Nicolaus of Damascus, in his ninety-sixth book, hath a particular relation about them; where he speaks thus: [95] "There is a great mountain in Armenia, over Minyas, called Baris,[2] upon which it is reported that many who fled at the time of the Deluge were saved; and that one who was carried in an ark came on shore upon the top of it; and that the remains of the timber were a great while preserved. This might be the man about whom Moses the legislator of the Jews wrote."

Source: Translated by William Whiston in *The Genuine Works of Flavius Josephus*, vol. 1 (New York: David Huntington, 1815), 93.

Commentary: *We have encountered this legend from Berossus (20), who was referring to the Ark of Xisithrus from the Babylonian version of the Flood myth, preserving a late version of a story that in the Old Babylonian* Atrahasis *once referred to the Ark coming to rest "beyond Urartu" (Ararat), on a mountain at the edge of the world. The collection of Ark relics transferred from pagan to Christian tourists largely uninterrupted until the peak in question, located far up the Tigris and known by the Arabic name Al-Judi (Judi Dagh near Silopi in Turkey), corrupted from the name given above, fell out of favor as the proposed landing site in the eighteenth century, replaced by the mountain called Masis in Armenian, now known as Ararat, though Judi too once bore the same title of Masis (Strabo,* Geography *11.12.4). Islam, which preserved the Al-Judi tradition (Qur'an 11:44) continues to locate the ark in this spot. The name Ararat originally referred to the entire region, not a single peak. Eusebius quotes the text of Berossus* *again in his* Onomasticon *(entry for Ararat), to which he adds no further evidence in support of the existence of said relics. About eighty years after Josephus wrote, Theophilus of Antioch noted, by contrast, in his* Apology for Autolycus *that "the remains are to this day to be seen in the Arabian mountains" (3.19, trans. Marcus Dods).*

HIPPOLYTUS OF ROME

Refutation of All Heresies 10.26
Early 3rd c. CE
Greek
General

This *Noah*, inasmuch as he was a most religious and God-loving man, alone, with wife and children, and the three wives of these, escaped the flood that ensued. And he owed his preservation to an ark; and both the dimensions and relics of this *ark* are, as we have explained, shown to this day in the mountains called Ararat, which are situated in the direction of the country of the Adiabeni.

Source: Translated by J. H. McMahon in *The Ante-Nicene Fathers*, vol. 5: Hippolytus, Cyprian, Caius, Novatian, Appendix, eds. Alexander Roberts and James Donaldson (New York: Charles Scribner's Sons, 1903), p. 149.

Commentary: *Josephus confirmed the same in his* Antiquities *(20.22), where the places the Ark in the region of Carra or Carron, north of Adiabene, which is to say the Gordyaean Mountains. Such claims had a long life. Around 375, Epiphanius wrote in his* Panarion *(1.18.3) that "even to this day the remnants of the Ark are still shown in the region of the Cardyaei" (my trans.). Cardyaei was another variant on Gordyaei (also: Corduene and Carduchi), later corrupted into Al-Judi and also giving rise, via the people of the region, to the name Kurds. In the sixth century, Isidore of Seville, in the* Etymologies *(14.521), repeats the same claim.*

FAUSTUS OF BYZANTIUM (P'AVSTOS BUZAND)

History of the Armenians 3.10
5th c. CE
Armenian
General

By this time, the great bishop of Mitspin (Nisibis[3]), this admirable old man, tireless in performing works of truth, chosen by God, Jacob by name and Persian in origin, left his city heading toward the mountains of Armenia, which is to say toward the mountain of Sararad,[4] in the territory of the principality of Ayrarat, in the district of Korduk.[5] He was a man filled with the graces of Christ and who had the power to do miracles and wonders. Arriving (at this place), he addressed God with the keenest desire to receive the opportunity to see the ark of deliverance built by Noah, which came to rest on this mountain during the flood. Jacob obtained from God all that he asked. As he climbed the stony sides of the inaccessible and arid mountain of Sararad, he and those with him felt thirsty as a result of fatigue. Then the great Jacob bent his knees and prayed before the Lord, and in the place where he laid his head, a spring burst forth in which he and those with him quenched their thirst. To this very day it is still called the "Spring of Jacob." However it did not reduce his zeal to see the object of his desire, and he never ceased praying to the Lord God.

When he had neared the top of the mountain, exhausted and tired as he was, he fell asleep. Then the angel of God came and said to him: "Jacob! Jacob!" And he responded:

"Here I am, Lord." And the angel said: "The Lord grants your prayer and fulfills your request; that which you find beneath where you lie is the wood of the ark. I brought it for you from there. Now cease your desire to see the ark, for this is the will of the Lord." Jacob awoke with great joy, worshiping the Lord and thanking him; he saw the board that appeared to have been split by an ax from a larger piece of wood. Having taken it, he turned back with that which had been granted, followed by his companions. [...]

While the man of God brought the wood of deliverance, the symbol of the ark built by our father Noah, that eternal symbol of the great punishment inflicted by God on rational beings and those deprived of reason, the inhabitants of the city and the surrounding area came to meet him (Jacob) with joy and boundless elation. When they saw the holy man, they swarmed him as an Apostle of Christ and an angel from heaven; they regarded him as a brave shepherd and as a prophet who had seen God; they kissed the footprints of his tired feet. They eagerly accepted this wood, this graceful gift, which is preserved to this day among them as the visible sign of the ark of the patriarch Noah.

Source: Translated by Jason Colavito from the French translation of Victor Langolis in *Fragmenta historicum graecorum*, vol. 5, ed. Victor Langolis (Paris: Didot, 1872), 218–219.

Commentary: *Faustus of Byzantium is a shadowy figure who existence is the subject of much debate. His work was once thought to have been composed in Greek but is now believed to have been written in Armenian. His tale of St. Jacob of Nisibis (also called St. James) (died c. 338 CE) is the first recorded Christian effort to find Noah's Ark, implying that the trade in ark amulets (20) had died out sometime before Jacob's time. The story is repeated nearly a thousand years later and almost verbatim by the fictitious but famous medieval traveler John (Jehan) Mandeville, who differs only in omitting the angel's presentation of the plank, as the original had it.*

THEOPHILUS OF EDESSA

World Chronicle
8th c. CE
Greek or Syriac
Preserved in Agapius of Hierapolis, *Kitab al-'Unwan*
10th c. CE
General

Then Heraclius turned back and encamped at a village which was called Thamanin. This is the village where the ark stopped during the flood, in the time of Noah. He climbed the mountain which is called Al-Judi, examined the location of the ark, surveyed the world to the four cardinal points, and then headed for Amida where he remained throughout the winter.

Source: Translated by Jason Colavito from the edition of Alexander Vasiliev in A. A. Vasiliev, "Kitab-Al-'Unwan," part 2, tract 2, *Patrologia orientalis*, vol. 8, eds. R. Graffin and F. Nau (Paris: Firmin-Didot, 1912), 465.

Commentary: *Heraclius was a Byzantine emperor (610–641 CE), and the passage preserved by the Christian-Arab writer Agapius here suggests that the Al-Judi tradition was the one followed by the Byzantine Greeks. He made his trek to Al-Judi in the eighteenth year of his reign, in the spring of 628 CE. Following the Qur'an, Agapius' Islamic contemporaries Al-Mas'ūdī and Ibn Ḥawqal both identified Al-Judi as the site of the Ark and described an area near what* *is now Judi Dagh. Around 1260, the story of Heraclius is repeated nearly verbatim in the* al-Majmu' al-Mubarak *of the Christian Arab writer George Elmacin (Girgis Al-Makin) (2.1.1).*

SIR JOHN MANDEVILLE

Travels, Chapter 16
c. 1357–1371
French
General

From that city of Erzurum go men to a mountain called Sabissa. And there beside it is another mountain that men call Ararat, but the Jews call it Taneez [or Thano],[6] where Noah's ship rested, and yet remains upon that mountain. And men may see it from afar in clear weather. And that mountain is fully seven miles high. And some men say that they have seen and touched the ship, and put their fingers in the parts where the Devil went out when Noah said "Benedicite."[7] But they that say such words say them ignorantly, for a man may not go up the mountain due to the great deal of snow that is always on that mountain both in summer and winter. Thus no man may go up there, and indeed no man ever did, since the time of Noah, save a monk that, by the grace of God, brought one of the planks down, that yet is in the monastery at the foot of the mountain. [...] But to go up upon that mountain, this monk had a great desire. And so one day, he went up. And when he was a third of the way up the mountain he was so weary that he could go no further, and so he rested and fell asleep. And when he awoke he found himself lying at the foot of the mountain. And then he prayed devoutly to God that he would allow him to go up. And an angel came to him, and said that he should go up. And so he did. And since that time no other ever has, which is why men should not believe such words.

Source: Adapted from the English edition reprinted in *The Travels of Sir John Mandeville: The Version of the Cotton Manuscript in Modern Spelling* (London: Macmillan and Company, 1905), 100. In the ellipses, "Mandeville" presents undigested geographical data marking where he changed the authority from whom he copied without collating or merging the texts.

Commentary: *Mandeville took the geographical details from the* History of the Tartars *(1.9) of the Armenian monk Hayton of Corycus, its inaccessibility from Odoric's* Travels *(1), and its ascent by the monk from Vincent of Beauvais'* Speculum Historiale *(30.97.440). A century before Mandeville, William of Rubuck independently reported the same story in his* Travels *(387), saying a bishop in Armenia told him "that there had been a monk who was most desirous (of climbing it), but that an angel appeared to him bearing a piece of wood of the ark and told him to try no more" (trans. William Woodville Rockhill). Other medieval writers seem to draw on elements of the story. Benjamin of Tudela said the Ark's wood was used to make a mosque, while later medieval writers Ibn Al-Mid and Zakariya Qazvini repeat the Heraclius story (above) and assert the Ark's wood was used to build a monastery, almost certainly a confusion of the tradition reported by Mandeville, Vincent, and Rubuck that the plank resides in the monastery at the base of Al-Judi. Armenians believe that the plank was taken to Armenia and is preserved in the Armenian cathedral of Echmiadzin.*

Notes

1. The text given by Josephus varies slightly from that of Syncellus (**20**), who gives the mountains as plural.
2. Most scholars identify the unusual name Baris with Mt. Judi, as Josephus implies both here and in *An-*

tiquities 20.22 where the location is explicitly listed as Carra, north of Adiabene; i.e., the Gordyaean Mountains. It is possibly a Greek corruption of Mt. Lûbâr in Jubilees 5:28, on which the Ark landed and which Epiphanius (*Panarion* 1.2.2) equated with Mt. Judi in 375 CE, writing that it was located "between Armenia and Cardyaei" (i.e., Corduene, the site of Judi). Alternately, the Greek name Baris (*baros*, "heavy") could be an attempted translation of Masis ("great"), a name associated with today's Mt. Ararat but in Classical times also applied to Mt. Judi, as Strabo confirms in writing of "Mount Masius, which is situated above Nisibis" (*Geography* 11.12.4; see also Faustus of Byzantium below). Minyas refers to the territory of the Mannai or Minni south of Lake Urmia in modern Iran.

3. Nisibis is the Classical Greek name for what is now called Nusaybin in Mardin Province, Turkey. The city was variously ruled by Mesopotamia, Greece, Persia, and Rome in ancient times. It is about 70 miles (110 km) from Mount Judi and was long associated with that peak (Strabo, *Geography* 11.12.4, 16.1.22).

4. Mount Judi. The name *Sararad* is apparently a running together of *sar* (peak, mountain) and *Ararad* (Ararat).

5. Although the exact borders are disputed, this is usually identified as Corduene (Gordyene), the region surrounding Mt. Judi, which Faustus has here identified with the mountains of Ararat, sharing a name with the Armenian province of Ayrarat. Corduene had many rulers in ancient times but was geographically considered part of Armenia.

6. Possibly a corruption of the Persian name for the mountain of the Ark, *kuh-i-nuh* (Noah's Hill).

7. In medieval legendry and mystery plays, first attested in *Queen Mary's Psalter* around 1300, Noah allegedly expelled from the Ark the Devil, who had stowed away, by saying "Benedicite," or "Bless you."

IV

Flying Chariots and Ancient Astronauts

The emergence of the ancient astronaut theory during the twentieth century is closely tied to the rise of the UFO movement after 1947. Both have antecedents in the so-called Shaver Mystery of the 1940s (itself an outgrowth of pulp fiction and classic sci-fi like Bulwer-Lytton's *Coming Race*), a hoax that purported to report on a technologically-advanced subterranean race, as well as the pulp fiction of the 1920s and 1930s, particularly that of the American horror writer H. P. Lovecraft and other weird fiction writers like Robert E. Howard, creator of Conan the Cimmerian. Lovecraft's (fictional) stories of ancient aliens who came from the stars and built strange monoliths, drawn in part from the occult beliefs of Theosophy, influenced not just Shaver but also Jacques Bergier and Louis Pauwels, whose *Morning of the Magicians* (1960) became the template used (and sometimes appropriated wholesale) by Robert Charroux, Erich von Däniken, and those who followed. Bergier and Pauwels combined the esoteric and the occult with Soviet work attempting to rationalize Judeo-Christian mythology as tales of extraterrestrials. The Soviets of the 1950s considered this scientific-materialist propaganda against the values of the West, but in the hands of Theosophy-inspired European and American authors, ancient astronauts gradually became an eclectic New Age millenarian belief system where the "return of the gods" promised a Millennium of ecstasy and joy.

The competing points of origin—space age euhemerism, postmodern distrust of science, and New Age millenarianism—make it difficult to sort what used to be called "nuts and bolts" claims for physical contact with aliens and their craft from more recent claims about an all-pervasive "influence" from "non-human intelligences" that are functionally indistinguishable from the pagan gods ancient astronaut theorists proposed to replace with aliens. This chapter will examine texts specifically related to alleged "nuts and bolts" encounters with aliens and their craft, the type that gave their name to the genre's most famous book: *Chariots of the Gods*. Given the pervasive influence of the Watchers myth on fringe theories, it is not surprising that biblical and pseudo-biblical sources are among the most important "evidence" for prehistoric alien contact. We shall start there before widening our scope beyond the Holy Land.

31. Elijah Is Abducted by Aliens
2 Kings 2:9–12
After 500 BCE
Hebrew
Astro
Discussion in CG

[9] And it came to pass, when they were gone over, that Elijah said unto Elisha, Ask what I shall do for thee, before I be taken away from thee. And Elisha said, I pray thee, let a double portion of thy spirit be upon me.

[10] And he said, Thou hast asked a hard thing: nevertheless, if thou see me when I am taken from thee, it shall be so unto thee; but if not, it shall not be so.

[11] And it came to pass, as they still went on, and talked, that, behold, there appeared a chariot of fire, and horses of fire, and parted them both asunder; and Elijah went up by a whirlwind into heaven.

[12] And Elisha saw it, and he cried, My father, my father, the chariot of Israel, and the horsemen thereof. And he saw him no more: and he took hold of his own clothes, and rent them in two pieces.

Source: King James Version.

Commentary: *Although it is frequently claimed that the prophet Elijah was taken up in the fiery chariot (almost certainly meant to be the flaming chariot of the sun god in Near Eastern myth, possibly referring here to an actual Babylonian ceremonial procession), which alternative historians read as a spaceship, the text says it was a storm. According to the Psalms (104:4)*

Although the Biblical account has Elijah carried away in a whirlwind, the prior appearance of a fiery chariot in the passage led to the belief that the chariot carried Elijah away, as in this 1547 etching by Augustin Hirschvogel. Similar stories were also told of the prophet Enoch, who sometimes also said to have fiery chariot for a heavenly transport. Ancient astronaut theorists believe such chariots were spacecraft (National Gallery of Art).

storms were considered messengers of God, as they were in other Near East religions (cf. Baal "the rider of the clouds"). Ancient astronaut theorists often conflate Elijah's transfer to heaven with that of Enoch in Genesis 5:24 ("God took him") because in 1 Enoch he rises to heaven in "a whirlwind" (39:3) and in the Book of Jasher *in "a whirlwind, with horses and chariots of fire" (3:36), modelled on the ascent of Elijah, causing some writers to attribute to Enoch a ride in a fiery spaceship through the transitive property of fringe history.*

32. Ezekiel Has a Close Encounter

Ezekiel 1:1–28
c. 580 BCE
Hebrew
Astro
Discussion in CG, TG, etc.

[1] Now it came to pass in the thirtieth year, in the fourth month, in the fifth day of the month, as I was among the captives by the river of Chebar, that the heavens were opened, and I saw visions of God.

[2] In the fifth day of the month, which was the fifth year of king Jehoiachin's captivity,

[3] The word of the Lord came expressly unto Ezekiel the priest, the son of Buzi, in the land of the Chaldeans by the river Chebar; and the hand of the Lord was there upon him.

[4] And I looked, and, behold, a whirlwind came out of the north, a great cloud, and a fire infolding itself, and a brightness was about it, and out of the midst thereof as the colour of amber, out of the midst of the fire.

[5] Also out of the midst thereof came the likeness of four living creatures. And this was their appearance; they had the likeness of a man.

[6] And every one had four faces, and every one had four wings.

[7] And their feet were straight feet; and the sole of their feet was like the sole of a calf's foot: and they sparkled like the colour of burnished brass.

[8] And they had the hands of a man under their wings on their four sides; and they four had their faces and their wings.

[9] Their wings were joined one to another; they turned not when they went; they went every one straight forward.

[10] As for the likeness of their faces, they four had the face of a man, and the face of a lion, on the right side: and they four had the face of an ox on the left side; they four also had the face of an eagle.

[11] Thus were their faces: and their wings were stretched upward; two wings of every one were joined one to another, and two covered their bodies.

[12] And they went every one straight forward: whither the spirit was to go, they went; and they turned not when they went.

[13] As for the likeness of the living creatures, their appearance was like burning coals of fire, and like the appearance of lamps: it went up and down among the living creatures; and the fire was bright, and out of the fire went forth lightning.

[14] And the living creatures ran and returned as the appearance of a flash of lightning.

[15] Now as I beheld the living creatures, behold one wheel upon the earth by the living creatures, with his four faces.

[16] The appearance of the wheels and their work was like unto the colour of a beryl:

To pierce the veil of the universe and see the mechanics of the universe beyond animates not just scientists but also ancient astronaut writers. This illustration depicts a seeker of truth piercing the dome of the heavens to see the operation of the celestial spheres beyond, symbolized by the wheels in the upper left, reminiscent of Ezekiel's wheels, often claimed to be spaceships (Camille Flammarion, *L'Atmosphere: Météorologie Populaire* [Paris, 1888], p. 163).

and they four had one likeness: and their appearance and their work was as it were a wheel in the middle of a wheel.

[17] When they went, they went upon their four sides: and they turned not when they went.

[18] As for their rings, they were so high that they were dreadful; and their rings were full of eyes round about them four.

[19] And when the living creatures went, the wheels went by them: and when the living creatures were lifted up from the earth, the wheels were lifted up.

[20] Whithersoever the spirit was to go, they went, thither was their spirit to go; and the wheels were lifted up over against them: for the spirit of the living creature was in the wheels.

[21] When those went, these went; and when those stood, these stood; and when those were lifted up from the earth, the wheels were lifted up over against them: for the spirit of the living creature was in the wheels.

[22] And the likeness of the firmament upon the heads of the living creature was as the colour of the terrible crystal, stretched forth over their heads above.

[23] And under the firmament were their wings straight, the one toward the other: every one had two, which covered on this side, and every one had two, which covered on that side, their bodies.

[24] And when they went, I heard the noise of their wings, like the noise of great waters, as the voice of the Almighty, the voice of speech, as the noise of an host: when they stood, they let down their wings.

[25] And there was a voice from the firmament that was over their heads, when they stood, and had let down their wings.

[26] And above the firmament that was over their heads was the likeness of a throne, as the appearance of a sapphire stone: and upon the likeness of the throne was the likeness as the appearance of a man above upon it.

[27] And I saw as the colour of amber, as the appearance of fire round about within it, from the appearance of his loins even upward, and from the appearance of his loins even downward, I saw as it were the appearance of fire, and it had brightness round about.

[28] As the appearance of the bow that is in the cloud in the day of rain, so was the appearance of the brightness round about. This was the appearance of the likeness of the glory of the Lord. And when I saw it, I fell upon my face, and I heard a voice of one that spake.

Source: King James Version.

Commentary: *One of the most popular ancient astronaut claims, the vision of Ezekiel is frequently likened to a flying saucer. Ezekiel here seemingly describes typical Babylonian imagery for divine thrones, with four-winged, four-faced throne-bearers. In 1:16, for example, a more magnificent version of the Babylonian wheeled chariots for transporting divine statues is quite clearly indicated. However, because fringe writers are unfamiliar with ancient Near East culture, they are able to propose that Ezekiel saw a spaceship. The most famous version of this claim was NASA scientist Josef F. Blumrich's* Spaceships of Ezekiel *(1974), in which he used his NASA training to design a futuristic spacecraft to reflect his reading of the Ezekiel sighting. He explicitly credited his efforts to the inspiration of Erich von Däniken's CG, where that author calls the passage an encounter with a "vehicle" or "craft" full of "creatures" who cannot be gods, for gods don't need flying craft!*

33. Ezekiel Is Abducted by Aliens
Ezekiel 3:12–14
c. 580 BCE
Hebrew
Astro

[12] Then the spirit took me up, and I heard behind me a voice of a great rushing, saying, Blessed be the glory of the Lord from his place.

[13] I heard also the noise of the wings of the living creatures that touched one another, and the noise of the wheels over against them, and a noise of a great rushing.

[14] So the spirit lifted me up, and took me away, and I went in bitterness, in the heat of my spirit; but the hand of the Lord was strong upon me.

Source: King James Version

Commentary: *Ancient astronaut writers suggest this represents an alien abduction, but there is no indication of entry into a craft.*

34. Abraham Sees a UFO on a Trip to Space
Apocalypse of Abraham 15, 16, and 18
c. 75–150 CE
Old Slavonic, from a Hebrew or Aramaic original
Astro
Discussion in CG

CHAPTER 15

And it came to pass when the sun went down, and lo! a smoke as of a furnace. And the angels who had the portions of the sacrifice ascended from the top of the smoking furnace. And the Angel took me with the right hand and set me on the right wing of the pigeon, and set himself on the left wing of the turtle dove, which (birds) had neither been slaughtered nor divided. And he bore me to the borders of the flaming fire [and we ascended as with many winds to the heaven which was fixed upon the surface. And I saw on the air] on the height, to which we ascended a strong light, which it was impossible to describe, and lo! in this light a fiercely burning fire for people, many people of male appearance, all (constantly) changing in aspect and form, running and being transformed, and worshipping and crying with a sound of words which I knew not.

CHAPTER 16

And I said to the Angel: "Why hast thou brought me up here now, because I cannot now see, for I am already grown weak, and my spirit departeth from me?" And he said to me: "Remain by me; fear not! And He whom thou seest come straight towards us with great voice of holiness—that is the Eternal One who Loveth thee; but Himself thou canst not see). But let not thy spirit grow faint [on account of the loud crying], for I am with thee, strengthening thee."

CHAPTER 18

And while I still recited the song, the mouth of the fire which was on the surface rose up on high. And I heard a voice like the roaring of the sea; nor did it cease on account of the rich abundance of the fire. And as the fire raised itself up, ascending into the height, I saw under the fire a throne of fire, and, round about it all-seeing ones, reciting the song, and under the throne four fiery living creatures singing, and their appearance was one, *each one of them with four faces*. And such was the appearance of their countenances, *of a lion, of a man, of an ox, of an eagle:* four heads [were upon their bodies] [so that the four creatures had sixteen faces]; and each had six wings; from their shoulders, [and their sides] and their loins. And with the (two) wings from their shoulders they covered their faces, and with the (two) wings which (sprang) from their loins they covered their feet, while the (two) middle wings they spread out for flying straightforward. And when they had ended the singing, they looked at one another and threatened one another. And it came to pass when the angel who was with me saw that they were threatening each other, he left me and went running to them and turned the countenance of each living creature from the countenance immediately confronting him, in order that they might not see their countenances threatening each other. And he taught them the song of peace which hath its origin [in the Eternal One]. And as I stood alone and looked, I saw behind the living creatures a chariot with fiery wheels, each wheel full of eyes round about; and over the wheels was a throne; which I saw, and this was covered with fire, and fire encircled it round about, and lo! an indescribable fire environed a fiery host. And I heard its holy voice like the voice of a man.

Source: Translated by G. H. Box in *The Apocalypse of Abraham* (London: Society for Promoting Christian Knowledge, 1918), 55–63. Bracketed text are manuscript variants.

Commentary: *In CG, Erich von Däniken does not recognize the literary dependence of this much later passage on Ezekiel (31) and instead takes it as independent confirmation of an alien spacecraft. As always, he assumes that a text records faithfully the actual events it describes, no matter how long after the fact it was actually composed.*

35. Eve Sees a Flying Saucer
Apocalypse of Moses 33:1–5
3rd–5th c. CE
Greek
From a lost Hebrew or Aramaic original
c. 100 CE
Astro
Discussion in CG

[1] And Eve arose, and covered her face with her hand; and the angel says to her: Raise yourself from the things of earth. [2] And Eve gazed up into heaven, and she saw a chariot of light going along under four shining eagles—and it was not possible for any one born of woman to tell the glory of them, or to see the face of them—and angels going before the chariot. [3] And when they came to the place where your[1] father Adam was lying, the chariot stood still, and the seraphim between your father and the chariot. [4] And I saw golden censers, and three vials; and, behold, all the angels with incense, and the censers, and the vials, came to the altar, and blew them up, and the smoke of the incense covered the firmaments. [5] And the angels fell down and worshipped God, crying out and saying: Holy Jael, forgive; for he is Your image, and the work of Your holy hands.

Source: Translated by Alexander Walker in Alexander Roberts and James Donaldson (eds.), *Ante-Nicene Fathers*, vol. 8 (New York: Charles Scribner's Sons, 1903), 569.

Commentary: *The pseudo-epigraphic* Apocalypse of Moses *and several other apocryphal texts derived from the same original, conventionally called the* Life of Adam and Eve, *contain an early version of the myth, preserved in the Qur'an (7:11–13), that Satan rebelled because he refused to bow before Adam. The Latin version, as we saw (12), also preserves a variant of the prophecy of the tablets derived ultimately from a Mesopotamian original. In the passage above, Eve witnesses the chariot of God at Adam's death, again drawing on Mesopotamian models.*

Note
1. The text switches from third to first person narration here, and Eve is speaking to her children about Adam's death.

36. Unas Becomes a Cannibal, Flies Pyramid to Orion
Pyramid Texts, Utterances 273 and 274
c. 2345 BCE
Egyptian
Astro
Discussion in AA

273. Now heaven rains, and trembles every star
With terror; bowmen scamper to escape;
And quakes old Aker, lion of the earth,
While all his worshippers betake to flight,
For Unas rises and in heaven appears
Like to a god who lived upon his sires
And on his mothers fed.

Unas the lord
Of wisdom is; the secret of his Name
Not e'en his mother knows.... His rank is high
In heaven above; his power is like to Tum's,
His sire divine.... Greater than Tum is he.

His shadowy doubles follow him behind
As he comes forth. The uræus on his brow
Uprears; the royal serpent guides him on;
He sees his Ba [soul] a flame of living fire.

The strength of Unas shields him.... He is now
The Bull of Heaven, doing as he wills,
Feeding on what gives life unto the gods—
Their food he eats who would their bellies fill
With words of power from the pools of flame.

Against the spirits shielded by his might,
Unas arises now to take his meal—
Men he devours; he feasts upon the gods
This lord who reckons offerings: he who makes
Each one to bow his forehead, bending low.

Amkenhuu is snarer; Herthertu
Hath bound them well; and Khonsu killer is
Who cuts the throats and tears the entrails out—
'Twas he whom Unas sent to drive them in ...
Divided by Shesemu, now behold
The portions cooking in the fiery pots.

274. Unas is feasting on their secret Names;
Unas devours their spirits and their souls—
At morn he eats the largest, and at eve
The ones of middle girth, the small at night:
Old bodies are the faggots for his fire.
Lo! mighty Unas makes the flames to leap
With thighs of agèd ones, and into pots
Are legs of women flung that he may feast.

Unas, the Power, is the Power of Powers!
Unas, the mighty god, is god of gods!
Voraciously he feeds on what he finds,
And he is given protection more assured
Than all the mummies 'neath the western sky.

Unas is now the eldest over all—
Thousands he ate and hundreds he did burn;
He rules o'er Paradise.... Among the gods
His soul is rising up in highest heaven—
The Crown is he as the horizon lord.

He reckoned livers as he reckoned knots;
The hearts of gods he ate and they are his;
He swallowed up the White Crown and the Red,
And fat of entrails gulped; the secret Names
Are in his belly and he prospers well—
Lo! he devoured the mind of every god,
And so shall live for ever and endure
Eternally, to do as he desires.

The souls of gods are now in his great soul;
Their spirits in his spirit; he obtains
Food in abundance greater than the gods—
His fire has seized their bones, and lo! their souls
Are Unas's; their shades are with their forms.

Unas ascends.... Unas ascends with these—
Unas is hidden, is hidden.... An One
For him hath ploughed.... The seat of every heart is
Unas's among all living men.

Source: Translated by Donald A. Mackenzie in *Egyptian Myth and Legend* (London: Gresham Publishing, 1907), 168–170.

Commentary: *Often called the "Cannibal Hymn," this text represents a metaphorical consumption of the essence of the gods (represented as sacrificial bulls) by the pharaoh to give him the divine power needed to reach the afterlife. The text is comparatively rare, known only from the pyramid of Unas, the later pyramid of Teti, and Coffin Text spell 573. Such texts, including the Pyramid Texts and Coffin Texts, embodied sacred knowledge and the spells needed for the deceased to advance through the afterlife and are inherently magical rather than scientific or historical in nature. Ancient astronaut theorists sometimes relate this hymn to the Holy Bloodline Conspiracy and suggest that the pharaoh was an alien consuming special blood, or a human consuming alien blood to achieve extraterrestrial communion. On AA, Giorgio Tsoukalos suggested that the text recorded a literal journey to a planet near one of the stars of the constellation Orion in a pyramid-shaped spaceship because the god Osiris was represented by the constellation Orion, so by becoming Osiris the king literally traveled to Orion.*

37. Alexander the Great Sees Flying Saucers
Quintus Curtius Rufus
History of Alexander 4.3
c. 45–75 CE
Latin
Astro, UFO
Discussion in AA, TG, WS

Further, the besieged heated brazen targets [i.e., shields] to a red heat, which, filled with burning sand and boiling slime, they suddenly discharged from the walls. None of their pestiferous devices was more terrible: whenever the burning sand insinuated between the armour and the body, it was impossible to dislodge it; and where the caustic touched, it consumed the flesh: the wretches tortured by it, flinging down their weapons, and tearing off every defensive covering, lay, unrevenged, receiving incessant wounds. The crows and grappling-irons shot from engines swept off a number of men.

Source: Translated anonymously (but likely by P. Pratt) in Quintus Curtius Rufus, *The Life and Reign of Alexander the Great,* vol. 1 (London: Samuel Bagster, 1809), 370–371.

Commentary: *The text refers to an episode in the siege of Tyre in 332 BCE in which Alexander's army was attacked by the people they besieged. In* Stranger than Science *(1959), Frank Edwards paraphrases this passage incorrectly and alleges that it states that "great shining silvery shields" came from the sky, meaning UFOs, and caused men and war elephants to jump into the river to escape. Some believe Edwards incorporated into the text parts of a fire prodigy in the Hellenistic forgery the* Letter of Alexander of Macedonia to His Teacher Aristotle, *surviving in Greek summary and full Latin translation, but I wonder if his source is not the similar passage in* Mahabharata *7.202 (53) where men and elephants flee into a river to escape the burns caused by a heat weapon. Later writers such as Raymond Drake, David Childress, and Jacques Vallée repeated Edwards without verifying the source. Although Vallée and Aubeck concluded in WS that the story was likely exaggerated by ufologists, an illustration of the claim, complete with flying saucers, served as the cover image for the 2009 edition of WS.*

38. A UFO in the Roman Republic
Julius Obsequens
Liber prodigiorum 54
c. 350 CE
Latin
Astro, UFO
Discussion in WS

In Spoletium a gold-colored ball of fire rolled down to the ground and, becoming larger, appeared to be carried off from the ground toward the east, concealing the sun with its magnitude.

Source: Translated by Jason Colavito from the Latin edition published as Iulius Obsequens, *De Prodigiis Liber,* ed. Ioannus Shefferus (Amsterdam: Hernicus and Theodorus Boomus, 1679), 61.

Commentary: *Obsequens compiled a collection of the miraculous and wondrous events* *recorded by the Roman historian Livy before 17* CE, *and this incident refers to events of 91* BCE *that would have been in one of Livy's lost books. The story is repeated almost verbatim at around the same time and almost certainly from Livy by Orosius in* History against the Pagans *5.18. Taken at face value, it appears to describe the breakup of a meteor as seen from a distance, with some parts falling to earth and others shooting into the sky. In* Flying Saucers on the Attack *(1954), Harold T. Wilkins purposely mistranslates this to make the sphere "gyrate" like a rotating flying saucer. Obsequens' work did not survive in full, and it was reconstructed by Conrad Lycosthenes, who added much he believed had been in the original. The passage is No. 114 in his edition but 54 in modern editions of the original surviving Obsequens text.*

39. A UFO in Roman-Era Scotland
Hector Boece
Historia Gentis Scotorum 4.58
1527
Latin
Astro, UFO
Discussion in WS

Sundry marvels were seen in Albion before this last battle that Galdus fought with the Romans. Many fiery brands were seen flying in the air. And a great part of the wood of Caledonia appeared on fire all night, but no fire appeared therein in the day. And a vision of ships appeared in the sky. And a shower of stones was in Athole; similarly, in Angus it rained frogs. And a monster was borne in Tulina with both the genitals of men and women, so abominable a figure that it was destroyed by the people. The uncouth and wonderful marvels made the people astonished and divided their opinions, for they were given to interpreting them in sundry ways, sometimes to the good, sometimes to the evil.

Source: Adapted from the first English translation of 1536 by John Bellenden, published in *The History of Scotland*, vol. 1 (Edinburgh: W. and C. Tait, 1821), 155.

Commentary: *Hector Boece's work has frequently been criticized for its credulity in the miraculous and for its bias toward the patriotic, making it unreliable for the historian and thus a rich source of incident for the pseudo-historian. Harold T. Wilkins, in* Flying Saucers on the Attack *(1954), mistranslates this passage to make the phantom ships appear in the time of the fictitious "Roman emperor Agricola" (he was a general) and makes the "ships" into a single ship, with the implication that it was a fast-moving UFO. WS repeats Wilkins's version verbatim. The version given here has been modernized in spelling and slightly translated from the Scots-English dialect of the original translation.*

40. Irish Gods Arrive in Flying Saucers
Lebor Gabála Érenn, First Redaction 7.304–307
c. 1150 CE
Middle Irish
Astro
Discussion in AA

[304] Thereafter the progeny of Bethach son of Iarbonel the Soothsayer son of Nemed were in the northern islands of the world, learning druidry and knowledge and prophecy and magic, till they were expert in the arts of pagan cunning.

[306] So that they were the Tuatha De Danand who came to Ireland. In this wise they came, in dark clouds. They landed on the mountains of Conmaicne Rein in Connachta and they brought a darkness over the sun for three days and three nights.

[307] They demanded battle or kingship of the Fir Bolg. A battle was fought between them, to wit the first battle of Mag Tuired, in which a hundred thousand of the Fir Bolg fell. Thereafter they (the Tuatha De Danann) took the kingship of Ireland. Those are the Tuath Dea—gods were their men of arts, non-gods their husbandmen. They knew the incantations of druids, and charioteers, and trappers, and cupbearers.

Source: Translated by R. A. Stewart Macalister in *Lebor Gabála Érenn: The Book of the Taking of Ireland,* part 4 (Dublin: Irish Texts Society, 1941), 107–111.

Commentary: *On AA* David Childress *and others claimed that this passage records the arrival of aliens in spacecraft with cloaking devices. The above translation follows the oldest manuscript, the* Book of Leinster *(c. 1150* CE*). A later version, called the* Book of Fermoy *(1373* CE*), adds additional details to most of the above lines, including an entire section, 305, not given here; but these are almost certainly later interpolations. The Tuatha Dé Danann (or Tuatha De Danand) were originally pre–Christian Irish gods but here have been euhemerized as an invading people from the north. A few pages later, the author further euhemerizes the story by making the clouds into a smokescreen created by the Tuatha Dé Danann when they burned their ships upon invading Ireland. The smokescreen is reminiscent of the clouds the Greek gods used to cloak Odysseus in the* Odyssey *and Jason in the* Argonautica.

41. Charlemagne Legislates Against UFOs

Charlemagne
Admonitio generalis, Cap. 65
March 23, 789 CE
Latin
Astro, UFO
Discussion in AQ, WS

Again we have in the law of the Lord the command: *do not practice soothsaying or divination*[1]; and in Deuteronomy: *there shall not be found among you any that uses divination, or an observer of dreams and omens*; and also: *let no one among you be a wizard, nor an enchanter, nor a consulter with familiar spirits.*[2] Therefore, we enjoin that there shall be neither prognosticators and spell-casters, nor weather-magicians or amulet-binders,[3] and that wherever they are found they either be reformed or condemned. Again, with regard to the trees, rocks, or springs where some fools make lights or conduct other observances,[4] we command that wherever it is found this most wicked custom, detestable to God, be removed and destroyed.

Source: Translated by Jason Colavito from the Latin in Ferdinand Walter, *Corpus Iuris Germanici Antiqui,* vol. 2 (Berlin: Impensis G. Reimeri, 1824), 93. There the law is given as cap. 63; the number varies by editor (anywhere from 62 to 65) but is usually given today as 65.

Commentary: *The above is the text of a law promulgated by Charlemagne, who was citing scripture to prohibit magic and witchcraft, associated with paganism in an era when many Europeans were not yet Christians and still practiced Germanic paganism. The reference to the lights (torches) and ceremonies in the woods harks back to aspects of German paganism condemned by the* Second Council of Arles *(canon 23) and repeated in later Church canons, as well as in the works of several medieval clerics. St. Eligius (Dado,* Vita Eligii *16) and Martin of Braga (*De correctione rusticorum *16) both condemned the practices a century before Charlemagne in words nearly identical to the above. The 1670 Rosicrucian novel* Comte de Gabalis *of the Abbé de Villars (Discourse V, sec. 127–128) tied this law to the legend of wizards who lived in the clouds (**42**). Jacques Vallée in WS (and* Passport to Magonia *before it) and Philip Coppens in AQ, who know the law only from the Rosicrucian version and not from the actual text, therefore conclude that Charlemagne passed a law against UFOs.*

Notes

1. Leviticus 19:26.
2. Deuteronomy 18:10–11.
3. The *obligatores* (binders) were users of magical amulets and other tokens to drive away evil. They attached these to their bodies with bindings (*ligaturae*), with the belief that the proximity would cure illness. See **20** for parallel Near Eastern use of such amulets.
4. This refers to the ceremonies of German paganism in which torches or candles were lit at sacred natural places.

42. Sky-Wizards from Magonia Live in the Clouds

Agobard
Contra Insulsam Vulgi Opinionem de Grandine et Tonitruis, Cap. 2
c. 815 CE
Latin
Astro, UFO
Discussion in WS

We have seen and heard many who are overwhelmed by such madness, carried away by such folly, that they believe and assert that there is a certain region called Magonia, whence ships come in the clouds: the which bear away the fruits of the earth, felled by hail and destroyed by storms, to that same country; and these sailors of the air forsooth give rewards to the weather-wizards, and receive in return the crops or other fruits. Certain ones have we seen, blinded by so dark a folly, who brought into an assembly of men four persons, three men and a woman, as having fallen from the said ships; whom they held in bonds for certain days and then presented before an assembled body of men, in our presence, as aforesaid, that they should be stoned. Howbeit the truth prevailed, after much reasoning, and they who brought them forward were confounded.

Source: Translated by Reginald Lane Poole in *Illustrations of the History of Medieval Thought and Learning,* 2nd ed. (London: Society for Promoting Christian Knowledge, 1920), 36.

Commentary: *A priest from Lyon, Agobard wrote a treatise "On Hail and Thunder" to counter the popular belief in weather-magic, inherited from the pagans, particularly Germanic peoples, who had similar stories of gods with heavenly ice palaces. Agobard tried to make plain* that people accused of coming from the sky were the victims of a pervasive mythology, not actual aeronauts. The treatise was lost for nearly 800 years, until its rediscovery and publication in 1605. It is from this popular superstition, used to explain hail, that Jacques Vallée took the name of his most famous book, Passport to Magonia (1969), which attempted to place UFO sightings within a folklore context. The book suggested that what we perceive as ETs were related to folklore fairies and monsters, and that all of them might be from other dimensions rather than outer space. The pagan weather-magicians, however, lived on. In Transylvania they became known as the Solomonari (due to a presumed connection between Solomon, magic, and alchemy), and their gathering-place became known as the Scholomance, or Devil's School. Bram Stoker later made Count Dracula its most famous student.

43. King John Born Under a UFO

ROBERT OF TORIGNI

Gesta Normanorum Ducum, Entry for 1167
Before 1186
Latin
UFO

Queen Eleanor crossed over into England, leading her daughter Matilda with her. During the fourth part of the night of Our Lord's Nativity, there appeared in the West two stars of a fiery color, of which one was great and the other small. And they were as if conjoined; afterward, they were separated by a large space, and they ceased to be visible. John was born the son of the King of England.

Source: Translated by Jason Colavito from the Latin published in Robert de Torigni, *Chronique de Robert de Torigni,* vol. 1, ed. Leopold Delisle (Rouen: A. Le Brument, 1872), 369.

NICHOLAS TRIVET

Annales sex Regum Angliae, Entry for 1167
After 1307
Latin
UFO
Discussion in WS

Crossing into England, Queen Eleanor gave birth to a son, whom she called John, in the fourth part of the night of the Lord's Nativity, in which there appeared in the west two stars of a fiery color, one large and the other small. At first they were conjoined, but afterward they were mutually separated by a great space.

Source: Translated by Jason Colavito from the Latin in F. Nicholas Trivet, *De ordine frat. Praedictatorum, Annales sex Regum Angliae,* ed. Thomas Hog (London: Literary Society, 1845), 60–61.

Commentary: *Robert's text makes plain that the phenomenon in question was a meteor breaking up and burning up in the atmosphere, but alternative authors like Jacques Vallée prefer Nicholas's much later copy because it can more easily be manipulated to sound like a spaceship. WS omits Eleanor and John and makes the large space between the separating meteors into a "long time" that two craft were visible.*

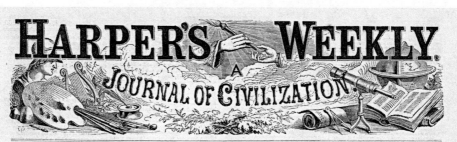

HARPER'S WEEKLY.
A JOURNAL OF CIVILIZATION.

Vol. IV.—No. 188.]   NEW YORK, SATURDAY, AUGUST 4, 1860.   [Price Five Cents.

Entered according to Act of Congress, in the Year 1860, by Harper & Brothers, in the Clerk's Office of the District Court for the Southern District of New York.

THE METEOR.

We engrave herewith three fine pictures of the Meteor which was witnessed in this section of country on Friday, 20th, from sketches by Mr. J. A. Adams at Saratoga Springs, by Mr. Avery at Brooklyn, and Mr. M'Nevin on Long Island.

The phenomenon is stated on all sides to have been one of the most wonderful of the kind ever witnessed. It was seen at Washington, District of Columbia, and in Virginia; at Buffalo, on Lake Erie, and at Detroit, Michigan; in the mountains of Pennsylvania; throughout New England; and at sea, 200 miles east of the Bay of New York.

By this time several volumes have been written and printed in the newspapers on the subject. Astronomers professional and astronomers dilettanti have all had their say; and now that we have heard it, what do we know about the meteor?

First, as to its shape. We have before us the reports of some forty observers, who declare that they saw it from various points, ranging from the Great Lakes to Norfolk, and from Pennsylvania to Boston. Most of them describe it as "two large balls of fire." But observers at Buffalo, Syracuse, Boston, Philadelphia, New York, Newburgh, and Long Island say that there was but "one ball."

An observer at Washington and others say that there were two balls connected; another at Norfolk describes it as "two dumb-bells tied together;" and another at Poughkeepsie says that it was in the shape of a "bar." A sharp amateur at Brooklyn says that it was composed of five balls; or, as an observer in Orange County puts it, "five distinct nuclei;" while another at New Haven is not disposed to admit that there were more than three, but allows that each had a distinct tail. At Philadelphia a leading authority saw "several distinct bodies."

Had it a tail? Several observers state that the meteor had a tail. Some, however, distinctly state that it had no tail, and was thus distinguishable from a comet. At Tarrytown a careful observer noticed a train of sparks following it, but separated from it; and most of the reports from this city confirm this view, though several do not. Those who deny the tail and say nothing about sparks, declare that it was followed by a train of smaller balls, which are variously stated at 2, 3, 5, and "several." At Newburgh, Poughkeepsie, Albany, in Connecticut, and in Pennsylvania, observers declare that the meteor threw off pieces, which were luminous—some say with a loud report, others say noiselessly.

As to the size of the meteor proper, and the length of the train, tail, or series of satellites, opinions are vastly divided. Many observers thought it was the moon, as it was about that size; a sapient watchman in Albany remarked naïvely that the moon was traveling more quickly than usual that night. Others report that it was the size of the planet Venus; at Newburgh it was found to measure three feet in diameter; several observers say that it was "as big as a man's head;" while two declare that it was "the size of a man's fist;" and in Westchester that it was only three inches in diameter. The length of the tail was reported at Boston to be ten feet lineal measure; on Long Island the tail measured 200 feet; at Albany, it extended "several degrees in length."

The color is as uncertain as the rest. On Staten Island it appeared red; red is also the color which met the eye of observers at New York, Buffalo, Hartford, and generally on the Hudson. But at Washington, District of Columbia, it was white; at Syracuse, New York, it was blue; in Jersey it was green; in Philadelphia, greenish; in Orange County, New York, bluish-white; on the Sound, silver and orange mixed.

It will thus be seen that, so far as the cause of astronomical science is concerned, but little advantage can be expected from the popular observations of the meteor. This will not surprise scientific students. The power of accurate observation of physical phenomena is an art only acquired by study and practice. Despite the proverb, very few men can afford to trust their own eyes. To say nothing of color blindness, which is more common than is supposed, there are but few persons in the world whose eye sight is so quick, and whose memory of perceptions so sure as to enable them to report accurately, even after a brief lapse of time, an image which has been impressed upon and then suddenly withdrawn from the retina. We do not suppose that any one of the forty observers whose reports are before us desired to mislead the public; yet, as the body seen by them all was the same (for all agree as to time and the direction taken by the meteor), it is evident that not much more than half a dozen of them saw and remembered it correctly. We are fortunate in being able to lay before the public the report of some whose profession it is to observe such phenomena, and to record them for future study. The astronomer Mitchell writes to the *Herald*:

Albany, July 23, 1860.

"The brilliant meteor seen by your correspondent at Brooklyn was seen at this place by several persons. One

THE METEOR OF JULY 20, AS SEEN BY J. A. ADAMS, ESQ., AT SARATOGA SPRINGS.

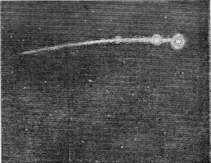

THE METEOR AS SEEN BY S. P. AVERY, ESQ., AT BROOKLYN.

THE METEOR AS SEEN BY J. M'NEVIN, ESQ., NEAR BEDFORD, LONG ISLAND.

The dramatic appearance of a meteor as it breaks up in the atmosphere has always caught the attention of observers below, as happened in 1860 when this meteor streaked across the sky. However, many fringe history writers wonder whether some ancient meteor sightings were really spaceships (Library of Congress).

44. A Renaissance Visit from Mysterious Men

Fazio Cardano
1491
Italian
Preserved in Gerolamo Cardano, *De Subtilitate*, book 19
1552
Astro
Discussion in EV, WS

August 13, 1491. When I had completed the customary rites, at about the twentieth hour of the day, seven men duly appeared to me clothed in silken garments, resembling Greek togas, and wearing, as it were, shining shoes. The undergarments beneath their glistening and ruddy breastplates seemed to be wrought of purple[1] and were of extraordinary glory and beauty. Nevertheless all were not dressed in this fashion, but only two who seemed to be of nobler rank than the others. The taller of them who was of ruddy complexion, was attended by two companions, and the second, who was fairer and of shorter stature, by three. Thus in all there were seven. He left no record as to whether their heads were covered. They were about forty years of age, but they did not appear to be above thirty. When asked who they were, they said that they were men composed, as it were, of air, and subject to birth and death. It was true that their lives were much longer than ours, and might even reach to three hundred years duration. [*The men then discuss philosophical issues.*] The shorter of the two leaders had three hundred disciples in a public academy, and the other, two hundred. Indeed both were in the habit of lecturing publicly. When my father asked them why they did not reveal treasures to men if they knew where they were, they answered that it was forbidden by a peculiar law under the heaviest penalties for anyone to communicate this knowledge to men. They remained with my father for over three hours. But when he questioned them as to the cause of the universe they were not agreed. The tallest of them denied that God had made the world from eternity. On the contrary, the other added that God created it from moment to moment, so that should He desist for an instant the world would perish. To prove this he brought forward certain statements from the Disquisitions of Averroës, although that particular book had not then been found. He referred, and by name, to certain books, some of which had been found and others which up to that time had remained undiscovered. They were all works of Averroës. Indeed he openly declared himself to be an Averroist. Be this fact or fable, so it stands.

Source: Translation of Gerolamo Cardano in Abbé N. de Montfaucon de Villars, *Comte de Gabalis,* trans. "The Brothers" (Paterson, N.J.: The News Printing Company, 1914), 208–210. Bracketed material is mine.

Commentary: *The above text claims to be a literal transcription of a manuscript left behind by the Italian jurist and occultist Fazio Cardano, a Hermetic scientist who consorted with spirits. Widely cited in ancient astronaut literature as an example of human-alien interaction, most authors omit the sentence about public lecturing in order to avoid explaining where the aliens' school was located or how so many could have come to see the aliens speak while leaving no record of them. In truth, Fazio's son Gerolamo Cardano was reporting what he alleged to be his father's allegory of men dressed in the costume of the Roman triumph advocating the Aristotelian philosophy of the Islamic scholar Averroës (Ibn Rushd). The triumphators cast the rumors of consorting with spirits in a more positive light and seem to represent the predicted tri-*

umph of Averroist philosophy, which was of great importance to Gerolamo. The reader will of course note that the text containing the translation, the Comte de Gabalis, *is the same from which fringe writers also derive Charlemagne's anti–UFO law (40). The opening lines of the passage recall alien abduction narratives, particularly in the sudden appearance of glistening beings in the twilight hours.*

Note

    1. The translator gives this as "crimson," but the Latin clearly states "purple."

45. Ojibwa Close Encounter of the Third Kind

Jonas George (Wah-sah-ghe-zik)
c. 1915
English
Recorded in G. E. Laidlaw, "The Man from the Sky."
1916
Astro, UFO

    About four hundred years ago there were five or six hundred Indians living together somewheres south from Barrie, on what is now called "Pine Plains." These Indians had a big time at that place.

    Two Indians walked up and looked around those plains. They went a little ways (about 200 yards) and saw somebody sitting on the grass. This was a man, so they went to see. The man put up his hand to keep them back, so they stopped and looked. After a while the man spoke and said, "I don't belong to this land, I dropped down from above, yesterday, so I am here now." Those two men wanted him to go with them down home. "Yes," he said, "you go home and clean the place where I will stay, and come back again, then I will go with you in a few days."

    The two men went home and told the people about it. They began to clean the place where they were to keep the Skyman for two days, then they went to get him. Skyman was a nice looking man, clean and shining bright. Just at sundown he looked up just like he was watching. He spoke sometimes in a clear voice. Just after dark he spoke. He said, "Stay in two days. I'll go up, something will come down and get me to go up."

    This wise man said that he was running from where he came. There was an open place and he couldn't stop running, so he got in and dropped. The next day he said, "It's a nice country where we live, everything good. To-morrow noon I am going up, I will leave you, and you people all be good. Every Indian must be home to-morrow to see me go up."

    Just after noon the next day he looked up and said. "It's coming." Everybody looked up but could see nothing for a long time. The man that kept Skyman at his home could see good, and saw something like a bright star shining away up. The other people didn't see anything till it came near the ground. This thing was the nicest thing ever seen in this world. Two men got hold of it and pulled down heavy, then Skyman got in and said, "All right." and away he went up happy. I guess he's living there yet.

    Source: G. E. Laidlaw, "The Man from the Sky," in "Ojibwa Myths and Tales," *Twenty-Eighth Annual Archaeological Report* (Toronto: Ministry of Education, 1916), 91–92.

    Commentary: *Of a piece with Old World tales of sky people and flying ships, the Ojibwa tale is popular in UFO circles. In recording this story, G. E. Laidlaw noted that his Native* *informant was "mixed and forgetful." He was also the only informant among the many inter-viewed to place mythic stories in fixed time. His account most likely describes a far more recent event, such as a sighting of a hot air balloon or large kite,*[1] *like the kite that caused the 1910 "balloon panic" in Dunkirk, N.Y. reported by Charles Fort in* Lo!*[2] Sailors on Lake Erie thought it a weird craft. Several weather balloons were also known to have been launched in Toronto in 1910, and by 1915 there was an air school in Toronto training pilots for the Great War.*

Notes

1. John Robert Colombo, *The Big Book of Canadian Hauntings* (Toronto: Dundurn Press, 2009), 427.
2. Charles Fort, *Lo!* (New York: Claude Kendall, 1931), 45.

V

Atlantis and Other Lost Civilizations

There is no more romantic an adventure than the discovery of the ruins of a lost city somewhere in the far corners of the earth, and it is no surprise that no single topic in fringe history has received more attention than the search for the lost continent of Atlantis seemingly anywhere and everywhere on earth. Indeed, no fringe history topic has spawned so many and varied interpretations as the lost world created by the Greek philosopher Plato in two dialogues around 360 BCE to illustrate moral points about the society of Athens. Although it is commonplace to note that there is not a shred of evidence for the lost continent, nor any mention of it prior to Plato, the point bears repeating: So far as history knows, Plato invented Atlantis out of whole cloth. Nor was he the only Greek to do so; Euhemerus invented the imaginary island of Panchaea (**50**), though even fringe historians admit this to be a fiction.

The Atlantis myth is remarkably malleable. From Plato's brief dialogues the lost continent has taken on so many forms. For Ignatius Donnelly, it was the home of the mighty men of renown who perished in Noah's Flood, a lost race who civilized the whole earth after the death-knell of the antediluvian world. For Helena Blavatsky and the Theosophists, it was one of the lands where prehistoric extraterrestrials came to earth to spur on the evolution of the planet. As we shall see in Chapter IX, for still others it was a cipher for the Americas.

The myth of Atlantis gave rise to other claims for lost civilizations, Atlantis offered the template for an imaginary globe-spanning Afrocentric Egyptian culture, for the lost continents of Lemuria and of Mu (itself named for an alleged princess of Atlantis), and notably for the work of Graham Hancock, whose *FG* reused the same evidence Ignatius Donnelly marshalled for Atlantis in service of a "lost civilization" that was Atlantis in all but name.

46. Plato's First Atlantis Dialogue
Plato
Timaeus 21b–25e
c. 360 BCE
Greek
Atlantis, Prehistoric, Theo
Discussion in AW

Critias: I will tell an old-world story which I heard from an aged man; for Critias, at the time of telling it, was as he said, nearly ninety years of age, and I was about ten. Now the day was that day of the Apaturia which is called the Registration of Youth, at which, according to custom, our parents gave prizes for recitations, and the poems of several poets were recited by us boys, and many of us sang the poems of Solon, which at that time had not gone out of fashion. One of our tribe, either because he thought so or to please Critias, said that in his judgment Solon was not only the wisest of men, but also the noblest of poets.[1] The old man, as I very well remember, brightened up at hearing this and said, smiling: Yes, Amynander, if Solon had only, like other poets, made poetry the business of his life, and had completed the tale which he brought with him from Egypt, and had not been compelled, by reason of the factions and troubles which he found stirring in his own country when he came home, to attend to other matters, in my opinion he would have been as famous as Homer or Hesiod, or any poet.

And what was the tale about, Critias? said Amynander.

About the greatest action which the Athenians ever did, and which ought to have been the most famous, but, through the lapse of time and the destruction of the actors, it has not come down to us.

Tell us, said the other, the whole story, and how and from whom Solon heard this veritable tradition.

He replied:—In the Egyptian Delta, at the head of which the river Nile divides, there is a certain district which is called the district of Sais, and the great city of the district is also called Sais,[2] and is the city from which King Amasis came. The citizens have a deity for their foundress; she is called in the Egyptian tongue Neith, and is asserted by them to be the same whom the Hellenes call Athene; they are great lovers of the Athenians, and say that they are in some way related to them. To this city came Solon, and was received there with great honour; he asked the priests who were most skilful in such matters, about antiquity, and made the discovery that neither he nor any other Hellene knew anything worth mentioning about the times of old. On one occasion, wishing to draw them on to speak of antiquity, he began to tell about the most ancient things in our part of the world—about Phoroneus,[3] who is called "the first man," and about Niobe; and after the Deluge, of the survival of Deucalion and Pyrrha; and he traced the genealogy of their descendants, and reckoning up the dates, tried to compute how many years ago the events of which he was speaking happened. Thereupon one of the priests, who was of a very great age, said: O Solon, Solon, you Hellenes are never anything but children, and there is not an old man among you. Solon in return asked him what he meant. I mean to say, he replied, that in mind you are all young; there is no old opinion handed down among you by ancient tradition, nor any science which is hoary with age. And I will tell you why. There have been, and will be again, many destructions of mankind arising out of many causes; the greatest have been brought about by the agencies of fire and water, and other lesser ones by innumerable other causes. There is a story, which even you have preserved, that once upon a time Phaethon, the son of Helios, having yoked the steeds in his father's chariot, because he was not able to drive them in the path of his father, burnt up all that was upon the earth, and was himself destroyed by a thunderbolt. Now this has the form of a myth, but really signifies a declination of the bodies moving in the heavens around the earth, and a great conflagration of things upon the earth, which recurs after long intervals; at such times those who live upon the mountains and in dry and lofty places are more liable to destruction than those who dwell by rivers or on the seashore. And from this calamity the Nile, who is our never-failing saviour, delivers and preserves us. When, on the other hand, the gods purge the earth with a deluge of water, the survivors in your country are herdsmen and shepherds who dwell on the mountains, but those who, like you, live in cities are carried by the rivers into the sea. Whereas in this land, neither then nor at any other time, does the water come down from above on the fields, having always a tendency to come up from below; for which reason the traditions preserved here are the most ancient.

The fact is, that wherever the extremity of winter frost or of summer does not prevent, mankind exist, sometimes in greater, sometimes in lesser numbers. And whatever happened either in your country or in ours, or in any other region of which we are informed—if there were any actions noble or great or in any other way remarkable, they have all been written down by us of old, and are preserved in our temples. Whereas just when you and other nations are beginning to be provided with letters and the other requisites of civilized life, after the usual interval, the stream from heaven, like a pestilence, comes pouring down, and leaves only those of you who are destitute of letters and education; and so you have to begin all over again like children, and know nothing of what happened in ancient times, either among us or among yourselves. As for those genealogies of yours which you just now recounted to us, Solon, they are no better than the tales of children. In the first place you remember a single deluge only, but there were many previous ones; in the next place, you do not know that there formerly dwelt in your land the fairest and noblest race of men which ever lived, and that you and your whole city are descended from a small seed or remnant of them which survived. And this was unknown to you, because, for many generations, the survivors of that destruction died, leaving no written word. For there was a time, Solon, before the great deluge of all, when the city which now is Athens was first in war and in every way the best governed of all cities, is said to have performed the noblest deeds and to have had the fairest constitution of any of which tradition tells, under the face of heaven.

Solon marvelled at his words, and earnestly requested the priests to inform him exactly and in order about these former citizens. You are welcome to hear about them, Solon, said the priest, both for your own sake and for that of your city, and above all, for the sake of the goddess who is the common patron and parent and educator of both our cities. She founded your city a thousand years before ours, receiving from the Earth and Hephaestus the seed of your race, and afterwards she founded ours, of which the constitution is recorded in our sacred registers to be eight thousand years old. As touching your citizens of nine thousand years ago, I will briefly inform you of their laws and of their most famous action; the exact particulars of the whole we will hereafter go through at our leisure in the sacred registers themselves. If you compare these very laws with ours you will find that many of ours are the counterpart of yours as they were in the olden time. In the first place, there is the caste of priests, which is separated from all the others; next, there are the artificers, who ply their several crafts by themselves and do not intermix; and also there is the class of shepherds and of hunters, as well as that of husbandmen; and you will observe, too, that the warriors in Egypt are distinct from all the other classes, and are commanded by the law to devote themselves solely to military pursuits; moreover, the weapons which they carry are shields and spears, a style of equipment which the goddess taught of Asiatics first to us, as in your part of the world first to you. Then as to wisdom, do you observe how our law from the very first made a study of the whole order of things, extending even to prophecy and medicine which gives health, out of these divine elements deriving what was needful for human life, and adding every sort of knowledge which was akin to them. All this order and arrangement the goddess first imparted to you when establishing your city; and she chose the spot of earth in which you were born, because she saw that the happy temperament of the seasons in that land would produce the wisest of men. Wherefore the goddess, who was a lover both of war and of wisdom, selected and first of all settled that spot which was the most likely to produce men likest herself. And there you dwelt, having such laws as these and still better ones, and excelled all mankind in all virtue, as became the children and disciples of the gods.

Many great and wonderful deeds are recorded of your state in our histories. But one of them exceeds all the rest in greatness and valour. For these histories tell of a mighty power which unprovoked made an expedition against the whole of Europe and Asia, and to which your city put an end. This power came forth out of the Atlantic Ocean, for in those days the Atlantic was navigable; and there was an island situated in front of the straits which are by you called the Pillars of Heracles; the island was larger than Libya and Asia put together,[4] and was the way to other islands, and from these you might pass to the whole of the opposite continent which surrounded the true ocean; for this sea which is within the Straits of Heracles is only a harbour, having a narrow entrance, but that other is a real sea, and the surrounding land may be most truly called a boundless continent. Now in this island of Atlantis there was a great and wonderful empire which had rule over the whole island and several others, and over parts of the continent, and, furthermore, the men of Atlantis had subjected

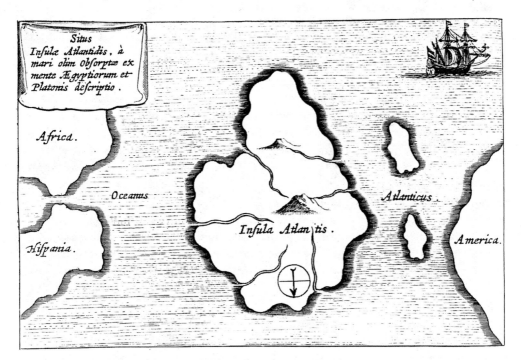

Jesuit scholar Athanasius Kircher's famous but fanciful map of Atlantis was published in 1664. North is at the bottom. The legend reads "The site of the island of Atlantis, long ago swallowed up by the sea, according to the opinion of the Egyptians and the description of Plato." Although Kircher drew the map from his reading of Plato, fringe authors like Rand Flem-Ath and Frank Joseph assert (through mistranslation) that Kircher had copied an Egyptian original. Kircher himself believed Atlantis was destroyed by Noah's Flood, as would Ignatius Donnelly (Library of Congress).

Working from the same texts as Athanasius Kircher, Ignatius Donnelly took a much broader view of the empire of Atlantis in his book *Atlantis: The Antediluvian World*. As seen on this map from the book, Donnelly envisioned Atlantis as a hub controlling territories from America to Asia and giving rise to all of the great civilization of Antiquity except for those of East Asia (Library of Congress).

the parts of Libya within the columns of Heracles as far as Egypt, and of Europe as far as Tyrrhenia. This vast power, gathered into one, endeavoured to subdue at a blow our country and yours and the whole of the region within the straits; and then, Solon, your country shone forth, in the excellence of her virtue and strength, among all mankind. She was pre-eminent in courage and military skill, and was the leader of the Hellenes. And when the rest fell off from her, being compelled to stand alone, after having undergone the very extremity of danger, she defeated and triumphed over the invaders, and preserved from slavery those who were not yet subjugated, and generously liberated all the rest of us who dwell within the pillars. But afterwards there occurred violent earthquakes and floods; and in a single day and night of misfortune all your warlike men in a body sank into the earth, and the island of Atlantis in like manner disappeared in the depths of the sea. For which reason the sea in those parts is impassable and impenetrable, because there is a shoal of mud in the way; and this was caused by the subsidence of the island.

Source: Translated by Benjamin Jowett in Plato, *The Dialogues of Plato,* trans. B. Jowett, vol. 2 (New York: Scribner, Armstrong, and Co., 1873), 517–521.

Commentary: *Widespread consensus holds that Plato invented the story of Atlantis as a political allegory meant to chide Athens for its hubristic pretensions. No mention of the continent predates Plato, and no physical evidence of its existence has ever been found. Nevertheless, with the discovery of the New World efforts began to find a historical foundation for Atlantis when some writers identified America with the lost continent (see **92**). Locations proposed for the continent by modern writers have included the Greek islands of Thera and Crete, southern Spain, the Canaries, the Bahamas, Cuba, the Yucatán, Peru, Bolivia, Indonesia, and Antarctica. All* *share the same fundamental problem: to fit any of these sites to Plato's narrative requires asserting that some details from Plato are accurate while others (typically the continent's location, its size, or the date of its destruction) are fictitious or erroneous, rendering these identifications problematic at best and impossible at worst.*[5]

The story given by Plato cannot be literally true for many reasons. The oldest archaeological evidence of humans at Athens dates to perhaps 7000 BCE or earlier, but the city itself flourishes first around 1400 BCE—long after Plato's date of c. 9600 BCE. What is notable, too, is what is absent from this account: There is no mention of death rays, high technology, or the other trappings of the Atlantis myth as it developed after 1882. Today, the futuristic sci-fi Atlantis of twentieth century fiction has largely been replaced by visions of a powerful culture of a Bronze Age level of sophistication, which is at least closer to Plato's conception.

Notes

1. Solon lived c. 638–558 BCE.
2. Sais was the capital of Egypt from 664–525 BCE.
3. A primordial civilizing hero from the dawn of time.
4. The Pillars of Heracles are usually identified as the straits of Gibraltar, while Libya refers to North Africa west of Egypt, and Asia to Asia Minor and the Levant.
5. One this, see Paul Jordan, *The Atlantis Syndrome* (Sutton Publishing, 2001) and the classic work on the subject, L. Sprague de Camp, *Lost Continents: The Atlantis Theme in History, Science, and Literature* (New York: Dover, 1970 [1954]).

47. Plato's Second Atlantis Dialogue

Plato
Critias 108e–121c
c. 360 BCE
Greek
Atlantis, Prehistoric, Theo
Discussion in AW

Critias: ... Let me begin by observing first of all, that nine thousand was the sum of years which had elapsed since the war which was said to have taken place between those who dwelt outside the Pillars of Heracles and all who dwelt within them; this war I am going to describe.[1] Of the combatants on the one side, the city of Athens was reported to have been the leader and to have fought out the war; the combatants on the other side were commanded by the kings of Atlantis, which, as was saying, was an island greater in extent than Libya and Asia, and when afterwards sunk by an earthquake, became an impassable barrier of mud to voyagers sailing from hence to any part of the ocean. [...]

Yet, before proceeding further in the narrative, I ought to warn you, that you must not be surprised if you should perhaps hear Hellenic names given to foreigners. I will tell you the reason of this: Solon, who was intending to use the tale for his poem, enquired into the meaning of the names, and found that the early Egyptians in writing them down had translated them into their own language, and he recovered the meaning of the several names and when copying them out again translated them into our language. My great-grandfather, Dropides, had the original writing, which is still in my possession, and was carefully studied by me when I was a child. Therefore if you hear names such as are used in this country, you must not be surprised, for I have told how they came to be introduced. The tale, which was of great length, began as follows:—

I have before remarked in speaking of the allotments of the gods, that they distributed the whole earth into portions differing in extent, and made for themselves temples and instituted sacrifices. And Poseidon, receiving for his lot the island of Atlantis, begat children by a mortal woman, and settled them in a part of the island, which I will describe. Looking towards the sea, but in the centre of the whole island, there was a plain which is said to have been the fairest of all plains and very fertile. Near the plain again, and also in the centre of the island at a distance of about fifty stadia, there was a mountain not very high on any side.

In this mountain there dwelt one of the earth born primeval men of that country, whose name was Evenor, and he had a wife named Leucippe, and they had an only daughter who was called Cleito. The maiden had already reached womanhood, when her father and mother died; Poseidon fell in love with her and had intercourse with her, and breaking the ground, inclosed the hill in which she dwelt all round, making alternate zones of sea and land larger and smaller, encircling one another; there were two of land and three of water, which he turned as with a lathe, each having its circumference equidistant every way from the centre, so that no man could get to the island, for ships and voyages were not as yet. He himself, being a god, found no difficulty in making special arrangements for the centre island, bringing up two springs of water from beneath the earth, one of warm water and the other of cold, and making every variety of food to spring up abundantly from the soil. He also begat and brought up five pairs of twin male children; and dividing the island of Atlantis into ten portions, he gave to the first-born of the eldest pair his mother's dwelling and the surrounding allotment, which was the largest and best, and made him king over the rest; the others he made princes, and gave them rule over many men, and a large territory. And he named them all; the eldest, who was the first king, he named Atlas, and after him the whole island and the ocean were called Atlantic. To his twin brother, who was born after him, and obtained as his lot the extremity of the island towards the Pillars of Heracles, facing the country which is now called the region of Gades in that part of the world, he gave the name which in the Hellenic language is Eumelus, in the language of the country which is named after him, Gadeirus. Of the second pair of twins he called one Ampheres, and the other Evaemon. To the elder of the third pair of twins he gave the name Mneseus, and Autochthon to the one who followed him. Of the fourth pair of twins he called the elder Elasippus, and the younger Mestor. And of the fifth pair he gave to the elder the name of Azaes, and to the younger that of Diaprepes. All these and their descendants for many generations were the inhabitants and rulers of divers islands in the open sea; and also, as has been already said, they held sway in our direction over the country within the Pillars as far as Egypt and Tyrrhenia.

Now Atlas[2] had a numerous and honourable family, and they retained the kingdom, the eldest son handing it on to his eldest for many generations; and they had such an amount of wealth as was never before possessed by kings and potentates, and is not likely ever to be again, and they were furnished with everything which they needed, both in the city and country. For because of the greatness of their empire many things were brought to them from foreign countries, and the island itself provided most of what was required by them for the uses of life. In the first place, they dug out of the earth whatever was to be found there, solid as well as fusile, and that which is now only a name and was then something more than a name, orichalcum,[3] was dug out of the earth in many parts of the island, being more precious in those days than anything except gold. There was an abundance of wood for carpenter's work, and sufficient maintenance for tame and wild animals. Moreover, there were a great number of elephants in the island; for as there was provision for all other sorts of animals, both for those which live in lakes and marshes and rivers, and also for those which live in mountains and on plains, so there was for the animal which is the largest and most voracious of all. Also whatever fragrant things there now are in the earth, whether roots, or herbage, or woods, or essences which distil from fruit and flower, grew and thrived in that land; also the fruit which admits of cultivation, both the dry sort, which is given us for nourishment and any other which we use for food—we call them all by the common name pulse, and the fruits having a hard rind, affording drinks and meats and ointments, and good store of chestnuts and the like, which furnish pleasure and amusement, and are fruits which spoil with keeping, and the pleasant kinds of dessert, with which we console ourselves after dinner, when we are tired of eating—all these that sacred island which then beheld the light of the sun, brought forth fair and wondrous and in infinite abundance. With such blessings the earth freely furnished them; meanwhile they went on constructing their temples and palaces and harbours and docks. And they arranged the whole country in the following manner:

First of all they bridged over the zones of sea which surrounded the ancient metropolis, making a road to and from the royal palace. And at the very beginning they built the palace in the habitation of the god and of their ancestors, which they continued to ornament in successive generations, every king surpassing the one who went before him to the utmost of his power, until they made the building a marvel to behold for size and for beauty. And beginning from the sea they bored a canal of three hundred feet in width and one hundred feet in depth and fifty stadia in length, which they carried through to the outermost zone, making a passage from the sea up to this, which became a harbour, and leaving an opening sufficient to enable the largest vessels to find ingress. Moreover, they divided at the bridges the zones of land which parted the zones of sea, leaving room for a single trireme to pass out of one zone into another, and they covered over the channels so as to leave a way underneath for the ships; for the banks were raised considerably above the water. Now the largest of the zones into which a passage was cut from the sea was three stadia in breadth, and the zone of land which came next of equal breadth; but the next two zones, the one of water, the other of land, were two stadia, and the one which surrounded the central island was a stadium only in width. The island in which the palace was situated had a diameter of five stadia. All this including the zones and the bridge, which was the sixth part of a stadium in width, they surrounded by a stone wall on every side, placing towers and gates on the bridges where the sea passed in. The stone which was used in the work they quarried from underneath the centre island, and from underneath the zones, on the outer as well as the inner side. One kind was white, another black, and a third red, and as they quarried, they at the same time hollowed out double docks, having roofs formed out of the native rock. Some of their buildings were simple, but in others they put together different stones, varying the colour to please the eye, and to be a natural source of delight. The entire circuit of the wall, which went round the outermost zone, they covered with a coating of brass, and the circuit of the next wall they coated with tin, and the third, which encompassed the citadel, flashed with the red light of orichalcum.

The palaces in the interior of the citadel were constructed on this wise:—in the centre was a holy temple dedicated to Cleito and Poseidon, which remained inaccessible, and was surrounded by an enclosure of gold; this was the spot where the family of the ten princes first saw the light, and thither the people annually brought the fruits of the earth in their season from all the ten portions, to be an offering to each of the ten. Here was Poseidon's own temple which was a stadium in length, and half a stadium in width, and of a proportionate height, having a strange barbaric appearance. All the outside of the temple, with the exception of the pinnacles, they covered with silver, and the pinnacles with gold. In the interior of the temple the roof was of ivory, curiously wrought everywhere with gold and silver and orichalcum; and all the other parts, the walls and pillars and floor, they coated with orichalcum. In the temple they placed statues of gold: there was the god himself standing in a chariot—the charioteer of six winged horses—and of such a size that he touched the roof of the building with his head; around him there were a hundred Nereids riding on dolphins, for such was thought to be the number of them by the men of those days. There were also in the interior of the temple other images which had been dedicated by private persons. And around the temple on the outside were placed statues of gold of all the descendants of the ten kings and of their wives, and there were many other great offerings of kings and of private persons, coming both from the city itself and from the foreign cities over which they held sway. There was an altar too, which in size and workmanship corresponded to this magnificence, and the palaces, in like manner, answered to the greatness of the kingdom and the glory of the temple.

In the next place, they had fountains, one of cold and another of hot water, in gracious plenty flowing; and they were wonderfully adapted for use by reason of the pleasantness and excellence of their waters. They constructed buildings about them and planted suitable trees, also they made cisterns, some open to the heavens, others roofed over, to be used in winter as warm baths; there were the kings' baths, and the baths of private persons, which were kept apart; and there were separate baths for women, and for horses and cattle, and to each of them they gave as much adornment as was suitable. Of the water which ran off they carried some to the grove of Poseidon, where were growing all manner of trees of wonderful height and beauty, owing to the excellence of the soil, while the remainder was conveyed by aqueducts along the bridges to the outer circles; and there were many temples built and dedicated to many gods; also gardens and places of exercise, some for men, and others for horses in both of the two islands formed by the zones; and in the centre of the larger of the two there was set apart a race-course of a stadium in width, and in length allowed to extend all round the island, for horses to race in. Also there were guardhouses at intervals for the guards, the more trusted of whom were appointed—to keep watch in the lesser zone, which was nearer the Acropolis while the most trusted of all had houses given them within the citadel, near the persons of the kings. The docks were full of triremes and naval stores, and all things were quite ready for use. Enough of the plan of the royal palace.

Leaving the palace and passing out across the three you came to a wall which began at the sea and went all round: this was everywhere distant fifty stadia from the largest zone or harbour, and enclosed the whole, the ends meeting at the mouth of the channel which led to the sea. The entire area was densely crowded with habitations; and the canal and the largest of the harbours were full of vessels and merchants coming from all parts, who, from their numbers, kept up a multitudinous sound of human voices, and din and clatter of all sorts night and day.

I have described the city and the environs of the ancient palace nearly in the words of Solon, and now I must endeavour to represent the nature and arrangement of the rest of the land. The whole country was said by him to be very lofty and precipitous on the side of the

sea, but the country immediately about and surrounding the city was a level plain, itself surrounded by mountains which descended towards the sea; it was smooth and even, and of an
oblong shape, extending in one direction three thousand stadia, but across the centre inland
it was two thousand stadia. This part of the island looked towards the south, and was sheltered from the north. The surrounding mountains were celebrated for their number and
size and beauty, far beyond any which still exist, having in them also many wealthy villages
of country folk, and rivers, and lakes, and meadows supplying food enough for every animal,
wild or tame, and much wood of various sorts, abundant for each and every kind of work.

I will now describe the plain, as it was fashioned by nature and by the labours of many
generations of kings through long ages. It was for the most part rectangular and oblong, and
where falling out of the straight line followed the circular ditch. The depth, and width, and
length of this ditch were incredible, and gave the impression that a work of such extent, in
addition to so many others, could never have been artificial. Nevertheless I must say what I
was told. It was excavated to the depth of a hundred, feet, and its breadth was a stadium everywhere; it was carried round the whole of the plain, and was ten thousand stadia in length. It
received the streams which came down from the mountains, and winding round the plain
and meeting at the city, was there let off into the sea. Further inland, likewise, straight canals
of a hundred feet in width were cut from it through the plain, and again let off into the ditch
leading to the sea: these canals were at intervals of a hundred stadia, and by them they brought
down the wood from the mountains to the city, and conveyed the fruits of the earth in ships,
cutting transverse passages from one canal into another, and to the city. Twice in the year
they gathered the fruits of the earth—in winter having the benefit of the rains of heaven, and
in summer the water which the land supplied by introducing streams from the canals.

As to the population, each of the lots in the plain had to find a leader for the men who
were fit for military service, and the size of a lot was a square of ten stadia each way, and the
total number of all the lots was sixty thousand. And of the inhabitants of the mountains and
of the rest of the country there was also a vast multitude, which was distributed among the
lots and had leaders assigned to them according to their districts and villages. The leader
was required to furnish for the war the sixth portion of a war-chariot, so as to make up a
total of ten thousand chariots; also two horses and riders for them, and a pair of chariot-
horses without a seat, accompanied by a horseman who could fight on foot carrying a small
shield, and having a charioteer who stood behind the man-at-arms to guide the two horses;
also, he was bound to furnish two heavy armed soldiers, two slingers, three stone-shooters
and three javelin-men, who were light-armed, and four sailors to make up the complement
of twelve hundred ships. Such was the military order of the royal city—the order of the other
nine governments varied, and it would be wearisome to recount their several differences.

As to offices and honours, the following was the arrangement from the first. Each of
the ten kings in his own division and in his own city had the absolute control of the citizens,
and, in most cases, of the laws, punishing and slaying whomsoever he would. Now the order
of precedence among them and their mutual relations were regulated by the commands of
Poseidon which the law had handed down. These were inscribed by the first kings on a pillar
of orichalcum, which was situated in the middle of the island, at the temple of Poseidon,
whither the kings were gathered together every fifth and every sixth year alternately, thus
giving equal honour to the odd and to the even number. And when they were gathered
together they consulted about their common interests, and enquired if any one had trans-

gressed in anything and passed judgment and before they passed judgment they gave their pledges to one another on this wise:—There were bulls[4] who had the range of the temple of Poseidon; and the ten kings, being left alone in the temple, after they had offered prayers to the god that they might capture the victim which was acceptable to him, hunted the bulls, without weapons but with staves and nooses; and the bull which they caught they led up to the pillar and cut its throat over the top of it so that the blood fell upon the sacred inscription. Now on the pillar, besides the laws, there was inscribed an oath invoking mighty curses on the disobedient. When therefore, after slaying the bull in the accustomed manner, they had burnt its limbs, they filled a bowl of wine and cast in a clot of blood for each of them; the rest of the victim they put in the fire, after having purified the column all round. Then they drew from the bowl in golden cups and pouring a libation on the fire, they swore that they would judge according to the laws on the pillar, and would punish him who in any point had already transgressed them, and that for the future they would not, if they could help, offend against the writing on the pillar, and would neither command others, nor obey any ruler who commanded them, to act otherwise than according to the laws of their father Poseidon. This was the prayer which each of them offered up for himself and for his descendants, at the same time drinking and dedicating the cup out of which he drank in the temple of the god; and after they had supped and satisfied their needs, when darkness came on, and the fire about the sacrifice was cool, all of them put on most beautiful azure robes, and, sitting on the ground, at night, over the embers of the sacrifices by which they had sworn, and extinguishing all the fire about the temple, they received and gave judgment, if any of them had an accusation to bring against any one; and when they given judgment, at daybreak they wrote down their sentences on a golden tablet, and dedicated it together with their robes to be a memorial.

There were many special laws affecting the several kings inscribed about the temples, but the most important was the following: They were not to take up arms against one another, and they were all to come to the rescue if any one in any of their cities attempted to overthrow the royal house; like their ancestors, they were to deliberate in common about war and other matters, giving the supremacy to the descendants of Atlas. And the king was not to have the power of life and death over any of his kinsmen unless he had the assent of the majority of the ten.

Such was the vast power which the god settled in the lost island of Atlantis; and this he afterwards directed against our land for the following reasons, as tradition tells: For many generations, as long as the divine nature lasted in them, they were obedient to the laws, and well-affectioned towards the god, whose seed they were; for they possessed true and in every way great spirits, uniting gentleness with wisdom in the various chances of life, and in their intercourse with one another. They despised everything but virtue, caring little for their present state of life, and thinking lightly of the possession of gold and other property, which seemed only a burden to them; neither were they intoxicated by luxury; nor did wealth deprive them of their self-control; but they were sober, and saw clearly that all these goods are increased by virtue and friendship with one another, whereas by too great regard and respect for them, they are lost and friendship with them. By such reflections and by the continuance in them of a divine nature, the qualities which we have described grew and increased among them; but when the divine portion began to fade away, and became diluted too often and too much with the mortal admixture, and the human nature got the upper hand, they then, being unable to bear their fortune, behaved unseemly, and to him who had an eye to see grew visibly debased, for they were losing the fairest of their precious gifts; but to those who had no eye to see the true happiness, they appeared glorious and blessed at the very time when they were full of avarice and unrighteous power. Zeus, the god of gods, who rules according to law, and is able to see into such things, perceiving that an honourable race was in a woeful plight, and wanting to inflict punishment on them, that they might be chastened and improve, collected all the gods into their most holy habitation, which, being placed in the centre of the world, beholds all created things. And when he had called them together, he spake as follows—

[The dialogue breaks off here, and the rest is lost.]

Source: Translated by Benjamin Jowett in Plato, *The Dialogues of Plato,* trans. B. Jowett, vol. 2 (New York: Scribner, Armstrong, and Co., 1873), 595–607.

Commentary: *The final sections of this dialogue share much in common with the Mesopotamian, Greek, and Genesis flood myths (**19–21, 23, 24**), to the extent that Ignatius Donnelly thought it reflected events that actually occurred during the Noachian Flood. More likely, Plato modeled the fall of Atlantis on the Near Eastern version of the myth. Compare, for example, the loss of divine status due to unrestrained mating with mortal women with the parallel passages about the Watchers-Nephilim in Genesis, Enoch, and Jubilees (**8–10**). The ten kings of Atlantis recall the ten kings who reigned before the Flood in Mesopotamia according to Berossus (Eusebius, Chronicle **15**). At the same time, the social organization of Atlantis, its divine rulers, and its sacred pillar recall the parallel account in Euhemerus' Sacred History (see **50**) regarding Panchaea because Euhemerus used Plato as a model for his own work.*

Notes

1. This means Atlantis sank c. 9600 BCE.
2. The Titan Atlas was believed to hold up the heavens from the Atlas Mountains in Morocco.
3. Literally "mountain copper," the exact alloy is not known for certain but may have been of gold and bronze.
4. The bull was sacred to Poseidon.

48. Marcellus on the Reality of Atlantis

Marcellus
Ethiopic History
c. 100 BCE (?)
Greek
Preserved in Proclus, *Commentary on Timaeus,* Book 1 (at 24e)
5th c. CE
Atlantis, Hyper, Prehistoric
Discussion in AW

That such and so great an island once existed, is evident from what is said by certain historians respecting what pertains to the external sea [i.e., the Atlantic]. For according to them, there were seven islands in that sea, in their times, sacred to Persephone, and also three others of an immense extent, one of which was sacred to Hades, another to Ammon, and the middle [or second] of these to Poseidon, the magnitude of which was a thousand stadia. They also add that the inhabitants of it preserved the remembrance from their ancestors of the Atlantic island which existed there and was truly prodigiously great; which for many periods had dominion over all the islands in the Atlantic sea, and was itself likewise sacred to Poseidon. *These things, therefore, Marcellus writes in his Ethiopic History.*

Source: Adapted from the translation by Thomas Taylor in Proclus, *Commentaries of Proclus on the Timaeus of Plato,* trans. Thomas Taylor, vol. 1 (London: 1820), 148.

Commentary: *Nothing is known of when Marcellus lived, but consensus places him in the Hellenistic period. His fragment, preserved only in Proclus, is often taken as independent confirmation of Atlantis' reality, though this cannot be proved. Afrocentrists takes this as proof that Atlantis was in Ethiopia and thus the font of civilization is in sub–Saharan Africa. It is reminiscent of accounts of the Azores or Canaries found in* **93**.

49. Egyptians Receive Survivors from Atlantis

Herodotus
The Histories 2.143–144
c. 440 BCE
Greek
Astro, Prehistoric, Atlantis
Discussion in CG, FG, AW

[143] And formerly when Hecataios the historian was in Thebes, and had traced his descent and connected his family with a god in the sixteenth generation before, the priests of Zeus did for him much the same as they did for me (though I had not traced my descent). They led me into the sanctuary of the temple, which is of great size, and they counted up the number, showing colossal wooden statues in number the same as they said; for each chief-priest there sets up in his lifetime an image of himself: accordingly the priests, counting and showing me these, declared to me that each one of them was a son succeeding his own father, and they went up through the series of images from the image of the one who had died last, until they had declared this of the whole number. And when Hecataios had traced his descent and connected his family with a god in the sixteenth generation, they traced a descent in opposition to this, besides their numbering, not accepting it from him that a man had been born from a god; and they traced their counter-descent thus, saying that each one of the statues had been piromis son of piromis, until they had declared this of the whole three hundred and forty-five statues, each one being surnamed piromis; and neither with a god nor a hero did they connect their descent. Now piromis means in the tongue of Hellas "honourable and good man."

[144] From their declaration then it followed, that they of whom the images were had been of form like this, and far removed from being gods: but in the time before these men they said that gods were the rulers in Egypt, not mingling with men, and that of these always one had power at a time; and the last of them who was king over Egypt was Oros the son of Osiris, whom the Hellenes call Apollo: he was king over Egypt last, having deposed Typhon. Now Osiris in the tongue of Hellas is Dionysos.

Source: Translated by G. C. Macaulay in Herodotus, *The History of Herodotus,* trans. G. C. Macaulay, vol. 1 (London: Macmillan, 1890), 183–184.

Commentary: *In CG, Erich von Däniken suggests that the "gods" were aliens, while Ignatius Donnelly in AW asserts they were humans from Atlantis, a sentiment picked up by Graham Hancock in FG, assigning them to a lost civilization. All alternative authors believe them to be real in some way. Alan B. Lloyd, a scholar of Herodotus, believes the Egyptians simply humored Herodotus, who already assumed 341 generations from Menes to Sethos, and four more thereafter, and told him the number he wanted to hear.*[1]

Note

1. Alan B. Lloyd, *Herodotus Book II: Commentary 1–98* (Leiden: E. J. Brill, 1988), 108.

50. Panchaea: The Other Atlantis

Euhemerus
Sacred History
c. 295 BCE
Greek
Preserved in Diodorus Siculus, *Library of History* 5.42–46
c. 60–30 BCE
Atlantis, Prehistoric

[42] [...] There are many things observable in Panchaea that deserve to be taken notice of. The natural inhabitants are those they call Panchaeans; the strangers that dwell among them are people of the western parts, together with Indians, Cretans, and Scythians. In this island there is a famous city, called Panara, not inferior to any for wealth and grandeur. The citizens are called the suppliants of Zeus Triphylius, and are the only people of Panchaea, that are governed by a democracy, without a monarch. They choose every year the presidents or governors that have all matters under their cognizance, but what concerns life and death; and the weightiest matters they refer to the college of their priests. The temple of Zeus Triphylius is about sixty furlongs distant from the city, in an open and level plain. It is in great veneration because of its antiquity and the stateliness of the structure, and the fertility of the soil.

[43] The fields round about the temple are planted with all sorts of trees, not only for fruit, but for pleasure and delight; for they abound with tall cypresses, plane trees, laurels, and myrtles, the place abounding with fountains of running water: for near the temple there is such a mighty spring of sweet water rushes out of the earth, as that it becomes a navigable river: thence it divides itself into several currents and streams, and waters all the fields thereabouts, and produces thick groves of tall and shady trees; amongst which, in summer, abundance of people spend their time, and a multitude of birds of all sorts build their nests, which create great delight, both by affecting the eye with the variety of their colours, and taking the ear with the sweetness of their notes. Here are many gardens, sweet and pleasant meadows decked with all sorts of herbs and flowers, and so glorious is the prospect, that it seems to be a paradise worthy of the gods themselves. There are here likewise large and fruitful palms, and abundance of walnut trees, which plentifully furnish the inhabitants with pleasant nuts. Besides all these, there are a multitude of vines of all sorts, trained to climb up on high, and so curiously interwoven one amongst another, that they are exceeding pleasant to the view, and greatly advance the delights of the place.

[44] The temple was built of white marble, most artificially jointed and cemented, two hundred yards in length, and as many in breadth, supported with great and thick pillars, curiously adorned with carved work. In this temple are placed huge statues of the gods, of admirable workmanship, and amazing largeness. Round the temple are built apartments for the priests that attend the service of the gods, by whom everything in that sacred place is performed. All along from the temple, is an even course of ground, four furlongs in length, and a hundred yards in breadth; on either side of which are erected vast brazen statues, with four-square pedestals; at the end of the course, breaks forth the river from the fountains before mentioned, from whence flows most clear and sweet water, the drinking of which conduces much to the health

of the body. This river is called the water of the sun. The whole fountain is lined on both sides and flagged at the bottom with stone at a vast expense, and runs out on both sides for the space of four furlongs. It is not lawful for any but the priests to approach to the brink of the fountain.

All the land about for two hundred furlongs round, is consecrated to the gods, and the revenues bestowed in maintaining the public sacrifices, and service of the gods: beyond these consecrated lands, is a high mountain, dedicated likewise to the gods, which they call the throne of Coelus and Triphylius Olympus; for they report that Uranus, when he governed the whole world, pleasantly diverted himself in this place; and from the top of the mount observed the motion of the heavens and stars, and that he was called Triphylius Olympus, because the inhabitants were composed of three several nations, Panchaeans, Oceanites, and Doians, who were afterwards expelled by Ammon; for it is said, that he not only rooted out this nation, but utterly destroyed all their cities, and laid Doia and Asterusia even with the ground. The priests every year solemnize a sacred festival in this mountain, with great devotion.

[45] Behind this mount, in other parts of Panchaea, they say there are abundance of wild beasts of all kinds, as elephants, lions, leopards, deer, and many other wonderful creatures both for strength and proportion. In this island there are three chief cities, Hyracia, Dalis, and Oceanis. The whole country is very fertile, and especially in the production of all sorts of wine in great plenty. The men are warlike, and use chariots in battles, after the ancient manner.

The whole nation is divided into three parts: the first class is of the priests, with whom are joined the artificers. The other tribe consists of the husbandmen; and the third are the militia and the shepherds. The priests govern all, and are the sole arbitrators in every matter; for they give judgment in all controversies, and have the power and authority in all public transactions of state. The husbandmen till the land, but the fruit is brought into the common treasury, and who is judged the most skilful in husbandry, receives the largest share of the fruits for a reward in the first place; and so the second, and the rest in order to the tenth, as everyone merits less or more, receives his reward by the judgment of the priests. In the same manner the shepherds and herdsmen carefully bring into the public stock, the victims and other things both by number and weight, as the nature of the things are; for it is not lawful for any to appropriate anything to themselves particularly, except a house and a garden. For all the young breed of cattle, and other things, and all the revenues, are received by the priests, and they justly distribute to every one as their necessity does require; only the priests have a double proportion.

They wear soft and fine garments; for their sheep's wool is much finer here than anywhere else; both men and women likewise deck themselves with golden ornaments; for they wear necklaces of gold, and bracelets about their arms, and like the Persians, have rings hanging in their ears. Their shoes are such as others wear, but richly beautified with divers sorts of colours.

[46] Their soldiers, for ordinary pay, defend the country, fortifying themselves within camps and bulwarks; for there is a part of the island infested with most daring thieves and robbers, who often lurch and surprise the husbandmen.

To conclude, these priests for delicacy, state, and purity of life, far excel all the rest of the inhabitants: their robes are of white linen, and sometimes of pure soft wool. They wear likewise miters, embroidered with gold. Their shoes are sandals curiously wrought with exquisite workmanship, and in their ears hang golden ear-rings like to the women's.

They attend chiefly upon the service of the gods, singing melodious songs in their praises, setting forth their glorious acts and benefits bestowed upon men. The priests say they came originally from Crete, and were brought over into Panchaea by Zeus, when he was upon earth, and governed all the world; and allege their language for a confirmation of this assertion, inasmuch as they retain many words of the Cretan speech among them. And further say, that they derived from their ancestors that civility and kindness wherewith they entertain the Cretans, the fame and report of their ancient consanguinity descending continually in a perpetual succession to their posterity: they show likewise a record written, as they say, by Zeus' own hand, at the time when he was on earth, and laid the foundation of the temple.

There are in this island likewise mines of gold, silver, brass, and iron, but not lawful for any to export them. Nay, it is not lawful, for any of the priests to go out of the verge of the consecrated ground; and if any do it is lawful for any man that finds them to kill them. They have under their charge innumerable vast vessels, and other consecrated things, both of gold and silver, which have been laid up there in honor of the gods for many ages. The gates of the temple are of admirable workmanship, beautified with gold, silver, ivory, and thyme wood.

The bed of the god is six cubits long, and four broad, of massy gold, most curiously wrought in every part; near adjoining, stands the table, as large, and of the like materials and workmanship with the other in every respect.

In the middle of the bed is placed a great golden pillar, whereon are letters inscribed, called by the Egyptians, sacred writing, expressing the famous actions of Uranus, Zeus, Artemis, and Apollo, written, they say, by Hermes himself. But this may suffice concerning the islands lying in the ocean over against Arabia.

Source: Translation adapted and modernized from that of G. Booth in Diodorus the Sicilian, *The Historical Library of Diodorus the Sicilian,* vol. 1 (London: 1814), 325–239.

Commentary: *Despite the obvious similarity to the Atlantis story, most fringe writers prefer to ignore the "other" Atlantis, even at the risk of excluding another sacred pillar crafted by the divine Hermes, not unlike those of the Watchers myth (12–13). This is especially odd since most fringe writers rely on Euhemerus in some way to justify their equation of gods with humans or space aliens and myth with history. The occult writer Lewis Spence, for one, cited Euhemerus on the gods (1, 2) but declined to discuss his Panchaea.*

51. A Lost Civilization Maps Antarctica
Oronteus Finaeus
New and Complete Description of the Whole World (Map)
1531
Latin
Prehistoric
Discussed in FG

Legend on Terra Australis
The Southern Land recently discovered but not yet completely known.

Legend for the Map as a Whole
Behold! For you, dear Reader, Oronteus Finaeus Delphinus offers an elegantly produced and accurately printed Geography, never before seen, which has the shape of the human heart (at least it should appear to you as a heart from a distance), and he presents for your gaze provinces, islands, seas, rivers, and mountains unseen before now, known neither to

Ptolemy, nor Eudoxus, nor Eratosthenes, or Macrobius, but which have lain in shadows up to the present day. Therefore, please accept (if you have sense) this small present with both arms, and consult it usefully.

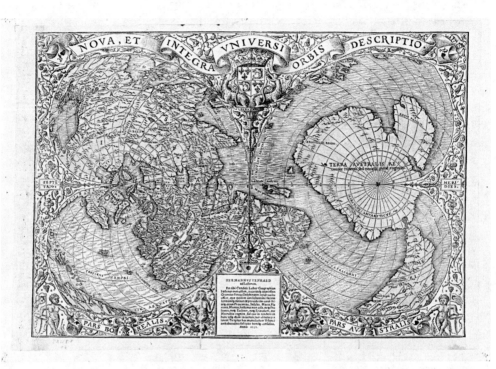

Since the 1960s, fringe writers have taken Oronteus Finaeus's 1531 map of the world as proof that Antarctica was known prior to its official discovery in 1818. However, few take the time to read the legend on the map, which makes clear that the mapmaker was extrapolating a continent from reports of discoveries of what we now know as the southern tip of South America (Library of Congress, Geography and Maps Division).

    Source: Translated by Jason Colavito from the Latin appearing on the map housed at the Library of Congress, Geography and Maps Division, Washington, D.C., G3200 1531 .F5 Vault.

    Commentary: *Charles Hapgood in* Maps of the Ancient Sea Kings *and Graham Hancock in* FG *assert that Oronteus Finaeus's map, which depicts a wildly exaggerated and semi-mythical southern continent, was made from pre–Ice Age maps drawn by a lost civilization. Neither read the map's legend, given above, which asserts that the map is entirely new and not reliant on older maps. The unknown lands he describes and labels* Terra Australis *on a landmass superficially similar to Antarctica were meant to be* Tierra del Fuego,[1] *discovered only in 1520.*

Note

    1. Robert J. King, "Terra Australis Not Yet Known," in National Library of Australia, *Mapping Our World: Terra Incognita to Australia* (Canberra: National Library of Australia, 2013), 83.

VI

Lost Wisdom of the Ancients

Fringe historians are united in their belief that ancient people possessed extraordinary scientific and spiritual knowledge which, if rediscovered, could transform human society and restore a lost golden age. These historians differ, however, in their understanding of where this ancient wisdom originated. Some see it as the product of a deeply ancient but human civilization that developed a high culture before being destroyed in the Flood, by a nuclear disaster, by a comet strike, or some other cataclysm. The remnants of this civilization encoded their wisdom in religion and mythology to preserve it for all time (see **12–17**). Others view this wisdom as the product of extraterrestrial intervention, brought from the stars and garbled by uncomprehending humans, to be understood only by ancient astronaut theorists.

Such claims for superior prehistoric wisdom have a long history, for the ancients themselves believed that the further one went into the past, the closer humanity was to the gods. They saw the bones of Ice Age megafauna and mistook them for human (Suetonius, *Twelve Caesars* 2.72), imagining that the men of the past and their works were bigger and grander than those of the present. Hesiod captures the sentiment in his *Works and Days* (lines 109–201), which describes the decline of the world from the Golden Age to the Silver, Bronze, Heroic, and Iron Ages. The same imagery appears in Daniel 2:31–45, and Dante adapts Daniel in *The Divine Comedy* (Inferno 14.103–116); scholars believe that the Hebrew and Greek texts are not wholly independent. In India, the concept of cyclical time told that the universe was in perpetual decline before periodic renewal. For a Greek or Roman standing before the pyramids, decline from a gigantic past might have seemed both logical and justified.

Although all the extant archaeological evidence contradicts this philosophy of decline, so powerful is this ancient belief that modern fringe theorists mine ancient texts for proof that the people of the distant past knew far more than we today.

52. An Alien Provides Plans for the Pyramids
Famine Stela
Ptolemaic Period (c. 200 BCE)
Egyptian
Astro
Discussion in AQ

In the year 18 of the king, Neterkhet, the divine incarnation, the "golden Horus," Djoser, when Mesir was prince of the cities of the South land and director of the Nubians in Elephantine, this message of the king was brought to him:

"I am sorrowing upon my high throne over those who belong to the palace. In sorrow is my heart for the vast misfortune, because the Nile flood in my time has not come for seven years. Light is the grain, there is lack of crops and of all kinds of food. Each man has become a thief to his neighbor. They want to hurry and cannot walk, the child cries, the youth creeps along and the old man, their souls are bowed. Their legs are bent together and drag along the ground and their hands rest in their bosoms. The counsel of the great ones of the coast is but emptiness. Torn open are the chests of provisions, but instead of contents there is air. Everything is exhausted. Then my soul, turning itself to the past, consulted a member of the staff of the Ibis, the chief script-sage, Imhotep,[1] the son of Ptah South-of-His-Wall. Tell me, where is the birthplace of the Nile? Which god or which goddess dwells there as its great protector?"

He stood and said, "I shall journey to Hermopolis (literally: Mansion-of-the-Net) where Thoth has uttermost patience for all men according to their deeds. I will enter the house of the sacred writer. I will spell out the Souls of Re (papyrus rolls) and will take guidance from them!"

Then he made the journey and came immediately back to me. He informed me concerning the Nile flood and everything that had been written about it. He disclosed to me the secret to which the forefathers fled for refuge, and whose second has been with no king since the beginning of time.

He said to me: "There is a place in the midst of the stream, where the Nile flood comes to view. Elephantine has been its name from the beginning. So since the beginning the city has been called, and so the district since the beginning has been called Wawat because there is the beginning of the land. It is the great arched terrace of the Sun's rising.... 'Sweet is Life' is the dwelling called. The water is called 'The Dual Caverns.' It is the double breast which nourishes everything good. It is the restful couch of the Nile. He increases on it to his (right) time in order that he may pour forth the floods. He disports himself in his course as a young man with his bride. He renews his youth that his desires may be satisfied. He rises twenty-eight yards and he sinks at Sema-behdet (Diospolis Inferior) to seven yards.... The conjunction is the same in Elephantine as the god Khnum. He strikes the ground with the soles of his feet. He opens the bolts of the portals with his hands and the doors of the water-gates fall open. Otherwise he is the same as the god Shu, an original possessor of the island. He takes into account the land to the south and the north, in order to give to all gods a portion of it, in that he brings along birds and fish and everything that they live on. The measuring stick is there and the writing tablet.

His divine house opens towards the southeast, the daily sun stands about it, its water is dangerous towards the south, ... mountains buttress it on the east. The peasantry come with all their possessions to build a divine house on the west and in the south, and a dwelling place for holy animals, and the royal pyramid, and every kind of obelisk. They stand in the temple in the crypt with salutations, opposite the god Khnum in his environment. In the same way they hand fresh wreaths of all flowers.... Learn the names of the gods in the Temple of Khnum: The goddess Satis [note: written as Sothis], the goddess Anukis, Hapy the Nile god, god Shu, god Geb, the goddess Nut, the god Osiris, the god Horus, the goddess Isis, and the goddess Nephthys."

[Then follows a list of the minerals of Elephantine, etc.]

My soul was glad when I heard this. I entered. The director opened what was concealed. The purification was performed, a great sacrifice offered to the gods whose names are praised in the place "Resting Place of the Soul in Life and Strength." I found the god standing before me who was pleased to be praised. I besought him. He opened his eye. His heart was moved and his voice resounded:

"I am Khnum thy Creator; my hand rested on thee in order to make your body healthy. I have sent unto you precious stones upon stones, previously unknown and on which no work has yet been done, so you may build temples, rebuild ruins, and inlay the eyes of statues. For I am the Lord of Fashioning, the one who created himself, the powerfully great original Water which was in the beginning, Hapy of the Nile Flood, who rises as he wishes, creator of all humanity. I am leader and director of all men in their time, Tatenen, the father of the gods, the god Shu, the great one, the first possessor. The two hemispheres serve me as a dwelling place. A spring stands open to me which I know (the Nile) which embraces the land, and whose embrace brings forth nourishment to all, according to the order of the embrace. With increasing age, a state of weakness approaches. I will let the Nile rise for you without missing a year. He shall let himself down on every portion of the land. All plants shall sprout and the Hour-bearing fruit shall bow. The divine harvest blessings shall be everywhere, and all things shall flourish a million fold. The servants shall have plenty, and hope shall rise in their hearts and in that of their masters. The famine shall pass away and the lack in their houses of provisions. The Egyptian folk shall go into the fields when the acres shall shine with grain, and the meadow-grass shall be according to their wish, more than has ever been known."

I awoke with a racing heart. My courage returned and correspondingly my fatigue left me. I read the following edict in the place of my father Khnum: "I, the king, provide support for thee, my father, the divine Khnum, the sun, the master of the cataract district in the Nubian land, as surety for that which you will do for me. Given over to you as your possession shall be the right and left banks in the west, in the district of Elephantine, with a circuit of twenty miles on the right and left banks so far as it is covered with plant growth along the stream in the portion given to you."

There shall be required from all peasants who till the ground and from those who revere the dead and water the fields with all the islands which lie within the measurement, a part of all harvests as your portion. Of that which is found in the net of every fisher and hunter; what the anglers and bird-catchers win, together with all hunting booty and all animals caught on the mountains, I demand a tithe. Of all the calves which are born within the prescribed limit one-tenth shall be offered as burnt offerings according to their daily count; together with this shall be the gift of a tithe of gold, ivory, ebony, carob wood, ochre, carnelian, *shrt*, *diw*-plants, *nfw*-plants, all kinds of wood and all other products which the Nubians of southern Nubia, and all those under supervision of them, shall bring in to Egypt. One shall release their hands, and no officer shall speak a word in these places in order to require anything from them or to withdraw anything from thy provision stores. I give to you the flat lands belonging to the city district which bear stones and good soil. Nothing shall be stolen from it or diminished. In order not to cast suspicion on the scribes, the officers and the royal supervisors who must take account of them all: Let it be ordered that the stonecutter and the copper-smith and the metal-worker of all works which they carry out in order to work up the stones with the help of gold, silver, copper, lead; and that all strangers[2] who fell trees or do anything else; that all these workers give a tithe of everything according to the reckoning—including the rare stones which are brought from abroad and of all stones from the East. Let there also be a director appointed for the weighing according to direction of the gold, silver, precious stones and all other things which the artists, goldsmiths and architects require for the erection of the divine statues which, with their material, are exceptional, and have not been enumerated in the preceding classes of work. Let everything be granted to you from the provision-house, even to their children. Let there be abundance of whatever is in your Temple, so that it may be as it was before.

This decree shall be engraved in writing on a tablet in a conspicuous place, which writing shall agree with the original on the wooden tablets. The god and the directors of the temple shall be represented there. Whoever spits upon the contents shall be punished. The directors of the priests and every director of the people of the temple shall provide for the preservation of my name in the temple of Khnum-Re, the lord of Elephantine, mighty forever.

Source: Adapted from the translation of Camden M. Cobern in "The Seven Biblical Years of Famine," *Biblia* 4, no. 7 (1891): 182–184. Cobern's translation was made from the 1891 German translation of Heinrich Brugsch. Both being somewhat incorrect in light of current knowledge of Egyptian, it has been corrected against modern editions of the text.

Commentary: *The Famine Stela is a piece of historical fiction created around 200 BCE to justify claims of Khnum's priesthood to lands south of Elephantine by imagining events from 2,500 years earlier featuring the "donation" of these lands to Imhotep, architect of the first pyramid, that of Djoser, whom he served as vizier.[3] In AQ and in public discussions with me before his death,[4] Philip Coppens asserted that this text relates a non-human intelligence's delivery of plans for the pyramid to Imhotep in a dream. The text, however, explains that Khnum promised "stones" (gems) for decorating and restoring temples, with no mention made of pyramids. More interesting is the history of this text, which upon its discovery was initially thought to offer proof of the seven year famine under Joseph (Genesis 47:13–27). Although this was proven false (seven year famines were a stock phrase in ancient literature), some fringe writers and some biblical apologists still allege that Imhotep himself was Joseph, and the pyramids his granaries (Genesis 41:48; cf. chapter 7 of Mandeville's* Travels).

Notes

1. The architect Imhotep was later deified and in this late period text is anachronistically designated the son of a god. Some English translations insert a genitive, making Pharaoh consult a member of the divine Imhotep's staff, but Egyptologist Robert K. Ritner argues that this is an error and Imhotep himself is the figure indicated (Robert K. Ritner, "The Famine Stela," in *The Literature of Ancient Egypt*, 3rd ed., ed. William Kelly Simpson [New Haven: Yale University Press, 2003], 387).

2. *Apiru*, a term for semi-nomadic foreign laborers from the Near East, sometimes thought to include the Hebrews, though no solid evidence for this connection exists.

3. See, for example, Miriam Lichtheim, *Ancient Egyptian Literature,* vol. 3: The Late Period (University of California Press, Berkeley, 2006 [1980]), 94–95.

4. "Philip Coppens Responds," JasonColavito.com, October 3, 2012 <http://www.jasoncolavito.com/blog/philip-coppens-responds>.

53. Fallen Angels Teach Alchemy and Magic
Sextus Julius Africanus
Chronography
c. 221 CE
Greek
Preserved in George Syncellus, *Chronicle* 19–20
Astro

When men multiplied on the earth, the angels of heaven came together with the daughters of men. In some copies[1] I found "the sons of God." What is meant by the Spirit, in my opinion, is that the descendants of Seth are called the sons of God on account of the righteous men and patriarchs who have sprung from him, even down to the Saviour Himself; but that the descendants of Cain are named the seed of men, as having nothing divine in them, on account of the wickedness of their race and the inequality of their nature,[2] being a mixed people,[3] and having stirred the indignation of God. But if it is thought that these refer to angels, we must take them to be those who deal with magic and sorcery,[4] who taught the women the motions of the stars and the knowledge of things celestial, by whose power they conceived the giants as their children, by whom wickedness came to its height on the earth, until God decreed that the whole race of the living should perish in their impiety by the deluge.

Source: Translated by S. D. F. Salmond in *The Writings of Hippolytus, Bishop of Rome, vol. II and Fragments of Writings of the Third Century* (Edinburgh: T. & T. Clark, 1869), 172.

Commentary: *The Christian writer Africanus was skeptical of the myth of the Fallen Angels, preferring to see them as referring to corrupt members of Seth's lineage, making him our oldest writer to attest to this belief, which seems to have existed in the time of Josephus (see* **12***). Nevertheless, Africanus documents the widespread influence of the Enoch narrative (***9***), which here has changed from teaching the sciences, of which Africanus apparently approved,[5] to all manner of wizardry, which was for Christians actually evil (Leviticus 19:26; Deuteronomy 18:10–11). Africanus seems to differ from Enoch by exonerating science and condemning as evil only the magic forbidden by the Bible.*

ZOSIMUS OF PANOPLIS

Imouth 9
c. 400 CE
Greek
Preserved in George Syncellus, *Chronicle* 14
Astro

The Holy Scriptures, which is to say the books,[6] say, O woman,[7] that a race of demons had commerce with the female sex. Hermes relates this in his *Physics*; and nearly universal report, both public and private, records it. Thus, the ancient and divine writings say that the angels became enamoured of women; and, descending, taught them all the works of nature. Having fallen due to these women, he says, they were barred from heaven, for from them came all that miserable knowledge which is of no use to the soul. The same scriptures say that from them were birthed the Giants. From them, therefore, is the first tradition of Chemeu, concerning these arts; for they called this book *Chemes* and hence the science of alchemy takes its name.

Source: Adapted from the translation of William Drummond, "On the Sciences of the Egyptians and Chaldeans," *The Classical Journal* 18 (1818): 298–299, with additions from the editor of *The Works of Thomas Moore*, vol. 5 (Paris: A. and W. Galignani, 1823), 116 and Jason Colavito.

Commentary: *Zosimus was the most famous early alchemist, though his works survive only in Greek, Syriac, and Arabic fragments. Obviously drawing on the Watchers myth of 1 Enoch (***9***), he makes several innovations: first, to give Hermes direct knowledge of the Watchers and* *second to attribute to them the invention of alchemy, and authorship of the subject's first books. Zosimus' own book's title, the* Imouth, *is likely a Hellenization of Imhotep, whose alien encounters were discussed in* 52.

Ibrāhīm ibn Waṣīf Shāh

History of Egypt and Its Wonders
Late 12th c.
Arabic
Preserved in Al-Maqrīzī, *Al-Khitat* 1.10
c. 1400 CE
Astro

Master Ibrāhīm ibn Waṣīf Shāh said that King ʿĀdim (=ʿĀd), son of Naqtarim, was a violent and proud prince, tall in stature. It was he who ordered the rocks cut to make the pyramids, as had been done by the ancients. In his time there lived two angels cast out of heaven, and who lived in the well of Aftarah; these two angels taught magic to the Egyptians, and it is said that ʿĀdim, the son of al-Budasheer, learned most of their sciences, after which the two angels went to Babel. Egyptians, especially the Copts, assure us that these were actually two demons named Mahla and Bahala, not two angels, and that the two are at Babel in a well, where witches meet, and they will remain there until the Day of Judgment. Since that time they worshiped idols. It is Satan, they say, who made them known to men and raised them for men. According to others, it was Badoura who raised the first idol, and the first idol erected was the Sun; yet others claim that Nimrod ordered the first idols raised and the worship of them. It was also said that ʿĀdim first made use of the crucifixion, for this purpose: a woman married to a person of the court had adulterous relations with a man of the artisan class. The king ordered them crucified on two poles, the back of one of the culprits facing the back of the other; and on each post was written the names of perpetrators, their crime, and the date of punishment. Therefore adultery ceased. This king built four cities where all kinds of wonderful objects and talismans were deposited, and there he buried considerable treasures.

Source: Translated by Jason Colavito from the French in Maqrīzī, *Description topographique et historique de l'Égypte,* part 1, trans. U. Bouriant, Mémoires de la mission archéologique française du Caire 17 (Paris: 1895), 89–90.

Commentary: *On* Ancient Aliens *Giorgio Tsoukalos cited this passage as evidence that the Egyptians received the plans for the pyramids from space aliens. The text, of course, is a medieval legend recorded nearly 4,000 years after the pyramids were built, and the text further states that ʿĀdim—of Iram of the Pillars (see* **60, 61**)*—learned magic, not architecture, from the angels. The story of these fallen angels is probably again derived from the Watchers (**9**) via the well-known Islamic myth of the angels Harut and Marut (Qur'an 2:102), who taught forbidden magic and were suspended upside-down at Babylon in punishment. But Lucian, in the* Menippus (**10**), *reports that the Babylonians worshiped chthonic gods in a watery underground cave, which may be the point of origin for these specific demons.*

Notes

1. Of Genesis 6:1 (**8**). The Septuagint version reads "angels," but the Hebrew has "sons of God."
2. When compared with the godly, or with God.
3. The text is corrupt here and intends to convey the meaning that intermarriage (mixing) between the seed of Cain and the children of Seth led to God's anger.

4. Salmond gave this as "jugglery," but this obsolete word for deceptive tricks carries too humorous a connotation to retain.

5. Africanus is traditionally believed to be the author of a scientific encyclopedia, the *Kestoi.*

6. Βίβλοι. This is ambiguous and could refer to the Bible or possibly the Holy Books of Hermes.

7. Theosebeia, a wealthy woman with alchemical interests. Nothing more is known of her.

54. A Lost Civilization's Secret Cosmology
Snæbjörn Galti
Unknown poem
c. 1000 CE
Old Norse
Preserved in Snorri Sturlson, *Prose Edda,* Skáldskaparmal 25
c. 1220 CE
Prehistoric
Discussion in FG

Men say that the nine maidens of the island-mill, the ocean, are working hard at the host-devouring skerry-quern (the sea), out beyond the skirts of the earth; yea, they have for ages past been grinding at Amlódi's meal-bin (the sea). Let us furrow the waves with the prow of my ship.

Source: Translated by Gudbrand Vigfusson and F. York Powell (eds. and trans.), *Corpus Poeticum Boreale,* vol. 2 (Oxford: Clarendon Press, 1883), 54–55.

Commentary: *This brief reference to the great world mill that churned in the ocean is the foundational text for the elaborate theoretical framework of* Hamlet's Mill *(1969), the book by Giorgio de Santillana and Hertha von Dechend which claimed that this mill represented the 26,000-year slow rotation of the stars in the nighttime sky, giving rise to dozens of fringe theories, including those of Graham Hancock, that claimed advanced astronomical understanding in prehistory, likely from a lost civilization. Snorri Sturlson reported that the myth referred to churning of the sea, and many scholars think on Indo-European analogies that it originally referred to the mill the Indo-European gods churned each night to rekindle the sun's fire by dawn. The figure of Amlódi is oldest reference to the Scandinavian mythological character who would eventually become Shakespeare's Hamlet.*[1]

Note

1. Kenneth Muir, *The Sources of Shakespeare's Plays* (Oxon: Routledge, 1977), 159; Kemp Malone, *The Literary History of Hamlet: The Early Tradition* (New York: Haskell House, 1964 [1923]), 184–188.

55. The Argonauts' Secret Star Knowledge from Sirius
Aratos
Phainomena, lines 342–351
c. 3rd c. BCE
Greek
Astro
Disussion in SM

Sternforward *Argo* by the *Great Dog's* tail
Is drawn: for hers is not a usual course.
But backward turned she comes, as vessels do
When sailors have transposed the crooked stern

On entering the harbor; all the ship reverse,
And gliding backward on the beach it grounds.
Sternforward thus is Jason's *Argo* drawn.
And part moves dim and starless from the prow
Up to the mast, but all the rest is bright.
The slackened rudder has been placed beneath
The hind-feet of the Dog, who goes in front.

Source: Translated by Robert Brown, Jr. in *The* Phainomena *or "Heavenly Display" of Aratos: Done into English Verse* (London: Longmans, Green, and Co., 1885), 40–41.

Commentary: *Aratos' text was translated and adapted into Latin by Cicero, in the* Phaenomena Aratea, *from which Hyginus includes the above text in* Fabula *14 in the more elaborate Latin version. In* SM, *Robert Temple asserts that this poem, which describes the* constellation *of Argo Navis, located near the Dog-Star Sirius, actually describes the mythological ship* Argo *and thus encodes hidden knowledge of the star Sirius given by amphibious alien frog-people, specifically Oannes (see* **6**). *He further identifies* Argo *with Noah's Ark on the authority of nineteenth century religious thinkers.*

56. Anubis Worship Tied to Aliens from Sirius
Plutarch
Moralia 5.26.61 (*Isis and Osiris* 61)
1st century CE
Greek
Prehistoric, General
Discussion in SM

But Osiris had his name from ὅσιος and ἱερός (*pious* and *sacred*) compounded; for he is the common idea of things in heaven and things in the lower world, the former of which the ancients thought fit to style ἱερά, and the latter ὅσια. But the principle which discloses things heavenly, and which appertains to things whose motion tends upwards (ἄνω), is called Anubis, and sometimes he is also named Hermanubis, the former name referring to things above, and the latter to things beneath. For which reason they also sacrifice to him two cocks, the one whereof is white and the other of a saffron color, as esteeming the things above to be entire and clear, and the things beneath to be mixed and various. Nor need any one to wonder at the formation of these words from the Grecian tongue; for there are many thousand more of this kind, which, accompanying those who at several times removed out of Greece, do to this very day sojourn and remain among foreigners; some whereof when poetry would bring back into use, it hath been falsely accused of barbarism by those men, who love to call such words strange and outlandish. They say, moreover, that in the so-called books of Hermes there is an account given of the sacred names; and that power which presides over the circulation of the sun is called Horus, and by the Greeks Apollo; and that which is over the winds is by some called Osiris, and by others Serapis, and by others again in the Egyptian tongue Sothi. Now the word Sothi signifies in Greek *to breed* (κύειν) and *breeding;* and therefore, by an obliquation of the word κύειν, the star which they account proper to the Goddess Isis is called in Greek κύων, which is as well *dog* as *breeder.* And although it be but a fond thing to be over contentious about words, yet I had rather yield to the Egyptians the name of Serapis than that of Osiris, since I account the former to be foreign, and the latter to be Greekish, but believe both to appertain to one God and to one power.

Source: Translation by William Baxter in *Plutarch's Morals,* vol. 4, ed. William Goodwin (Boston: Little, Brown, and Company, 1874), 119–120.

Commentary: *In SM Robert Temple knows this passage only secondhand from a brief excerpt of Samuel Squire's 1744 translation in E. A. Wallis Budge's* The Gods of the Egyptians,[1] *terminating with what in our translation is "mixed and various." As a result he asserts that Anubis' sacrifice is a symbol of Sirius A (bright) and Sirius B (dim), unaware that Plutarch discusses actual Sirius beliefs from the Greek period of Egypt immediately following his quoted lines. The "Book of Hermes" is a reference to the Hermetic literature, inspiration for medieval pyramid myths (16), for the* Kore Kosmou *(57), and for the Emerald Tablet (58).*

Note

1. E. A. Wallis Budge, *The Gods of the Egyptians, or Studies in Egyptian Mythology,* vol. 2 (Chicago: Open Court, 1904), 265. Budge provides Squire's full translation of *Isis and Osiris* on pp. 186–194, but Temple seems not to have read it, quoting instead Budge's later paraphrase and partial quotation.

57. The Wisdom of Hermes and the Retreat of the Alien Gods

Kore Kosmou, Part 1
Uncertain date, probably Ptolemaic or Roman period
Greek
Preserved in Joannes Stobaeus, *Anthology* 1.44 (Hermetic fragment 23.64–5)
5th c. CE
Astro, Prehistoric
Discussion in SM

Having thus spoken, Isis first pours out for Horos the sweet draught of immortality which souls receive from the Gods, and thus begins the most holy discourse.

Heaven, crowned with stars, is placed above universal nature, O my son Horos, and nothing is wanting to it of that which constitutes the whole world. It is necessary, then, that all nature should be adorned and completed by that which is above her, for this Order could not proceed from below to above. The supremacy of the greater mysteries over the lesser is imperative. Celestial order reigns over terrestrial order, as being absolutely determined, and inaccessible to the idea of death. Wherefore, the things below lament, being filled with fear before the marvellous beauty and eternal permanence of the heavenly world. For, indeed, a spectacle worthy of contemplation and desire were these magnificences of heaven, revelations of the God as yet unknown, and this sumptuous majesty of night illumined with a penetrating radiance, albeit less than that of the sun, and all these other mysteries which move above in harmonious cadence, ruling and maintaining the things below by secret influences. And so long as the Universal Architect refrained from putting an end to this incessant fear, to these anxious investigations, ignorance enveloped the universe. But when He judged good to reveal Himself to the world, He breathed into the Gods the enthusiasm of love, and poured into their mind the splendour which His bosom contained, that they might first be inspired with the will to seek, next with the desire to find, and lastly with the power to readjust.

Now, my wondrous child Horos, all this could not happen among mortals, for as yet they did not exist; but it took place in the universal Soul in sympathy with the mysteries of heaven. This was Hermes, the Kosmic Thought. He beheld the universe of things, and having seen, he understood, and having understood, he had the power to manifest and to reveal. That which he thought, he wrote; that which he wrote, he in great part concealed, wisely silent and speaking by turns, so that while the world should last, these things might be sought. And thus, having enjoined upon the Gods, his brethren, that they should follow in his train, he ascended to the stars. But he had for successor his son, and the heir of his knowledges, Tat, and a little later, Asclepios, son of Imouthè, by the counsels of Pan and Hephaistos, and all those for whom sovereign Providence reserved an exact knowledge of heavenly things.

Hermes then justified himself in the presence of those who surrounded him, in that he had not delivered the integral theory to his son, on account of his youth. But I, having arisen, beheld with mine eyes, which see the invisible secrets of the beginnings of things and at length, but with certainty, I understood that the sacred symbols of the Kosmic elements were hidden near the secrets of Osiris. Hermes returned to heaven, having, pronounced an invocatory speech.

It is not fitting, O my Son, that this recital be left incomplete; thou must be informed of the words of Hermes when he laid down his books. "O sacred books," he said, "of the Immortals, ye in whose pages my hand has recorded the remedies by which incorruptibility is conferred, remain for ever beyond the reach of destruction and of decay, invisible and concealed from all who frequent these regions, until the day shall come in which the ancient heaven shall bring forth instruments worthy of you, whom the Creator shall call souls."

Having pronounced upon his books this invocation, he wrapped them in their coverings, returned into the sphere which belonged to him, and all remained hidden for a sufficient space.

And Nature, O my Son, was barren until the hour in which those who are ordained to survey the heavens, advancing towards God, the King of all things, deplored the general inertia, and affirmed the necessity of setting forth the universe. No other than Himself could accomplish this work.

"We pray Thee," said they, "to consider that which already is, and that which is necessary for the future."

At these words, the God smiled benignant, and commanded Nature to exist. And, issuing with His voice, the feminine came forth in her perfect beauty. The Gods with amaze beheld this marvel. And the great Ancestor, pouring out for Nature an elixir, commanded her to be fruitful; and forthwith, penetrating the universe with His glance, He cried, "Let heaven be the plenitude of all things, and of the air, and of the ether." God spake, and it was done. But Nature, communing with herself, understood that she might not transgress the commandment of the Father, and, uniting herself to Labour, she produced a most beautiful daughter, whom she called Invention, and to whom God accorded being.

And having differentiated created forms, He filled them with mysteries, and gave the command of them to Invention.

Then, not willing that the upper world should be inactive, He saw fit to fill it with spirits, in order that no region should remain in immobility and inertia; and in the accomplishment of His work He used His sacred art. For, taking of Himself such essence as was necessary and mingling with it an intellectual flame, He combined with these other materials by unknown ways. And having achieved by secret formulas the union of these principles, He endowed with motion the universal combination. Gradually, in the midst of the protoplasm, glittered a substance more subtle, purer, more limpid, than the elements from which it was generated. It was transparent, and the Artist alone perceived it. Soon, it attained its perfection, being neither melted by the fire, nor chilled by the breath, but possessing the stability of a special combination, and having its proper type and constitution. He bestowed on it a happy name, and, according to the similitude of its energies, He called it Self-Consciousness.

Of this product he formed myriads of Souls, employing the choicest part of the mixture for the end which He had in view, proceeding with order and measure, according to His knowledge and His reason. The souls were not necessarily different, but the choicest part, animated by the Divine motion, was not identical with the rest The first layer was superior to the second, more perfect and pure; the second, inferior truly to the first, was superior to the third; and thus, until sixty degrees, was completed the total number. Only, God established this law, that all equally should be eternal, being of one essence, whose forms He alone determines.

He traced the limits of their sojourn on the heights of nature, so that they might turn the wheel according to the laws of Order and of wise discretion, for the joy of their Father.

Then, having summoned to these splendid regions of ether the souls of every grade, He said to them: "O souls, beautiful children of my breath and of my care, you whom I have produced with my hands, in order to consecrate you to my universe, hear my words as a law:—Quit not the place assigned to you by my will. The abode which awaits you is heaven, with its galaxy of stars and its thrones of virtue. If you attempt any transgression against my decree, I swear by my sacred breath, by that elixir of which I formed you, and by my creative hands, that I will speedily forge for you chains and cast you into punishment."

Having thus spoken, God, my Master, mingled together the rest of the congenial elements, earth and water, and pronouncing certain powerful and mystic words—albeit different from the first—He breathed into the liquid protoplasm motion and life, rendered it thicker and more plastic, and formed of it living beings of human shape. That which remained He gave to the loftiest souls inhabiting the region of the Gods in the neighbourhood of the stars, who are called the Sacred Genii. "Work," said He, "my children, offspring of my nature; take the residue of my task, and let each one of you make beings in his image. I will give you models."

Therewith He took the Zodiac and ordained the world in conformity with vital movements, placing the animal signs after those of human form. And after having given forth the creative forces and generative breath for the whole range of beings yet to come, He withdrew, promising to unite to every visible work an invisible breath and a reproductive principle, so that each being might engender its similar without necessity to create continually new entities.

And what did the souls do, O my Mother? And Isis answered:—They took the mingled material, O my Son Horos, and began to reflect thereon, and to adore this combination, the work of the Father. Next, they sought to discover of what it was composed, which, indeed, it was not easy to find. Then, fearing that this search might excite the anger of the Father, they set themselves to carry out His commands. Therefore, taking the upper portion of the protoplasm, that which was lightest, they created of it the race of birds. The compound having now become more compact and assuming a denser consistency, they formed of it the quadrupeds; while of the thickest part which needed a moist vehicle for its support, they made fishes. The remainder, being cold and heavy, was employed by the souls in the creation of reptiles.

Forthwith, O my Son, proud of their work, they were not afraid to transgress the Divine law, and, in spite of the prohibition, they receded from their appointed limits. Not willing to remain longer in the same abode, they moved ceaselessly, and repose seemed to them death.

But, O my Son—(thus Hermes informed me)—their conduct could not escape the eye of the Lord God of all things; He minded to punish them, and to prepare for them hard bonds. The Ruler and Master of the universe resolved then for the penance of the souls, to mould the human organism, and having called me to Him, said Hermes, He spoke in this wise:—"O soul of my soul, holy thought of my thought, how long shall earthly Nature remain sad? How long shall the creation already produced continue inactive and without praise? Bring hither before me all the Gods of heaven."

Thus God spake, quoth Hermes, and all obeyed His decree. "Look upon the earth," He said to them, "and upon all things beneath."

Straightway they looked, and understood the will of the Lord. And when He spoke to them of the creation of Man, asking of each what he could bestow upon the race about to be born, the Sun first replied:—"I will illumine mankind." Then the Moon promised enlightenment in her turn, adding that already she had created Fear, Silence, Sleep, and Memory. Kronos announced that he had begotten Justice and Necessity. Zeus said, "In order to spare the future race perpetual wars, I have generated Fortune, Hope, and Peace." Ares declared himself already father of Conflict, impetuous Zeal, and Emulation, Aphrodite did not wait to be called upon: "As for me, O Master," she said, "I will bestow upon mankind Desire, with voluptuous Joy and Laughter, that the penalty to which our sister Souls are destined may not weigh on them too hardly." These words of Aphrodite, O my Son, were welcomed gladly. "And I," said Hermes, "will endow human nature with Wisdom, Temperance, Persuasion, and Truth; nor will I cease to ally myself with Invention. I will ever protect the mortal life of such men as are born under my signs, seeing that to me the Creator and Father has attributed in the Zodiac, signs of Knowledge and Intelligence; above all, when the movement which draws thereto the stars is in harmony with the physical forces of each."

He Who is Master of the world rejoiced at hearing these things, and decreed the production of the human face. As for me—said Hermes—I sought what material ought to be employed in the work, and invoked the Lord. He commanded the Souls to give up the residue of the protoplastic substance, which having taken, I found it entirely dried up. Therefore, I used a great excess of water wherewith to renew the combination of the substance, in such wise that the product might be resolvable, yielding, and feeble, and that Force should not be added therein to Intelligence. When I had achieved my work it was beautiful, and I rejoiced in seeing it. And from below I called upon the Lord to behold what I had done. He saw it, and approved. Straightway He ordained that the Souls should be incorporated; and they were seized with horror on learning what should be their condemnation.

These words, said Isis, struck me. Hearken, my son Horos, for I teach thee a mystery. Our ancestor Kamephes had it also from Hermes, who inscribes the recital of all things; I, in turn, received it from the ancient Kamephes when he admitted me to the initiation of the black veil; and thou, likewise, O marvellous and illustrious child, receive it from me.

The Souls were about to be imprisoned in bodies, whereat some sighed and lamented, as when some wild and free animal suddenly enchained, in the first moment of subjection to hard servitude and of severance from the beloved habits of the wilderness, struggles and revolts, refusing to follow its conqueror, and if occasion presents itself, slaying him. Others, again, hissed like serpents, or gave vent to piercing cries and sorrowful words, glancing aimlessly from height to depth.

"Great Heaven," said one, "principle of our birth, ether, pure airs, hands, and sacred breath of the sovereign God, and you, shining Stars, eyes of the Gods, unwearying light of Sun and Moon, our early brethren, what grief, what rending is this! Must we quit these vast, effulgent spaces, this sacred sphere, all these splendors of the empyrean and of the happy republic of the Gods, to be precipitated into these vile and miserable abodes? What crime. O wretched ones, have we committed? How can we have merited, poor sinners that we are, the penalties which await us? Behold the sad future in store for us—to minister to the wants of a fluctuating and dissoluble body! No more may our eyes distinguish the souls divine! Hardly through these watery spheres shall we perceive, with sighs, our ancestral heaven; at intervals even we shall cease altogether to behold it. By this disastrous sentence direct vision is denied to us; we can see only by the aid of the outer light; these are but windows that we possess—not eyes. Nor will our pain be less when we hear in the air the fraternal breathing of the winds with which no longer can we mingle our own, since that will have for its dwelling, instead of the sublime and open world, the narrow prison of the breast! But Thou, Who drivest us forth, and causest us from so high a seat to descend so low, assign a limit to our sufferings! O Master and Father, so quickly become indifferent to Thy handiwork, appoint a term to our penance, deign to bestow on us some last words, while yet we are able to behold the expanse of the luminous spheres."

This prayer of the Souls was granted, my son Horos, for the Lord was present; and sitting upon the throne of Truth, thus He addressed them:—

"O Souls; you shall be governed by Desire and Necessity; after me, these shall be your masters and your guides. Souls, subjected to my sceptre which never fails, know that inasmuch as you remain stainless you shall inhabit the regions of the skies. If among you any be found to merit reproach, they shall inhabit abodes destined to them in mortal organisms. If your faults be light, you shall, delivered from the bond of the flesh, return to heaven. But if you become guilty of graver crime, if you turn away from the end for which you have been formed, then indeed you shall, dwell neither in heaven nor in human bodies, but thenceforth you shall pass into those of animals without reason."

Having thus spoken, O my son Horos, He breathed upon them, and said, "It is not according to chance that I have ordained your destiny; if you act ill, it will be worse; it will be better if your actions are worthy of your birth. It is myself and not another who will be your witness and your judge. Understand that it is because of your past errors that you are to be punished and shut up in fleshly bodies. In different bodies, as I have already told you, your re-births will be different. Dissolution shall be a benefit, restoring your former happy condition. But if your conduct be unworthy of me, your prudence, becoming blinded and guiding you backwards, will cause you to take for good fortune that which is really a chastisement, and to dread a happier lot as though it were a cruel injury. The most just among you shall, in their future transformations, approximate to the divine, becoming among men, upright kings, true philosophers, leaders and legislators, true seers, collectors of salutary plants, cunning musicians, intelligent astronomers, wise augurs, instructed ministrants: all beautiful and good offices; as among birds are the eagles which pursue not nor devour those of their own kind, and do not permit weaker ones to be attacked in their presence, because justice is in the nature of the eagle; among quadrupeds, the lion, for he is a strong animal, untamed by slumber, in a mortal body performing immortal toils, and by nothing tired nor beguiled; among reptiles, the dragon, because he is powerful, living long, innocent, and a friend of men, allowing himself to be tamed, having no venom, and, leaving old age, approximating to the nature of the Gods; among fishes, the dolphin, for this creature, taking pity on those who fall into the sea, will carry them to land if they still live, and will abstain from devouring them if dead, although it is the most voracious of all aquatic animals."

Having spoken these words, God became an Incorruptible Intelligence (*i.e.,* resumed the unmanifest).

After these things, my son Horos, there arose out of the earth an exceeding powerful Spirit, unencumbered with any corporeal envelope, strong in wisdom, but savage and fearful; although he could not be ignorant of the knowledge he sought, seeing the type of the human body to be beautiful and august of aspect, and perceiving that the souls were about to enter into their envelopes:—

"What are these," said he, "O Hermes, Secretary of the Gods?" "These are men," replied Hermes. "It is a rash work," said he, "to make man with such penetrating eyes, such a subtle tongue, such a delicate hearing that can hear even those things which concern him not, such a fine scent, and in his hands a sense of touch capable of appropriating everything. O generating Spirit, thinkest thou it is well that he should be free from care—this future investigator of the fine mysteries of Nature? Wilt thou leave him exempt from suffering—he whose thought will search out the limits of the earth? Mankind will dig up the roots of plants, they will study the properties of natural juices they will observe the nature of stones, they will dissect not only animals but themselves, desiring to know how they have been formed. They will stretch forth their daring hands over the sea, and, cutting down the timber of the wild forest, they will pass from shore to shore seeking one another. They will pursue the inmost secrets of Nature even into the heights, and will study the motions of heaven. Nor is this enough; when nothing yet remains to be known than the furthest boundary of the earth, they will seek even there the last extremities of night. If they apprehend no obstacle, if they live exempt from trouble, beyond reach of any fear or of any anxiety, even heaven itself will not arrest their audacity; they will seek to extend their power over the elements. Teach them, then, desire and hope, in such wise that they may know likewise the dread of accident and of difficulty, and the painful sting of expectation deceived. Let the curiosity of their souls have for balance, desire and fear, care and vain hope. Let their souls be a prey to mutual love, to aspirations and varied longings, now satisfied, now deceived, so that even the sweetness of success may be an allurement to draw them towards misfortune. Let the weight of fevers oppress them, and break in them all desire." Thou sufferest, Horos, in hearing this thy mother's recital? Surprise and wonder seize thee in presence of the evils which now fall upon poor humanity? That which thou art about to hear is still more sad. The speech of Momos pleased Hermes; he deemed his advice good, and he followed it.

"O, Momos," said he, "the nature of the divine breath which enwraps all things shall not be ineffectual! The Master of the universe has charged me to be His agent and overseer. The Deity of the penetrating eye (Adrastia) will observe and direct all events; and for my part, I will design a mysterious instrument, a measure inflexible and inviolable, to which everything shall be subject from birth even to final destruction, and which shall be the bond of created entities. This instrument shall rule that which is on the earth, and all the rest."

It is thus—quoth Hermes—that I spoke to Momos; and forthwith the instrument operated. Straightway the souls were incorporated, and I was praised for my work.

Then the Lord summoned anew the assembly of the Gods. They gathered together, and He thus addressed them:—

"Gods, who have received a sovereign and imperishable nature, and the sway of the vast eternity, ye whose office it is to maintain unceasingly the mutual harmony of things, how long shall we govern an empire unknown? How long shall creation remain invisible to the sun and moon? Let each of us undertake his part in the universe. By the exercise of our power let us put an end to the cohesion of inertia. Let chaos become a fable, incredible to posterity. Inaugurate your great labours; I will direct you."

He said, and immediately the Kosmic unity, until now obscure, was opened, and in the heights appeared the heavens with all their mysteries. The earth, hitherto unstable, grew more solid beneath the brightness of the sun, and stood forth adorned with enfolding riches. All things are beautiful in the eyes of God, even that which to mortals appears uncomely, because all is made according to the divine laws. And God rejoiced in beholding His works filled with movement; and with outstretched hands grasping the treasures of nature. "Take these," He said, "O sacred earth, take these, O venerable one, who art to be the mother of all things, and henceforth let nothing be lacking to thee!"

With these words, opening His divine hands, He poured His treasures into the universal font. But yet they were unknown, for the souls newly embodied and unable to support their opprobrium, sought to enter into rivalry with the celestial Gods, and, proud of their lofty origin, boasting an equal creation with these, revolted. Thus men became their instruments, opposed to one another, and fomenting civil wars. And thus, force oppressing weakness, the strong burnt and massacred the feeble, and quick and dead were thrust forth from the sacred places.

Then the elements resolved to complain before the Lord of the savage condition of mankind. For the evil being already very grievous, the elements hastened to God the Creator, and pleaded in this wise—the fire being suffered to speak first:—

"O Master," he said, "Maker of this new world, Thou whose name, mysterious among the Gods, has hitherto been revered among all men; how long, O Divinity, hast Thou decreed to leave human life without God? Reveal Thyself to the world which calls for Thee, correct its savage existence by the institution of peace. Grant unto life, law, grant unto night oracles; fill all things with happy auguries; let men fear the judgment of the Gods, and no man shall sin any more. Let crimes receive their just punishment, and men will abstain from unrighteousness. They will fear to violate oaths, and madness will have an end. Teach them gratitude for benefits, so shall I devote my flame to pure offerings and libations, and the altars shall yield Thee exhalations of sweet savours. For now I am polluted, O Master, because the impious temerity of men forces me to consume flesh. They will not suffer me to remain in my nature; they pervert and corrupt my purity!"

The air spoke in its turn:—"I am defiled by the effluvium of corpses, O Master; I am becoming pestilent and unwholesome, and from on high I witness things which I ought not to behold."

Then the water took up the word, and spoke on this wise, O my illustrious son, and thus began:—

"Father and wondrous Creator of all things, Divinity incarnate, Author of Nature who brings forth all through Thee, command the waters of the streams to be always pure, for now both rivers and seas are compelled to bathe the destroyer and to receive his victims!"

Then at the last the earth appeared, O my glorious son, and thus began:—

"O King, Chief of celestial choirs and Lord of their orbits, Master and Father of the elements which lend to all things increase and decrease, and into which all must return; behold how the impious and insensate tribe of man overspreads me, O venerable One, since by Thy commands I am the habitation of all beings, bearing them all and receiving into my bosom all that is slain; such is now my reproach. Thy terrestrial world in which all creatures are contained is bereft of God. And because they revere nothing, they transgress every law and overwhelm me with all manner of evil works. To my shame, O Lord, I admit into myself the product of the corruption of carcases. But I, who receive all things, would fain also receive God. Grant to earth this grace, and if Thou comest not Thyself—for indeed I cannot contain Thee—let me at least receive some holy efflux of Thee. Let the earth become the most glorious of all the elements; and since she alone gives all things to all, may she revere herself as the recipient of Thy favours."

Thus the elements discoursed, and forthwith God filled the universe with His divine voice. "Go," said He, "sacred offspring, worthy of your Father's greatness, seek not to change anything, nor refuse to my creatures your ministry. I will send you an efflux of myself, a pure Being who shall investigate all actions, who shall be the dreadful and incorruptible Judge of the living; and sovereign justice shall extend its reign even into the shades beneath the earth. Thus shall every man receive his merited deserts."

Thereupon the elements ceased from their complaints, and each of them resumed its functions and its sway.

And in what manner, O my mother, said Horos, did the earth afterwards obtain this efflux of God?

I will not recount this Nativity, said Isis; I dare not, O powerful Horos, declare the origin of thy race, lest men in the future should learn the generation of the Gods. I will say only that the Supreme God, Creator and Architect of the world, at length accorded to earth for a season, thy father Osiris and the great Goddess Isis, that they might bring the expected salvation. By them life attained its fulness; savage and bloody wars were ended; they consecrated temples to the Gods their ancestors, and instituted oblations. They gave to mortals law, nourishment, and raiment. "They shall read," Hermes said, "my mystic writings, and dividing them into two parts, they shall keep certain of them, and inscribe upon columns and obelisks those which may be useful to man." Institutors of the first tribunals, they established everywhere the reign of order and justice. With them began the faith of treaties, and the introduction into human life of the religious duty of oaths. They taught the rites of sepulture towards those who cease to live; they interrogated the horrors of death; they shewed that the spirit from without delights to return into the human body, and that if the way of entry be shut against it, it brings about a failure of life. Instructed by Hermes, they engraved upon secret stelae[1] that the air is filled with genii. Instructed by Hermes in the secret laws of God, they alone were the teachers and legislators of mankind, initiating them in the arts, the sciences, and the benefits of civilised life. Instructed by Hermes concerning the sympathetic affinities which the Creator has established between heaven and earth, they instituted religious representations and sacred mysteries. And, considering the corruptible nature of all bodies, they ordained prophetic initiation, so that the prophet who lifts his hands to the

Gods should be instructed in all things, and that thereby philosophy and magic might provide nourishment for the soul, and medicine might heal the sufferings of the flesh.

Having performed all these things, O my son, and seeing the world arrived at its fulness, Osiris and I were recalled by the inhabitants of heaven; but we could not return thither without having first praised the Lord, so that the celestial Vision might fill the expanse, and that the way of a happy ascension might open before us, since God delights in hymns.

O my mother, said Horos, teach me this hymn, that I also may be instructed in it. Hearken, my son, answered Isis. (...)

Source: Translated by Anna Kingsford and Edward Maitland in Hermes Mercurius Trismegistus, *The Virgin of the World of Hermes Trismegistus,* trans. Anna Kingsford and Edward Maitland (London: G. Redway, 1885), 1–22.

Commentary: *Although the text's native Egyptian origins are indisputable, the exact provenance of the Greek text is uncertain. Scholars believe it was written sometime in the late centuries BCE or first centuries CE, but it may contain doctrines dating earlier. The text bears clear evidence of having been extensively and clumsily revised from an earlier version to recast it as a dialogue between Horus and Isis, probably in adapting it for Greco-Egyptian Hermeticism. The above translation, made from the excerpts preserved by Stobaeus in the fifth century CE, is somewhat tentative, as the Greek text is in some places corrupt and others obscure, but the uncertainties do not affect the overall meaning. This rare text contains passages that parallel the Watchers narrative from the* Book of Enoch *(9), as well as sections that are apparently the oldest surviving versions of the Hermetic idea of Hermes' books (or stelae) of wisdom. Ancient astronaut theorists suggest the final section reflects the alien gods' return to their home planet, and Robert Temple in SM asserts that the text accurately preserves early Egyptian or prehistoric ideas.*

Note

1. The translators gave this as "hidden tables," but I have translated this important phrase more literally to better compare with the Stelae of Wisdom in Josephus (**12**).

58. The Emerald Tablet of Hermes
Attributed to Hermes
Quoted in Balinas, *Kitāb sirr al-alīqa*
c. 8th c. CE
Arabic
Translated as *Secretum Secretorum,* cap. 81
1234 CE
Latin
AA, Prehistoric
Discussion in AA

[1] I speak not of fictitious things but of that which is most certain and true. [2] Whatsoever is below is like that which is above, and that which is above is similar to that which is below to accomplish the miracles of one thing. [3] And as all things were produced by the meditation of one Being, so all things were produced from this one thing by adaptation. [4] Its father is *Sol,* its mother *Luna;* the wind carried it in its belly, the earth is its nurse. [5] It is the cause of all perfection throughout the whole earth. [6] Its power is perfect, if it be changed into earth. [7] Separate the earth from the fire the subtile from the gross, acting prudently and with judgment. [8] Ascend with the greatest sagacity from the earth to heaven,

and then again descend to the earth, und unite together the powers of things superior and things inferior. Thus you will possess the glory of the whole world, and all obscurity will fly far away from you. [9] This thing has more fortitude than fortitude itself, because it will overcome every subtile thing and penetrate every solid thing. [10] By it this world was formed. [11] Hence proceed wonderful things which in this wise were established. [12] For this reason I am called Hermes Trismegistus, because I possess three parts of the philosophy of the whole world. [13] What I had to say about the operation of *Sol* is completed.

Source: Translated by Henry Carrington Bolton in *The Follies of Science at the Court of Rudolph II: 1576–1612* (Milwaukee: Pharmaceutical Review Publishing Co., 1904), 35. Bolton's translation is an uncredited adaptation of Thomas Thomson's translation in the *History of Chemistry* (1830), smoothing out the language for modern readers.

Commentary: *Alleged to have been composed by Hermes Trismegistus ("Thrice-Great"), who is often identified as an ancient astronaut or an Atlantean, the text in question allegedly was discovered by Alexander the Great in a cave near Hebron. In reality, it is believed to be a medieval Arab work summarizing Hermetic principles later applied to alchemy. The text was first published in Arabic, though it claimed to be a translation from the Syriac of an older Greek text. Most scholars believe this to be fictional and Arabic the first language. In the West, the text was known from two Latin translations, those of John of Seville around 1120 and Philippus Tripolitanus from 1232. More translations were made from these in various European languages, with still further translations made in turn from these, becoming one of the most popular alchemical texts throughout the medieval and early modern periods. It remains the only non–Greek Hermetic text routinely included in Western Hermetic collections. The modern* Emerald Tablets of Thoth *are an apocryphal work written by Maurice Doreal that borrows the name of this text for a modern "channeled" text created in the 1940s from fairly direct copying from weird fiction writers like H. P. Lovecraft ("The Dunwich Horror") and Frank Belknap Long ("The Hounds of Tindalos"). Many fringe writers accept it as Atlantean.*

VII

High Technology in Ancient Times

In reviewing fringe literature, it is noticeable how claims for advanced technology in prehistoric times track with the development of modern technology in recent history. For Ignatius Donnelly, Atlantis was a grand civilization, but not one noticeably more advanced than the later cultures of the Bronze Age. For the Theosophists, prehistoric culture was marked by magic—by the spiritual power of the extraterrestrial gods. The discovery of the Antikythera Mechanism in 1901 would eventually change these views of the past when in time researchers began to recognize it as a Hellenistic clockwork astronomical computer that suggested a hitherto unknown level of technological sophistication among the ancients. Not long after the invention of the airplane, claims were suddenly emerging that texts like the *Mahabharata* contained prehistoric references to just such aircraft (see **119**).

The concurrent rise of science fiction helped to develop the theme, notably in works such as Garrett P. Serviss's *Edison's Conquest of Mars* (1898) in which high technology and prehistoric extraterrestrial invasions came together as an explanation for Egypt's wonders. The pulp fiction, comic books, and movie serials of the 1930s would help to shape the technological dreamscape of Atlantis, particularly *Undersea Kingdom* (1936), around the same time that the sleeping prophet Edgar Cayce made claims for the technological prowess of Atlantis, including a death ray[1] (reading 364–11), all while citing fringe literature (reading 364–1), his true inspiration. Robert Oppenheimer unwittingly contributed to the theme when he compared a nuclear explosion to a passage from the *Bhagavad Gita* in a November 8, 1948 *Time* magazine article. A decade later, the Soviet mathematician Matest M. Agrest had begun to speculate that Sodom and Gomorrah had been felled by prehistoric nuclear bombs.[2]

Alleged ancient references to spacecraft, televisions, and computers followed in short order whenever a new technology was invented. Fringe writers were seeking ancient precedents to help ground modern change.

Notes

1. A ray capable of destroying people and airplanes from afar caused a brief stir in 1924 when Edwin R. Scott tried to sell one to the British government, but similar beams were a staple of science fiction long before. In 1898 Serviss had given Edison a disintegration ray in *Edison's Conquest of Mars*, modeled on H. G. Wells's heat ray from *War of the Worlds*. *Undersea Kingdom*, borrowing from *Flash Gordon*, made a death ray a key part of the weapons of Atlantis four years after Cayce had done the same from similar source material.

2. His work was published in Russian but became known to the West through citation in ancient astronaut books. Louis Pauwels and Jacques Bergier cited him in *Morning of the Magicians*, Peter Kolosimo in *Not of This World*, and Erich von Däniken in *Chariots of the Gods*. For a scholarly take, see James A. Herrick, *Scientific Mythologies: How Science and Science Fiction Forge New Religious Beliefs* (Downer's Grove, Illinois: InterVarsity, 2008), 67.

59. Sodom and Gomorrah Destroyed by Nuclear Bombs
Genesis 19:1–29
c. 6th c. BCE
Hebrew
Astro, Prehistoric
Discussion in AA, CG, MM

CHAPTER 19

[1] And there came two angels to Sodom at even; and Lot sat in the gate of Sodom: and Lot seeing them rose up to meet them; and he bowed himself with his face toward the ground;

[2] And he said, Behold now, my lords, turn in, I pray you, into your servant's house, and tarry all night, and wash your feet, and ye shall rise up early, and go on your ways. And they said, Nay; but we will abide in the street all night.

[3] And he pressed upon them greatly; and they turned in unto him, and entered into his house; and he made them a feast, and did bake unleavened bread, and they did eat.

[4] But before they lay down, the men of the city, even the men of Sodom, compassed the house round, both old and young, all the people from every quarter:

[5] And they called unto Lot, and said unto him, Where are the men which came in to thee this night? bring them out unto us, that we may know them.

[6] And Lot went out at the door unto them, and shut the door after him,

[7] And said, I pray you, brethren, do not so wickedly.

[8] Behold now, I have two daughters which have not known man; let me, I pray you, bring them out unto you, and do ye to them as is good in your eyes: only unto these men do nothing; for therefore came they under the shadow of my roof.

[9] And they said, Stand back. And they said again, This one fellow came in to sojourn, and he will needs be a judge: now will we deal worse with thee, than with them. And they pressed sore upon the man, even Lot, and came near to break the door.

[10] But the men put forth their hand, and pulled Lot into the house to them, and shut to the door.

[11] And they smote the men that were at the door of the house with blindness, both small and great: so that they wearied themselves to find the door.

[12] And the men said unto Lot, Hast thou here any besides? son in law, and thy sons, and thy daughters, and whatsoever thou hast in the city, bring them out of this place:

[13] For we will destroy this place, because the cry of them is waxen great before the face of the Lord; and the Lord hath sent us to destroy it.

[14] And Lot went out, and spake unto his sons in law, which married his daughters, and said, Up, get you out of this place; for the Lord will destroy this city. But he seemed as one that mocked unto his sons in law.

[15] And when the morning arose, then the angels hastened Lot, saying, Arise, take thy wife, and thy two daughters, which are here; lest thou be consumed in the iniquity of the city.

[16] And while he lingered, the men laid hold upon his hand, and upon the hand of his wife, and upon the hand of his two daughters; the Lord being merciful unto him: and they brought him forth, and set him without the city.

[17] And it came to pass, when they had brought them forth abroad, that he said,

Escape for thy life; look not behind thee, neither stay thou in all the plain; escape to the mountain, lest thou be consumed.

[18] And Lot said unto them, Oh, not so, my Lord:

[19] Behold now, thy servant hath found grace in thy sight, and thou hast magnified thy mercy, which thou hast shewed unto me in saving my life; and I cannot escape to the mountain, lest some evil take me, and I die:

[20] Behold now, this city is near to flee unto, and it is a little one: Oh, let me escape thither, (is it not a little one?) and my soul shall live.

[21] And he said unto him, See, I have accepted thee concerning this thing also, that I will not overthrow this city, for the which thou hast spoken.

[22] Haste thee, escape thither; for I cannot do anything till thou be come thither. Therefore the name of the city was called Zoar.

[23] The sun was risen upon the earth when Lot entered into Zoar.

[24] Then the Lord rained upon Sodom and upon Gomorrah brimstone and fire from the Lord out of heaven;

[25] And he overthrew those cities, and all the plain, and all the inhabitants of the cities, and that which grew upon the ground.

[26] But his wife looked back from behind him, and she became a pillar of salt.

[27] And Abraham gat up early in the morning to the place where he stood before the Lord:

[28] And he looked toward Sodom and Gomorrah, and toward all the land of the plain, and beheld, and, lo, the smoke of the country went up as the smoke of a furnace.

[29] And it came to pass, when God destroyed the cities of the plain, that God remembered Abraham, and sent Lot out of the midst of the overthrow, when he overthrew the cities in the which Lot dwelt.

Source: King James Version.

Commentary: *The destruction of the two cities has attracted a wide range of explanations, including the claim, dating back to the 1700s, that a comet or meteor destroyed them. The Soviet writer Matest M. Agrest proposed in 1959, based solely on the Genesis text, that a nuclear bomb dropped by space aliens destroyed the cities, a claim ancient astronaut writers follow to this day. The site of the two cities has never been definitively identified,[1] and no likely candidate exhibits nuclear traits. The story of Lot bears striking structural and thematic similarities to that of Noah (21), including a sinful world destroyed, a single surviving family, and (in Genesis 9:21– 25 and 19:30–38), the hero's drunkenness and sexual misbehavior with his children.*

Note

1. Identifications of Sodom have a long history. Strabo (*Geography* 16.2.44) placed it at the southwestern tip of the Dead Sea, while in 1973 Walter E. Rast and R. Thomas Schaub identified it with Bab edh–Dhra to the north and east. A recent argument, but by no means definitive, places Sodom at the site of Tall el–Hammam. See Steven Collins, "Where Is Sodom?: The Case for Tall El-Hammam," *Biblical Archaeology Review* 39, no. 2 (2013), 32–41.

60. Iram of the Pillars Destroyed

Qur'an 69:5–8, 89:6–14
609–632 CE
Arabic

Astro, Prehistoric
Discussion in EV

69: [5] But Thamud were destroyed by a terrible noise, [6] and 'Ād were destroyed by a roaring and furious wind, [7] which *God* caused to assail them for seven nights and eight days successively: thou mightest have seen people during the same lying prostrate, as though they *had been* the roots of hollow palm-trees; [8] and couldest thou have seen any of them remaining?

89: [6] Hast thou not considered how thy Lord dealt with 'Ād, [7] *the people of* Iram, adorned with lofty buildings, [8] the like whereof hath not been erected in the land; [9] and with Thamud, who hewed the rocks in the valley *into houses*; [10] and with Pharaoh, the contriver of the stakes: [11] who had behaved insolently in the earth, [12] and multiplied corruption therein? [13] Wherefore thy Lord poured on them various kinds of chastisement: [14] for thy Lord *is* surely in a watch-tower, *whence he observeth the actions of men.*

Source: Translated by George Sale in *The Koran; Commonly Called the Alcoran of Mohammed* (Boston: T. O. H. P. Burnham, 1870), 437, 460.

Commentary: *This brief reference to Iram (or Irem), a lost city of the Arabian Desert, is more fully explained in the later legend given below from the* Arabian Nights. *Its destruction recalls that of Sodom, with which it is often compared. Fringe writer Philip Gardiner asserts falsely in* Secret Societies *(2007) that horror writer H. P. Lovecraft drew on genuine traditions in making the city the center of an extraterrestrial prehistoric cult in "The Call of Cthulhu" (1926). Jacques Bergier, in EV, mistakenly asserts that Lovecraft invented Iram.*

61. Elaboration of the Destruction of Iram

Arabian Nights, Nights 276–279
Early medieval
Arabic
Astro, Prehistoric

It is related that Abdullah bin Abi Kilabah went forth in quest of a she-camel which had strayed from him, and as he was wandering in the deserts of Al-Yaman and the district of Sabá, behold, he came a great city girt by a vast castle around which were palaces and pavilions that rose high into middle air. He made for the place thinking to find there folk of whom he might ask concerning his she-camel. But when he reached it, he found it desolate, without a living soul in it. So (quoth he) I alighted and, hobbling my dromedary, and composing my mind, entered into the city.—And Shahrazad perceived the dawn of day and ceased saying her permitted say.

And now when it was the two hundred and seventy-sixth night, she said it hath reached me now, O ausipicious King, that Abdullah bin Abi Kilabah continued:—I dismounted and hobbling my dromedary, and composing my mind, entered into the city. Now when I came to the castle, I found it had two vast gates (never in the world was seen their like for size and height) inlaid with all manner jewels and jacinths, white and red, yellow and green. Beholding this, I marveled with great marvel and thought the case mighty wondrous. Then, entering the citadel in a flutter of fear and dazed with surprise and affright, I found it long and wide, about equaling Al-Medinah in point of size. And therein were lofty palaces laid out in pavilions all built of gold and silver and inlaid with many colored jewels and jacinths and chrysolites and pearls. And the door leaves in the pavilions were like those of the castle for beauty, and their floors were strewn with great pearls and balls, no smaller than hazelnuts, of musk and ambergris and saffron.

Now when I came within the heart of the city and saw therein no created beings of the Sons of Adam, I was near swooning and dying for fear. Moreover, I looked down from the great roofs of the pavilion chambers and their balconies and saw rivers running under them, and in the main streets were fruit-laden trees and tall palms, and the manner of their building was one brick of gold and one of silver. So I said to myself, "Doubtless this is the Paradise promised for the world to come." Then I loaded me with the jewels of its gravel and the musk of its dust as much as I could carry, and returned to my own country, where I told the folk what I had seen.

After a time the news reached Mu'awiyah, son of Abu Sufyán, who was then Caliph in Al-Hijaz, so he wrote to his lieutenant in San'á of Al-Yaman to send for the teffer of the story and question him of the truth of the case. Accordingly the lieutenant summoned me and questioned me of my adventure and of all appertaining to it, and I told him what I had seen, whereupon he dispatched me to Mu'awiyah, before whom I, repeated the story of the strange sights, but he would not credit it. So I brought out to him some of the pearls and balls of musk and ambergris and saffron, in which latter there was still some sweet savor, but the pearls were grown yellow and had lost pearly color.—And Shahrazad perceived the dawn of day and ceased saying her permitted say.

Now, when it was the two-hundred and seventy-seventh night, she said, It hath reached me, O auspicious King, that Abdullah son of Abu Kilabah continued:—Now Mu'awiyah wondered at this and, sending for Ka'ab al-Ahbar, said to him, "O Ka'ab, I have sent for thee to ascertain the truth of a certain matter and hope that thou wilt be able to certify me thereof." Asked Ka'ab, "What is it, O Commander of the Faithful?" and Mu'awiyah answered, "Wottest thou of any city founded by man which is builded of gold and silver, the pillars whereof are of chrysolite and rubies and its gravel pearls and bans of musk and ambergris and saffron?" He replied, "Yes, O Commander of the Faithful, this is 'Iram with pillars decked and dight, the like of which was never made in the lands,'[1] and the builder was Shaddád son of 'Ád the Greater." Quoth the Caliph, "Tell us something of its history," and Ka'ab said:

"'Ád the Greater had two sons, Shadid and Shaddád, who when their father died ruled conjointly in his stead, and there was no King of the Kings of the earth but was subject to them. After awhile Shadid died and his brother Shaddád reigned over the earth alone. Now he was fond of reading in antique books, and happening upon the description of the world to come and of Paradise, with its pavilions and pileries and trees and fruits and so forth, his soul move him to build the like thereof in this world, after the fashion aforesaid. Now under his hand were a hundred thousand kings, each ruling over a hundred thousand chiefs, commanding each a hundred thousand warriors, so he called these all before him and said to them: 'I find in ancient books and annals a description of Paradise as it is to be in the next world, and I desire to build me its like in this world. Go ye forth therefore to the goodliest tract on earth and the most spacious, and build me there a city of gold and silver, whose gravel shall be chrysolite and rubies and pearls, and for support of its vaults make pillars of jasper. Fill it with palaces, whereon ye shall set galleries and balconies, and plant its lanes and thoroughfares with all manner trees bearing yellow-ripe fruits, and make rivers to run through it in channels of gold and silver.'

Whereat said one and all, 'How are we able to do this thing thou hast commanded, and whence shall we get the chrysolites and rubies and pearls whereof thou speakest?' Quoth he, 'What! Weet ye not that the kings of the world are subject to me and under my hand and that none therein dare gainsay my word?' Answered they, 'Yes, we know that.'"—And Shahrazad perceived the dawn of day and ceased saying her permitted say.

Now, when it was the two-hundred and seventy-eighth night, she said, It hath reached me, O auspicious King, that the lieges answered, "Yes, we know that"; whereupon the King rejoined, "Fare ye then to the mines of chrysolites and rubies and pearls and gold and silver and collect their produce and gather together all of value that is in the world, and spare no pains and leave naught. And take also for me such of these things as be in men's hands and let nothing escape you. Be diligent and beware of disobedience." And thereupon he wrote letters to all the kings of the world and bade them gather together whatso of these things was in their subjects' hands, and get them to the mines of precious stones and metals, and bring forth all that was therein, even from the abysses of the seas.

This they accomplished in the space of twenty years, for the number of rulers then reigning over the earth was three hundred and sixty kings. And Shaddād presently assembled from all lands and countries architects and engineers and men of art and laborers and handicraftsmen, who dispersed over the world and explored all the wastes and wolds and tracts and holds. At last they came to an uninhabited spot, a vast and fair open plain clear of sand hills and mountains, with founts flushing and rivers rushing, and they said, "This is the manner of place the King commanded us to seek and ordered us to find." So they busied themselves in building the city even as bade them Shaddād, King of the whole earth in its length and breadth, leading the fountains in channels and laying the foundations after the prescribed fashion. Moreover, all the kings of earth's several reigns sent thither jewels and precious stones and pearls large and small and carnelian and refined gold and virgin silver upon camels by land, and in great ships over the waters, and there came to the builders' hands of all these materials so great a quantity as may neither be told nor counted nor conceived.

So they labored at the work three hundred years, and when they had brought it to end, they went to King Shaddād and acquainted him therewith. Then said he: "Depart and make thereon an impregnable castle, rising and towering high in air, and build around it a thousand pavilions, each upon a thousand columns of chrysolite and ruby and vaulted with gold, that in each pavilion a wazir may dwell." So they returned forthwith and did this in other twenty years, after which they again presented themselves before King Shaddād and informed him of the accomplishment of his will. Then he commanded his wazirs, who were a thousand in number, and his chief officers and such of his troops and others as he put trust in, to prepare for departure and removal to Many-columned Iram, in the suite and at the stirrup of Shaddād, son of 'Ād, King of the world, and he bade also such as he would of his women and his harem and of his handmaids and eunuchs make them ready for the journey. They spent twenty years in preparing for departure, at the end of which time Shaddād set out with his host— And Shahrazad perceived the dawn of day and ceased saying her permitted say.

Now, when it was the two hundred and seventy-ninth nights, she said, it hath reached me, O auspicious King, that Shaddād bin 'Ād fared forth, he and his host, rejoicing in the attainment of his desire till there remained but one day's journey between him and Iram of the Pillars. Then Allah sent down on him and on the stubborn unbelievers with him a mighty rushing sound from the Heavens of His power, which destroyed them all with its vehement clamor, and neither Shaddād nor any of his company set eyes on the city. Moreover, Allah blotted out the road which led to the city, and it stands in its stead unchanged until the Resurrection Day and the Hour of Judgment.

So Mu'awiyah wondered greatly at Ka'ab al-Ahbar's story, and said to him, "Hath any mortal ever made his way to that city?" He replied, "Yes, one of the companions of Mohammed (on whom be blessing and peace!) reached it, doubtless and for sure after the same fashion as this man here seated." And (quoth Al-Sha'abi) it is related, on the authority of learned men of Himyar in Al-Yaman that Shaddād, when destroyed with all his host by the sound, was succeeded in his kingship by his son Shaddād the Less, whom he left viceregent in Hazramaut and Saba when he and his marched upon Many-columned Iram. Now as soon as he heard of his father's death on the road, he caused his body to be brought back from the desert to Hazramaut and bade them hew him out a tomb in a cave, where he laid the body on a throne of gold and threw over the corpse threescore and ten robes of cloth of gold, purfled with precious stones. Lastly at his sire's head he set up a tablet of gold whereon were graven these verses:

> Take warning O proud,
> And in length o' life vain!
> I'm Shaddād son of 'Ād,
> Of the forts castellain,
> Lord of pillars and power,
> Lord of tried might and main,
> Whom all earth sons obeyed
> For my mischief and bane,
> And who held East and West
> In mine awfulest reign.
> He preached me salvation
> Whom God did assain,[2]
> But we crossed him and asked,
> "Can no refuge be ta'en?"
> When a Cry on us cried
> From th' horizon plain,
> And we fell on the field
> Like the harvested grain,
> And the Fixt Day await
> We, in earth's bosom lain!

Al-Sa'alibi also relateth: It chanced that two men once entered this cave and found steps at its upper end, so they descended and came to an underground chamber, a hundred cubits long by forty wide and a hundred high. In the midst stood a throne of gold, whereon lay a man of huge bulk, filling the whole length and breadth of the throne. He was covered with jewels and raiment gold-and-silver wrought, and at his head was a tablet of gold bearing an inscription. So they took the tablet and carried it off, together with as many bars of gold and silver and so forth as they could bear away.

Source: Slightly adapted from Richard F. Burton, *A Plain and Literal Translation of the Arabian Nights' Entertainments, Now Entitled the Book of the Thousand Nights and a Night*, vol. 4 (Burton Club Private Printing, c. 1885): 113–119.

Commentary: *The hubristic Shaddād bin 'Ād is the legendary builder of the pyramids in some Arabic versions of the medieval pyramid myth (see **17**). His association with the chastisement of Iram is probably the origin of his later association with the chastisement of the earth in the Flood and thus with the preservation of knowledge in the pyramids, identified with the pillars of wisdom (**12, 13**), reminiscent of Iram's lofty pillars.*

Notes

1. Quoting Qur'an 89:6–7 (see **61**).
2. The prophet Hud, commissioned to preach to the 'Ādites (Qur'an 7:65).

62. Nuclear Explosion and Radioactive Fallout in Ancient India

Mahabharata 16.1–2
c. 400 BCE–400 CE
Sanskrit
Astro, Atlantis, Prehistoric
Discussion in CG, MM, TG

When the next day came, Cāmva actually brought forth an iron bolt through which all the individuals in the race of the Vrishnis and the Andhakas became consumed into ashes. Indeed, for the destruction of the Vrishnis and the Andhakas, Cāmva brought forth, through that curse, a fierce iron bolt that looked like a gigantic messenger of death. The fact was duly reported to the king. In great distress of mind, the king (Ugrasena) caused that iron bolt to be reduced into fine powder. [...]

Day by day strong winds blew, and many were the evil omens that arose, awful and foreboding the destruction of the Vrishnis and the Andhakas. The streets swarmed with rats and mice. Earthen pots showed cracks or broken from no apparent cause. At night, the rats and mice ate away the hair and nails of slumbering men. [...] That chastiser of foes commanded the Vrishnis to make a pilgrimage to some sacred water. The messengers forthwith proclaimed at the command of Keçava that the Vrishnis should make a journey to the seacoast for bathing in the sacred waters of the ocean.

Source: Translated by Kisari Mohan Ganguli in *The Mahabharata*, Açwamedha Parva (Calcutta: Bhārata Press, 1894), 3–5.

Commentary: *This is one of innumerable battle passages in the* Mahabharata. *After these passages were cited in* MM, *later authors, notably including David Childress, rewrote and reworked them to increase the similarity to nuclear events. The first paragraph became an atomic detonation, and the second lost its mice and rats to better approximate radiation poisoning, with the sacred water becoming a decontamination attempt. Writers like Childress merged this passage with an unrelated passage given next.*

Mahabharata 8.33–34

c. 400 BCE–400 CE
Sanskrit
Astro, Atlantis, Prehistoric
Discussion in CG, MM, TG

While the worlds were thus afflicted, Śakra,[1] surrounded by the Maruts, battled against the three cities by hurling his thunder upon them from every side. When, however, Purandra failed to pierce those cities made impenetrable, O king, by the Creator with his boons, the chief of celestials, filled with fear, and leaving those cities, repaired with those very gods to that chastiser of foes, viz., the Grandsire, for representing unto him the oppressions committed by the *Asuras*. [...]

Thus equipped, that car shone brilliantly like a blazing fire in the midst of the priests officiating at a sacrifice. Beholding that car properly equipped, the gods became filled with wonder. Seeing the energies of the entire universe united together in one place, O sire, the gods wondered, and at last represented unto that illustrious Deity that the car was ready. [...] Then He called Blue and Red, or smoke—that terrible deity robed in skins,—looking like 10,000 Suns, and shrouded by the fire of superabundant Energy, blazed up with splendour. [...] The triple city then appeared immediately before that god of unbearable energy [Maheswara, or Siva], that Deity of fierce and indescribable form, that warrior who was desirous of slaying the *Asuras*. The illustrious deity, that Lord of the universe, then drawing that celestial bow, sped that shaft which represented the might of the whole universe, at the triple city. Upon that foremost of shafts, O thou of great good fortune, being shot, loud wails of woe were heard from those cities as they began to fall down towards the Earth. Burning those *Asuras*, he threw them down into the Western ocean.

Source: Adapted slightly from the translation by Kisari Mohan Ganguli in *The Mahabharata,* Karna Parva (Calcutta: Bhārata Press, 1889), pp. 107, 112–113, 117–118.

Commentary: *This account of the destruction of the triple city, with its uncanny imagery,*

The destructive power of the heavens was terrifying to ancient people, who assigned to powerful gods control over lightning. This illustration from a scientific treatise of 1709 demonstrates the continuing fear of celestial power. Many of the cosmic weapons of the *Mahabharata* reflect the destructive power of lightning, meteors, and other celestial phenomena (NOAA).

became a staple of claims for prehistoric nuclear war, particularly when merged with the preceding passage into an ersatz account. In 1889 Ganguli transliterated the name Śakra as Cakra, and in French it was given as Çakra, from which MM renders it incorrectly as Cukra. Later writers, notably Erich von Däniken and then David Childress, misunderstood this and mangled the name into Gurkha (the name of a Nepalese people), in which form he became canonized in ancient astronaut literature as an alien. Unlike the canonical ancient astronaut version in CG and TG, Śakra (= Indra) is not the driver of the vehicle in the second section, but rather Maheswara (Siva). On all accounts the MM-CG-TG version completely mangles the passages. For a fabricated version of this passage, see 119.

Note

1. Śakra, meaning "powerful," is an epithet of Indra, the storm god.

63. Another Nuclear Event in Ancient India

Mahabharata 7.202
c. 400 BCE–400 CE
Sanskrit
Astro, Atlantis, Prehistoric, Theo
Discussion in CG

The valiant Açwatthāman, then, staying resolutely on his car, touched water and invoked the *Āgneya* weapon incapable of being resisted by the very gods. Aiming at all his visible and invisible foes, the preceptor's son, that slayer of hostile heroes, inspired with *mantras* a blazing shaft possessed of the effulgence of a smokeless fire, and let it off on all sides, filled with rage. Dense showers of arrows then issued from it in the welkin. Endued with fiery flames, those arrows encompassed Pārtha on all sides. Meteors flashed down from the firmament. A thick gloom suddenly shrouded the (Pāndava) host. All the points of the compass also were enveloped by that darkness. *Rākshasas* and *Piçāchas*, crowding together, uttered fierce cries. Inauspicious winds began to blow. The Sun himself no longer gave any heat. Ravens fiercely croaked on all sides. Clouds roared in the welkin, showering blood. Birds and beasts and kine, and *Munis* of high vows and souls under complete control, became exceedingly uneasy. The very elements seemed to be perturbed. The sun seemed to turn. The universe, scorched with heat, seemed to be in a fever. The elephants and other creatures of the land, scorched by the energy of that weapon, ran in fright, breathing heavily and desirous of protection against that terrible force. The very waters heated, the creatures residing in that element, O Bhārata, became exceedingly uneasy and seemed to burn. From all the points of the compass, cardinal and subsidiary, from the firmament and the very earth, showers of sharp and fierce arrows fell and issued with the impetuosity of Garuda or the wind. Struck and burnt by those shafts of Açwatthāman, that were all endued with the impetuosity of the thunder, the hostile warriors fell down like trees burnt down by a raging fire. Huge elephants, burnt by that weapon, fell down on the earth all around, uttering fierce cries loud as the rumblings of the clouds. Other huge elephants, scorched by that fire, ran hither and thither, and roared aloud in fear, as if in the midst of a forest conflagration. The steeds, O king, and the cars also, burnt by the energy of that weapon, looked, O sire, like the tops of trees burnt in a forest-fire. Thousands of cars fell down on all sides. Indeed, O Bhārata, it seemed that the divine lord *Agni* burnt the (Pāndava) host in that battle, like the

Samvarta fire consuming everything at the end of the *Yuga*. [...] Burnt by the energy of Açwatthāman's weapon, the forms of the slain could not be distinguished.

Source: Translated by Kisari Mohan Ganguli in *The Mahabharata*, Drona Parva (Calcutta: Bhārata Press, 1888), 677–679.

Commentary: *In CG, Erich von Däniken, in calling this a nuclear event, translated this passage into German from the Ganguli translation (which he wrongly credits to the publisher, Pratap Chandra Roy[1]). Michael Heron then re-translated it into English for the Anglo-American editions of CG without reference to the original. Uncannily similar to a nuclear event, the text makes plain that it references an imaginary sky canon shot from above by a single being, not an explosion rising up from the ground from a bomb. Several later authors repeated the re-translated version of CG without reference to the original. Theosophist Helena Blavatsky claimed that the Āgneya (literally, "fire") weapon was wielded by the residents of Atlantis.[2]*

Notes

1. An understandable error. Ganguli wished to publish anonymously, so (causing much confusion) his name appears only in the preface to the first volume; Roy's name is given on the title page of all eighteen volumes.
2. Helena Blavatsky, *The Theosophical Glossary* (London: Theosophical Publishing, 1892), 9.

64. An Ancient Indian War Plane
Mahabharata 7.155
c. 400 BCE–400 CE
Sanskrit
Astro, Prehistoric, Atlantis
Discussion in TG

Seeing him rush in that battle against the car of Cini's grandson, Bhimasena's son, the gigantic *Rākshasa*, Ghatotkacha, endued with great strength, rushed at him, riding on a huge and terrible car made of black iron covered with bear-skins. Both the height and the width of that large car measured thirty *nalwas*.[1] Equipped with machines set in proper places it was; its rattle resembled that of a mighty mass of clouds. No steeds or elephants were yoked unto it, but, instead, beings that looked like elephants. On its tall standard perched a prince of vultures with outstretched wings and feet, with eyes wide-expanded, and shrieking awfully. And it was equipped with red flags and decked with the entrails of various animals. And that huge vehicle was furnished with eight wheels.

Source: Translated by Kisari Mohan Ganguli in *The Mahabharata*, Drona Parva (Calcutta: Bhārata Press, 1888), 493.

Commentary: *In* Flying Saucers Have Landed *(1957), Desmond Leslie misquotes this passage to make into a description of a metallic spacecraft. The car here does not fly, and few planes are covered in bear skins and entrails.*

Note

1. A nalwa was 400 cubits.

65. Flying Chariots in Ancient India
Ramayana 5.9
c. 500 BCE

Sanskrit
Astro, Prehistoric
Discussion in AA, CG, TG

In the midst of that mansion the Wind-god's offspring found another, excellently constructed, having innumerable mad elephants;—that noble car embellished with all gems, entitled *Pushpaka,* which had been constructed in heaven by Viçva-karmā for Brahmā himself,—which Kuvera obtained from the Great-father through high austerities,—and which, vanquishing Kuvera by his prowess, the Rākshasa chief got possession of. And the mighty monkey ascended the splendid car *Pushpaka,* containing figures of wolves,—made of *Kárttaswara* and *Hiranya;* graced with ranges of goodly pillars; as if blazing in splendour; throughout garnished with narrow secret rooms and saloons, piercing the heavens, and resembling Meru or Mandara,[1] and like unto the flaming Sun; skilfully reared by Viçvakarmā; with golden staircases and graceful and grand raised seats, rows of golden and crystal windows, and daises composed of sapphires, emeralds and other superb gems; embellished with noble *vidrumas,* costly stones, and round pearls, as also with plastered terraces; pasted with red sandal, like unto gold, and furnished with a sacred aroma; and resembling the sun new risen. And stationed thereon, Hanumān smelt the rich odour of viands and drinks that was spreading on all sides;—and like one dear friend smelling another, he also smelt the mighty Air, impregnated with aroma, which seemed like embodied Odour.

Source: Translated by Āranya Kāndam in *The Ramayana,* trans. Āranya Kāndam and ed. Manmatha Nath Dutt (Calcutta: 1892), 911.

Commentary: *This is the earliest depiction of a self-propelled flying machine in Sanskrit literature and is widely cited by James Churchward, David Childress, and others as evidence of Indian flying machines. Earlier accounts made plain that the vehicles were chariots, drawn by flying horses. Beginning with the* Ramayana, *the chariots lost their horses but nevertheless retained their wheels, evidence that they began as horse-drawn chariots projected by human imagination into the sky. Claims that such chariots were actually UFO-style flying machines emerge not directly from this text but from a modern book, a supposedly psychically channeled volume called the* Vaimānika Shāstra, *whose author, Pandit Subbaraya Shastry, claimed it to be an ancient writing revealed to him from the spirit world. Our text of the* Vaimānika Shāstra *was allegedly recorded on paper in 1918 and first publicized in 1952 when G. R. Josyer announced its existence via press release.[2] It was published in Hindi in 1959 and in English translation in 1973, after which it became a fringe history staple.*

Notes

1. Sacred mountains in Vedic cosmology.

2. Scholarly analysis has concluded the document was composed in Sanskrit sometime between 1900 and 1922. See H. S. Mukunda, S. M. Deshpande, H. R. Nagendra, A. Prabhu, and S. P. Govindraju, "A Critical Study of the Work 'Vyamanika Shastra.'" *Scientific Opinion* (1974): 5–12.

66. Flying Chariots in Ancient Judaea

Kebra Nagast, Chapter 94
c. 1300 CE
Ge'ez
Astro
Discussion in TG

But King David, with his soldiers, and the armies of his soldiers, and all those who obeyed his word, ran by the wagons without pain or suffering, and without hunger or thirst, and without sweat or exhaustion, and travelled in one day a distance that [usually] took three months to traverse.

Source: Translated by Sir E.A. Wallis Budge in *The Queen of Sheba and Her Only Son, Menyelek* (London: Medici Society, 1922), 166. The bracketed word is the translator's own addition.

Commentary: *This passage comes from a thirteenth-century Ethiopian work attempting to connect Ethiopia's kings to Solomon. In* Signs of the Gods *(1981), Erich von Däniken alters this translation to replace "ran by" with "flew on," thus turning a supernaturally fast ground transport into a flying saucer. Later writers, including David Childress, repeat his claims.*

67. Ark of the Covenant: Killing Machine
2 Samuel 6:1–8
c. 640–530 BCE
Hebrew
Astro, Prehistoric
Discussion in AA, CG

[1] Again, David gathered together all the chosen men of Israel, thirty thousand.

[2] And David arose, and went with all the people that were with him from Baale of Judah, to bring up from thence the ark of God, whose name is called by the name of the Lord of hosts that dwelleth between the cherubims.

[3] And they set the ark of God upon a new cart, and brought it out of the house of Abinadab that was in Gibeah: and Uzzah and Ahio, the sons of Abinadab, drave the new cart.

[4] And they brought it out of the house of Abinadab which was at Gibeah, accompanying the ark of God: and Ahio went before the ark.

[5] And David and all the house of Israel played before the Lord on all manner of instruments made of fir wood, even on harps, and on psalteries, and on timbrels, and on cornets, and on cymbals.

[6] And when they came to Nachon's threshingfloor, Uzzah put forth his hand to the ark of God, and took hold of it; for the oxen shook it.

[7] And the anger of the Lord was kindled against Uzzah; and God smote him there for his error; and there he died by the ark of God.

[8] And David was displeased, because the Lord had made a breach upon Uzzah: and he called the name of the place Perezuzzah to this day.

Source: King James Version.

Commentary: *In* The Sign and the Seal *(1992), Graham Hancock read such accounts and became convinced that the Ark was a piece of high technology, spawning his interest in a lost, technologically-advanced civilization. He claimed to have become interested in the subject after watching* Raiders of the Lost Ark *(1981), which in turn depicts the powers of the Ark in terms that are very close to CG.*[1] *There von Däniken says it was "undoubtedly" an electrically-powered piece of technology, based on this passage, which he falsely claims states that Uzzah was killed "as if struck by lightning." He alleges that a "reconstruction" of the Ark would produce an electrical current of "several hundred volts."*

Note

1. On the possible connection between *Chariots of the Gods* and *Raiders of the Lost Ark*, see Peter Nicholls, *The World of Fantastic Films* (New York: Dodd, Mead, 1984), 98; von Däniken would hint that his claims inspired George Lucas and Steven Spielberg in interviews. See, e.g., his 2008 interview with Christian Düblin, <http://www.xecutives.net/24-monats-interviews/103-erich-von-daeniken-interviewed-by-christian-dueblin>.

68. The Fate of the Ark of the Covenant

2 Maccabees 2:1–7
c. 2nd or 1st c. BCE
Greek
Prehistoric, General

[1] It is also found in the records, that Jeremy the prophet commanded them that were carried away to take of the fire, as it hath been signified:

[2] And how that the prophet, having given them the law, charged them not to forget the commandments of the Lord, and that they should not err in their minds, when they see images of silver and gold, with their ornaments.

[3] And with other such speeches exhorted he them, that the law should not depart from their hearts.

[4] It was also contained in the same writing, that the prophet, being warned of God, commanded the tabernacle and the ark to go with him, as he went forth into the mountain, where Moses climbed up, and saw the heritage of God.

[5] And when Jeremy came thither, he found an hollow cave, wherein he laid the tabernacle, and the ark, and the altar of incense, and so stopped the door.

[6] And some of those that followed him came to mark the way, but they could not find it.

[7] Which when Jeremy perceived, he blamed them, saying, As for that place, it shall be unknown until the time that God gather his people again together, and receive them unto mercy.

Source: King James Version.

Commentary: *2 Maccabees is canonical to Catholics and the Orthodox but not to Protestants or Jews. This passage, in which the prophet Jeremiah secrets the Ark at what tradition identifies as Mt. Nebo, became the basis for later claims by a group known as British Israelists that Britain was the legitimate successor to ancient Israel after nineteenth century writers, building on the work of F. R. A. Glover, asserted that because Jeremiah's followers had not found the Ark, Jeremiah must have brought the Ark of the Covenant to Ireland (ruled in the 1800s by Britain) and buried it at Tara. Believers caused significant damage to the ancient Irish site while digging there for the Ark in 1899.[1] British Israelism claimed that white Anglo-Saxons were the true Chosen People, and in the United States it contributed directly to the Christian Identity movement and white supremacist ideologies, along with their anti–Semitic beliefs.[2]*

Notes

1. "Proceedings at Meetings of the Royal Archaeological Institute," *Archaeological Journal* 57 (1900): 334–335; for a fuller treatment of the Ark and Tara see Mairéad Carew, *Tara and the Ark of the Covenant: A Search for the Ark of the Covenant by British-Israelites on the Hill of Tara (1899–1902)* (Discovery Programme/Royal Irish Academy, 2003).

2. See Michael Barkun, *Religion and the Racist Right: The Origins of the Christian Identity Movement,* rev. ed. (Chapel Hill: University of North Carolina Press, 1997).

69. Archimedes' Mobile Planetarium
Cicero
De re publica 1.14
51 BCE
Latin
Astro, Prehistoric

But as soon as Gallus had begun to explain, in a most scientific manner, the principle of this [Archimedes'] machine, I felt that the Sicilian geometrician must have possessed a genius superior to anything we usually conceive to belong to our nature. For Gallus assured us that that other solid and compact globe was a very ancient invention, and that the first model had been originally made by Thales of Miletus. That afterward Eudoxus of Cnidus, a disciple of Plato, had traced on its surface the stars that appear in the sky, and that many years subsequently, borrowing from Eudoxus this beautiful design and representation, Aratus had illustrated it in his verses, not by any science of astronomy, but by the ornament of poetic description. He added that the figure of the globe, which displayed the motions of the sun and moon, and the five planets, or wandering stars, could not be represented by the primitive solid globe; and that in this the invention of Archimedes was admirable, because he had calculated how a single revolution should maintain unequal and diversified progressions in dissimilar motions. In fact, when Gallus moved this globe, we observed that the moon succeeded the sun by as many turns of the wheel in the machine as days in the heavens. From whence it resulted that the progress of the sun was marked as in the heavens, and that the moon touched the point where she is obscured by the earth's shadow at the instant the sun appears opposite ... [text breaks off]

Source: Translated by C.D. Yonge in Cicero, *The Treatises of M. Tullius Cicero*, ed. and trans. C.D. Yonge (London: Henry G. Bohn, 1853), 295.

Commentary: *Although not frequently cited by fringe writers, this text demonstrates that the Antikythera Mechanism discussed in the introduction to this chapter was no isolated work of genius; similar mechanical computers were also known to the Romans. Ancient astronaut writers, lost civilization advocates, and Atlantis theorizers all assert that the Antikythera Mechanism is proof of ancient high technology impossible without outside intervention. Cicero, however, had no doubt of the human genius behind such works.*

70. Frederick II's Celestial Tent
Chronica regia Coloniensis, continuatio IV, entry for 1232
c. 1238 CE
Latin
Astro, Prehistoric

The Sultan of Babylonia[1] [i.e., Egypt] sent to the emperor a tent constructed with wondrous artifice, in which images of the sun and the moon made to move with scientific precision traveled over their courses in a fixed and determined interval, and indicated infallibly the hours of day and night. Of the value of this tent, it is said that its price exceeded twenty thousand marks. This is stored among the royal treasures at Venosa.

Source: Translated by Jason Colavito from the Latin in *Chronica regia Coloniensis* (Scriptores Rerum Germanicum), ed. Georgius Waitz (Hanover: Impensis Bibliopolii Hahniani, 1880), 263.

Commentary: *The generally reliable* Royal Annals of Cologne *were composed sometime around 1175 CE, but the text above comes from a later continuation by an unknown hand who was contemporary with the events described. It is therefore a better and more direct source than the much later version below, which is the version known to ancient astronaut writers.*

JOHANN TRITHEMIUS

Annales Hirsaugienses, entry for 1232
1509–1514
Latin
Astro, Prehistoric
Discussion in CG

In the same year the Saladin [Sultan] of Egypt sent by his ambassadors as a gift to the emperor Frederic a valuable machine of wonderful construction worth more than five thousand ducats. For it appeared to resemble internally a celestial globe in which figures of the sun, moon, and other planets formed with the greatest skill moved, being impelled by weights and wheels, so that performing their course in certain and fixed intervals they pointed out the hour night and day with infallible certainty; also the twelve signs of the zodiac with certain appropriate characters, moved with the firmament, contained within themselves the course of the planets.

Source: Translated by William Francis and J. W. Griffith in John Beckmann, *History of Inventions, Discoveries, and Origins,* 4th ed., trans. William Johnston with enlargements by William Francis and J. W. Griffiths, vol. 1 (London: Henry G. Bohn 1846), 349–350.

Commentary: *In CG Erich von Däniken, who is unaware of the medieval source on which this Renaissance text is based, suggests this planetarium was a legacy from ancient originals inspired by aliens.*

Note

1. This term for Egypt comes from the name of a fort near Cairo.

71. An Android in Ancient China

Lie Yukou (traditional attribution)
Liezi, Book 5
Compiled 4th c. CE, but attributed to 5th c. BCE
Chinese
Astro, Prehistoric

King Mu of Chou made a tour of inspection in the west. He crossed the K'un-lun range, but turned back before he reached the Yen mountains—"The place where the sun sets."

On his return journey, before arriving in China, a certain artificer was presented to him, by name Yen Shih. King Mu received him in audience, and asked what he could do. "I will do anything," replied Yen Shih, "that your Majesty may please to command. But there is a piece of work, already finished, that I should like to submit first to your Majesty's inspection." "Bring it with you to-morrow," said the King, "and we will look at it together." So Yen Shih called again the next day, and was duly admitted to the royal presence. "Who is that man accompanying you?" asked the King. "That, Sire, is my own handiwork. He can sing and he can act." The King stared at the figure in astonishment. It walked with rapid strides, moving its head up and down, so that any one would have taken it for a live human being. The artificer touched its chin, and it began singing, perfectly in tune. He touched its hand, and it started posturing, keeping perfect time. It went through any number of movements suggested by its owner's fancy. The King, looking on with his favourite concubine and the other inmates of his harem, could hardly persuade himself that it was not real.

As the performance was drawing to an end, the automaton winked his eye and made sundry advances to the ladies in attendance on the King. This, however, threw the King into a passion, and he would have put Yen Shih to death on the spot had not the latter, in mortal terror, instantly pulled the automaton to pieces to let him see what it really was. And lo! it turned out to be merely a conglomeration of leather, wood, glue and paint, variously coloured white, black, red and blue. Examining it closely, the King found all the internal organs complete—liver, gall, heart, lungs, spleen, kidneys, stomach and intestines—and, over these, again, muscles and bones and limbs with their joints, skin and teeth and hair, all of them artificial. Not a part but was fashioned with the utmost nicety and skill; and when it was put together again, the figure presented the same appearance as when first brought in. The King tried the effect of taking away the heart, and found that the mouth would no longer utter a sound; he took away the liver, and the eyes could no longer see; he took away the kidneys, and the legs lost their power of locomotion.

Now the King was delighted. Drawing a deep breath, he exclaimed: "Can it be that human skill is really on a par with that of the Creator?" And forthwith he gave an order for two extra chariots, in which he took home with him the artificer and his handiwork.

Now, Pan Shu, with his cloud-scaling ladder, and Mo Ti, with his flying kite,[1] thought that they had reached the limits of human achievement. But when Yen Shih's wonderful piece of work had been brought to their knowledge, the two philosophers never again ventured to boast of their accomplishments, and ceased to busy themselves so frequently with the square and compasses.

Source: Translated by Lionel Giles in *Taoist Teachings from the Book of Lieh Tzŭ* (London: John Murray, 1912), 90–92.

Commentary: *The* Leizi *is a Daoist text of uncertain origin. Scholars are uncertain about the degree to which the text, which was finalized sometime in the 4th century CE, preserves ancient material dating back to the 400s BCE. King Mu of the Zhou dynasty reigned c. 950 BCE, four centuries before the traditional date of the composition of the* Liezi, *but he is a figure cloaked in myth. The story above is self-evidently a wonder story, projecting through fiction and myth astonishing levels of perfection to clockwork machinery, like the famous South-Pointing Chariot, a self-steering chariot that used a mechanical system to keep a pointer facing south no matter which way the chariot turned.[2] It had been in use for centuries before the text's creation.*

Notes

1. Commentary of Chang Chan (4th c. CE): "Pan Shu made a cloud-ladder by which he could mount to the sky and assail the heights of heaven; Mo Ti made a wooden kite which would fly for three days without coming down." (Giles' note.)

2. For discussion of the South-Pointing Chariot, see Hong-Sen Yan, *Reconstruction Designs of Lost Ancient Chinese Machinery* (Dordrecht: Netherlands, 2007), chapter 7.

72. China's First Emperor's Amazing Tomb
Sima Qian
Records of the Grand Historian, Chapter 6
109–91 BCE
Chinese
Astro, Prehistoric
Discussion in AA

From the beginning of his reign, Shi Huangdi had dug and remodeled Li Mountain. And when he had gathered in his hands the whole of the empire, he had sent to him seven hundred thousand workers; they dug into the ground until the water flowed from the third layer of springs, and they poured bronze for a sarcophagus. Replicas of palaces, scenic towers, and the hundred administrators, marvelous utensils, jewels, and art objects—all were transported to fill (the sepulcher) and were buried. Artisans were ordered to craft automatic bows and arrows so if someone wanted to make a hole and enter (into the grave), he would have been suddenly shot. Quicksilver was used to create imitations of the hundred rivers, the Yellow River, the Yangtze, and the vast seas, and machines made it so they seemed to flow from one to another. Above were all the signs of the heavens; below the whole geographical layout of the earth. Torches were manufactured with blubber, calculated not to extinguish for a long time. Er-Shi [the second emperor] said, "It would be unfitting to have those of the women in the former emperor's harem who bore no sons sent away." He ordered that all of the women accompany the former emperor in death, and those who were put to death were numerous. When the coffin had been lowered, someone said that the workers and artisans who built the machines and hidden treasures knew everything that was there, and the great value of what was buried might be disclosed. So when the funeral was completed, the gate leading to the central burial was hidden and blocked and the door to the outside entrance was closed, shutting in all those who were employed as laborers or artisans so they could not come out. Trees and bushes were planted so that (the grave) had the appearance of a mountain.

Source: Translated by Jason Colavito from Édouard Chavannes (trans.), *Mémoires Historiques de Se-Ma Ts'ien,* vol. 2 (Paris: Ernest Leroux, 1897), 193–195.

Commentary: *The generally reliable historian Sima Qian is the sole source for the fabulous interior of the tomb of China's first emperor, Qin Shi Huang (Shi Huangdi) (260–210 BCE). The suggestion of a model of heaven and earth run by machines has, of course, suggested to ancient astronaut theorists that this was the work of aliens. The pyramid itself is also a source of fringe theories relating it without evidence to various mounds and pyramids worldwide.*

73. Navigation Technology and the "Earth-Crust Displacement"
Plutarch
Moralia 5.26.62 (*Isis and Osiris* 62)
1st century CE
Greek
Prehistoric, General
Discussion in FG, SM

Moreover, they [the Egyptians] call the loadstone Horus's bone, and iron Typhon's bone, as Manetho relates. For as iron is oftentimes like a thing that is drawn to and follows the loadstone, and oftentimes again flies off and recoils to the opposite part; so the salutary, good, and intelligent motion of the universe doth, as by a gentle persuasion, invert, reduce, and make softer the rugged and Typhonian one; and when again it is restrained and forced back, it returns into itself, and sinks into its former interminateness.

Source: Translation by William Baxter in *Plutarch's Morals,* vol. 4, ed. William Goodwin (Boston: Little, Brown, and Company, 1874), 121.

Commentary: *Although the above passage seems to metaphorically relate natural magnets called loadstones (known since at least the time of Thales of Miletus in the sixth century BCE) to the philosophy of a balanced universe, Graham Hancock incongruously sees it as a coded prediction of a future catastrophe. In* FG *Hancock accepted Charles Hapgood's (false) claim that the earth's crust would slide over the surface of the earth when the magnetic poles reversed, as they do from time to time due to fluctuations in the earth's magnetic field. He interpreted this discussion of competing beneficial and dangerous forces governing the cosmos as a coded prediction of an upcoming earth crust displacement caused by a "harsh and deadly cosmic power," the knowledge of which was inherited from an Ice Age civilization. By contrast, in* SM *Robert Temple sees the passage as garbled and half-understood references to navigation devices and extraterrestrial technology and astronomy.*

VIII

Mysteries of the Americas

From the moment that Europeans discovered the New World and its inhabitants, denizens of the Old World struggled to understand how it fit into ancient cosmologies inherited from antiquity. Were the Americas populated by the Lost Tribes of Israel? Were they the Atlantis of Plato? Or were they the Devil's continents, a mockery of the Old World? For the first several centuries after Europeans were simultaneously fascinated and repelled by the similarities and differences between the Old World and the New. Some had correctly deduced that Native Americans came from Asia as early as the sixteenth century. The idea was famously advocated by Thomas Jefferson in his *Notes on the State of Virginia*. However, those who recorded early information about the cultures of the Western Hemisphere were not neutral observers, and all too often their documents betray the cultural assumptions that traveled with them across the Atlantic, particularly in the penchant of the *conquistadores* to see in native religions reflections of the Mosaic accounts, and in native gods various Christian saints.

The overarching theme—one repeated to this very day—is maddeningly the same: that there is a deep connection between the Americas and the Old World somehow invisible to mainstream archaeology, and that this connection extends to the ancient passage of Caucasians across the Atlantic, Caucasians who somehow, through moral, technological, and intellectual superiority, ruled over native peoples. Modern fringe writers deduce all manner of proof for this claim in a bewildering variety of forms, though at time this extends beyond Caucasians to encompass Chinese or African voyagers—who nonetheless are depicted as reigning over the benighted natives.

This chapter will look at evidence for "white" visitors and other prehistoric mysteries from texts written from (or attempting, however poorly, to convey) a native perspective, or, rather, how native myths and legends have been appropriated by European and American writers. Chapter XI will examine similar claims attributed to the historic period, down to the late Middle Ages, in texts relating accounts from non-native perspectives.

74. Maya Creation of the Earth
Popol Vuh, Part 1
Before 1700 CE
K'iche'
Astro

This is the first book (or leaf) written in olden times, but its sight is concealed to him who sees and who thinks. Its appearance is admirable, as the tale of the times in which everything in heaven and upon earth completed its shape, the signs, the measure of their angles and their distribution, also the parallels in the skies and on earth, at the four ends and four (cardinal) points,—as it was spoken by the Creator and the Moulder, the Mother, the Father of life and being, by whom every one lives and breathes, Him the Father and living source of the peace of the nations of His well-bred people. He, whose wisdom has planned the excellency of everything that exists in the sky and on earth, in the lakes and in the sea.

This now is the tale how everything was in suspense, everything was calm and silent, immovable and in peace,—the immensities of heaven being void.

Now this is the first word and speech: There was neither man, nor animal, neither bird nor fish or crab, no wood, no stones, no ravines, no thickets or herbs or shrubbery,—the heavens alone existed.

The face of the earth did not manifest itself yet, the peaceful sea alone existed and the spaces of heaven.

There was yet nothing which formed a body, nothing which held together, nothing that moved, not the least sound was heard in the skies.

This now is the tale how everything was in suspense, everything was calm and silent, immovable and in peace,—the immensities of heaven being void. Now this is the first word and speech: There was neither man, nor animal, neither bird nor fish or crab, no wood, no stones, no ravines, no thickets or herbs or shrubbery,—the heavens alone existed. The face of the earth did not manifest itself yet, the peaceful sea alone existed and the spaces of heaven. There was yet nothing which formed a body, nothing which held together, nothing that moved, not the least sound was heard in the skies. Nothing stood erect; the peaceful waters of the sea, calm within its limits, alone were, because nothing existed.

Nothing but the immobility and silence in darkness and night. But alone the Creator, the Moulder, the Ruler, the feathered serpent, those who engender, those who give being, they are on the waters like a growing light.

They are wrapt in green and in blue, therefore Gukumatz[1] is their name; his being is of the deepest knowledge. This is how the sky exists, thus also is the heart of heaven; such is the name of God, and thus he is called.

Then it happened that the word came thither, with the Ruler and the Gukumatz, in the darkness and night; and it spoke to the Ruler and to Gukumatz.

And they spoke: then, they advised together and pondered over it, they understood each other, joining their words and opinions. And while they were thus advising together, dawn appeared, and as day broke, man made its appearance, whilst they were consulting upon the bringing forth and growth of the woods and vines, upon the being of life and mankind in darkness and night,—through him who is the heart of heaven, whose name is Hurakan.

Its first token is lightning, its second one thunder, its third is the deadly ray; and these three together are of the heart of heaven.

Source: Translated by A. F. Bandelier in "On the Sources for Aboriginal History of Spanish America," *Proceedings of the American Association for the Advancement of Science,* twenty-seventh meeting, August 1878 (Salem: Author, 1879), 330–331.

Commentary: *The* Popol Vuh *is a late K'iche' Mayan text written sometime after the Conquest but preserving older material. It survives in a manuscript recorded by Father Francisco Ximénez in the early 1700s. In 1861, Charles-Étienne Brasseur de Bourbourg, who thought the*

Mayans were survivors of Atlantis, published the K'iche' text along with a French translation. Strangely, though, the complete text was not translated into English until the late twentieth century. The above translation was made from Brasseur's edition, though Bandelier did not specify whether the K'iche' or the French text was used; I have corrected it against modern editions.[2] The opening of the Popol Vuh *has long been recognized as an indigenous accommodation of the Christian teachings of Genesis, a pious cover for later, more authentic indigenous legends.*

Notes

1. A Postclassic version of the famous quetzal serpent god, roughly equivalent to Kukulkan or Quetzalcoatl.

2. For the standard scholarly translation, see Dennis Tedlock, *Popol Vuh: The Definitive Edition of the Mayan Book of the Dawn of Life and the Glories of Gods and Kings,* revised and expanded ed. (New York: Touchstone, 1996).

75. Destruction of the Wooden Race by Flood

Popol Vuh, Part 1
Before 1700 CE
K'iche'
Astro, Atlantis

Thus was the end of these men, their ruin and their destruction,—the end of these manikins made of wood, who were put to death. The waters were swelled by the will of the Heart of the Sky, and there was a mighty flood which reached above the heads of these manikins made of wood.

Thus were they destroyed: they were flooded, and a thick resin fell out of heaven. The bird Xecotcavach plucked out their eyes; the Camalotz cut off their heads; the Cotzbalam devoured their flesh; the Tecumbalam broke and brayed their bones and muscles, and scattered their dust, as a punishment, because they thought not of their father and mother, of him who is the Heart of the Sky, whose name is Hurakan; therefore the face of the earth was covered, and a black rain fell, rain by day, rain by night.

Source: Translated anonymously in "Art. VIII: The Popul Vuh," *The Christian Remembrancer* 54 (1867): 436.

Commentary: *Unlike its Near Eastern counterpart, the Maya flood myth envisions a separate and inferior creation completely obliterated, leaving no survivors save monkeys until the gods repopulate the world with human beings made of corn rather than wood. As in our previous selection, the above translation and the one which follows were made from Brasseur's edition, though the anonymous translator did not specify whether the K'iche' or the French text was used; I have corrected it against modern editions.*

76. The Origin of Maya Human Sacrifice

Popol Vuh, Part 2
Before 1700 CE
K'iche'
Astro, Atlantis

"In truth, there is your god, him whom you hold up, who is the symbol of the shadow of your Creator and Maker. Give not of your fire to these tribes, till they have given themselves to your god Tohil. Ask then of Tohil what recompense they shall make for the fire you give them," spake the messenger of Xibalba,[1] whose shape was that of a bat. "I have been sent by your Creator and Maker," he said.

Then they were filled with joy. The heart of Tohil was lifted up whilst spake the messenger of Xibalba. And when he had spoken, he vanished without ceasing to exist.

Then arrived other tribes perishing from cold; for there had been great frost and a frozen rain, a piercing chill. And all the tribes were gathered shivering and quaking with cold, when they came before (the leaders) Balam-Quitze, Balam-Agab, Mahucutah, and Iqui-Balam. Great was their misery. Their mouths, their faces were full of sorrow. "Will you not compassionate us?" they asked. "We only entreat a little fire. Were we not all one, and with one country, when we were first created? Have pity upon us!" they again exclaimed.

"What will you give us that we should compassionate you?" was the answer made to them.

"We will give silver," answered the tribes.

"We will not have silver," said Balam-Quitze and Balam-Agab.

"What do you require then?" they asked. It was answered, "We will inquire of Tohil." The tribes replied, "It is well."

"What shall the tribes give thee, O Tohil, in return for a little fire?" asked then Balam-Quitze, Balam-Agab, Mahucutah, and Iqui-Balam.

"Let them be united to me betwixt the armpit and the belt. Will their hearts agree to embrace me, Tohil? If not, let them have no fire." Thus spake the good Tohil; and he added, "Tell them that this shall be little by little, and that it will not be the union of themselves between the armpit and the belt." And thus he spake to Balam-Quitze, Balam-Agab, Mahucutah, and Iqui-Balam.

Then they repeated the message of Tohil. "It is well," they said, on hearing the words of Tohil, "We will embrace him." They were not long. They received the fire and they warmed themselves.

"But one tribe stole the fire in smoke, the house of Zotzel.... When they passed in the smoke, they passed gently, coming and stealing fire, and the Cakchiquels did not ask for fire and yield up themselves. But all the other tribes were taken in the snare, for when they yielded from the armpit to the belt, it was for the cutting open of the breast that Tohil spake, when the tribes are sacrificed before his face, and when they tear the hearts out of the breast."

This rite had not been practised, till death was enigmatically proposed by Tohil in horror and majesty by the hand of Balam-Quitze, Balam-Agab, Mahucutah, and Iqui-Balam.

Source: Translated anonymously in "Art. VIII: The Popul Vuh," *The Christian Remembrancer* 54 (1867): 442.

Commentary: *This myth, which explains why the Maya began the practice of human sacrifice, also serves as alleged evidence that extraterrestrials or Atlanteans instituted the practice.*

Note

1. The Underworld.

77. The Aztec Creation Myth

Gerónimo de Mendieta

Historia eclesiástica Indiana 2.1–2

c. 1596
Spanish
Astro, Prehistoric
Discussion in AA, FG

[1] ... But while the people of each province gave their accounts (of the creation) in various ways, for the most part they came to the conclusion that in the sky there was a god called Citlalatonac and a goddess called Citlalicue, and that the goddess gave birth to a large knife or flint (which in their language is called *técpatl*). On seeing this, her sons were frightened and agreed to cast the large knife from the sky, and so they undertook this action and the knife fell to a certain part of the earth which is called Chicmoztoc, meaning the Seven Caves. They say there emerged from it 1,600 gods (which seems to be an attempt to explain the fall of the evil angels[1]), and they say that these beings, seeing themselves thus fallen and banished and without servants, agreed to send a message to the goddess their mother saying that because they had been cast out and banished it would be good if she were to give them permission, power, and a way to create men who could provide service for them. And their mother responded that if they deserved them, they would always have been in their company; however, they were unworthy of this, and if they wanted to have servants here on earth, then they would have to go beg of Mictlan Tecutli, Lord or Chief of Hades, that he may give them a bone or some ashes of the dead that are with him; over which having received they shall sacrifice themselves, that from this a man and woman might emerge who would then multiply. This seems to be an attempt to understand the Flood, when all men died and none remained. Having heard their mother's response (which they say was brought by Tlotli, who is a hawk), the gods having consulted together, sent one of their number, called Xolotl, down to Hades for the bone and ash as their mother had advised. He succeeded in obtaining from the chief, Mictlan Tecutli, the bone and the ash his brothers hoped he would; and then, wary of his grisly host, he took an abrupt departure, running at the top of his speed. Wroth at this, the infernal chief gave chase; not causing to Xolotl, however, any more serious inconvenience than a hasty fall in which an arm bone was broken in pieces, great and small, which is why some men are smaller ones than others. The messenger gathered up what he could in all haste, and despite his stumble made his escape. Reaching the earth, he put the fragments of bone into a basin, and all the gods drew blood from their bodies (after which the Indians were later accustomed) and sprinkled it into the vessel. On the fourth day there was a movement among the wetted bones and a boy lay there before all; and in four days more, the blood-letting and sprinkling being still kept up, a girl was lifted from the ghastly dish. The children were given to Xolotl to bring up; and he fed then on the juice of the cardoon.

[2] Now man having been created, and having multiplied, each one of the gods took some men to be their devotees and servants. There had been (so they say) no sun in existence for many years; so the gods being assembled in a place called Teotihuacan, six leagues from Mexico, and gathered at the time round a great fire, told their devotees that he of them who should first cast himself into that fire should have the honor of being transformed into a sun. So one of them,[2] out of pure bravery, flung himself into the fire. Then the gods began to peer through the gloom in all directions for the expected sun and to make bets with quails, locusts,[3] butterflies, and snakes as to what part of heaven he should first appear in. And some said Here, and some said There; but when the sun rose they were all proved wrong, for not one of them had fixed upon the east. And in that same hour, though they knew it not, the

decree went forth that they should all die by sacrifice, which afterward they [the Natives] had quite the habit of doing before their idols.

The sun had risen indeed, and with a glory of the cruel fire about him that not even the eyes of the gods could endure; but he moved not. There he lay on the horizon; and when the deities sent Tlotli their messenger to him, with orders that he should go on upon his way, his ominous answer was, that he would never leave that place till he had destroyed and put an end to them all. Then a great fear fell upon some, while others were moved only to anger; and among the latter was one Citli, who immediately strung his bow and advanced against the glittering enemy. By quickly lowering his head the Sun avoided the first arrow shot at him; but the second and third had attained his body in quick succession, when, filled with fury, he seized the last and launched it back upon his assailant. And the brave Citli laid shaft to string nevermore, for the arrow of the sun pierced his forehead.

Then all was dismay in the assembly of the gods, and despair filled their heart, for they saw that they could not prevail against the shining one; and they agreed to die, and to cut themselves open through the breast. Xolotl was appointed minister, and he killed his companions one by one, and last of all he slew himself also. So they died like gods; and each left to the sad and wondering men who were his servants, his garments for a memorial. And these servants made up, each party, a bundle of the raiment that had been left to them, binding it about a stick into which they had bedded a small green stone to serve as a heart. These bundles were called *tlaquimilloli*, and each bore the name of that god whose memorial it was; and these things were more reverenced than the ordinary gods of stone and wood of the country. Fray Andres de Olmos found one of these relics in Tlalmanalco, wrapped up in many cloths, and half rotten with being kept hid so long.

Source: Adapted from the translation by Hubert Howe Bancroft in *The Works of Hubert Howe Bancroft*, Vol. 3: The Native Races (San Francisco: The History Company, 1886), 58–62 with corrections and original translation by Jason Colavito from Gerónimo de Mendieta, *Historia eclesiástica Indiana,* ed. Joaquin Garcia Icazbalceta (México: Antigua Libreria, 1870), 77–80. The parentheticals belong to Gerónimo de Mendieta; the brackets are mine.

Commentary: *Fray Gerónimo de Mendieta recorded the Aztec creation myth secondhand, from the telling of Fray Andrés de Olmos, who conflated various accounts. The entire text, moreover, is at somewhat of a remove from pre–Conquest myths, recorded by Christian friars through a Christian framework, from the telling by Aztecs who had converted to Catholicism. It is therefore something of a hybrid. Menieta's work was suppressed due to its millenarian ideas, but after it was rediscovered and published in 1870, its version of the Aztec creation myth became the standard account, thanks in large measure to Hubert Howe Bancroft's influential translation, adapted above to restore Mendieta's in-text commentary, to correct errors, and to re-translate more literally the beginning of chapter 1, which Bancroft adapted far too freely. On* Ancient Aliens, *Giorgio Tsoukalos declared the flint knife a spaceship and the gods who emerged from it extraterrestrial colonists. Note the coincidental similarity between this account and the Mesopotamian creation myth (4), down to the desire for servants and the blood rites used to make such human servants.*

Notes

1. The sons of God from Genesis 6:1 (**8**), traditionally identified as evil angels, following 2 Peter 2:4.

2. The Spanish missionary Bernadino de Sahagún names him as the god Nanahuatzin (*Historia general* 7.2).

3. The Spanish word *langosta* can refer to lobsters, locusts, crustaceans, and the like. Its use here is ambiguous.

78. Repeated Destruction of Earth in Aztec Cosmology

Francisco Javier Clavijero Echegaray
History of Mexico 6.24
1780
Italian
Atlantis, Prehistoric
Discussion in FG

The Mexicans, the Acolhuans, and all the other nations of Anahuac [the Basin of Mexico], distinguished four ages of time by as many suns. The first named *Alonatiuh,* that is the sun, or the age of water, commenced with the creation of the world, and continued until the time at which all mankind almost perished in a general inundation, along with the first sun. The second *Tlaltonatiuh,* the age of earth, lasted from the time of the general inundation until the ruin of the giants, and the great earthquakes, which concluded in like manner the second sun. The third, *Ehècatonatiuh,* the age of air, lasted from the destruction of the giants until the great whirlwinds, in which all mankind perished along with the third sun. The

The Aztec Calendar Stone was intentionally buried in Tenochtitlan at the time of the Spanish conquest and remained hidden until 1790. The stone features a central carving often thought to represent the sun god surrounded by images of the four previous suns, whose end was believed to cause periodic catastrophe for the earth. Fringe writers have associated the stone with such disparate ideas as Atlantis, the Maya 2012 apocalypse, and (according to Giorgio Tsoukalos) a two-dimensional depiction of a particle accelerator (William Henry Jackson/Library of Congress).

fourth *Tletonatiuh,* the age of fire, began at the last restoration of the human race, and was to continue, as we have already mentioned in their mythology, until the fourth sun, and the earth were destroyed by fire. This age it was supposed would end at the conclusion of one of their centuries; and thus we may account for these noisy festivals in honour of the god of fire, which were celebrated at the beginning of every century, as a thanksgiving for his restraining his voracity, and deferring the termination of the world.

Source: Translated by Charles Cullen, in Francesco Saverio Clavigero, *The History of Mexico,* trans. Charles Cullen, vol. 1 (London: G.G.J. and J. Robinson, 1787), 288–289.

Commentary: *The succession of ages in Aztec cosmology is often presented in fringe literature as proof of catastrophism and a prophecy of a coming catastrophe or the return of alien gods. Our author, Clavijero, was a Jesuit who lived and worked in the Americas, gathering information from Native informants; however, his romantic belief in the goodness of the Natives has led scholars to view his work as somewhat unreliable. His* History of Mexico *(1780) was composed in Spanish, but he translated it himself into Italian for publication. The translation here was made from the Italian edition. Various missionary writers and early historians give the ages in different orders, with sometimes four, sometimes five suns. Their accounts were based on native informants and limited Aztec codices, which used pictures and brief Nahuatl captions, such as the Codex Vaticanus A.*

79. Ancient Giants' Bones in the Americas
Peter Martyr d' Anghiera
Decades 5.9
1523
Latin
General, Hyper, Prehistoric

I wish to end this chapter with an account of giants, who, like the formidable and solid Atlas, will serve as an ending, and will support the outlines of what I have established. Diego de Ordaz,[1] whom I have mentioned above, explored many of the hidden places of this land, and he pacified many chiefs: one of whom in particular is of the province where the money tree[2] grows, where he [Ordaz] learned how the money tree is planted and grown, just as I had explained in his section [of my book]. He discovered in the vault of a temple a piece of the thigh bone of a Giant, worn and partially gnawed away by extreme age: A short time after your Holiness [Pope Adrian VI] had departed for Rome, the licentiate Allyón, one of the jurisconsults of the Hispaniola Senate, bought this thigh bone to the city of Victoria. This I had in my house for some days: From the knot of the hip to the knee it is five spans long, and proportionate in accordance with its great length. After this, those sent by Cortés to the Southern mountains reported that they had found the region where these men lived, and they were said, in proof of this, to have brought back a great many ribs from the dead.

Source: Translated by Jason Colavito from the first Latin edition, Petrus Martyrus ab Angleria, *De orbe nouo Petri Martyris ab Angleria Mediolanensis Protonotarii Cesaris senatoris decades* (Michael de Eguia, 1530), f83v.

Commentary: *The thigh bone in question is undoubtedly large, reported to be approximately 45 inches (114 cm) in length. It was probably the bone of a type of Pleistocene megafauna. However, this account is especially interesting because the standard English translation, made in 1912 by Francis MacNutt, mistakenly renders the partial thigh bone ("fœmorale osseum* frustum") as "half" of a "hip bone," leading to speculation about monumentally massive giants in the fringe literature due to later writers' failure to consult the original.

Notes

1. Diego de Ordaz was a Spanish explorer in the company of Hernán Cortés who tried and failed to find the mythical city of El Dorado. The bone he found arrived in Spain in 1521 and was in Peter's hands in mid–1522.

2. Presumably a tree whose fruits were used as currency.

80. God Kills the Giants during All-Male Orgy

Pedro Cieza de León
First Part of the Chronicle of Peru, Chapter 52
1553
Spanish
General, Hyper, Prehistoric

There are, however, reports concerning giants in Peru, who landed on the coast at the point of Santa Elena, within the jurisdiction of this city of Puerto Viejo, which require notice. I will relate what I have been told, without paying attention to the various versions of the story current among the vulgar, who always exaggerate everything. The natives relate the following tradition, which had been received from their ancestors from very remote times. There arrived on the coast, in boats made of reeds, as big as large ships, a party of men of such size that, from the knee downwards, their height was as great as the entire height of an ordinary man, though he might be of good stature. Their limbs were all in proportion to the deformed size of their bodies, and it was a monstrous thing to see their heads, with hair reaching to the shoulders. Their eyes were as large as small plates. They had no beards, and were dressed in the skins of animals, others only in the dress which nature gave them, and they had no women with them. When they arrived at this point, they made a sort of village, and even now the sites of their houses are pointed out. But as they found no water, in order to remedy the want, they made some very deep wells, works which are truly worthy of remembrance; for such are their magnitude, that they certainly must have been executed by very strong men. They dug these wells in the living rock until they met with water, and then they lined them with masonry from top to bottom in such sort that they will endure for many ages. The water in these wells is very good and wholesome, and always so cold that it is very pleasant to drink it. Having built their village, and made their wells or cisterns where they could drink, these great men, or giants, consumed all the provisions they could lay their hands upon in the surrounding country; insomuch that one of them ate more meat than fifty of the natives of the country could. As all the food they could find was not sufficient to sustain them, they killed many fish in the sea with nets and other gear. They were detested by the natives, because in using their women they killed them, and the men also in another way. But the Indians were not sufficiently numerous to destroy this new people who had come to occupy their lands. They made great leagues against them, but met with no success. After a few years of these giants being yet in these parts, either they began missing their own women and the natural agreement of their bodies for their height, or perhaps it was due to the counsel and inducement of the accursed Devil, but they began to indulge in vice, including using one another for the heinous sin of sodomy, both grave and horrendous, which they performed and committed publicly and openly, without fear of God and little ashamed of themselves. All the natives declare that God our Lord brought upon them a punishment in proportion to the enormity of their offence. While they were all together, engaged in their accursed sodomy, a fearful and terrible fire came down from heaven with a great noise, out of the midst of which there issued a shining angel with a glittering sword, with which, at one blow, they were all killed, and the fire consumed them. There only remained a few bones and skulls, which God allowed to remain without being consumed by the fire, as a memorial of this punishment. This is what they say concerning these giants, and we believe the account, because in this neighborhood they have found, and still find, enormous bones. I have heard from Spaniards who have seen part of a double tooth, that they judged the whole tooth would have weighed more than half a butcher's pound. They also have seen another piece of a shin bone, and it was marvellous to relate how large it was. These men are witnesses to the story, and the site of the village may be seen, as well as the wells and cisterns made by the giants. I am unable to say from what direction they came, because I do not know.

Source: Adapted from the translation of Sir Clements R. Markham in *The Travels of Pedro de Cieza de Leon, AD 1532–1550,* trans. Clements R. Markham (London: Hakluyt Society, 1864), 188–190. I have restored references to sodomy Markham refused to translate from Pedro Cieza de León, *La Crónica del Perú* (Madrid: Calpe, 1922), 181–183.

Commentary: *The influence of Christianity is here obvious, and the story seems to combine genuine Peruvian mythology with material from the traditional interpretation of Genesis 6:4 (8), which saw the sons of God as giants. Here, the Peruvians seem to be taking the story as literally as possible, wondering how giants would mate with human women, to violent ends. It is possible that the Peruvians intended to liken the rapacious giants to the conquering Spanish. The bones heralded as proof of the giants are almost certainly those of Pleistocene megafauna. The area around Puerto Viejo is known for its Ice Age fossils. In 1827, John Ranking, in his His-torical Researches, used this passage to conclude that the "giant" bones were those of elephants used by the Mongols to conquer the Americas in the Middle Ages. The same text can also be found quoted in Garcilaso de la Vega's* Royal Commentaries of the Incas *(9.9), where Marx Kaye used it to defend the existence of flesh and blood humanoid giants in a nonfiction column on Peruvian giants in the July 1947 issue of* Amazing Stories.

81. Giants Build the Great Pyramid of Cholula
Diego Durán
Historia de las Indias de Nueva-España y islas de Tierra Firme, Chapter 1
1585
Spanish
Atlantis
Discussion in AW, FG

In the beginning, before the light of the sun had been created, this land (Cholula) was in obscurity and darkness, and void of any created thing; all was a plain, without hill or elevation, encircled in every part by water, without tree or created thing; and immediately *after the light and the sun arose in the east* there appeared gigantic men of deformed stature and possessed the land, and desiring to see the nativity of the sun, as well as his occident, proposed to go and seek them. Dividing themselves into two parties, some journeyed to the west and others toward the east; these travelled; until the sea cut off their road, whereupon they determined to return to the place from which they started, and arriving at this place (Cholula),

The Great Pyramid of Cholula is the largest pyramid by volume in the world, encompassing more than 4.45 million cubic meters. It took a thousand years to reach its final form. When the Spanish conquered Mexico, they built a church atop the pyramid, seen in this photograph, and dedicated it to the Virgin in replacement of the rain goddess to whom it had been dedicated (Library of Congress).

not finding the means of reaching the sun, enamored of his light and beauty, they determined to build a tower so high that its summit should reach the sky. Having collected materials for the purpose, they found a very adhesive clay and bitumen, with which they speedily commenced to build the tower; and having reared it to the greatest possible altitude, so that they say it reached to the sky, the Lord of the Heavens, enraged, said to the inhabitants of the sky, "Have you observed how they of the earth have built a high and haughty tower to mount hither, being enamored of the light of the sun and his beauty? Come and confound them, because it is not right that they of the earth, living in the flesh, should mingle with us." Immediately the inhabitants of the sky sallied forth like flashes of lightning; they destroyed the edifice, and divided and scattered its builders to all parts of the earth.

    Source: Translated by Ignatius Donnelly in *Atlantis: The Antediluvian World* (New York: Harper & Brothers, 1882), 200–201.

    Commentary: *Durán here gives the words of a Native informant, which he immediately likened to the Tower of Babel story from Genesis. Although this is quite obviously a Christian-trained Native's application of the Genesis story to his homeland, Ignatius Donnelly in* AW *takes it as independent proof of Atlanteans in Mexico. Perhaps surprisingly given Donnelly's reputation as a fringe historian, his translation is exceptionally literal. It is interesting to compare this application of the Babel story to that of pseudo–Eupolemus (25). It is worth noting that emergence and migration myths were common across North and Central America, and the migration discussed here fits the pattern found across the Americas.*[1]

Note

    1. On such legends, see, e.g., George E. Lankford, *Native American Legends of the Southeast* (Tuscaloosa: University of Alabama Press, 2011), 112.

82. Quetzalcoatl Was a Toltec Giant

Bernadino de Sahagún
Historia General de Las Cosas de Nueva España 10.29
1590
Spanish and Nahuatl
Atlantis, Hyper
Discussion in AW, FG

The Toltecs were tall, of larger bodies than those living now, and being so tall they were able to run and advance quite far, for which they were called *tlanquacemilhuique*, which means that they ran a whole day without rest. They were also good singers, and while singing or dancing used drums and rattles called *aiacachtli*, with which they sang, composed, and organized curious songs in their heads. They were very devout, and frequently at prayer, and even worshiped one lord whom they held to be God, whom they called Quetzalcoatl, whose priest had the same name, that is to say Quetzalcoatl. This priest was very devout and fond of all the things of his god, and for this he was held in high esteem among them; and so, whatever he commanded of them, they fulfilled, with complete obedience; and he used to say many times that there was only one Lord and God, whose name was Quetzalcoatl, and that he did not want them to offer anything more than snakes and butterflies in sacrifice. All that he said, the Toltecs believed and obeyed, and they were no less followers of divine things than their priest, and, very fearful of their god, carried out his orders.

Source: Translated by Jason Colavito from Bernardino de Sahagún, *Historia General de Las Cosas de Nueva España*, ed. Carlos Maria de Bustamante, vol. 3 (Mexico: 1830), 112–113.

Commentary: *Bernadino de Sahagún was a Spanish missionary who drew on the accounts of Native informants in writing the history of New Spain. Although this passage is today used as evidence by fringe historians that Quetzalcoatl was from Atlantis, the risen Jesus, an apostle, or a European monk, Sahagún himself considered him to be only a man, writing elsewhere in his volume that Quetzalcoatl was a mere human who consorted with demons and whose soul now burned in Hell (*Historia general, *appendix to book 1*).*

83. Quetzalcoatl as White Visitor from Europe

Gerónimo de Mendieta
Historia eclesiástica Indiana 2.10
c. 1596
Spanish
Astro, Hyper, Prehistoric
Discussion in FG

The god or idol of Cholula, called Quetzalcoatl, was by universal account the most celebrated and had the greatest and most worth among the other gods. According to their histories, he came from the parts of Yucatán (although some said from Tula) to the city of Cholula. He was a white man, of portly person, broad brow, great eyes, long black hair, and large round beard; of exceedingly chaste and quiet life, and of great moderation in all things. The people had at least three reasons for the great love, reverence, and devotion with which they regarded him: first, he taught the silversmith's art, a craft the Cholulans greatly prided themselves on; second, he desired no sacrifice of the blood of men or animals, but delighted only in offerings of bread, roses and other flowers, of perfumes and sweet odors; third, he prohibited and forbade all war and violence. Nor were these qualities esteemed only in the city of his chiefest labors and teachings; from all the land came pilgrims and devotees to the shrine of the gentle god. Even the enemies of Cholula came and went secure, in fulfilling their vows; and the lords of distant lands had in Cholula their chapels and idols to the common object of devotion and esteem. And only Quetzalcoatl among all the gods was preeminently called Lord; in such sort, that when any one swore, saying, By Our Lord, he meant Quetzalcoatl and no other; though there were many other highly esteemed gods. For indeed the service of this god was gentle, neither did he demand hard things, but light; and he taught only virtue, abhorring all evil and hurt. Twenty years this good deity remained in Cholula, then he passed away by the road he had come, carrying with him four of the principal and most virtuous youths of that city. He journeyed for a hundred and fifty leagues, till he came to the sea, in a distant province called Coatzacoalco. Here he took leave of his companions and sent them back to their city, instructing them to tell their fellow citizens that a day should come in which white men would land upon their coasts, by way of the sea in which the sun rises; brethren of his and having beards like his; and that they should rule that land. The Indians always waited for the accomplishment of this prophecy, and when the Christians came they called them the sons of the gods and brothers of Quetzalcoatl, although when they came to know them and to experience their works, they no longer took them for heavenly.

Source: Adapted from the translation by Hubert Howe Bancroft in *The Works of Hubert Howe Bancroft*, vol. 3: The Native Races (San Francisco: The History Company, 1886), 250–252 with corrections by Jason Colavito from Gerónimo de Mednieta, *Historia eclesiástica Indiana,* ed. Joaquin Garcia Icazbalceta (México: Antigua Libreria, 1870), 92–93.

Commentary: *Mendieta is the oldest source to give the color of Quetzalcoatl's hair and skin in shades that cannot be found in indigenous depictions of the god. He is believed to have based his account on ethnographic research reported in the now-lost work of Fray Andrés de Olmos, who began studying the Aztecs in 1533 and whose work is referenced elsewhere in Mendieta's book. He was also one of Sahagún's key sources. It is from this account that the myth that Quetzalcoatl was white and European derives. Without actually citing the primary sources, writers like Ignatius Donnelly in AW and Graham Hancock in FG make use of his claims, ascribing them only to "legend."*

JUAN DE TORQUEMADA

Monarchia Indiana 6.24
1616
Spanish
Atlantis, Hyper
Discussion in AW, FG

The name Quetzalcoatl means Snake-plumage, or Snake that has plumage and the kind of snake referred to in this name is found in the province of Xicalanco, which is on the frontier of the kingdom of Yucatán as one goes thence to Tabasco. This god Quetzalcoatl was very celebrated among the people of the city of Cholula, and held in that place for the greatest of all.

He was, according to credible histories, high-priest in the city of Tulla. From that place he went to Cholula, and not, as Bishop Bartolomé de las Casas says in his *Apologia*, to Yucatán; though he went to Yucatán afterward, as we shall see. It is said of Quetzalcoatl that he was a white man, large-bodied, broad-browed, great-eyed, with long black hair, and a beard heavy and rounded. He was a great artificer, and very ingenious. He taught many mechanical arts, especially the art of working the precious stones called *chalchiuites*, which are a kind of green stone highly valued, and the art of casting silver and gold. The people, seeing him so inventive, held him in great estimation, and reverenced him as king in that city; and so it came about that though in temporal things the ruler of Tulla was a lord named Huemac, yet in all spiritual and ecclesiastical matters Quetzalcoatl was supreme, and as it were chief pontiff.

It is feigned by those that seek to make much of their god that he had certain palaces made of green stone like emeralds, others made of silver, others of shells, red and white, others of all kinds of wood, others of turquoise, and others of precious feathers. He is said to have been very rich, and in need of nothing. His vassals were very obedient to him, and very light of foot; they were called *tlanquacemilhuique*. When they wished to publish any command of Quetzalcoatl, they sent a crier up upon a high mountain called Tzatzitepec, where with a loud voice he proclaimed the order; and the voice of this crier was heard for a hundred leagues distance, and farther, even to the coasts of the sea: all this is affirmed for true. The fruits of the earth and the trees flourished there in an extraordinary degree, and sweet-singing birds were abundant. The great pontiff inaugurated a system of penance, pricking his legs, and drawing blood, and staining therewith maguey thorns. He washed also at midnight in a fountain called Xiuhpacoya. From all this, it is said, the idolatrous priests of Mexico adopted their similar custom.

While Quetzalcoatl was enjoying this good fortune with pomp and majesty, we are told that a great magician called Titlacahua (Tezcatlipoca), another of the gods, arrived at Tulla. He took the form of an old man, and went in to see Quetzalcoatl, saying to him, My lord, inasmuch as I know thine intent, and how much thou desirest to set out for certain distant lands; also, because I know from thy servants that thou art unwell, I have brought thee a certain beverage, by drinking which thou shalt attain thine end. Thou shalt so make thy way to the country thou desirest, having perfect health to make the journey; neither shalt thou remember at all the fatigues and toils of life, nor how thou art mortal. Seeing all his projects thus discovered by the pretended old man, Quetzalcoatl questioned him, Where have I to go? Tezcatlipoca answered, That it was already determined with the supreme gods that he had to go to Tlapalla, and that the thing was inevitable, because there was another old man waiting for him at his destination. As Quetzalcoatl heard this, he said that it was true, and that he desired it much; and he took the vessel and drank the liquor it contained. Quetzalcoatl was thus easily persuaded to what Tezcatlipoca desired, because he wished to make himself immortal and to enjoy perpetual life. Having swallowed the draught, he became beside himself, and out of his mind, weeping sadly and bitterly. He determined to go to Tlapalla. He destroyed or buried all his plate and other property, and set out. First he arrived at the place Quauhtitlan, where the great tree was, and where he, borrowing a mirror from his servants, found himself "already old." The name of this place was changed by him to Huehuequauhtitlan, that is to say, "near the old tree, or the tree of the old man"; and the trunk of the tree was filled with stones that he cast at it. After that he journeyed on, his people playing flutes and other instruments, till he came to a mountain near the city of Tlal-nepantla, two leagues from the city of Mexico, where he sat down on a stone and put his hands on it, leaving marks embedded therein that may be seen to this day. The truth of this thing is strongly corroborated by the inhabitants of that district; I myself have questioned them upon the subject, and it has been certified to me. Further more, we have it written down accurately by many worthy authors; and the name of the locality is now Temacpalco, that is to say, in the palm of the hand. Journeying on to the coast and to the kingdom of Tla-palla, Quetzalcoatl was met by the three sorcerers, Tezcatlipoca and other two with him, who had already brought so much destruction upon Tulla. These tried to stop or hinder him in his journey, questioning him, Whither goest thou? He answered, To Tlapalla. To whom, they inquired, hast thou given the charge of thy kingdom of Tulla, and who will do penance there? But he said that that was no longer any affair of his, and that he must pursue his road. And being further questioned as to the object of his journey, he said that he was called by the lord of the land to which he was going, who was the sun. [...]

The three wizards, seeing then the determination of Quetzalcoatl, made no further attempt to dissuade him from his purpose, but contented themselves with taking from him all his instruments and his mechanical arts, so that though he departed, those things should not be wanting to the state. It was here that Quetzalcoatl threw into a fountain all the rich jewels that he carried with him; for which thing the fountain was called from that time Coz-caapan, that is to say, "the water of the strings or chains of jewels." The same place is now called Coaapan, that is to say, "in the snake-water," and very properly, because the word Quetzalcoatl means "feathered snake." In this way he journeyed on, suffering various molesta-tions from those sorcerers, his enemies, till he arrived at Cholula, where he was received (as we in another part say), and afterward adored as god. [...]

Having lived twenty years in that city, he was expelled by Tezcatlipoca. He set out for the kingdom of Tlapalla, accompanied by four virtuous disciples of noble birth, and in Goatzacoalco, a province distant from Cholula toward the sea a hundred and fifty leagues, he embarked for his destination. Parting with his disciples, he told them that there should surely come to them in after times, by way of the sea where the sun rises, certain white men with white beards like him, and that these would be his brothers and would rule that land. [...] After that the four disciples returned to Cholula, and told all that their master and god had prophesied when departing. Then the Cholulans divided their province into four prin-cipalities, and gave the government to those four, and some four of their descendants always ruled in like manner over these tetrarchies till the Spaniard came; being, however, subordinate to a central power.

This Quetzalcoatl was god of the air, and as such had his temple, of a round shape and very magnificent. [...] He was made god of the air for the mildness and gentleness of all his ways, not liking the sharp and harsh measures to which the other gods were so strongly inclined. [...] It is to be said further that his life on earth was marked by intensely religious characteristics; not only was he devoted to the careful observance of all the old customary forms of worship, but he himself ordained and appointed many new rites, ceremonies, and festivals for the adoration of the gods; and it is held for certain that he made the calendar. He had priests who were called *quequetzalcohua*, that is to say, priests of the order of Quet-zalcoatl. The memory of him was engraved deeply upon the minds of the people, and it is said that when barren women prayed and made sacrifices to him, children were given them.

He was, as we have said, god of the winds, and the power of causing them to blow was attributed to him as well as the power of calming or causing their fury to cease. It was said further that he swept the road, so that the gods called Tlaloques could rain; this the people imagined because ordinarily a month or more before the rains began there blew strong winds throughout all New Spain. Quetzalcoatl is described as having worn during life, for the sake of modesty, garments that reached down to the feet, with a blanket over all, sown with red crosses. The Cholulans preserved certain green stones that had belonged to him, regarding them with great veneration and esteeming them as relics. Upon one of these was carved a monkey's head, very natural. In the city of Cholula, there was to be found dedicated to him a great and magnificent temple, with many steps, but each step so narrow that there was not room for a foot on it. His image had a very ugly face, with a large and heavily bearded head. It was not set on its feet, but lying down, and covered with blankets. This, it is said, was done as a memorial that he would one day return to reign. For reverence of his great majesty, his image was kept covered, and to signify his absence it was kept lying down, as one that sleeps, as one that lies down to sleep. In awaking from that sleep, he was to rise up and reign. The people also of Yucatán reverenced this god Quetzalcoatl, calling him Kukulcan, and saying that he came to them from the west, that is, from New Spain, for Yucatan is eastward therefrom. From him it is said the kings of Yucatán are descended, who call themselves Cocomes, that is to say, judges or hearers.

Source: Translated by Hubert Howe Bancroft in *The Works of Hubert Howe Bancroft*, vol. 3: The Native Races (San Francisco: The History Company, 1886), 255–260.

Commentary: *Much of Torquemada's account was derived from parallel passages in Sahagún and Mendieta's accounts but are better known in Torquemada's account, which is more detailed and adds some novelties not found in his predecessors' accounts.*

84. The Mixtecs' Glowing Stone Idol

Francisco Burgoa
Geográphica descripción de la América setentrional, Chapter 28
1674
Spanish
Astro, Hyper, Prehistoric
Discussion in FG

At the highest part of the hill of boulders to the east of the city of Achiotlan,[1] amidst the roughness and cragginess of the eminence, these Indians had their greatest shrine, where presided their false Pope. There they celebrated their sacrifices, and among their nefarious altars, one had an idol which they called "the heart of the place or of the country (*Corazón de Pueblo*)," and which received great honor. The material was of marvelous value, for it was an emerald of the size of a thick pepper-pod (capsicum), upon which a small bird was engraved with the greatest skill, and, with the same skill, a small serpent coiled ready to strike. The stone was so transparent that it shone from its interior with the brightness of a candle flame. It was a very old jewel, and there is no tradition extant concerning the origin of its veneration and worship.

Source: Adapted from the translation by Charles P. Bowditch in Eduard Seler, "The Wall Paintings of Mitla," *Mexican and Central American Antiquities, Calendar Systems, and History*, trans. Charles P. Bowditch, Smithsonian Institution Bureau of American Ethnology

Bulletin 28 (Washington, D.C.: Government Printing Office, 1904), 292. The first lines down to "idol" are my own translation, omitted from Seler's partial quotation.

Commentary: *Believers in the myth of the Crystal Skulls myth point to this and the monkey-jewel of 83 as testament to the existence of similar objects in the remote past. This particular idol suffered a terrible fate. The first Spanish missionary to visit the site rejected a fellow Spaniard's offer of 3,000 ducats for the gem and instead had it ground to dust, mixed it with water, poured out the liquid onto the earth, and stomped on it to show the powerlessness of the Mixtec gods.*

Note

1. Located in Tlachquiauhco tributary province, now known as Santa María Ascunción Tlaxiaco.

85. A Flying Saucer Emerges from Lake Titicaca, Deposits White Man
Pedro de Cieza de León
Chronicle of Peru 2.5
1540
Spanish
Astro, Hyper, Prehistoric
Discussion in FG

Before the Incas reigned in these kingdoms, or had ever been heard of, the Indians relate another thing much more notable than all things else they say. For they declare that they were a long time without seeing the sun, and that, suffering much evil from its absence, great prayers and vows were offered up to their gods, imploring for the light they needed. Things being in this state, the sun, shining very brightly, came forth from the island of Titicaca, in the great lake of the Collao, at which everyone rejoiced. Presently afterwards, they say, that there came from a southern direction a white man of great stature, who, by his aspect and presence, called forth great veneration and obedience. This man who thus appeared had great power, insomuch that he could change plains into mountains, and great hills into valleys, and make water flow out of stones. As soon as such power was beheld, the people called him the Maker of created things, the Prince of all things, Father of the Sun. For they say that he performed other wonders, giving life to men and animals, so that by his hand marvellous great benefits were conferred on the people. And such was the story that the Indians who told it to me say that they heard from their ancestors, who in like manner heard it in the old songs which they received from very ancient times. They say that this man went on towards the north, working these marvels along the way of the mountains; and that he never more returned so as to be seen. In many places he gave orders to men how they should live, and he spoke lovingly to them and with much gentleness, admonishing them that they should do good, and no evil or injury one to another, and that they should be loving and charitable to all. In most parts he is generally called *Ticiviracocha,* but in the province of the Collao they call him *Tuapaca,* and in other places *Arnauan.* In many parts they built temples in which they put blocks of stone in likeness of him, and offered up sacrifices before them. It is held that the great blocks at Tiahuanaco were from that time. Although, from the fame of what formerly had passed, they relate the things I have stated touching Ticiviracocha, they know nothing more of him, nor whether he would ever return to any part of this kingdom.

Besides this, they say that, a long time having passed, they again saw another man resembling the first, whose name they do not mention; but they received it from their forefathers as very certain that wherever this personage came and there were sick, he healed them, and where there were blind he gave them sight by only uttering words. Through acts so good and useful he was much beloved by all. In this fashion, working great things by his words, he arrived at the province of the Canas, in which, near to a village which has the name of Cacha, and in which the Captain Bartolomé de Terrazas holds an *encomienda,* the people rose against him, threatening to stone him. They saw him upon his knees, with his hands raised to heaven, as if invoking the divine favour to liberate him from the danger that threatened him. The Indians further state that presently there appeared a great fire in the heaven, which they thought to be surrounding them. Full of fear and trembling, they came to him whom they had wanted to kill, and with loud clamour besought him to be pleased to forgive them. For they knew that this punishment threatened them because of the sin they had committed in wishing to stone the stranger. Presently they saw that when he ordered the fire to cease, it was extinguished, so that they were themselves witnesses of what had come to pass; and the stones were consumed and burnt up in such wise as that large blocks could be lifted in the hand, as if they were of cork. On this subject they go on to say that, leaving the place where these things happened, the man arrived on the sea coast, where, holding his mantle, he went in amongst the waves and was never more seen. And as he went, so they gave him the name of *Viracocha,* which means "the foam of the sea."

Source: Translated by Sir Clements R. Markham in Pedro de Cieza de León, *The Second Part of the Chronicle of Peru,* trans. Clements R. Markham (London: Hackluyt Society, 1883), 5–7.

Commentary: *Pedro de Cieza de León was a Spanish conquistador and chronicler who recorded important information about Peru in a book of four parts. Only one of those parts was published in his lifetime, and the section translated here appeared first in Markham's 1871 translation. In their 1974 book* In Search of Ancient Mysteries, *Alan and Sally Landsburg edited an excerpt of this passage that had appeared in* National Geographic *in 1971 to eliminate the mythic material about the missing sun and instead presented this myth as relating the emergence of a glowing UFO from the island. Because Cieza de León went on to note that the Spanish considered Viracocha to be a memory of one of Christ's apostles, in FG Graham Hancock cited this same passage as proof that white Caucasians from a "lost" civilization civilized Peru. Most scholars believe the legends include influence from Catholic teachings.*

86. A Lost Race Builds Tiahuanaco
Pedro de Cieza de León
Chronicle of Peru 1.105
1553
Spanish
Atlantis, Hyper, Prehistoric
Discussion in FG

Tiahuanaco is not a very large village, but it is celebrated for the great edifices near it, which are certainly things worth seeing. Near the buildings there is a hill made by the hands of men, on great foundations of stone. Beyond this hill there are two stone idols, of the human shape and figure, the features very skilfully carved, so that they appear to have been done by the hand of some great master. They are so large that they seem like small giants, and it is clear that they have on a sort of clothing different from those now worn by the natives of these parts. They seem to have some ornament on their heads. Near these stone statues there is another building. Their antiquity and the want of letters, are the causes why it is not known who built such vast foundations, and how much time has since elapsed; for at present there is only a wall very well built, and which must have been standing for many ages. Some of the stones are much worn. At this part there are stones of such enormous size that it causes wonder to think of them, and to reflect how human force can have sufficed to move them to the place where we see them, being so large. Many of these stones are carved in different ways, some of them having the shape of the human body, which must have been their idols. Near the wall there are many holes and hollow places in the ground. In another, more to the westward, there are other ancient remains, among them many doorways, with their jambs, lintels, and thresholds, all of one stone. But what I noted most particularly, when I wandered about over these ruins writing down what I saw, was that from these great doorways there came out other still larger stones, upon which the doorways were formed, some of them thirty feet broad, fifteen or more long, and six in thickness. The whole of this,

The Gate of the Sun at Tiahuanaco was carved from a single ten-ton block of stone. Many claims have been made for the monument. Graham Hancock wrote in *FG* that the 48 condor-headed winged effigies on the face of the monument were actually Ice Age depictions of wooly mammoths. Arthur Posnansky and others have claimed the gate is a sophisticated calendar, though fringe writers can't agree whether it was a solar, lunar, or Venusian calendar (Library of Congress).

with the doorway and its jambs and lintel, was all one single stone. The work is one of grandeur and magnificence, when well considered. For myself I fail to understand with what instruments or tools it can have been done; for it is very certain that before these great stones could be brought to perfection and left as we see them, the tools must have been much better than those now used by the Indians. It is to be noted, from what now appears of these edifices, that they were not completed, for there is nothing but these portals, and other stones of strange big ness which I saw, some of them shaped and dressed ready to be placed on the edifice, which was a little on one side. Here there was a great idol of stone, which must have been placed there to be worshipped. It is rumoured that some gold was found near this idol; and all round there are more stones, large and small, all dressed and fitted like those already described.

There are other things to be said concerning Tiahuanaco, which I pass over, concluding with a statement of my belief that this ruin is the most ancient in all Peru. It is asserted that these edifices were commenced before the time of the Yncas, and I have heard some Indians affirm that the Yncas built their grand edifices at Cuzco on the plan which they had observed at the wall near these ruins. They even say that the first Yncas thought of establishing their court at Tiahuanaco. Another remarkable thing is, that in all this district there are no quarries whence the numerous stones can have been brought, the carrying of which must have required many people. I asked the natives, in presence of Juan de Varagas (who holds them in *encomienda*), whether these edifices were built in the time of the Yncas, and they laughed at the question, affirming that they were made before the Yncas ever reigned, but that they could not say who made them. They added that they had heard from their fathers that all we saw was done in one night. From this, and from the fact that they also speak of bearded men on the island of Titicaca, and of others who built the edifice of Vinaque, it may, perhaps, be inferred that, before the Yncas reigned, there was an intelligent race who came from some unknown part, and who did these things. Being few, and the natives many, they may all have been killed in the wars.

Seeing that all these things are hidden from us, we may well say. Blessed be the invention of letters! by virtue of which the memory of events endures for many ages, and their fame flies through the universe. We are not ignorant of what we desire to know when we hold letters in our hands. But in this new world of the Indies, as they knew nothing of letters, we are in a state of blindness concerning many things. Apart from these ruins there are the buildings of the Yncas, and the house where Manco Ynca, the son of Huayna Ccapac, was born. Close by are the tombs of the native chiefs of this place, as high as towers, broad and square, with doors towards the rising sun.

Source: Translated by Sir Clements R. Markham in *The Travels of Pedro de Cieza de Leon, AD 1532–1550,* trans. Clements R. Markham (London: Hakluyt Society, 1864), 374–379.

Commentary: *This text is often used to support the idea that refugees from Atlantis or a lost civilization built Tiahuanaco, though the author makes plain that this is not a fact but a supposition, based only on the local peoples' ignorance of their history. This same passage is summarized by the chronicler Garcilasao de la Vega (El Inca), the half–Incan son of a conquistador, in* Royal Commentaries of the Incas *3.1 (1609), in which El Inca adds on the authority of the half–Incan priest Diego de Alcobasa that "for the great sins of the people" the ancient inhabitants of Tiahuanaco were converted into the city's many statues.*

87. Atlantis in Bolivia

Juan de Santa Cruz Pachacuti-yamqui Salcamayhua
An Account of the Antiquities of the Kings of Peru
c. 1613–1630 CE
Spanish, with Quechua and Aymara
Atlantis, Prehistoric

This worthy, named *Thonapa*, is said to have visited all the provinces of the Colla-suyu, preaching to the people without cessation, until one day he entered the town of *Yamquesupa*. There he was treated with great insolence and contempt, and driven away. They say that he often slept in the fields, without other covering than the long shirt he wore, a mantle, and a book. They say that *Thonapa* cursed that village, so that it was covered with water. The site is now called *Yamqnisupaloiga*. It is a lake, and nearly all the Indians of that time knew that it was once a village, and was then a lake.

Source: Translated by Sir Clements R. Markham in *Narrative of the Rites and Laws of the Yncas,* ed. and trans. Clements R. Markham (London: Hakluyt Society, 1873), 72.

Commentary: *Written in the seventeenth century but not published until 1873, this myth inspired fringe writers to suggest that the Peruvians had a myth of Atlantis, or that Atlantis was located in Bolivia. However, the text states that a small village flooded, not that an island sank into the sea. It is one of many parallel stories recorded by the author in which the god Tunupa (Thonapa here) punishes various individuals and peoples for offending him.*

88. Viracocha Arrives in Peru after Atlantis Sinks

José de Acosta
Natural and Moral History of the East and West Indies 1.25
1590
Spanish
Atlantis, Hyper, Prehistoric
Discussion in AW, FG

It is no matter of any great importance to know what the Indians themselves report of their beginning, being more like unto dreams than to true Histories. They make great mention of a deluge that happened in their country, but we cannot well judge if this deluge were universal (whereof the scripture makes mention) or some particular inundation of those regions where they are. Some expert men say that in those countries are many notable signs of some great inundation, and I am of their opinion which thinks that these marks and signs of a deluge was not that of Noah, but some other particular, as that which Plato speaks of, or Deucalion's flood, which the Poets sing of; whatsoever it be, the Indians say that all men were drowned in this deluge; and they report that out of the great Lake Titicaca came one Viracocha, who stayed in Tiahuanaco, where at this day there is to be seen the ruins of ancient and very strange buildings, and from thence came to Cuzco, and so began mankind to multiply. They show in the same lake a small island, where they feign that the sun hid himself, and so was preserved; and for this reason they make great sacrifices unto him in that place, both of sheep and men. Others report that six, or I know not what number of men, came out of a certain cave by a window, by whom men first began to multiply; and for this reason they call them Paccari-tampu [literally: morning inn]. And therefore they are of the opinion that the Tampus are the most ancient race of men.

Source: Adapted from the 1604 translation by Edward Grimston in Father Joseph de Acosta, *The Natural & Moral History of the Indies*, vol. 1, trans. Edward Grimson and ed. Clements R. Markham (London: Hakluyt Society, 1880), 70–71. The text has been slightly modernized.

Commentary: *Ignatius Donnelly in AW suggested that such myths represented the survivors of Atlantis dispersing to new lands. In FG, Graham Hancock concurred, but replaced Atlantis with an unnamed lost civilization drowned by the post–Ice Age glacial melting. This passage is also used as evidence that Atlantis was located in modern-day Bolivia, on the strength of the author's identification of the flood with the deluge that ended Plato's island city, for the author noted that many believed Plato's Atlantis was the Americas (1.12) but that he himself thought it fiction (1.22). Instead, Acosta was the first to suggest that there was a land bridge between America and the Old World through which the Native Americans crossed (1.24), which turned out to be right.*

89. Men from a Lost Civilization Civilize Peru

Francisco de Avila
Narrative of the Errors, False Gods, and Other Superstitions and Diabolical Rites etc., Chapters 1–2
1608
Spanish
Atlantis, Hyper, Prehistoric
Discussion in FG

It is a most ancient tradition that, before any other event of which there is any memory, there were certain huacas or idols, which, together with the others of which I shall treat, must be supposed to have walked in the form of men. These huacas were called *Yananamca Intanamca*; and in a certain encounter they had with another huaca called *Huallallo Caruincho,* they were conquered and destroyed by the said *Huallallo,* who remained as Lord and God of the land. He ordered that no woman should bring forth more than two children, of which one was to be sacrificed for him to eat, and the other,—whichever of the two the parents chose,—might be brought up. It was also a tradition that, in those days, all who died were brought to life again on the fifth day, and that what was sown in that land also sprouted, grew, and ripened on the fifth day; and that all these three provinces were then a very hot country, which the Indians call *Yunca or Ande;* and they say that these crops were made visible in the deserts and uninhabited places, such as that of Pariacaca and others; and that in these Andes there was a great variety of most beautiful and brilliant birds, such as macaws, parrots, and others. All this, with the people who then inhabited the land (and who, according to their account, led very evil lives), and the said idol, came to be driven away to other Andes by the idol *Pariacaca,* of whom I shall speak presently, and of the battle he had with this *Huallallo Carrincho.*

It is also said that there was another idol called *Coniraya,* of which it is not known certainly whether it existed before or after the rise of *Pariacaca.* It is, however, certain that it was invoked and reverenced almost down to the time when the Spaniards arrived in this land. For when the Indians worshipped it they said, "*Coniraya Viracocha* (this name is that which they gave, and still give, to the Spaniards), thou art Lord of all: thine are the crops, and thine are all the people." In commencing any arduous or difficult undertaking, they threw a piece of coca (a well-known leaf) on the ground, as an oblation, and said, "Tell me,

O Lord *Coniraya Viracocha,* how I am to do this?" The same custom prevailed among the weavers of cloths, when their work was toilsome and difficult. This invocation and custom of calling the idol by the name of Viracocha certainly prevailed long before there were any tidings of Spaniards in the country. It is not certain whether *Coniraya* or *Pariacaca* were first; but as it is more probable that *Coniraya* was the more ancient, we will first relate his origin and history, and afterwards that of *Pariacaca.* [...] They say that in most ancient times the *Coniraya Viracocha* appeared in the form and dress of a very poor Indian clothed in rags, insomuch that those who knew not who he was reviled him and called him a lousy wretch. They say that this was the Creator of all things; and that, by his word of command, he caused the terraces and fields to be formed on the steep sides of ravines, and the sustaining walls to rise up and support them.

Source: Translated by Sir Clements R. Markham in *Narrative of the Rites and Laws of the Yncas,* ed. and trans. Clements R. Markham (London: Hakluyt Society, 1873), 123–124.

Commentary: *This passage is widely quoted in the diffusionist literature, cited by many authors as "proof" that an advanced civilization, almost always white (as Graham Hancock maintains in* FG), *launched civilization in Peru. As the full title of the work in question indicates, this was not an entirely unbiased work:* A Narrative of the Errors, False Gods, and Other Superstitions and Diabolical Rites in which the Indians of the Provinces of Huarochiri, Mama, and Chaclla Lived in Ancient Times, and in which They Even Now Live, to the Great Perdition of Their Souls. *Its author, although born in Peru, was a Spanish-educated clergyman who nevertheless recorded important myths and ethnographic details.*

90. White Rulers in Pre-Conquest Peru
Pedro Pizarro
Relation of the Discovery and Conquest of the Kingdoms of Peru
1571
Spanish
Atlantis, Hyper

The Indian women of the Guancas and Chachapoyas and Cañares were the common women, most of them being beautiful. The rest of the womanhood of this kingdom were thick, neither beautiful nor ugly, but of medium good-looks. The people of this kingdom of Peru were white, the color of wheat, and among them the Lords and Ladies were whiter, like Spaniards. I saw in this land an Indian woman and a child who would not stand out among white blonds. These people [of the upper class] say that they were the children of the idols.

Source: Adapted from the translation of Philip Ainsworth Means in Pedro Pizarro, *Relation of the Discovery and Conquest of the Kingdoms of Peru*, trans. Philip Ainsworth Means, vol. 2 (New York: The Cortes Society, 1921), 471.

Commentary: *In his 1963 work* In Quest of the White God, *Philip Honoré explicitly revised this passage to make all the upper class Native people blond, giving rise to the myth of blond Atlanteans in Peru. Genetic variation accounts for the appearance of varying skin tones in the Native populations. The key word in Pizarro's text is* rubios, *which Means translates as "blonds," but which can also mean "fair-haired," not necessarily yellow in color. In other words, Pizarro simply meant that their hair was light in color, as some Native Americans' hair remains to this day. Means also incorrectly said they were whiter "than" Spaniards.*

91. Caucasian Atlantis Descendant's Peruvian Mummy

Garcilaso de la Vega
Royal Commentaries of the Inca 5.29
1609
Spanish
Atlantis, Hyper
Discussion in AW

The Inca Viracocha died in the height of his power and majesty. He was universally regretted throughout the empire, and adored as a god, and child of the Sun, to whom they offered many sacrifices. He left as his heir his son Pachacutec Inca, and many other legitimate sons and daughters of the blood royal, as well as illegitimate. He subdued eleven provinces, four to the south of Cuzco, and seven to the north. It is not certainly known how many years he lived, nor how many he reigned, but his reign is generally said to have lasted more than fifty-years, and his body confirms this belief. I saw it in Cuzco in the beginning of the year 1570. Being on the point of starting for Spain, I went to the lodging of the licentiate Polo Ondegardo, a native of Salamanca, who was then Corregidor of Cuzco, to take leave, and kiss hands before setting out. Amongst other favours that he showed me, he said: "Well, as you are going to Spain, come first into this building, and you will see some of your own people that have been brought to light, and then you can give an account of them where you are going." I found in the building five bodies of the Kings Incas, three of men and two of women. The Indians said that one of them was the Inca Viracocha; and it proved his great age, the head being as white as snow. The second, they said, was the great Tupac Inca Yupanqui, great grandson of the Inca Viracocha. The third was Huayna Ccapac, son of Tupac Inca Yupanqui, and great-great-grandson of Viracocha. The two others did not appear to have been so old, for, though they had grey hairs, they were fewer than those of the Inca Viracocha.

Source: Translated by Sir Clements R. Markham in the Ynca Garcilaso de la Vega, *First Part of the Royal Commentaries of the Yncas*, vol. 2, trans. Clements R. Markham (London: Hakluyt Society, 1871), 91. I have modernized the spelling of Inca Viracocha's name for clarity.

Commentary: *In AW Ignatius Donnelly claims this passage suggests Aryan inhabitants of Atlantis colonized Peru. In the 1963 work* In Quest of the White God, *Philip Honoré explicitly revised this passage to eliminate references to Inca Viracocha's great age in order to claim that the mummy's hair was not white due to age and he was therefore Caucasian and blond rather than old. Viracocha could not have been less than fifty at the time of his death (c. 1438) and is routinely described as elderly in early Incan and Spanish accounts.*

IX

Pre-Columbian Trans-Atlantic Contacts

Europeans struggled to understand exactly how two continents full of people could have gone unrecognized for so many centuries until the Age of Exploration opened the Americas to the Old World. Not surprisingly, countless efforts have attempted to link the Old World and the New through long but secretive contact hiding beneath the surface of history. Known as "hyperdiffusionism," this body of thought suggests that cultural traits and genetic traits passed from the Old World (primarily Europe) to the Americas, where they decisively influenced the development of Native American cultures. The upshot was centuries of claims that Native people were degenerate Europeans or Jews, their culture a degraded simulacrum of superior Old World models, or worse—that they were savages who killed off a lost white race when they stormed into the Americas from Asia, squatting in the lost race's mounds and pyramids.

So prevalent was this belief that a lost race, almost certainly European and white, once were the dominant people of the ancient Americas that it gave rise to a religion (Mormonism) and served as the justification for the Indian Removal Act. U.S. President Andrew Jackson in his 1830 state of the union address charged that "In the monuments and fortresses of an unknown people, spread over the extensive regions of the west, we behold the memorials of a once powerful race, which was exterminated, or has disappeared, to make room for the existing savage tribes." In his mind, the presence of a lost white race justified removal of Native peoples, who had no claim to the lands that actually belonged to white Euro-Americans by dint of history.

Our previous chapter touched on this theme in exploring claims for contact in deepest prehistory, before the rise of historic civilizations like Phoenicia and Rome. This chapter will review texts that have been used to support trans–Atlantic contact with known historical civilizations, both in service of lost white race theories and in Afrocentric and native reactions against these ideas.

92. Classical and Biblical Voyages to the Americas
Francisco López de Gómara
Historia general de las Indias, Chapter 220
1552
Spanish
Atlantis, Hyper

Plato writes in the dialogues *Timaeus* and *Critias* that in the most ancient times there were great lands in the Atlantic sea and the Ocean, and one island called Atlantis, greater than Africa and Asia, affirming that these lands were truly solid and large, and that the kings of this island had ruled over a large part of Africa and of Europe. But with a great earthquake and rain, the island sank, drowning the people, and there was so much silt that it was not possible to sail the Atlantic sea. Some take this for a fable and many for a true history, and Proclus, as Marsilius Ficinus says, cites certain histories of the Ethiopians written by one Marcellus,[1] where this is confirmed.

But there is no cause to dispute or doubt about the island of Atlantis, for the discovery and conquest of the Indies simply clarify what Plato wrote of those lands; and in Mexico they call water *atl*, a word that seems like, if not actually to be, the name of the island. Therefore, we can say that the Indies are the island and the continent of Plato, and not the Hesperides, nor Ophir and Tarshish, as some have recently said, for the Hesperides are the islands of Cape Verde and the Gorgons, from which Hanno[2] brought back apes. Albeit there is some doubt of the navigation of forty days which Solinus assigns to it.[3] Also, it may be that Cuba, or Haiti, or some other islands of the Indies were those which the Carthaginians[4] found and forbade their population to journey toward, according to the accounts of Aristotle and Theophrastus in their works on the unknown marvels of nature. It is not known where Ophir and Tarshish were nor what they are, although many learned men, as St. Augustine says,[5] have sought which city or land Tarshish might be; St. Jerome, who knew the Hebrew

Many have tried to identify Atlantis with the New World. When the ruins of Maya temples and palaces were first uncovered in the nineteenth century, no one knew how old they were. Romantic illustrations, like this one by the artist Frederick Catherwood, and those of Jean Frederic Waldeck helped to make Maya ruins seem glamorous and exotic, and Europeans had a hard time believing Native peoples could have built them. Believing them much older than they were, Charles Etienne Brasseur de Bourbourg and Augustus Le Plongeon, among others, proposed that they were built by the descendants of Atlantis (from *Views of Ancient Monuments*, Frederick Catherwood, 1844/Library of Congress).

language very well, says in many places upon the prophets that "Tarshish" was used to indicate the sea[6]; and so when it says Jonah fled to Tarshish,[7] it means to the sea, where there are many ways to escape without a trace. Nor did the fleet of Solomon travel to our Indies because to go to them they would have to sail to westward, departing from the sea of Bermejo [i.e. the Red Sea], and not eastward as they actually sailed; and because our Indies have no unicorns, nor elephants, nor diamonds, nor other things which they brought from their navigations and took in trade.[8]

Source: Translated by Jason Colavito from Francisco López de Gómara, *Historia general de las Indias,* vol. 2 (Madrid: Calpe, 1922), 248–249.

Commentary: *Gómara was the first to identify Atlantis with America, and his elaborate speculation about ancient voyages to and from America launched the modern diffusionist school of fringe history. Today his work forms the basis for recent claims that the wealthy overseas Biblical land of Tarshish, found in the books of 1 Kings and 2 Chronicles, was Atlantis.*

Notes

1. See **49**.
2. Hanno voyaged to Africa in the 6th c. BCE and reported his adventures in his *Periplus,* wherein he describes his encounter with what appears to be chimpanzees.
3. Julius Solinus, a third century epitomizer, said the Hesperides or Gorgons' islands were forty days' sail into the ocean (*De mirabilibus mundi* 57).
4. See **93**.
5. Augustine, *Exposition on the Psalms* 48.6.
6. Jerome, *Commentary on the Prophet Isaiah* 18 at 2.16.
7. Jonah 1:3.
8. Referencing the products of Tarshish from 2 Chronicles 9:21 (= 1 Kings 10:22).

93. Carthaginians Discover America
Pseudo-Aristotle
De mirabilibis auscultationibus 84 (Aristotle 836b–837a)
c. 300 BCE
Greek
Atlantis, Hyper

In the sea outside the Pillars of Hercules they say that an island was discovered by the Carthaginians, desolate, having wood of every kind, and navigable rivers, and admirable for its fruits besides, but distant several days' voyage from them. But, when the Carthaginians often came to this island because of its fertility, and some even dwelt there, the magistrates of the Carthaginians gave notice that they would punish with death those who should sail to it, and destroyed all the inhabitants, lest they should spread a report about it, or a large number might gather together to the island in their time, get possession of the authority, and destroy the prosperity of the Carthaginians.

Source: Translated by Launcelot D. Dowdall in Launcelot D. Dowdall, *De mirabilis auscultationibus* (Oxford: Clarendon Press, 1909), at 836b–837a (not paginated).

DIODORUS SICULUS

Library of History 5.19–20
c. 60–30 BCE
Greek
Atlantis, Hyper

19. Since we have gone through the islands lying eastward, on this side within the Pillars of Heracles, we shall now launch into the main ocean to those that lie beyond them; for over against Libya, lies a very great island in the vast ocean, of many days' sail from Libya, westward. The soil here is very fruitful, a great part whereof is mountainous, but much likewise of level plains, which is the most sweet and pleasant part of all the rest; for it is watered with several navigable rivers, beautified with many gardens of pleasure, planted with divers sorts of trees, and abundance of orchards, interlaced with currents of sweet water. The towns are adorned with stately buildings, and banqueting-houses up and down, pleasantly situated in their gardens and orchards. And here they recreate themselves in summertime, as in places accommodated for pleasure and delight. The mountainous part of the country is clothed with many large woods, and all manner of fruit-trees; and for the greater delight and diversion of people in these mountains, they ever and anon open themselves into pleasant vales, watered with fountains and refreshing springs: and indeed the whole island abounds with springs of sweet water: whence the inhabitants not only reap pleasure and delight, but improve in health and strength of body. There you may have game enough in hunting all sorts of wild beasts, of which there is such plenty, that in their feasts there is nothing wanting either as to pomp or delight. The adjoining sea furnishes them plentifully with fish, for the ocean there naturally abounds with all sorts. The air and climate in this island is very mild and healthful, so that the trees bear fruit (and other things that are produced there are fresh and beautiful) most part of the year; so that this island (for the excellency of it in all respects) seems rather to be the residence of some of the gods than of men.

20. Anciently, by reason of its remote situation, it was altogether unknown, but afterwards discovered upon this occasion. The Phoenicians in ancient times undertook frequent voyages by sea, in way of traffic as merchants, so that they planted many colonies both in Africa and in these western parts of Europe. These merchants succeeding in their undertaking, and thereupon growing very rich, passed at length beyond the Pillars of Heracles, into the sea called the ocean: and first they built a city called Gadeira (Cadiz), near to Heracles' Pillars, at the sea-side, in an isthmus in Europe, in which, among other things proper for the place, they built a stately temple to Heracles, and instituted splendid sacrifices to be offered to him after the rites and customs of the Phoenicians. This temple is in great veneration at this day, as well as in former ages; so that many of the Romans, famous and renowned both for their births and glorious actions, have made their vows to this god, and after success in their affairs, have faithfully performed them. The Phoenicians therefore, upon the account before related, having found out the coasts beyond the pillars, and sailing along by the shore of Africa, were on a sudden driven by a furious storm afar off into the main ocean; and after they had lain under this violent tempest for many days, they at length arrived at this island; and so, coming to the knowledge of the nature and pleasantness of this isle, they caused it to be known to everyone; and therefore the Tyrrhenians, when they were masters at sea, designed to send a colony thither; but the Carthaginians opposed them, both fearing lest most of their own citizens should be allured through the goodness of the island to settle there, and likewise intending to keep it as a place of refuge for themselves, in case of any sudden and unexpected blasts of fortune, which might tend to the utter ruin of their government: for, being then potent at sea, they doubted not but they could easily transport themselves and their families into that island unknown to the conquerors.

Source: Translation adapted and modernized from that of G. Booth in Diodorus the Sicilian, *The Historical Library of Diodorus the Sicilian,* vol. 1 (London: 1814), 308–309.

Commentary: *Fringe historians have variously identified the islands discussed here (or, rather, the same island in two differing accounts) as Atlantis, North America, Brazil, the Azores, and the Canaries. Mainstream historians suggest that the islands were either heavily distorted accounts of ventures near western Africa or Spain, or that the accounts are entirely fictional.*[1]

Note

1. On the latter view: James S. Romm, *The Edges of the Earth in Ancient Thought: Geography, Exploration and Fiction* (Princeton: Princeton University Press, 1992), 127. On the former, C. H. Oldfather offered the suggestion in his notes to 5.20 in the Loeb edition of Diodorus.

94. Native Americans Reach Europe in 60 BCE

Pomponius Mela
De situ orbis 3.45
43 CE
Latin
Hyper
Discussion in BC

When he [Quintus Caecilius Metellus Celer] was proconsul in Gaul, he was presented with certain Indians as a present by the king of the Boti; asking whence they had come to these lands, he learned they had been seized by strong storms from Indian waters, that they had traveled across the regions between, and that at last they had landed on the shores of Germany.

Source: Translated by Jason Colavito from the Latin in Pomponius Mela, *De situ orbis libri tres*, ed. Karl Heinrich Tzschucke (Leipzig: 1816), 252. I am following the modern numbering system; Tzschucke labels this as the end of Book 3, chapter 5.

Commentary: *Q. Caecilius Metellus Celer was proconsul in Gaul from 62 to 59 BCE. The "Indians" refer to people of India, not Native Americans, with whom they were only identified more than 1,500 years later. Pomponius Mela, like Pliny after him, wrongly believed it possible to sail from India to the Atlantic by a northern water route. The tribe given here as the Boti are also translated as the Boii.*

PLINY THE ELDER

Natural History 2.67
77–79 CE
Latin
Hyper
Discussion in BC

The same Cornelius Nepos, when speaking of the northern circumnavigation, tells us that Q. Metellus Celer, the colleague of L. Afranius in the consulship, but then a proconsul in Gaul, had a present made to him by the king of the Suevi, of certain Indians, who sailing from India for the purpose of commerce, had been driven by tempests into Germany.

Source: Translated by John Bostock and H. T. Riley in *The Natural History of Pliny*, vol. 1, trans. John Bostock and H. T. Riley (London: George Bell & Sons, 1893), 99.

Commentary: *Cornelius Nepos (c. 110–c. 25 BCE) was a Roman biographer who later became confused for the protagonist of the story when Pliny's text was adapted in Late Antiquity (see below). He was also Mela's acknowledged source for the anecdote reported above.*

MARTIANUS CAPELLA

Marriage of Philology and Mercury 6.621
c. 411–428 CE
Latin
Hyper
Discussion in BC

The same Cornelius, after capturing Indians, sailed by Germany.

Source: Translated by Jason Colavito from the Latin in Martianus Capella, *Nuptiis Philologiae et Mercurii et de Septem Artibus Liberalibus,* ed. Ulrich Frederick Kopp (Frankfurt: 1835), 512.

Commentary: *Corruption is suspected in this variant of Pliny's and Mela's story, which both misidentifies Celer as Cornelius Nepos and makes him capture Indians and return to Germany with them. This version inspired Otto of Friesingen, the uncle of Frederick Barbarossa, who updated the tale to place it "in the time of the German emperors" and wrote that "an Indian ship with Indian merchants was taken on the coast of Germany which evidently had been driven there from the east," as recorded by Aeneas Sylvius Piccolomini (Pope Pius II) in his* Historia rerum ubique gestarum *(1477).*[1] *Columbus read Piccolomini's text and found in it the germ of the idea that one could sail to India.*

FRANCISCO LÓPEZ DE GÓMARA

Historia general de las Indias 10
1552
Spanish
Hyper
Discussion in BC

To sail from India to Caliz by the other part of the north, where there is extreme cold, is difficult and dangerous. And thus there is no memory among the ancients of any who came that way excepting one ship, which, according to the writings of Pliny and Mela, referring to Cornelius Nepos, came to rest in Germany; and the king of the Suevi, whom others call Saxons, presented certain Indians to Quintus Metellus Celer, who in that time governed France for the Roman people. If not, otherwise they were from the land of Labrador, and they (the Suevi) took them for Indians, deceived by their (skin) color. They also say that in the time of the Emperor Frederick Barbarossa, there arrived at port in Lübeck certain Indians in a canoe.

Source: Translated by Jason Colavito from Francisco López de Gómara, *Historia general de las Indias,* vol. 1 (Madrid: Calpe, 1922), 25–26.

Commentary: *Gómara was the first to link the "Indians" of the Classical story with the Native Americans. In so doing, he spawned a school of diffusionist literature, beginning with the Portuguese writer António Galvão in* Discoveries of the World *(1563) and continuing through Ivan Van Sertima's BC and even James Loewen's* Lies My Teacher Told Me[2] *(1995), that advocated pre–Columbian trans–Atlantic voyages. This story was a key piece of evidence for Native American activist and scholar Jack D. Forbes in* The American Discovery of Europe *(2007).*[3]

Notes

1. Translated by Henry F. Brownson in Francesco Tarducci, *John and Sebastian Cabot* (Detroit: H. F. Brownson, 1893), 280.

2. "Two Indians shipwrecked in Holland around 60 BC became major curiosities in Europe." James Loewen, *Lies My Teacher Told Me* (New York: Simon and Schuster, 1996), 46.

3. Jack D. Forbes, *The American Discovery of Europe* (Urbana-Champaign: University of Illinois, 2007), chapter 5.

95. Chinese Discover America in the Fifth Century

Yao Silian
Liang Shu, geography section entry for "Fusang-guo"
635 CE
Chinese
Hyper

During the reign of the dynasty *Tsi*, in the first year of the year-naming, "Everlasting Origin" [499 CE], came a Buddhist priest from this kingdom, who bore the cloister-name of Hui Shen, *i.e.*, Universal Compassion, to the present district of Hukuang, and those surrounding it, who narrated that Fusang is about twenty thousand *li* in an easterly direction from Da-han, and east of the Middle Kingdom. Many Fusang trees grow there, whose leaves resemble the *Dryanda cordifolia*; the sprouts, on the contrary, resemble those of the bamboo-tree, and are eaten by the inhabitants of the land. The fruit is like a pear in form, but is red. From the bark they prepare a sort of linen which they use for clothing, and also a sort of ornamented stuff. The houses are built of wooden beams; fortified and walled places are there unknown. They have written characters in this land, and prepare paper from the bark of the Fusang. The people have no weapons, and make no wars; but in the arrangements for the kingdom they have a northern and a southern prison. Trifling offenders were lodged in the southern prison, but those confined for greater offences in the northern; so that those who were about to receive grace could be placed in the southern prison, and those who were not, in the northern. Those men and women who were imprisoned for life were allowed to marry. The boys resulting from these marriages were, at the age of eight years, sold as slaves; the girls not until their ninth year.

If a man of any note was found guilty of crimes, an assembly was held; it must be in an excavated place. There they strewed ashes over him, and bade him farewell. If the offender was one of a lower class, he alone was punished; but when of rank, the degradation was extended to his children and grandchildren. With those of the highest rank it attained to the seventh generation.

The name of the king is pronounced Ichi. The nobles of the first-class are termed Tuilu; of the second, Little Tuilu; and of the third, Na-to-scha. When the prince goes forth, he is accompanied by horns and trumpets. The colour of his clothes changes with the different years. In the two first of the ten-year cycles they are blue; in the two next, red; in the two following, yellow; in the two next, red; and in the last two, black.

The horns of the oxen are so large that they hold ten bushels. They use them to contain all manner of things. Horses, oxen, and stags are harnessed to their wagons. Stags are used here as cattle are used in the Middle Kingdom, and from the milk of the hind they make butter. The red pears of the Fusang-tree keep good throughout the year. Moreover, they have apples and reeds. From the latter they prepare mats.

No iron is found in this land; but copper, gold, and silver are not prized, and do not serve as a medium of exchange in the market. Marriage is determined upon in the following manner:—The suitor builds himself a hut before the door of the house where the one longed for dwells, and waters and cleans the ground every morning and evening. When a year has passed by, if the maiden is not inclined to marry him, he departs; should she be willing, it is completed. When the parents die, they fast seven days. For the death of the paternal or maternal grandfather they lament five days; at the death of elder or younger sisters or brothers, uncles or aunts, three days. They then sit from morning to evening before an image of the ghost, absorbed in prayer, but wear no mourning-clothes. When the king dies, the son who succeeds him does not busy himself for three years with State affairs.

In earlier times these people lived not according to the laws of Buddha. But it happened that in the second year-naming "Great Light," of Song [458 CE], five beggar-monks from the kingdom of Kipin [in northeastern Afghanistan] went to this land, extended over it the religion of Buddha, and with it his holy writings and images. They instructed the people in the principles of monastic life, and so changed their manners.

Source: Translated by Charles G. Leland in Leland, *Fusang: The Discovery of America by Chinese Buddhist Priests in the Fifth Century* (New York: J. W. Bouton, 1875), 25–29. Because Leland did not translate unbroken, I have followed the paragraphing of G. Schlegel in "Problèmes géographiques: Les Peuples Étrangers Chez les Historiens Chinois," *T'oung Pao* 3, no. 2 (1892): 120–123.

Commentary: *This account of the land of Fusang from Yao Silian's official account of events during the Liang Dynasty (502–557 CE) was written at more than a century's remove from events, and then from hearsay collected by Yao's father, Yao Cha. In Chinese myth Fusang originally referred to the tree of sunrise in the mythic east, and in poetry it was later identified with Japan. However, Joseph de Guignes identified Fusang with America in 1761 (in turn identifying the Chinese as descendants of the Egyptians!), and Charles G. Leland revived the idea in 1875, placing Fusang in Mesoamerica. The 20,000 li distance would be 5,200 miles using Han-era measurements or 4,000 miles using Tang-era measurements. Some eighteenth century European maps based on Guignes's work claimed Fusang was British Columbia, California, or Mexico. Diligent research by scholars like Gustaaf Schlegel demonstrated the impossibility of this identification, not least because there were no horses in the Americas until the Spanish Conquest. Nevertheless, some still identify Fusang with Mesoamerica today, and the Fusang controversy contributed directly to later efforts to "discover" various Chinese voyages to America, such as those of Gavin Menzies.*

96. Vikings and the Magic Grapes of Vinland
Isidore of Seville
Etymologiae 14.6.8
c. 630 CE
Latin
Hyper

The Fortunate Islands signify by their name that they produce all manner of good things, as if they were happy and blessed with an abundance of fruit. For suited by their nature they produce fruit from precious trees; grape vines of their own accord clothe the hillsides; instead of grass, crops [i.e., wheat] and vegetables are common.

Source: Translated by Jason Colavito from the Latin in Isidorus, *Etymologiarum sive orginum*, vol. 1, ed. W. M. Lindsay (Oxford: Clarendon Press, 1911), at 14.6.8 (not paginated).

Commentary: *This myth, deriving ultimately from Classical sources (Pliny, Natural History 6.37), was later applied to the Vikings' American colony of Vinland on the strength of Isidore's introduction of grapes, not found in Classical antecedents. Isidore's text is repeated verbatim in Rabanus*

Maurus Magnetius, De Universo *12.5 (c. 844 CE). Geoffrey of Monmouth borrows it almost whole-sale to describe the Fortunate Island to which King Arthur is brought in the* Life of Merlin *(c. 1150).*

THE VOYAGE OF ST. BRENDAN 25

c. 900 CE
Latin
Hyper

Three days after, they [St. Brendan and his companions] saw near at hand an island covered all over with trees, closely set, and laden with such grapes as those, in surprising abundance, so that all the branches were weighed down to the ground, with fruit of the same quality and colour, and there was no tree fruitless or of a different kind in the whole island.

Source: Translated by Denis O'Donoghue in O'Donoghue, *Brendaniana: St. Brendan the Voyager in Story and Legend,* 2nd ed. (Dublin: Browne & Nolan Ltd., 1893), 155.

Commentary: *Mythic accounts of voyages across the ocean, like that of St. Brendan, were influenced by Isidore's descriptions of the Fortunate Islands and set the stage for what Europeans expected trans-oceanic lands to be like.*

ADAM OF BREMEN

Descriptio Insularum Aquilonis 38 (Gesta Hammaburgensis 4.38)
c. 1075 CE
Latin
Hyper

Moreover he (King Sweyn II Estridsson of Denmark) spoke of an island in that ocean[1] discovered by many, which is called Wineland,[2] for the reason that vines grow wild there, which yield the best of wine. Moreover that grain unsown grows there abundantly, is not a fabulous fancy, but, from the accounts of the Danes, we know to be a fact. Beyond this island, it is said, that there is no habitable land in that ocean, but all those regions which are beyond are filled with insupportable ice and boundless gloom, to which Martianus thus refers: "One day's sail beyond Thule the sea is frozen."[3] This was essayed not long since by that very enterprising Northmen's prince, Harald,[4] who explored the extent of the northern ocean with his ship, but was scarcely able by retreating to escape in safety from the gulf's enormous abyss, where before his eyes the vanishing bounds of earth were hidden in gloom.

Source: Translated by Arthur M. Reeves in Arthur M. Reeves (ed. and trans.), *The Finding of Wineland the Good: The History of the Icelandic Discovery of America* (London: Henry Frowde, 1895), 92–93.

Commentary: *The oldest reference to Vinland, Adam's text—a supplement often printed as the fourth part of his* Gesta Hammmaburgensis—*is very clearly informed by the Fortunate Island tradition of Isidore, which Adam appears to explicitly reference (as "fabulous fancy") even in telling his audience his version, obtained directly from King Sweyn II at his court, is actually true. Elaborations of the same story can be found below in the two Icelandic sagas that describe Leif Erikson's voyage to Vinland.*

THE SAGA OF ERIK THE RED 7

c. 13th century
Old Icelandic
Preserved, with variants, in the *Hauksbók* (c. 1302–1310) and the *Skálholtsbók* (c. 1450)
Hyper

During this time much talk took place in Brattahlid about making ready to go to Vinland the Good, and it was asserted that they would there find good choice lands. The discourse came to such conclusion that Karlsefni and Snorri prepared their ship, with the intention of seeking Vinland during the summer. Bjarni and Thorhall ventured on the same expedition, with their ship and the retinue which had accompanied them. [...] Now, before this, when Leif was with King Olaf Tryggvason, and the king had requested him to preach Christianity in Greenland, he gave him two Scotch people, the man called Haki, and the woman called Hækja. The king requested Leif to have recourse to these people if ever he should want fleetness, because they were swifter than wild beasts. Eirik and Leif had got these people to go with Karlsefni. Now, when they had sailed by Furdustrandir, they put the Scotch people on land, and requested them to run into the southern regions, seek for choice land, and come back after three half-days were passed. They were dressed in such wise that they had on the garment which they called *biafal*. It was made with a hood at the top, open at the sides, without sleeves, and was fastened between the legs. A button and a loop held it together there; and elsewhere they were without clothing. Then did they cast anchors from the ships, and lay there to wait for them. And when three days were expired the Scotch people leapt down from the land, and one of them had in his hand a bunch of grapes, and the other an ear of wild wheat.

Source: Translated by the Reverend J. Sephton in *Eirik the Red's Saga: A Translation* (Liverpool: D. Marples & Co., 1880), 22–24.

GREENLANDER SAGA

c. 13th century
Old Icelandic dialect of Old Norse
Preserved in the *Flateyjarbók* (1387–1394)
Hyper

Leif observed at once that his foster-father was in lively spirits. Tyrker had a prominent forehead, restless eyes, small features, was diminutive in stature, and rather a sorry-looking individual withal, but was, nevertheless, a most capable handicraftsman. Leif addressed him, and asked: "Wherefore art thou so belated, foster-father mine, and astray from the others?" In the beginning Tyrker spoke for some time in German, rolling his eyes, and grinning, and they could not understand him; but after a time he addressed them in the Northern tongue: "I did not go much further [than you], and yet I have something of novelty to relate. I have found vines and grapes." "Is this indeed true, foster-father?" said Leif. "Of a certainty it is true," quoth he, "for I was born where there is no lack of either grapes or vines." They slept the night through, and on the morrow Leif said to his shipmates: "We will now divide our labours, and each day will either gather grapes or cut vines and fell trees, so as to obtain a cargo of these for my ship." They acted upon this advice, and it is said, that their after-boat was filled with grapes. A cargo sufficient for the ship was cut, and when the spring came, they made their ship ready, and sailed away; and from its products Leif gave the land a name, and called it Wineland.

Source: Translated by Arthur M. Reeves in Arthur M. Reeves (ed. and trans.), *The Finding of Wineland the Good: The History of the Icelandic Discovery of America* (London: Henry Frowde, 1895), 66–67.

Commentary: *European voyagers expected that new lands across the sea would feature* *wild grapes and wheat based on Isidore's description of the Fortunate Islands, but later researchers instead took the above descriptions for literal accounts of the fruits of the New World. The search for North American territory where grapes grew wild consumed much of the modern search for Vinland, even after the discovery of L'anse-aux-Meadows, the only confirmed Viking settlement in North America. The grapes, however, play the role of the magical fruit of the Fortunate Islands in the sagas—they grow year round, even in winter—rather than any known fruit. There is no wheat indigenous to North America despite its appearance in the Fortunate Islands and in the literary accounts of Vinland.*

Notes

1. The northernmost Atlantic, to the west of Greenland, around the Arctic Circle.
2. The Latin literally reads "Winland."
3. Martianus Capella, *Marriage of Philology and Mercury* 6.666. Adam spelled the name of the mythic island, often identified with Iceland, as "Thile," while versions of Martianus give "Thyle," "Tile," "Thile," etc. The varying spellings derive from the Greek original, Θούλη.
4. Almost certainly King Harald III Hardrada of Norway (1015–1066). He fought Sweyn II of Denmark (c. 1019–1076) for control of the Danish throne. Harald renounced his claim to Denmark in 1064, after which he set out to explore the northern limits of his kingdom.

97. Medieval Africans Discover America

Bartolomé de Las Casas
General History of the Indies 1.130–131
1561
Spanish
Hyper
Discussion in BC

130. ... it was concluded that the King of Portugal should have 370 leagues to the west from the islands of the Azores and Cape Verde, from north to south, from pole to pole. And the Admiral [Columbus] says further that the said King Don Juan was certain that within those limits famous lands and things must be found. Certain principal inhabitants of the island of Santiago came to see them and they say that to the south-west of the island of Huego, which is one of the Cape Verdes distant 12 leagues from this, may be seen an island, and that the King Don Juan was greatly inclined to send to make discoveries to the south-west, and that canoes had been found which start from the coast of Guinea and navigate to the west with merchandise. [...]

131. Wednesday, July 4 [1498], he ordered sail made from that island in which he says that since he arrived there he never saw the sun or the stars, but that the heavens were covered with such a thick mist that it seemed they could cut it with a knife and the heat was so very intense that they were tormented, and he ordered the course laid to the way of the south-west, which is the route leading from these islands to the south, in the name, he says, of the Holy and Individual Trinity, because then he would be on a parallel with the lands of the sierra of Loa and cape of Sancta Ana in Guinea, which is below the equinoctial line, where he says that below that line of the world are found more gold and things of value: and that after, he would navigate, the Lord pleasing, to the west, and from there would go to this Hispaniola, in which route he would prove the theory of the King John aforesaid: and that he thought to investigate the report of the Indians of this Hispaniola who said that there had come to Hispaniola from the south and south-east,[1] a black people who have the tops of their spears made of a metal

which they call "guanin," of which he had sent samples to the Sovereigns to have them assayed, when it was found that of 32 parts, 18 were of gold, 6 of silver and 8 of copper.

Source: Translated by John Boyd Thatcher in *Christopher Columbus: His Life, His Work, His Remains*, vol. 2 (New York: G. P. Putnam's Sons, 1903), 379–380. The chapter numbered in modern editions as 131 is given as 132 in older Spanish editions, which have no 131.

Commentary: *Afrocentrists, beginning with Leo Wiener in 1920, use this text to suggest that the "black people" are Africans who discovered America before Columbus. However, Jack D. Forbes, a Native American activist and scholar who supported hyperdiffusionism, and others have noted that Columbus, who did not speak the Natives' language, could have been referring to the peoples of South America or Mesoamerica, who came to Hispaniola from time to time, and sometimes painted themselves black,[2] or may have had darker skin tones. Columbus may also have been interpreting material in light of his preexisting expectation about finding an "African" land southwest of the Cape Verde islands as noted above.*

Notes

1. The word translated here as "south-east" (*sueste*) was also an abbreviation for southwest in the 1500s and was interpreted as such by Antonio de Herrera y Tordesillas in his 1601 summary.

2. Jack D. Forbes, *Africans and Native Americans: The Language of Race and the Evolution of Red-Black Peoples*, 2nd ed. (Urbana-Champaign: University of Illinois Press, 1993), 15.

98. A Moor of Spain Discovers America
Al-Mas'ūdī
Meadows of Gold and Mines of Gems 12
c. 947 CE
Arabic
Hyper

On the limits where these two seas, the Mediterranean and the Ocean join, pillars of copper and stone, have been erected by King Hirakl the giant [i.e. Heracles]. Upon these pillars are inscriptions and figures, which show with their hands that one cannot go further, and that it is impracticable to navigate beyond the Mediterranean into that sea (the ocean), for no vessel sails on it: there is no cultivation nor a human being, and the sea has no limits neither in its depths nor extent, for its end is unknown. This is the sea of darkness, also called the green sea or the surrounding sea. Some say that these pillars are not on this strait, but in some islands of the ocean and their coast.

Some people consider this sea as the origin of all others. There are some wonderful stories related respecting it, for which we refer the reader to our book the *Akhbār al-zamān*; there he will find an account of those crews who have risked their lives in navigating this sea, and who of them have escaped, and who have been shipwrecked, also what they have encountered and seen. Such an adventurer was a Moor of Spain, of the name of Khashkhāsh.[1] He was a young man of Cordoba: having assembled some young men they went on board a vessel which they had ready on the ocean, and nobody knew for a long time what had become of them. At length they came back loaded with rich booty. Their history is well known among the people of al-Andalus (the Moors in Spain).

Source: Translated by Aloys Sprenger in *El-Mas'údí's Historical Encyclopædia entitled "Meadows of Gold and Mines of Gems,"* trans. Aloys Sprenger, vol. 1 (London: Oriental Translation Fund, 1841), 282–283.

Commentary: *Advocates of Islamic discovery of America routinely omit the first paragraph in order to make Khashkhāsh's voyage seem to be to America. Masʿūdī suggests that it was the ancient belief that no one lives on the other side of the ocean, and his passage makes no mention of where Khashkhāsh may have gone. Presumably Old World locations cannot be excluded.*

Note

1. Khashkhāsh ibn Saʿīd, according to modern Islamic writers, who identify him with Khashkhāsh al-Baḥrī ("the sailor"), said by al-ʿUdhrī to have died in 859 CE fighting the Norse. Al-Masʿūdī gives but one name, and I cannot identify whence his patronymic derives. Sprenger transliterated his name as Khoshkhash.

99. Columbus Allegedly Finds a Mosque in Cuba

Christopher Columbus
Journal of the First Voyage
Entry for October 29, 1492
Spanish
Hyper
Discussion in BC

Remarking on the position of the river and port, to which he [Columbus] gave the name of San Salvador, he describes its mountains as lofty and beautiful, like the *Peña de las Enamoradas*, and one of them has another little hill on its summit, like a graceful mosque. The other river and port, in which he now was, has two round mountains to the S.W., and a fine low cape running out to the W.S.W.

Source: Translated by Clements R. Markham in *The Journal of Christopher Columbus (During His First Voyage, 1492–1493)* (London: Hakluyt Society, 1893), 62–63.

Commentary: *Afrocentrists and advocates of Islamic discovery of America before Columbus purposely falsify this entry from Columbus' journal, given in Bartolomé de Las Casas's summary-transcription, to support the idea that Columbus actually found an Islamic mosque in Cuba, not just that the hill resembled one. In the above translation, Markham has followed the handwritten abstract of the journal made by Las Casas and later published in the original Spanish by Martin Fernandez de Navarette in* Colección de los viajes y descubrimientos *(1825). Las Casas later used the abstract in writing his* Historia de las Indias, *where a near-verbatim summary of the passage appears at 1.44. The original journal is now lost and survives primarily in Las Casas's summary.*

100. Columbus Finds White People on Hispaniola

Christopher Columbus
Journal of the First Voyage
Entry for December 13, 1492
Spanish
Hyper

The Christians reported to the Admiral that this was a handsomer and finer people than any that had hitherto been met with. But the Admiral says that he does not see how they can be a finer people than the others, giving to understand that all those he had found in the other islands were very well conditioned. As regards beauty, the Christians said there was no comparison, both men and women, and that their skins are whiter than the others. They saw two girls whose skins were as white as any that could be seen in Spain.

Source: Translated by Clements R. Markham in *The Journal of Christopher Columbus (During His First Voyage, 1492–1493)* (London: Hakluyt Society, 1893), 109.

Commentary: *Columbus's men saw these people on the northern coast of Hispaniola. As the text implies, the Native peoples had diverse skin tones (see **101**). The Europeans equated lighter skin with beauty, which would become a key element of the New World caste system. As with **99**, this passage appears in Las Casas's summary-transcription of Columbus' journal. In his* Historia de las Indias *a near-verbatim summary of the passage appears at 1.53.*

101. Pirate Finds Viking Descendants in Panama

Lionel Wafer
A New Voyage and Description of the Isthmus of America
"Of the Indian Inhabitants; their Manners, Customs, &c."
1699
English
Hyper
Discussion in AF

There is one complexion so singular among a sort of people of this country [the Kuna people of Darién, in Panama], that I never saw nor heard of any like them in any part of the world. The account will seem strange, but any privateers who have gone over the Isthmus must have seen them, and can attest the main of what I am going to relate; though few have had the opportunity to of so particular an information about these people as I have had.

They are white, and there are of them of both sexes; yet there are but few of them in comparison of the copper-coloured, possibly, but one to two or three hundred. They differ from the other Indians chiefly in respect of colour, though not in that only, their skins are not of such a white as those of fair people among Europeans, with some tincture of a blush or sanguine complexion; yet neither is it like that of our paler people, but it is rather a milk-white, lighter than the colour of any Europeans, and much like that of a white horse.

For there is this further remarkable in them, that their bodies are beset all over, more or less, with a fine short milk-white down; yet they are not so thick-set with this down, especially on the cheeks and forehead, but that the skin appears distinct from it. The men would probably have white bristles for beards, did not they prevent them by their custom of plucking the young beard up by the roots continually: But for the down all over their bodies, they never try to get rid of it. Their eye-brows are milk-white also, and so is the hair of their heads, and very fine withal; about the length of six or eight inches, and inclining to a curl.

They are not so big as the other Indians, and what is yet more strange, their eye-lids bend and open in an oblong figure, pointing downward at the corners, and forming an arch or figure of a crescent, with points downwards. From hence, and from their seeing so clearly as they do in a moonshiny night, we used to call them the moon-eyed; for they see not well in the sun, poring in the clearest day; their eyes being but weak, and running with water if the sun shine toward them; so that in the day-time they care not to go abroad, unless it be in a cloudy dark, day: besides, they are a weak people in comparison of the others, and not very fit for hunting, or other laborious exercises; nor do they delight in any such. But, notwithstanding their being thus sluggish and dull in the day time, yet, when the moon-shiny nights come, they are all life and activity, running abroad into the woods, and skipping about like wild bucks, and running as fast by moonlight, even in the gloom and shade of the woods, as the other Indians by day, being as nimble as they though not so strong and lusty.

The copper-coloured Indians seem not to respect them so much as those of their own complexion, looking on them as something monstrous. They are not a distinct race by themselves, but now and then one is bred of a copper-coloured father and mother, and I have seen a child of less than a year old of this sort. Some might be apt to suspect they might be the offspring of some European father; but besides that the Europeans come little here, and have little commerce with the Indian women, when they do come there, white people are as different from the Europeans in some respects, as from the copper-coloured Indians in others. And besides, where an European lies with an Indian woman, the child is always a *mostese* [= *mestizo*] or tawny, as is well known to all who have been in the West Indies, where there are mostesas, mulattoes, of several gradations, between the white and the black, or copper-coloured, according as the parents arc, even to decompounds, as a *mulatto-fina*, the child of a mulatto man, and mostesa woman, &c.

But neither is the child of a man and woman of these white Indians white like the parents, but copper-coloured, as their parents were: for so Lacenta [the Kuna Chief] told me, and gave me this as his conjecture how these came to be white, that it was through the force of the mother's imagination looking on the moon at the time of conception; but this 1 leave others to judge of. He told me withal that they were but short-lived.

Source: Lionel Wafer, *A New Voyage and Description of the Isthmus of America*, ed. George Parker Winship (Cleveland: The Burrows Brothers Company, 1903), 133–136. I have slightly modernized the orthography.

Commentary: *Wafer, a privateer, visited Panama in the spring of 1681 and spent many months with the Kuna people. He wrote about this after he returned to England in 1691. His description of the so-called "white Indians" of Darién (who still live in the region today) makes quite plain that the individuals involved were Native Americans with a genetic condition related to albinism, as twentieth century scientific investigation later showed.*[1] *Nevertheless, in the nineteenth and early twentieth centuries, these people became "evidence" of a Caucasian presence in the pre–Columbian Americas. When R. O. Marsh brought two "whites" to America in 1925 and claimed them as "Aryans," the Association for the Advancement of Science called on the U.S. government to pressure Panama to create a reservation for "white Indians" to preserve them from "destructive infusions of low-caste mixed white and negro blood."*[2] *Nazi scientists thought them the descendants of the Teutons or Vikings. Scott Wolter, in AF, calls them the descendants of the Knights Templar.*

Notes

1. Margot Lynn Iverson, "Blood Types: A History of Genetic Studies of Native Americans, 1920–1955," (doctoral dissertation, University of Minnesota, 2007), 2n3.
2. "Scientists Urge White Indian Reservation," *American Journal of Physical Anthropology* 9 (1926): 144.

102. The Lost Templar Fleet Leaves for America
Interrogation of Jean de Châlons at Potiers
Vatican Secret Archives, *Registra Avenionensia* 48, f450r
June 1308
Latin

Holy, Hyper

Discussion in AF

Then he [Jean de Châlons] said that, learning beforehand about this trouble,[1] the leaders of the [Templar] Order fled, and he himself met Brother Gerard de Villiers leading fifty horses; and he heard it said that he set out to sea with eighteen galleys and that Brother Hugues de Châlons fled with the whole treasure of Brother Hugues de Pairaud. When asked how he was able to keep this fact secret for so long, he responded that no one would have dared reveal it for anything, if the Pope and the King had not opened the way, for if it were known in the Order that anyone had spoken, he would at once be killed.

Source: Translation by Jason Colavito from document 155 in Heinrich Finke (ed.), *Papsttum und Untergang des Templerordens*, Vol. 2: Band: Quellen (Vorreformationsgeschichtlighe Forschungen, no. 5) (Münster: Aschendorff, 1907), 339.

Commentary: *The events described above allegedly occurred during the suppression of the Templar order in 1307. The above statements were made before Pope Clement V by a captive Templar whose other claims (that, for example, he managed a Templar prison where brothers*

The Old Stone Mill in Newport, Rhode Island was a windmill built for Gov. Benedict Arnold in the 1600s, but after the Danish antiquarian Carl Rafn said it was the medieval work of the Vikings of Vinland in 1839, the so-called Newport Tower entered fringe history as a major piece of "evidence." Today, based on the testimony of Jean de Châlons that the Knights Templar fled Europe in eighteen oared ships, fringe figures like Scott Wolter attribute the Tower to the Templars and their secret allies (Library of Congress).

were condemned to death for failing to deny Christ) are almost certainly false. It is the sole support for claims that the Templars had a fleet and used it to cross the Atlantic. Most scholars consider the coerced testimony of the Templars extremely suspect.[2] *The word translated as "galleys" (*galea, *ablative plural* galeis) *was in 1308 a Byzantine Greek term for an oared vessel, not an oceangoing sailing ship (galleon, derived from the same word after 1520).*

Notes

1. The arrest of the Knights Templar on October 13, 1307 on orders from French King Philip IV.
2. Malcolm Barber, *The Trial of the Templars* (Cambridge: Cambridge University Press, 1978); see pp. 101–103 for Jean de Châlons's testimony and its context.

103. Henry Sinclair Discovers America in 1398

Nicolò Zeno (the younger)
Concerning the Discovery, etc.
1558
Italian 1
Holy, Hyper

[HEADING OR SUB-TITLE.]

[Folio 45.] "Concerning the Discovery of the Islands Frislanda, Eslanda, Engroueland Estotilanda, and Icaria made by the two brothers Zeni Messire Nicolò, the Knight, and, Messire Antonio. One book, with a map of the said Islands."

[FAMILY HISTORY OF THE ZENI. By Nicolò Zeno the Younger, the Compiler of the Work.]

"In the year of our Salvation 1200, Messire Marin Zeno, a man very famous in Venice, was elected, on account of his great abilities and the force of his character, Governor in some of the Republics of Italy, in the administration of which he always bore himself so well, that he was beloved, and his name greatly reverenced, even by those who had never known him personally. Amongst other good works of his, it is particularly recorded that he quelled certain grave civil discords that arose amongst the Veronese, which might have been expected to give rise to war, if his extreme activity and good counsel had not been interposed. To this man was born a son, Messire Pietro, who was the father of the Doge Rinieri, which Doge, dying without leaving any children of his own, made Messire Andrea, the son of his brother Messire Marco, his heir. This Messire Andrea was Captain-General and Procurator, and had a very high reputation on account of the many rare qualities which he possessed. His son, Messire Rinieri, was an illustrious Senator, and many times a Councillor. From him descended Messire Pietro, Captain-General of the League of Christians against the Turks, who was called *Dragone* because he bore upon his shield a Dragon, instead of a *Manfrone* which he had first. He was the father of the great Messire Carlo, the most illustrious Procurator and Captain-General against the Genoese, in those perilous wars which were carried on whilst almost all the greater Princes of Europe were fighting against our liberty and Empire, in which, by his own valour, as Furius Camillus did for Rome, he delivered his country from the imminent risk which it ran of becoming the prey of its enemies; for which reason he acquired the cognomen *The Lion*, bearing the figure of a lion, in perpetual memory of his prowess, depicted upon his shield. The brothers of Messire Carlo were [*folio 46*] Messire

Nicolò, the Knight, and Messire Antonio, the father of Messire Dragone, to whom was born a son, Messire Caterino, who begat Messire Pietro, from whom descended another Messire Caterino, who died last year, the father of Messire Nicolò, who is still living."

[THE VOYAGE OF NICOLÒ ZENO. From His Letter to His Brother Antonio.]

"Now Messire Nicolò, the Knight, being a man of high spirit, after the termination of the aforesaid Genoese war in Chioggia, which gave our ancestors so much to do, conceived a very great desire to see the world, and to travel, and to make himself acquainted with the various customs and languages of men, in order that, when occasion arose, he might be better able to do service to his country, and to acquire for himself fame and honour. Therefore, having built and fitted out a ship from his own private means, of which he possessed an abundance, he left our seas, and, having passed the Straits of Gibraltar, sailed for some days across the Ocean, always holding his course towards the North, with the intention of seeing England and Flanders. While in these seas, he was assailed by a great tempest. For many days he was carried by the waves and the winds without knowing where he might be, until, at last, discovering land, and not being able to steer against such an exceedingly fierce storm, he was wrecked upon the Island Frislanda. The crew and a great part of the goods which were in the ship were saved; and this was in the year one thousand three hundred and eighty. The Islanders, running together in great numbers, all ready-armed, attacked Messire Nicolò and his men, who, all wearied by the storm they had passed through, and not knowing in what country they might be, were not able to make the least counter attack, or even to defend themselves against the enemy so vigorously as the danger demanded. Under these circumstances, they would probably have been badly treated if good fortune had not so ordered that, by chance, a Prince with an armed following happened to be in the neighbourhood. He, understanding that a large ship had just been wrecked upon the Island, hastened up, on hearing the uproar and cries which were made against our poor sailors; and, after chasing away the people of the country, he spoke in Latin, and demanded of what nation they were, and whence they came; and, when he discovered that they came from Italy, and were men of the same country, he was filled with the greatest joy. Then, assuring them all that they should receive no injury, and that they were come into a place in which they should be most kindly treated, and well looked after, he took them under his protection on his good faith."

"This man was a great Lord, and possessed some Islands called Porlanda, near to Frislanda[1] on the south side, the richest and most populous in all those parts. He was named Zichmni,[2] and, besides the aforesaid little Islands, he ruled over the dominion of the Duchy of Sorant, situate on the side towards Scotland."

[BY THE COMPILER.]

"Of these parts of the North it occurred to me to draw out a copy of a navigating chart[3] which I once found [*folio* 47] that I possessed among the ancient things in our house, which, although it is all rotten and many years old, I have succeeded in doing tolerably well, and which, placed before the eyes of those who delight themselves with such things, will serve as a light to make intelligible that which, without it, they would not be so well able to understand."

[From Nicolò Zeno's Letter to His Brother Antonio.]

"Besides being a man of such position as I have stated, Zichmni was warlike and valiant, and, above all, most famous in maritime affairs. Having gained a victory the year before over the King of Norway, who ruled over the Island, Zichmni, being a man who desired by deeds of arms to make himself yet more illustrious than he was already, had come down with his people to attack and acquire for himself the country of Frislanda, which is an Island much larger than Ireland. Therefore, perceiving that Messire Nicolò was a prudent person, and greatly skilled in maritime and military matters, he commissioned him to go on board the fleet with all his men, directing the Captain to pay him respect, and to avail himself of his counsel in all things, as that of one who knew and understood much from his long experience in navigation and arms. This fleet of Zichmni's consisted of thirteen ships (two only propelled by oars, the rest small vessels, and one ship), with which they sailed towards the West, and with little trouble made themselves masters of Ledovo and Ilofe, and of some other small Islands. Turning into a bay called Sudero, they took, in a port of the country called Sanestol, some boats laden with salt fish. At this place finding Zichmni, who, with his army, had come by land, having taken possession of all the country behind him, they stayed there a little.

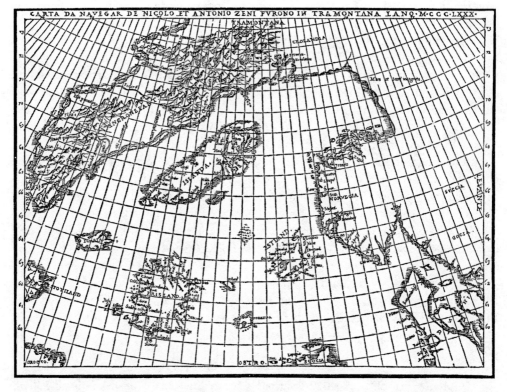

The Zeno map was long thought to be the oldest accurate medieval map of Greenland, despite Nicolò Zeno's own admission that the map was redrawn in 1558. Early explorers used the map to try to find the Northwest Passage, but most modern scholars now recognize that key elements of the map were copied from Renaissance-era maps available to Zeno. Charles Hapgood suggested that the map dated to the Ice Age (scanned from the *Facsimile Atlas to the Early History of Cartography* [1889]).

Then making sail towards the West, they came at last to the other headland of the Bay; thence turning round again, they found some Islands and lands which were all reduced into the possession of Zichmni. The sea in which they were sailing was, so to speak, full of Shoals and Rocks, so that, if Messire Nicolò had not been their Pilot, with his Venetian mariners, all that fleet, in the judgment of all that were in it, would have been lost, because of the little experience which Zichmni's men had in comparison with that of ours, who were, so to say, born, bred and grown old in the art [of navigation]. The fleet having thus done those things which have been mentioned, the Captain, by the advice of Messire Nicolò, decided to put into port at a place called Bondendon, to enquire as to the success of Zichmni's campaign. There they learnt, to their great pleasure, that he had fought a great battle and routed the enemy's army. In consequence of that victory, the whole island sent Ambassadors to make submission to him, raising his standards throughout the whole country and in the villages. Therefore, they decided to wait in that place for his coming, assuring themselves confidently that he must soon be there."

"Upon his arrival they made great [*folio* 48] demonstrations of joy, as well on account of the victory by land as of that by sea; for which latter all the Venetians were so much honoured and extolled that no one could speak of anything else than of them, and of the valour of Messire Nicolò. Then the Prince, who was very fond of valiant men, and especially of those who bore themselves well in naval affairs, sent for Messire Nicolò, and, after having commended him with many honouring words, and having praised his great activity and genius in the two matters (namely, the preservation of his fleet and the acquisition of so many places without any trouble to himself [Zichmni]), in which, as he said, he acknowledged a very great and important benefit, he made Messire Nicolò a Knight, and honoured, and made very rich presents to, all his people. Departing from that place, in the manner of a triumph for the victory achieved, he went in the direction of Frislanda, the principal city of the Island. This place is situated on its South-eastern side, at the entrance to a bay, of which there are many in that Island, in which they take fish in such abundance that they lade many ships with them, and supply Flanders, Brittany, England, Scotland, Norway and Denmark, deriving very great riches from this traffic."

[NICOLÒ JOINED BY ANTONIO. NICOLÒ'S VOYAGE TO GREENLAND, from his own written account.]

"All the above information, Messire Nicolò wrote in one of his letters to Messire Antonio his brother, praying him to come to find him, with some ships. And, as he [Antonio] was no less desirous than his brother had been to see the world and to have converse with various nations, and so to make himself illustrious and a great man, he bought a ship, and, steering in that direction, after a long voyage, and many perils passed, finally joined Messire Nicolò, safe and sound, who received him with the greatest delight, both because he was his natural brother and because he was his brother in valour also."

"Messire Antonio stayed in Frislanda and lived there fourteen years, four with Messire Nicolò and ten alone. There they grew into such grace and favour with the Prince that, partly to gratify Nicolò, but even more because he was excessively useful to him, he made him Captain of his fleet, and sent him with a great armament to attack Estlanda [Shetland], which is on the side between Frislanda and Norway. There they inflicted many injuries, but, understanding that the King of Norway was coming against them, with a large fleet of ships, to divert them from that war, they set sail in a Tempest so terrible that, being driven upon certain rocks, a great number of their ships were lost, and the remainder sought safety in Grislanda, a large Island, but uninhabited. The fleet of the King of Norway, likewise assailed by the same storm, was wrecked and totally lost in those seas. Zichmni, being informed of this by a small ship of the enemy which ran by good fortune into Grislanda, having first repaired his fleet, [*folio* 49] and perceiving himself to be near Islande[4] on the North, determined to attack Islanda, which, exactly in the same manner as the others, belonged to the King of Norway; but he found the country so well fortified and furnished for defence[5] that he could not but have been repulsed, as he had such a small fleet, and that, small as it was, likewise very badly provided both with arms and men. On this account, he abandoned that enterprise without having done anything, and attacked, in the same channels, the other Islands called Islande, which are seven in number, that is to say, Talas, Broas, Iscant, Trans, Mimant, Damberc, and Bres. Taking possession of them all, he built a fort in Bres, in which he left Messire Nicolò, with some small ships, some men and provisions; and, as it appeared to him that he had done enough for the time with so small a fleet, he returned safely to Frislanda with the remainder. Messire Nicolò, remaining in Bres, determined to set forth in the spring on a voyage of discovery. So, fitting out his not very large ships, in the month of July, he made sail towards the North, and arrived in Engroueland [Greenland]. There he found a Monastery of the order of Preaching Friars, and a Church dedicated to St. Thomas, near to a mountain which cast out fire like Vesuvius and Etna.[6] There is there a spring of hot water with which they warm the buildings in the Church of the Monastery, and the chambers of the Friars, the water in the kitchen being so boiling that, without any other fire, it serves all their needs; and bread, being put into copper cooking-pots without water, is cooked as in a well-heated And there are little gardens covered in in the winter, which, being watered with this water, are preserved from the snow and the cold, which in these parts, on account

This illustration of volcanoes in Iceland from Olaus Magnus's 1555 *Historia de gentibus septentrionalibus* (2.2), inspired Nicolò Zeno as he created a fictional geography for Greenland. This particular illustration shows heated rivers of lava or pitch emerging from the volcanoes to power a heating system, a detail Zeno took over for his version of Greenland. He also adopted uncritically Olaus Magnus's false belief that volcanoes burned from the bottom, illustrated here (scanned from the 1909 reprint of *Historia de gentibus septentrionalibus* [1555]).

This second illustration from Olaus Magnus's *Historia de gentibus septentrionalibus* (2.1) depicts a lake of burning pitch beside a village nestled at the foot of a volcano. Its arrangement exactly duplicates that of the Monastery of St. Thomas in Nicolò Zeno's fictional Greenland. The burning pitch would eventually inspire Fredrick Pohl to go looking for a real-life counterpart in Nova Scotia, where he wrongly thought the story actually occurred (scanned from the 1909 reprint of *Historia de gentibus septentrionalibus* [1555]).

of their situation being so very close under the Pole, are exceedingly severe. From these [gardens] are produced flowers and fruits and herbs of various kinds, just as they are in temperate climates in their seasons, so that the rough and wild people of these countries, seeing these supernatural effects, consider the Friars as Gods, and bring them fowls, flesh, and other things, and hold them all as Lords in the greatest reverence and respect. In the manner, then, which has been described, these Friars warm their habitations when the ice and snow are severe, and they can, in a moment, warm or cool a room by increasing the water to certain limits, or by opening the windows and letting in the fresh air."

"In the fabric of the Monastery no other materials are used than those which are furnished by the fire [volcano], for the hot stones, which issue like sparks from the fiery mouth of the mountain, are taken at the time when they are at their hottest, and water is thrown upon them, which causes them to split open and to become pitch, or very white and very tenacious lime, which, when once set [*folio* 50], never deteriorates. And the scoriae, likewise, when they have become cool, serve in place of stone to make walls and arches, as, when once they have grown cold, it is no longer possible to dissolve them or to break them, unless indeed they are cut with iron; and arches made of these are so light that they need no buttresses, but always last well and remain in good order. In consequence of their possessing such conveniences, these good fathers have erected such dwellings and walls that it is a wonder to see them. Most of the roofs are made in the following manner: the wall being carried to its proper height, they then incline it inwards little by little as they go on, so that in the middle it forms a rain-proof arch[7]; but they have not much apprehension of rain in those parts, because the Pole being, as has been said, very cold, the first-fallen snow melts no more until nine months of the year have passed, for so long does their winter last."

"They live on wildfowl and fish, since, in the place where the warm water enters the sea, there is a tolerably large and capacious harbour, which, by reason of the boiling water, never freezes even in the winter. Here, therefore, there is such a concourse of sea-fowl and fish that they catch an almost infinite number, which provides support for a great many people of the vicinity, who are kept in continual employment, as well in working on the buildings as in catching birds and fish, and in a thousand other matters which are required in the Monastery."

"The houses of these people surround the mountain, and are all circular in shape and twenty-five feet in diameter. They make them narrow in towards the top, in such a way as to leave above a little aperture, by which the air enters, and which gives light to the place; and the earth is so warm below that they do not feel any cold within. Hither, in the summer, come many boats from the neighbouring islands, and from the cape upon Norway, and from Treadon [Trondhjem], and bring to the Friars all the things which they can desire, and they trade with these for fish, which they dry in the open air and in the cold, and for skins of different sorts of animals. Thus they acquire wood for burning, and timber, excellently worked, for building, and grain, and cloth for clothing; for, in exchange for the two things mentioned,[8] nearly all the neighbouring people are desirous of selling their merchandise; and so, without trouble or expense, they have whatever they wish."

"There come together in this Monastery Friars from Norway, Sweden, and other countries, but the greater part are from Islande; and there are always in this port many ships, which cannot get away because the sea is frozen, awaiting the spring thaw."

"The boats of the fishermen they make like the shuttles which the weavers use to make cloth. Taking the skins of fishes, they fit them over the bones of the same fish, of which they make a flame, and sew them together, and lay them over many times double. They turn these boats out so strong and sound, that it is [*folio* 51] certainly a miraculous thing to observe how, during tempests, they fasten themselves inside, and allow them to be carried over the sea by the waves and the winds without any fear of being wrecked or drowned; and, if they do strike on the land, they stand safely many blows. They have a sleeve at the bottom which they keep tied in the middle, and, when water enters the boat, they take it in one half [of the sleeve] and close it above with two wooden shutters, then taking the ligature from below, they drive out the water. However many times they have to do this, they do it without any trouble or danger."

"Since the water of the Monastery is sulphurous, it is conduced into the rooms of the Superiors by means of certain vessels of copper, tin, or stone, so hot that, like a stove, it warms the habitation very well, without introducing any stench or other noxious odour. Besides this, they lead other spring water through a culvert underground, so that it may not freeze, as far as the middle of the courtyard, where it falls into a large copper vessel which stands in the midst of a boiling spring, and so they warm the water for drinking and for watering their gardens."

"They have in the mountains all the commodities which they can most desire. Nor do these good fathers put themselves to any other trouble than that of cultivating their gardens, and making beautiful, charming, and, above all, commodious buildings; nor tor this do they want for good, clever, and industrious workmen, although pagans, and they pay them largely. To those who bring them fruits and seeds they are liberal without limit, and lavish in their expenditure. On these accounts, there is a very great concourse of people there seeking employment and instruction, in order to earn in that place such good wages and better living. They use, for the most part, the Latin language, especially the Superiors and the principal men of the Monastery."

[By the Compiler.]

"So much is known of Engroueland [Greenland], concerning which Messire Nicolò described all the foregoing particulars, and more especially the river discovered by him, as may be seen in the map made by me. At last, not being used to such severe cold, he sickened, and, soon after returning to Frisland, he died there."

"Messire Antonio succeeded to his riches and honours, but, although he tried many ways, and begged and prayed much, he could never succeed in getting back to his own home, because Zichmni, being a man of spirit and valour, had resolved from the bottom of his heart to make himself master of the sea. Wherefore, availing himself of the services of Messire Antonio, he desired that he should sail with several small ships towards the West, to obtain information as to the existence of some very rich and populous Islands on that side, discovered by some of his fishermen; which discovery Messire Antonio narrates in one of his letters, written to his brother Messire Carlo, with so much detail that, except that we have changed the old language and style, we have let the matter stand as it was."

[The Frisland Fisherman's Story.[9] From Antonio Zeno's Letter to His Brother Carlo.]

[*folio* 52.] "Twenty-six years ago, four fishing boats sailed [from Frisland], which, driven by a great tempest, wandered many days, lost, as it were, upon the sea, until, when at last the weather moderated, they found an Island, called Estotilanda, lying to the Westward, and distant from Frislanda more than a thousand *miglia*, on which one of the boats was wrecked. Six men who were in it were seized by the islanders, and conducted to a most beautiful and largely populated city. The King who ruled there summoned many interpreters, but found none who had any knowledge of the language of these fishermen, except one who spoke Latin, and who had been cast upon the same Island by a similar tempest. This man, demanding of the castaways, on behalf of the King, who they were and whence they came, gathered all their statements, and reported their effect to the King, who, when he fully understood their case, willed that they should stay in that country. Wherefore, obeying this command, because they could not do otherwise, they remained five years in the Island and learnt the language. One of them in particular, having been in different parts of the Island, reports that it is very rich, and abundant in all the good things of this world; that it is rather smaller than Iceland, but more fertile, having in the middle a very high mountain from which spring four rivers, which water it. The inhabitants are quick-witted, and possess all the arts which we have. It is believed that in earlier times they have had commerce with our countrymen, because this man said that he saw Latin books in the King's library, which none of them at the present time understand. They have a distinct language, and letters. They get, by mining, metals of all sorts, and, above all, they have abundance of gold. Their trade is with Engroueland [Greenland], whence they receive furs, and sulphur, and pitch. And, towards the South, he says, there is a great country very rich in gold, and populous. They sow grain and make beer, which is a kind of beverage which the Northern people use as we do wine. They have woods of immense extent. They construct their buildings with walls, and there are many cities and villages. They make small ships and navigate them, but they have not the loadstone, nor can they indicate the North by the compass. On this account, these fishermen were held in great esteem, so much so that the king despatched them, with twelve small ships, towards the South, to the country which they call Drogio[10]; but during the voyage they met with so

great a tempest that they gave themselves up for lost. Nevertheless, in trying to escape from
one cruel death, they delivered themselves into the clutches of another much more terrible,
for, being taken into the country,[11] most of them were eaten by the ferocious inhabitants,
who feed upon human flesh, which they consider a most savoury viand."

"But this fisherman, with his companions, by showing the natives the method of taking
fish with nets, saved their lives; and, fishing every day in the sea, and in the fresh waters, they
caught many fish, and gave them to the Chiefs; by which means [*folio* 53] the fisherman
acquired so much favour that he was held dear, and was beloved and much honoured by
everyone. His fame spread among the adjacent nations, and a neighbouring Chief conceived
so great a desire to have him in his service, and to see how he exercised his wonderful art of
taking fish, that he made war upon the other Chief, by whom the fisherman was protected;
and prevailing at last, because he was the more powerful and warlike, the fisherman was
handed over to him, with his companions. During the thirteen years which he spent continuously in the parts aforesaid, he says that he was transmitted in this manner to more than
twenty-five Chiefs, they being constantly stirred up to make war one against another, solely
for the sake of having him in their service; and so, as he went on wandering, without ever
having a fixed abode in one place for any length of time, he came to know from actual experience almost all those parts."

"He says that it is a very large country, and like a new world[12]; but the people are ignorant, and destitute of all good qualities, for they all go naked, and suffer cruelly from the
cold; nor have they learnt how to cover themselves with the skins of the beasts which they
take in hunting. They have no metal of any sort. They live by hunting, and carry lances of
wood sharpened at the point, and bows, the strings of which are made of the skins of animals.
They are a people of great ferocity, and fight together to the death, and eat one another.
They have Chiefs, and certain laws, which differ much amongst them."

"But, the further one goes towards the South-west, the greater civilization one finds,
because there the climate is more temperate, so that there are cities, and temples of idols
wherein they sacrifice men, whom they afterwards eat. In these parts they have some knowledge of gold and silver, and use them."

"Now this fisherman, having dwelt in these countries so many years, purposed, if he
could, to return to his fatherland; but his companions, despairing of the possibility of ever
seeing it again, let him depart, wishing him a successful journey, and they themselves
remained where they were. Then he, commending them to God, fled through the woods
towards Drogio, and was made most welcome, and kindly treated by a neighbouring Chief
who knew him, and who had great enmity against the other Chief [from whom he had run
away]; and so, going from the hand of one to that of another of the same Chiefs with whom
he had been before, after much time and considerable hardships and fatigues, he arrived
finally in Drogio, where he dwelt the three following years. Then, by good fortune, he learnt
from the Countryfolk that some ships had arrived upon the coast, and he conceived good
hopes of accomplishing his desire. He went to the coast, and, enquiring from what country
the ships came, learnt to his great pleasure that they were from Estotilanda. Then, having
begged to be taken away, he was willingly received, because he knew the language of the
country; and, there being no one among the sailors who understood it, they used him as
their interpreter. Afterwards, he frequently made [*folio* 54] that voyage with them, until he
grew very rich, and, having built and equipped a ship of his own, returned to Frislanda, bear-

ing to the Lord of it [Zichmni] news of the discovery of that very rich country. In all this he was credited, because the sailors confirmed as true many other new things which he reported. It is on account of this affair that the Lord Zichmni has resolved to send me with a fleet towards those parts; and there are so many who wish to go over there, on account of the novelty of the thing, that I think we shall be a very strong force, without any public expense."

[BY THE COMPILER.]

"This is what is contained in the letter which I have cited above. I have stated its tenor here in order that another voyage which Messire Antonio made may be better understood. On this voyage he sailed with many people and ships, not, however, being appointed Captain, as he thought at first he would have been, because Zichmni decided to make the exploration in person; and I have a letter about this expedition, which states as follows":

[THE LETTER FROM ANTONIO ZENO TO HIS BROTHER CARLO ZENO DESCRIBING HIS WESTERN VOYAGE IN VAIN SEARCH OF ESTOTILANDA AND DROGIO, AND THE FINDING OF ICARIA AND GREENLAND.]

"Our great preparations to go into Estotilanda were commenced under an evil omen; for, three days exactly before our departure, the fisherman, who was to have been our guide, died. Notwithstanding this, our Chief would not abandon the intended voyage, and took with him as guides, instead of the dead fisherman, some of the sailors who had returned from that Island with the latter. And so we steered our course towards the West, and discovered some islands subject to Frislanda; and, passing certain rocks, we stopped at Ledovo, where we remained seven days for the sake of the repose, and to furnish the Beet with some necessary things. Departing from thence, we arrived, on the 1st of July, at the Island of Ilofe; and, because the wind made for us, we passed onward, without the least thing to hinder us, and went far out into the deepest ocean. Not long after, a storm assailed us, so fierce that, for eight days at a stretch, it kept us at work, and cast us about so that we knew not where we might be, and we lost a large proportion of the ships. At last, the weather having become calm, we got together the ships which had been separated from the others, and, sailing with a good wind, we discovered land in the West. Keeping our course directly for it, we arrived in a quiet and secure port, and we saw people, almost infinite in number, armed and ready to strike, running towards the shore to defend the Island. Thereupon, Zichmni ordered his people to make signs of peace, and the Islanders sent to us ten men, who could speak ten languages, but we could not understand any of them, except one who was from Islanda [Iceland]. This man, being conducted into the presence of our Prince, and asked by him how they called the Island, and what people inhabited it, and who ruled over it, replied, that the Island was called Icaria, and that all the Kings who had ruled over it were called Icarus,[13] after its first King, who, as they said, [*folio* 55] was the son of Daedalus, King of Scotland, who, having made himself master of the Island, left his son there as King, and left also those laws which the Islanders still used; and that, after these things were done, purposing to sail further on, he was drowned in a great storm; that, on account of his death in this manner, they still called that sea Icarian, and the King of the Island Icarus. Also that, because they were satisfied with that state which God had given them, they did not wish to change their customs in any particular, nor would they receive any foreigner; that they therefore prayed our Prince that he would not seek to violate those laws which they had preserved in happy memory of their King, and had observed down to that time; adding that he would not be able to do it without his own certain destruction, they being all prepared to abandon life, rather than to give up, on any account, the use of those laws. Nevertheless, in order that it might not appear that they altogether refused intercourse with other men, they said, in conclusion, that they were willing to receive one of us, and to give him a high position amongst them, and to do so solely in order to learn my (*sic*) language and to have an account of our customs, just as they had already received those other ten men who had come to the Island from ten other different countries. To these things our Prince made no other reply than to make enquiry as to where there was a good harbour. Then he feigned to depart, and, making a circuit of the Island, in full sail, put into a port pointed out to him on the Eastern side. There the sailors disembarked, to obtain wood and water, with as much despatch as possible, as they doubted whether they might not be attacked by the Islanders; nor was their fear vain, for those who dwelt near by, making signs to the others with fire and smoke, quickly armed themselves, and, the others joining them, they came down to the shore, armed with weapons and arrows, in such numbers against our people that many were left killed and wounded; nor did it avail us that we made signs of peace to them, for, as if they were fighting for their all, they grew more and more exasperated. Therefore, we were forced to set sail, and to go along in a great circle round the Island, being always accompanied, along the mountains and shores, by an infinite number of armed men. Then, doubling the Cape at the North of the Island, we found very great shoals, amongst which, for ten days continuously, we were in much danger of losing the fleet, but, luckily for us, the weather was very fine all the while. Passing thence as far as the Cape on the hast of the island, we saw the Islanders, always keeping pace with us on the summits of the mountains and along the shore, with cries and arrow-shots from afar, showing towards us more and more the same inimical mind. We therefore determined to stop in some safe port, and to see if we could not speak [*folio* 56] once more to the Icelander, but we did not succeed in this design, for the people, little better than beasts in this respect, remained continually in arms, with the deliberate intention of resisting us if we should attempt to land. Wherefore Zichmni, seeing that he could not do anything, and that, if he should remain obstinate in his purpose, victuals would soon be wanting in the fleet, set sail with a fair wind and sailed six days to the Westward; but, the wind changing to the South-west, and the sea therefore becoming rough, the fleet ran before the wind for four days. At last land was discovered, but we greatly feared to approach it, on account of the swelling seas, and because the land observed was unknown to us. Nevertheless, by God's aid, the wind dropped and it became calm. Then some men from the fleet went to the land in rowing boats, and not long after returned and reported, to our very great delight, that they had found a very good country and a still better harbour. At which news, having hauled up our ships and small vessels, we went on shore, and, having entered a good harbour, we saw afar off a great mountain which cast forth smoke[14]; this gave us hope that inhabitants would be found in the Island, nor, for all that it was so far off, did Zichmni delay sending a hundred good soldiers to reconnoitre the country and to report what kind of people inhabited it. In the meanwhile, the fleet was supplied with water and wood, and many fishes and sea-fowl were caught; they also found there so many birds' eggs that the half-famished men were able to eat their fill."[15]

"While we remained here, the month of June[16] came in, during which season the air in the island was more temperate and mild than can be expressed. In spite of this, not seeing anyone there, we began to suspect that so beautiful a place was, nevertheless, uninhabited, and we gave to the port and to the point of land which ran out into the sea the names of Trin and Capo di Trin. The hundred soldiers who had gone away returned, after eight days, and reported that they had been over the island and to the mountain; that the smoke proceeded from it because, as they had proved, at the bottom of it was a great fire; that there was a spring from which was produced a certain matter, like pitch, which ran into the sea[17]; that many people inhabited the neighbouring parts, half savage, and sheltering themselves in caves; that these were of small stature and very timid, for, directly they saw the soldiers, they fled into their caves; and that there was a large river there, and a good and safe harbour.[18] Zichmni, being informed of these things, and seeing that the place had a healthy and pure climate, and very good soil, and rivers, and so many peculiar advantages, began to think of making his dwelling there, and of building a city. But his people, who had already endured a voyage so full of hardships, began to rebel, and to say that they wished to return home, because, [*folio* 57] as the winter was near, if they let it come in, they would not be able afterwards to get away until the following summer; so he retained only the rowing boats, with those men who were willing to remain there, sending back all the others in the remaining ships; and he desired, against my will, that I should be the Captain. I departed therefore, because I could not do otherwise, and sailed towards the East for twenty days continuously without ever seeing land; then, turning towards the South-east, after five more days I sighted land, and found that I had reached the Island Neome. Knowing this country, I perceived that I had passed Islanda. Wherefore, having procured fresh provisions from the Islanders, who were under the dominion of Zichmni, I sailed in three days, with a fair wind, to Frislanda, where the people, who believed that they had lost their Prince, because of the long time that we had spent upon the voyage, received us with signs of the greatest joy.

[BY THE COMPILER.]

"After this letter I find nothing further, except what I judge from conjecture. I gather, from a clause in another letter, which I give below, that Zichmni built a town in the port of the island newly discovered by him; also, that he did his best to explore the whole country, together with the rivers in various parts of Engroueland [Greenland], because I see these described in detail in the map, but the description is lost. The clause in the letter is as follows:—"

[EXTRACT FROM ANOTHER LETTER FROM ANTONIO ZENO TO CARLO ZENO.]

"As to those things which you seek to know from me concerning the customs of the men, the animals, and the neighbouring countries, I have written about all these a separate book, which, please God, I shall bring home with me. In it I have described the countries, the monstrous fishes, the customs and laws of Frislanda, of Islanda [Iceland], of Estlanda [Shetland], of the Kingdom of Norway, of Estotilanda, of Drogio, and, lastly, the life of Nicolò the Knight, our brother, with the discoveries made by him, and matters relating to Grolanda [Greenland]. I have also written the life and exploits of Zichmni, a Prince certainly as worthy of immortal remembrance as any other who has ever lived in this world, on account of his great valour and many good qualities. In this life may be read of his discoveries in

Engrouiland (*sic*) [Greenland] on both sides, and of the city built by him. Wherefore, I will say no more to you in this letter, hoping soon to be with you, and to satisfy you concerning many other things *vivá voce*."

[By the Compiler.]

"All these letters were written by Messire Antonio to Messire Carlo, his brother, and I grieve that the book and many other writings, in which perhaps these very same projects may have been carried out, have come, I know not how, unhappily to harm; because, being still a boy when they came into my hands, and not understanding what they were, I tore them in pieces and destroyed them, as boys will do, which I cannot, except with the keenest regret, now call to mind. Nevertheless, in order that so fair a memorial of such things may not be lost [*folio* 58], I have placed in order in the above narrative what I have been able to recover of the aforesaid materials, to the end that I may, to some extent, make reparation to this present age, which, more than any other yet gone by, is interested in the many discoveries of new lands in those parts where, it might have been thought, they would be least expected, and which is very much given to the study both of recent accounts, and of the discoveries of unknown countries made by the great spirit and enterprise of our ancestors."

"the end."

Source: Translated by Fred W. Lucas, *Annals of the Voyages of the Brothers Nicolò and Antonio Zeno in the North Atlantic about the End of the Fourteenth Century and the Claim Founded Thereon to a Venetian Discovery of America: A Criticism and Indictment* (London: Henry Stevens Son and Stiles, 1898), 6–23.

Commentary: *The so-called* Zeno Narrative *is one of fringe history's strange sidelights, spawning an astonishing array of claims, largely due to the question of whether it is a genuine medieval document, a question Fred W. Lucas settled in the negative in 1898. The text was first published in 1558 by the "compiler" of the narrative, Nicolò Zeno the younger, who claimed to be reconstructing from memory letters of his ancestors, the brothers Zeno, he read in his youth but who actually fabricated the narrative from several identifiable sources. These sources include works by the Swedish writer Olaus Magnus and other Renaissance writers, some of which are indicated in my notes to the text and which are discussed at greater and exhaustive length by Lucas.*[19]

Zeno paired his written text with a map that he claimed showed the Arctic with unusual accuracy. The explorers Martin Frobisher and John Davis both relied on this map in seeking the Northwest Passage, resulting in several major geographical errors that persisted on European maps for a century. Lucas and others showed the map to be a hoax compiled from maps available to the younger Zeno, including Olaus Magnus' Carta marina *(1539), Cornelius Anthoniszoon's* Caerte van Oostlant *(1543), and derivatives of Claudius Clavus' early map of the North (c. 1427). Charles Hapgood, a hyperdiffusionist writer, instead declared it a copy of a fabulously ancient map of an ice-free Greenland in* Maps of the Ancient Sea Kings *(1966).*

In 1784 Johann Reinhold Forster identified the Zichmni of the text with Henry I Sinclair, Earl of Orkney: "This name of Sinclair appears to me to be expressed by the word Zichmni," he wrote.[20] *In 1873, Richard Henry Major, a geographer with the British Museum, translated the text and wrote a massive essay defending the identification of Sinclair with Zichmni, arguing that the Zeno text described actual Norse outposts in the Orkneys, Iceland, and Greenland.*

(*Sinclair was a vassal of the Norse king.*) *Nevertheless, no independent evidence outside the Zeno narrative exists to support such a claim; indeed, no medieval record makes any mention of Henry as a navigator of any note. Nevertheless, historian John Fiske, Sinclair family apologist Thomas Sinclair,*[21] *and fringe writers Frederick J. Pohl (not the science fiction writer*[22]*), Andrew Sinclair, and Scott Wolter, among others, have built on the the Sinclair identification, eventually tying in such seemingly unrelated themes as Oak Island's Money Pit, the Holy Bloodline Conspiracy, and the Knights Templar, based on claims made in the 1982 book* The Holy Blood and the Holy Grail *that identified the Sinclair family as participants in a conspiracy to hide the truth about the descendants of Jesus.*

This document remains the single and sole support for Sinclair's supposed discovery of America, and all of the later claims made for Sinclair's adventures in America, which today are legion.[23]

Notes

1. Although this island is fictional, Clements R. Markham, writing in the *Life of Christopher Columbus* (London: George Philip & Son, 1892, pp. 22–23), believed that Bartolomé de las Casas added a reference to it in his 1561 *Historia de las Indias* (1.3) as though Columbus had himself made mention of Frisland. Nearly identical lines can be found in the 1571 *Historie* by Columbus's son Fernando (ch. 4). As Fernando died in 1539, before the Zeno text was published, John Fiske in vol. 1 of his *Discovery of America* (Boston: Houghton, Mifflin and Company, 1892, p. 383) argued that this meant Frisland had been independently confirmed. Markham and Lucas view the line as an interpolation after Las Casas, added by the 1571 Italian translator of the original Spanish manuscript, which no longer exists.

2. Alternative thinkers claim Zichmni is a corruption of either "Sinclair" or "d'Orkney," titles of Henry Sinclair of Orkney.

3. The Zeno map has repeatedly been shown to be a hoax derived from early modern maps.

4. Here the text is either corrupt or the author did not understand what he was copying in creating the hoax; the word is meaningless.

5. According to Lucas, Zeno here has misread Olaus Magnus's *History of the Northern Peoples* or *Opera Breve,* which said that the Icelanders "wage wars with sufficient cruelty" in the former (21.3) and have "armed knights [and] very cruel wars" in the latter (A, sec. o). Zeno erroneously deduced defensive structures that did not exist.

6. Lucas writes that the following description is taken from drawings of Iceland appearing in Olaus Magnus' 1555 book *History of the Northern Peoples* (2.1–2) along with descriptions of the Royal Fortress of Aaranes in Sweden from the same book (2.21).

7. The translation here is uncertain; Zeno again seems to have only partially understood his source material about ventilation holes in Greenlandic and Icelandic houses derived from Olaus Magnus (*History of the Northern Peoples* 12.2–3), which he has presented in a confused way.

8. Dried fish and skins.

9. This section is modeled closely on the shipwreck of Gerónimo de Aguilar given in Book 6 of Peter Martyr's *Fourth Decade* (1521) and chapter 12 of Francisco López de Gomará's *Conquest of Mexico* (1554).

10. Many fringe historians identify Drogio with America.

11. Apparently Drogio.

12. Lucas demonstrated that the following sections are plagiarized quite closely from accounts of South America from Amerigo Vespucci, Benedetto Bordone, and Fracanzano da Montalboddo's *Paesi Novamente* anthology.

13. This strange reference to Greek myth is borrowed directly from Bordone's *Isolario* (1528), folio 46.

14. There are no volcanoes on Greenland. Zeno here appears to be again referencing material about Iceland he learned from Olaus Magnus and Bordone.

15. The birds' eggs can be found in Olaus Magnus' *History of the Northern Peoples* (19.37).

16. The author has obviously given the wrong date.

17. Frederick J. Pohl assumed this referred to a burning pitch field in Nova Scotia and thus to a Sinclair voyage to America, but that river of pitch was the result of modern mining operations and did not exist in the 1300s.

18. Lucas notes that these fellows appear to derive from descriptions in Bordone's *Isolario* (folio 5) and Olaus Magnus's *History of the Northern Peoples* (2.9), both of which discuss cave-dwelling dwarves.

19. Fred W. Lucas, *Annals of the Voyages of the Brothers Nicolò and Antonio Zeno in the North Atlantic about the End of the Fourteenth Century and the Claim Founded Thereon to a Venetian Discovery of America: A Criticism and Indictment* (London: Henry Stevens Son and Stiles, 1898).

20. Johann Reinhold Forster, *History of the Voyages and Discoveries Made in the North* (London, 1786), 181n.

21. Thomas Sinclair preferred to identify Zichmni with Henry II Sinclair, son of Henry I, and proposed that the U.S. honor Henry II instead of Columbus with a holiday to help prevent "Spanish or Latin domination" of the country through immigration from southern Europe. Thomas Sinclair was the first to propose that the Sinclairs once ruled over Native peoples in the Middle Ages: "It is already pretty certain that the Norse and Scotch heroes left a sprinkling of population, who ruled the Red Indians to some extent, and amalgamated with them" (Thomas Sinclair, *Caithness Events,* 2nd ed. [Wick: W. Rae, 1899], 167). Scott Wolter repeats the claim virtually unchanged in *AF.*

22. They are sometimes confused; for example, James J. Bloom in *The Imaginary Sea Voyage* (Jefferson, NC: McFarland, 2013, p. 89) asserts that the science fiction writer Frederik Pohl was the source for claims that the Mi'kmaq god Glooscap was actually Henry Sinclair; that dishonor goes to the other Pohl, who made the claim based on an imaginative conflation of unrelated Mi'kmaq myths from Silas Rand's *Legends of the Micmac* (1894) (Frederick J. Pohl, "A Nova Scotia Project," *Journal of the Massachusetts Archaeological Society* 20, no. 3 [1959]: 39–42).

23. For an overview of claims made for Sinclair, see David Goudsward, *The Westford Knight and Henry Sinclair: Evidence of at 14th Century Scottish Voyage to North America* (Jefferson, NC: McFarland, 2010).

X

Holy Blood and Holy Grail

Controversies over the nature and divinity of Christ are as old as Christianity itself, from the Gnostics to the Cathars to the New Age movement. However, it was only with the 1982 publication of *The Holy Blood and the Holy Grail* by Michael Baigent, Richard Leigh, and Henry Lincoln that the modern Holy Bloodline conspiracy emerged. These authors argued that Jesus was mortal, that he married Mary Magdalene, and that their children gave rise to a royal bloodline that yielded Europe's Merovingian royal family. The Knights Templar, they said, protected this bloodline and kept it safe from the machinations of popes and kings. Some fringe figures, such as *Ancient Aliens* pundit Kathleen McGowan, the widow of ancient astronaut theorist Philip Coppens, claim descent from this bloodline,[1] even though their claims are based on fabricated French documents about the fictitious Priory of Sion created in the 1960s by draftsman Pierre Plantard and the surrealist Philippe de Chérisey.

The progression of Holy Bloodline claims between 1982 and the present has been nothing short of astonishing. The most famous, and tamest, version of the theory emerged from *The Da Vinci Code* (2003), which cloaked *Holy Blood* in the clothes of fiction. In *Bloodline of the Holy Grail* (1996) and its sequels, Laurence Gardner attributed the Holy Bloodline to space aliens who mined the earth for so-called "monoatomic gold" (a nonexistent substance misunderstood from colloidal gold) and drank human menstrual blood. David Icke gives this as the food of the reptile people who live beneath the earth. Scott Wolter believes the United States is the ultimate Holy Bloodline kingdom, claimed for the descendants of the Magdalene by the Knights Templar in the Kensington Rune Stone (**123**).

The claim that Mary Magdalene's womb and royal blood (*sang real*) were the true Holy Grail (*san greal*) contrasts with other efforts to see in the chalice of Christ a pagan cauldron from Celtic lore, the alchemical philosopher's stone, or a meteor.[2]

Notes

1. Carol Memmet, "Is This Woman Living the 'Code'?," *USA Today*, July 18, 2006.
2. On the various interpretations of the Grail through history, see Richard Barber, *The Holy Grail: Imagination and Belief* (Cambridge: Harvard University Press, 2004).

104. Jesus Survives the Crucifixion
Irenaeus
Against Heresies 1.24.4
c. 180 CE
Originally Greek but survives in Latin
Holy

Those angels who occupy the lowest heaven, that, namely, which is visible to us, formed all the things which are in the world, and made allotments among themselves of the earth and of those nations which are upon it. The chief of them is he who is thought to be the God of the Jews; and inasmuch as he desired to render the other nations subject to his own people, that is, the Jews, all the other princes resisted and opposed him. Wherefore all other nations were at enmity with his nation. But the father without birth and without name, perceiving that they would be destroyed, sent his own first-begotten Nous (he it is who is called Christ) to bestow deliverance on those who believe in him, from the power of those who made the world. He appeared, then, on earth as a man, to the nations of these powers, and wrought miracles. Wherefore he did not himself suffer death, but Simon, a certain man of Cyrene, being compelled, bore the cross in his stead; so that this latter being transfigured by him, that he might be thought to be Jesus, was crucified, through ignorance and error, while Jesus himself received the form of Simon, and, standing by, laughed at them. For since he was an incorporeal power, and the Nous (mind) of the unborn father, he transfigured himself as he pleased, and thus ascended to him who had sent him, deriding them, inasmuch as he could not be laid hold of, and was invisible to all.

Source: Translated by Alexander Roberts and W. H. Rambaut in *The Ante-Nicene Christian Library,* eds. Alexander Roberts and James Donaldson, vol. 5: The Writings of Irenæus, vol. 1 (Edinburgh: T. & T. Clark, 1868), 91.

Commentary: *Irenaeus here reports the beliefs of the Gnostic thinker Basilides, whom he condemns. Although Basilides considered Christ a completely divine figure who therefore had no human body, others instead interpreted such beliefs as involving a fully human Christ. This belief, the foundation for so much Holy Bloodline speculation, can also be found later in the Gnostic text called* The Second Treatise of the Great Seth *(3rd c. CE), as well as still later in the Qur'an, where we read:*

QUR'AN 4:155–8

c. 609–632 CE
Arabic
Holy

[155] Therefore for that they [the Jews] have made void their covenant, and have not believed in the signs of God, and have slain the prophets unjustly, and have said, Our hearts are uncircumcised (but God hath sealed them up, because of their unbelief; therefore they shall not believe, except a few of them):

[156] and for that they have not believed *in Jesus*, and have spoken against Mary a grievous calumny;

[157] and have said, Verily we have slain Christ Jesus the son of Mary, the apostle of God; yet they slew him not, neither crucified him, but he was represented *by one* in his likeness; and verily they who disagreed concerning him, were in a doubt as to this *matter*, and had no *sure* knowledge thereof, but followed only on *uncertain* opinion.

[158] They did not really kill him; but God took him up unto himself: and God is mighty and wise.

Source: Translation by George Sale in *The Koran; Commonly Called the Alcoran of Mohammed* (Boston: T. O. H. P. Burnham, 1870), 117.

Commentary: *In this passage, the Qur'an records the continued existence of crucifixion* *beliefs similar to those of Basilides down to the time of Muhammad, though here with a fully human rather than divine Christ, in keeping with Islam's view of Christ as a prophet of Allah. It is held by Islam to be the true account of the end of Jesus' time on earth. In this account, a double dies on earth while Jesus is taken up to heaven by Allah. A medieval gospel written under Islamic influence repeats the tale with suprising additions and details:*

Gospel of Barnabas 217

c. 13th c. CE
Italian
Holy

The soldiers took Judas and bound him, not without derision. For he truthfully denied that he was Jesus; and the soldiers, mocking him, said: "Sir, fear not, for we are come to make thee king of Israel, and we have bound thee because we know that thou dost refuse the kingdom."

Judas answered: "Now have ye lost your senses! Ye are come to take Jesus of Nazareth, with arms and lanterns as [against] a robber; and ye have bound me that have guided you, to make me king!"

Then the soldiers lost their patience, and with blows and kicks they began to flout Judas, and they led him with fury into Jerusalem.

John and Peter followed the soldiers afar off; and they affirmed to him who writeth that they saw all the examination that was made of Judas by the high priest, and by the council of the Pharisees, who were assembled to put Jesus to death. Whereupon Judas spake many words of madness, insomuch that every one was filled with laughter, believing that he was really Jesus, and that for fear of death he was feigning madness. Whereupon the scribes bound his eyes with a bandage, and mocking him said: "Jesus, prophet of the Nazarenes," (for so they called them who believed in Jesus), "tell us, who was it that smote thee?" And they buffeted him and spat in his face.

When it was morning there assembled the great council of scribes and elders of the people; and the high priest with the Pharisees sought false witness against Judas, believing him to be Jesus: and they found not that which they sought. And why say I that the chief priests believed Judas to be Jesus? Nay, all the disciples, with him who writeth, believed it; and more, the poor virgin mother of Jesus, with his kinsfolk and friends, believed it, insomuch that the sorrow of every one was incredible. As God liveth, he who writeth forgot all that Jesus had said: how that he should be taken up from the world, and that he should suffer in a third person, and bthat he should not die until near the end of the world. Wherefore he went with the mother of Jesus and with John to the cross.

The high priest caused Judas to be brought before him bound, and asked him of his disciples and his doctrine.

Whereupon Judas, as though beside himself, answered nothing to the point. The high priest then adjured him by the living God of Israel that he would tell him the truth.

Judas answered: "I have told you that I am Judas Iscariot, who promised to give into your hands Jesus the Nazarene; and ye, by what art I know not, are beside yourselves, for ye will have it by every means that I am Jesus."

The high priest answered: "O perverse seducer, thou hast deceived all Israel, beginning from Galilee even unto Jerusalem here, with thy doctrine and false miracles: and now thinkest thou to flee the merited punishment that befitteth thee by feigning to be mad? As God liveth, thou shalt not escape it!" And having said this he commanded his servants to smite him with buffetings and kicks, so that his understanding might come back into his head. The derision which he then suffered at the hands of the high priest's servants is past belief. For they zealously devised new inventions to give pleasure to the council. So they attired him as a juggler, and so treated him with hands and feet that it would have moved the very Canaanites to compassion if they had beheld that sight.

But the chief priests and Pharisees and elders of the people had their hearts so exasperated against Jesus that, believing Judas to be really Jesus, they took delight in seeing him so treated.

Afterwards they led him bound to the governor, who secretly loved Jesus. Whereupon he, thinking that Judas was Jesus, made him enter into his chamber, and spake to him, asking him for what cause the chief priests and the people had given him into his hands.

Judas answered: "If I tell thee the truth, thou wilt not believe me; for perchance thou art deceived as the (chief) priests and the Pharisees are deceived."

The governor answered (thinking that he wished to speak concerning the Law): "Now knowest thou not that I am not a Jew? But the (chief) priests and the elders of thy people have given thee into my hand; wherefore tell us the truth, that I may do what is just. For I have power to set thee free and to put thee to death."

Judas answered: "Sir, believe me, if thou put me to death, thou shalt do a great wrong, for thou shalt slay an innocent person; seeing that I am Judas Iscariot, and not Jesus, who is a magician, and by his art hath so transformed me."

When he heard this the governor marvelled greatly, so that he sought to set him at liberty. The governor therefore went out, and smiling said: "In the one case, at least, this man is not worthy of death, but rather of compassion." "This man saith," said the governor, "that he is not Jesus, but a certain Judas who guided the soldiery to take Jesus, and he saith that Jesus the Galilean hath by his art magic so transformed him. Wherefore, if this be true, it were a great wrong to kill him, seeing that he were innocent. But if he is Jesus and denieth that he is, assuredly he hath lost his understanding, and it were impious to slay a madman."

Then the chief priests and elders of the people, with the scribes and Pharisees, cried out with shouts, saying: "He is Jesus of Nazareth, for we know him; for if he were not the malefactor we would not have given him into thy hands. Nor is he mad; but rather malignant, for with this device he seeketh to escape from our hands, and the sedition that he would stir up if he should escape would be worse than the former."

Pilate (for such was the governor's name), in order to rid himself of such a case, said: "He is a Galilean, and Herod is King of Galilee: wherefore it pertaineth not to me to judge such a case, so take ye him to Herod."

Accordingly they led Judas to Herod, who of a long time had desired that Jesus should go to his house. But Jesus had never been willing to go to his house, because Herod was a Gentile, and adored the false and lying gods, living after the manner of unclean Gentiles. Now when Judas had been led thither, Herod asked him of many things, to which Judas gave answers not to the purpose, denying that he was Jesus.

Then Herod mocked him, with all his court, and caused him to be clad in white as the fools are clad, and sent him back to Pilate, saying to him, "Do not fail in justice to the people of Israel!"

And this Herod wrote, because the chief priests and scribes and the Pharisees had given him a good quantity of money. The governor having heard that this was so from a servant of Herod, in order that he also might gain some money, feigned that he desired to set Judas at liberty. Whereupon he caused him to be scourged by his slaves, who were paid by the scribes to slay him under the scourges. But God, who had decreed the issue, reserved Judas for the cross, in order that he might suffer that horrible death to which he had sold another. He did not suffer Judas to die under the scourges, notwithstanding that the soldiers scourged him so grievously that his body rained blood. Thereupon, in mockery they clad him in an old purple garment, saying: "It is fitting to our new king to clothe him and crown him": so they gathered thorns and made a crown, like those of gold and precious stones which kings wear on their heads. And this crown of thorns they placed upon Judas' head, putting in his hand a reed for scepter, and they made him sit in a high place. And the soldiers came before him, bowing down in mockery, saluting him as King of the Jews. And they held out their hands to receive gifts, such as new kings are accustomed to give; and receiving nothing they smote Judas, saying: "Now, how art thou crowned, foolish king, if thou wilt not pay thy soldiers and servants?"

The chief priests with the scribes and Pharisees, seeing that Judas died not by the scourges, and fearing lest Pilate should set him at liberty, made a gift of money to the governor, who having received it gave Judas to the scribes and Pharisees as guilty unto death. Whereupon they condemned two robbers with him to the death of the cross.

So they led him to Mount Calvary, where they used to hang malefactors, and there they crucified him naked, for the greater ignominy.

Judas truly did nothing else but cry out: "God, why hast thou forsaken me, seeing the malefactor hath escaped and I die unjustly?"

Verily I say that the voice, the face, and the person of Judas were so like to Jesus, that his disciples and believers entirely believed that he was Jesus; wherefore some departed from the doctrine of Jesus, believing that Jesus had been a false prophet, and that by art magic he had done the miracles which he did: for Jesus had said that he should not die till near the end of the world; for that at that time he should be taken away from the world.

But they that stood firm in the doctrine of Jesus were so encompassed with sorrow, seeing him die who was entirely like to Jesus, that they remembered not what Jesus had said. And so in company with the mother of Jesus they went to Mount Calvary, and were not only present at the death of Judas, weeping continually, but by means of Nicodemus and Joseph of Abarimathia they obtained from the governor the body of Judas to bury it. Whereupon, they took him down from the cross with such weeping as assuredly no one would believe, and buried him in the new sepulchre of Joseph; having wrapped him up in an hundred pounds of precious ointments.

Source: Translated by Lonsdale and Laura Ragg in *The Gospel of Barnabas*, eds. and trans. Lonsdale and Laura Ragg (Oxford: Clarendon Press, 1907), 473–481.

Commentary: *After these events, a very much living Jesus shows himself, and his disciples think him resurrected. He is then carried up to heaven by four angels. The story given in the Gospel of Barnabas is clearly influenced by Islam, and many scholars believe that this late medieval text, known from an Italian manuscript and a now-lost Spanish translation, originated in an attempt to synthesize Christian and Islamic doctrines, agreeing fully with neither.[1] (The text, for example, makes Jesus predict the coming of Muhammad but contradicts the Qur'an in* *making Muhammad the Messiah.) Scholars are divided about the degree to which the medieval text preserves early heretical material, but it has nevertheless served as fuel for conspiracy theories, including claims that Pope Benedict XVI resigned in 2013 because of its revelations following rumors that a genuinely ancient copy of the gospel had been recovered in Turkey the year before.*

Note

1. See, for example, David Sox, *The Gospel of Barnabas* (London: Allen and Unwin, 1984).

105. Jesus Kisses Mary Magdalene
Gospel of Philip 59
c. 3rd c. CE
Coptic
Holy

The Wisdom which they call "the Barren," she herself is the mother of the Angels. And the companion of [...] was Mary Magdalene. [...] loved her more than all of the disciples, and he used to kiss her often on her [...].

Source: Translated by Jason Colavito from a facsimile manuscript.

Commentary: *The damaged papyrus is missing key words. Most translators believe the first two ellipses refer to Christ, while the last is usually given as "mouth," though "hand," "forehead," "cheek," and "feet" have also been proposed. Based on the reading of "mouth," many fringe theorists have used this Gnostic text, discovered in the Nag Hammadi corpus in 1945, to propose a sexual relationship between Jesus and Mary. Even taken at face value, it is hundreds of years too late to be an eye-witness account of Jesus' life.*

106. Jesus Takes Mary Magdalene as Concubine
Peter of les Vaux-de-Cernay
Historia Albigensis 10–11 (Older numbering: Chapter 2)
c. 1212–1218
Latin
Holy

First, it should be known that the heretics [the Cathars] propose the existence of two creators, one of things invisible, whom they call the benign God, and one of things visible, whom they name the evil God. They attribute the New Testament to the benign God and the Old to the malign God, and they repudiate all of the Old Testament except for certain passages included in the New Testament, which they judge to be appropriate because of their respect for the New Testament. They assert that the author of the Old Testament is a liar, for he said to the first created man: "But of the tree of the knowledge of good and evil, thou shalt not eat of it: for in the day that thou eatest thereof thou shalt surely die,"[1] yet they did not die after eating of it, as he had said they would—though in reality after eating of the forbidden fruit they became subject to death. They also called him a murderer because he incinerated the people of Sodom and Gomorrah, destroyed the world by the waters of the Flood, and overwhelmed Pharaoh and the Egyptians with the sea. They declared that all of the patriarchs of the Old Testament were damned; they asserted that John the Baptist was one of the greatest devils. And they also said in their secret meetings that the Christ who was born in the earthly and visible Bethlehem and crucified in Jerusalem was evil; and that

Mary Magdalene was his concubine; and that she was the woman taken in adultery of whom we read in Scripture.[2] Indeed, the good Christ they say neither ate nor drank nor assumed the true flesh, nor was he ever in this world except spiritually in the body of Paul. But for this reason we say "in the earthly and visible Bethlehem": The heretics believe there to be another earth, new and invisible, and in this second earth some of them believe the good Christ was crucified. Likewise, the heretics say the good God had two wives, Oolla and Ooliba,[3] and from these he begat sons and daughters. There were other heretics who said that there was one Creator, but that he had as sons both Christ and the Devil. They said that all creatures were once good but that from the vials[4] of which we read in the Apocalypse,[5] all were corrupted.

Source: Translated by Jason Colavito from the Latin in Petrus Vallium Sarnaii Monachus, *Hystoria albigensis*, eds. P. Guébin and E. Lyon (Paris: Honoré Champion, 1926), 9–12.

Commentary: *Font for many claims about the New Age spirituality of the Cathars, the text also provides a rare legend about Jesus' alleged sexual relationship with Mary Magdalene. Obviously, this text cannot support claims that the Cathars considered Mary Magdalene an object of veneration, as they identify her as the concubine of an evil demon-god. The names of God's wives Oolla and Ooliba are the symbolic sister-whores Oholah and Oholibah (Vulgate: Oolla and Ooliba) of Ezekiel 23:4, where they stand for Israel and Judah and are the brides of God.*

Notes

1. Genesis 2:17.
2. John 8:3.
3. The manuscript gives Collant and Colibant, but scholars assume corruption.
4. This term is subject to dispute. The Latin in older editions reads "filias" (daughters), but the modern critical editors read this as a misprint for "fialas" (vials) used in the Vulgate version of Revelation. If not, then the reference to Revelation is wrong and the daughters would be the human women from Genesis 6:1–4 (**8**) who consorted with the Sons of God. Either version could be supported from Peter's text.
5. Revelation 16:1–21.

107. Mary Magdalene Arrives in France
Sigebert of Gembloux
Chronicon sive Chronographia, entry for 745
1111 or 1112 CE
Latin
Holy

A persecution having arisen after the stoning of Stephen proto-martyr,[1] Maximinus, one of the seventy disciples of Christ, crossing to Gaul, took Mary Magdalene with him. Furthermore, he buried her body in the city of Aix, over which he presided. Verily, the city of Aix was despoiled by the Saracens, so the body of Mary herself was transferred by Gerard, count of Burgundy, to the monastery of Vézelay, which had been constructed by him. And yet some people write that this woman rests in Ephesus, having no covering over her.

Source: Translated by Jason Colavito from the Latin in George Heinrich Pertz (ed.), *Monumenta Germaniae Historica,* vol. 8 (Hanover: Impensis Bibliopolii Avlici Hahniani, 1844), 331.

Commentary: *Sigebert's text is the oldest surviving reference to the transfer of Mary Mag-*

dalene's relics from Aix to Vézelay. Medieval Catholic writers claimed Mary's body had been brought to Aix, later amended to the living Magdalene, while Greek Orthodox writers claimed Ephesus or Constantinople as her burial site (cf. Modestus in Photius, Biblioteca 275). The new legend arose to help Vézelay attract lucrative pilgrims to its monastery over rival Aix and was adopted into Catholic tradition (see below) only after 1112. In the final line, Sigebert references Gregory of Tours' In gloria martyrum 1.30, where the sixth-century author writes an unexplained line that "In this city [Ephesus] Mary Magdalene rests, having no covering over her" (my trans.).

Note

   1. Acts 7:57–60–8:1.

108. Mary Magdalene's Life in France
Jacobus de Voragine
Golden Legend, Life of S. Mary Magdalene
c. 1260 CE
Latin
Holy

   ... then after the ascension of our Lord, the fourteenth year from his passion, long after that the Jews had slain S. Stephen, and had cast out the other disciples out of the Jewry, which went into various countries, and preached the word of God. There was at that time with the apostles St. Maximin, who was one of the seventy-two disciples of our Lord, to whom the blessed Mary Magdalene was committed by S. Peter, and then, when the disciples were departed, St. Maximin, Mary Magdalene, and Lazarus her brother, Martha her sister, Marcella, chamberer of Martha, and St. Cedon who was born blind and afterward given sight by our Lord; all these together, and many other Christian men were taken of the miscreants and put in a ship in the sea, without any tackle or rudder, for to be drowned. But by the purveyance of Almighty God they came all to Marseilles, where, as none would receive them to be lodged, they dwelled and abode under a porch before a temple of the people of that country. And when the blessed Mary Magdalene saw the people assembled at this temple for to do sacrifice to the idols, she arose up peaceably with a glad visage, a discreet tongue and well speaking, and began to preach the faith and law of Jesus Christ, and withdrew from the worshipping of the idols. Then were they marveled at the beauty, of the reason, and of the fair speaking of her. And it was no marvel that the mouth that had kissed the feet of our Lord so debonairly and so goodly, should be inspired with the word of God more than the other. And after that, it happed that the prince of the province and his wife made sacrifice to the idols for to have a child. And Mary Magdalene preached to them Jesus Christ and forbade them those sacrifices.

   [...] And then they destroyed all the temples of the idols in the city of Marseilles, and made churches of Jesus Christ. And with one accord they chose the blessed St. Lazarus for to be bishop of that city. And afterward they came to the city of Aix, and by great miracles and preaching they brought the people there to the faith of Jesus Christ. And there St. Maximin was ordained to be bishop. In this meanwhile the blessed Mary Magdalene, desirous of sovereign contemplation, sought a right sharp desert, and took a place which was ordained by the angel of God, and abode there by the space of thirty years without knowledge of anybody. In which place she had no comfort of running water, nor solace of trees, nor of herbs.

Although Eastern tradition held that Mary Magdalene died and was buried in Ephesus, in the West competition for pilgrims' patronage led French monasteries to claim to have Mary's relics. Later this expanded to claims that she had actually lived in southern France. The legend that angels carried her to heaven from her home in France, seen in this Albrecht Dürer woodcut, emerged in the Middle Ages and contributed to the much later development of the Holy Bloodline myth (National Gallery of Art).

And that was because our Redeemer did do show it openly, that he had ordained for her refection celestial, and no physical meats. And every day at every canonical hour she was lifted up in the air of angels, and heard the glorious song of the heavenly companies with her bodily ears.

[At the hour of her death] Mary Magdalene received the body and blood of our Lord of the hands of the bishop with great abundance of tears, and after, she stretched her body before the altar, and her right blessed soul departed from the body and went to our Lord. And after it was departed, there issued out of the body an odour so sweet-smelling that it remained there by the space of seven days to all them that entered in. And the blessed Maximin anointed the body of her with diverse precious ointments, and buried it honourably, and after commanded that his body should be buried by hers after his death.

Source: Slightly adapted from the translation by William Caxton, reprinted and modernized in *The Golden Legend or the Lives of the Saints as Englished by William Caxton,* vol. 4, ed. F. S. Ellis (London: J. M. Dent and Co., 1900), 75–85.

Commentary: *This is the most developed version of the Magdalene legend in France, showing the final form of the story, which Holy Bloodline writers have adopted uncritically. Jacobus de Voraigne was not composing history, however, but hagiography, and his stories were compilations of miracle tales, folklore, allegory, and tradition.*

109. The Holy Grail as Stone from Heaven
Wolfram von Eschenbach
Parzival, Book 9
c. 1205 CE
German
Astro, Prehistoric, Holy

> Quoth Parzival, "Here I thank thee, from my heart, that such faithful rede
> Thou hast given of him who withholdeth from no man his rightful meed,
> But evil, as good, requiteth—Yet my youth hath been full of care,
> And my faith hath but brought me sorrow, and ill to this day I fare!"
>
> Then the hermit he looked on the Waleis, "If a secret be not thy grief,
> Right willing thy woe I'll hearken, I may bring thee perchance relief;
> Of some counsel may I bethink me such as yet to thyself dost fail!"
> Quoth Parzival, "Of my sorrows the chiefest is for the Grail,
> And then for my wife—none fairer e'er hung on a mother's breast,
> For the twain is my heart yet yearning, with desire that ne'er findeth rest."
> Quoth his host, "Well, Sir Knight, thou speakest, such sorrow is good to bear;
> If thus for the wife of thy bosom thy heart knoweth grief and care,
>
> And Death find thee a faithful husband, tho' Hell vex thee with torments dire
> Yet thy pains shall be swiftly ended, God will draw thee from out Hell-fire.
> But if for the *Grail* thou grievest, then much must I mourn thy woe,
> O! foolish man, since fruitless thy labours, for thou shalt know
> That none win the Grail save those only whose names are in Heaven known.
> They who to the Grail do service, they are chosen of God alone;

And mine eyes have surely seen this, and sooth is the word I say!"
Quoth Parzival, "Thou hast been there?" "Sir Knight," quoth the hermit, "Yea!"
But never a word spake our hero of the marvels himself had seen,
But he asked of his host the story, and what men by "The Grail" should mean?
Spake the hermit, "Full well do I know this, that many a knightly hand
Serveth the Grail at Monsalväsch, and from thence, throughout all the land,
On many a distant journey these gallant Templars fare,
Whether sorrow or joy befall them, for their sins they this penance bear!"

"And this brotherhood so gallant, dost thou know what to them shall give
Their life, and their strength and their valour—then know, by a *stone* they live,
And that stone is both pure and precious—Its name hast thou never heard?
Men call it *Lapis Exilis*—by its magic the wondrous bird,
The Phœnix, becometh ashes, and yet doth such virtue flow
From the stone, that afresh it riseth renewed from the ashes glow,
And the plumes that erewhile it moulted spring forth yet more fair and bright—
And tho' faint be the man and feeble, yet the day that his falling sight
Beholdeth the stone, he dies not, nor can, till eight days be gone,
Nor his countenance wax less youthful—If one daily behold that stone,
(If a man it shall be, or a maiden 'tis the same,) for a hundred years,
If they look on its power, their hair groweth not grey, and their face appears
The same as when first they saw it, nor their flesh nor their bone shall fail
But young they abide for ever—And this stone all men call the Grail."

"And its holiest power, and the highest shall I ween be renewed to-day,
For ever upon Good Friday a messenger takes her way.
From the height of the highest Heaven a Dove on her flight doth wing,
And a Host, so white and holy, she unto the stone doth bring.
And she layeth It down upon It; and white as the Host the Dove
That, her errand done, swift wingeth her way to the Heaven above.
Thus ever upon Good Friday doth it chance as I tell to thee:
And the stone from the Host receiveth all good that on earth may be
Of food or of drink, the earth beareth as the fulness of Paradise.
All wild things in wood or in water, and all that 'neath Heaven flies,
To that brotherhood are they given, a pledge of God's favour fair,
For His servants He ever feedeth and the Grail for their needs doth care!"

"Now hearken, the Grail's elect ones, say who doth their service claim?
On the Grail, in a mystic writing, appeareth each chosen name,
If a man it shall be, or a maiden, whom God calls to this journey blest.
And the message no man effaceth, till all know the high behest,
But when all shall the name have read there, as it came, doth the writing go:
As children the Grail doth call them, 'neath its shadow they wax and grow.
And blessèd shall be the mother whose child doth the summons hear,
Rich and poor alike rejoiceth when the messenger draweth near,

And the Grail son or daughter claimeth! They are gathered from every land,
And ever from shame and sorrow are they sheltered, that holy band.
In Heaven is their rewarding, if so be that they needs must die,
Then bliss and desire's fulfilment are waiting them all on high!"

"They who took no part in the conflict, when Lucifer would fight
With the Three-in-One, those angels were cast forth from Heaven's height.
To the earth they came at God's bidding, and that wondrous stone did tend,
Nor was It less pure for their service, yet their task found at last an end.
I know not if God forgave them, or if they yet deeper fell,
This one thing I know of a surety, what God doeth, He doeth well!
But ever since then to this service nor maiden nor knight shall fail,
For God calleth them all as shall please Him!—and so standeth it with the Grail!"

Source: Translated by Jessie L. Weston in Wolfram von Eschenbach, *Parzival: A Knightly Epic by Wolfram von Eschenbach,* vol. 1, trans. Jessie L. Weston (London: David Nutt, 1894), 269–271.

Commentary: *This text is a key source for many fringe accounts of the Holy Grail, including Otto Rahn's quest for the Grail at the behest of Nazi authorities. Ancient astronaut theorists and Holy Grail speculators often confuse this description with a later one attributed to Wolfram (see below). Holy Bloodline Conspiracy writers take references to the Templars in the poem, referring here to a fictional order who guard the Grail Temple, to be the Knights Templar, the order of knights they believe were privy to ancient secrets and the true history of Jesus.*

110. The Holy Grail as Lucifer's Crown Jewel

Der Wartburgkrieg 143
c. 1250 CE
German
Astro

Wolfram:
Shall I bring forth the crown?
It was made by sixty thousand angels
Who wished to drive God from Heaven's kingdom.

Behold, Lucifer, it was yours!
Wherever there remain wise master-priests,
They know well that I sing the truth.
St. Michael saw God's wrath at such brazen arrogance
And with his sword he dashed the crown
From his (Lucifer's) head: Behold! A stone sprang loose from it
That afterward on earth became Parzival's.

Source: Translated Jason Colavito from the Middle High German and the modern German translation of Karl Joseph Simrock in *Der Wartburgkrieg* (Stuttgart: J.G. Cotta'scher Verlag, 1858), 176–177.

Commentary: *The text attributes these lines to Wolfram von Eschenbach during a fictitious minstrel contest, leading to much confusion between this and Wolfram's* Parzival *in its* *description of the Grail (see above). The story appears to be an adaptation of an earlier legend that the Morning Star was Lucifer's gem. This led in turn to a misreading by Princess Carolyne Sayn-Wittgenstein in a work on Wagner, following a faulty 1832 interpolation by Albert Schuz (San Marte), who wrongly attributed the myth to Eschenbach in a poor paraphrase of* Parzival *without distinguishing between the poet's ideas and his own. Wagner was reportedly distressed at the misreading.*[1] *Today the passage is best known from a quotation of the original given in Karl Joseph Simrock's appendix to his 1842 modern German translation of Eschenbach, which was actually a paraphrase: "Sixty-thousand angels who wished to drive God from Heaven ... had a crown made for Lucifer. When the archangel Michael tore this from Lucifer's head, a stone sprang loose from it, and that stone is the Grail" (trans. William Ashton Ellis). Nearly all English-language Grail writers rely on Simrock's 1842 paraphrase (available in English translation since the 1870s) rather than his 1858 edition of the original.*

Note

1. On this, see William Ashton Ellis, *Life of Richard Wagner*, vol. 4 (London: Kegan Paul, Trench, Trübner & Co., 1904), 478–482.

XI

Miscellaneous Mysteries

The preceding chapters have reviewed some of the major themes that run through the fringe history literature, but fringe historians are hardly doctrinaire in adhering strictly to a theme. No matter what branch of fringe history one consults, it quickly becomes clear that fringe history writers are happy to expand their vision to encompass an eclectic mix of mysteries, essentially anything that suggests that mainstream science is incorrect. This is why fringe history works contain seemingly unrelated stories of flying people, surviving populations of dinosaurs, and prophecies of the end of the world—anything that suggests wonders and mysteries in the deep past. Such stories are more likely to be found in books focusing on "mysteries" like Brad Steiger's *Mysteries of Time and Space* or David Childress's *Lost Cities* series, but can appear in almost any fringe history work. The following passages represent some of the many miscellaneous mysteries that appear in fringe history literature.

111. Berossus Predicts the End of the World for May 5, 2000
Berossus
Babyloniaca
c. 290–278 BCE
Greek
Preserved in Seneca, *Natural Questions* 3.29
c. 65 CE
Latin
General
Discussion in FG

Some suppose that in the final catastrophe the earth, too, will be shaken, and through clefts in the ground will uncover sources of fresh rivers which will flow forth from their full source in larger volume. Berossus, the translator of [the records of] Belus, affirms that the whole issue is brought about by the course of the planets. So positive is he on the point that he assigns a definite date both for the conflagration and the deluge. All that the earth inherits will, he assures us, be consigned to flame when the planets, which now move in different orbits, all assemble in Cancer, so arranged in one row that a straight line may pass through their spheres. When the same gathering takes place in Capricorn, then we are in danger of the deluge.

Source: Translated by John Clarke, *Physical Science in the Time of Nero: Being a Translation of the* Quaestiones Naturales *of Seneca* (London: Macmillan and Co., 1910), 150–151.

Commentary: *Seneca's discussion of the end of the world, in which he goes on to outline* *his own thoughts about its end, is notable for preserving a fragment of Berossus that predicted the exact time of the destruction of the world. In* FG, *Graham Hancock speculated that Berossus referred to the conjunction of five planets (including Neptune and Uranus, unknown to Berossus) on May 5, 2000, which other fringe writers, particularly Richard Noone in* 5/5/2000: Ice, the Ultimate Disaster *(1982), feared would herald an "earth-crust displacement" and pole shift. Hancock praised Noone's work as "brilliant" in the 1990s.[1] Obviously, this was not the end of the world. More interesting is the fact that the Babylonian belief in a deluge and conflagration exactly parallels the prophecy of Adam (12) later adapted into medieval pyramid myths (16, 17).*

Note

1. "*5/5/2000* is an extraordinary treasury of knowledge, hard facts, brilliant intuition and formidable research," Hancock said in the cover blurb to the 1997 paperback edition I own.

112. The Oldest Unicorn Legend

Ctesias
Indica
5th c. BCE
Greek
Preserved Photius, *Biblioteca*, codicil 72
9th c. CE

In India there are wild asses as large as horses, or even larger. Their body is white, their head dark red, their eyes bluish, and they have a horn in their forehead about a cubit in length. The lower part of the horn, for about two palms distance from the forehead, is quite white, the middle is black, the upper part, which terminates in a point, is a very flaming red. Those who drink out of cups made from it are proof against convulsions, epilepsy, and even poison, provided that before or after having taken it they drink some wine or water or other liquid out of these cups. The domestic and wild asses of other countries and all other solid-hoofed animals have neither huckle-bones nor gall-bladder, whereas the Indian asses have both. Their huckle-bone is the most beautiful that I have seen, like that of the ox in size and appearance; it is as heavy as lead and of the colour of cinnabar all through. These animals are very strong and swift; neither the horse nor any other animal can overtake them. At first they run slowly, but the longer they run their pace increases wonderfully, and becomes faster and faster. There is only one way of catching them. When they take their young to feed, if they are surrounded by a large number of horsemen, being unwilling to abandon their foals, they show fight, butt with their horns, kick, bite, and kill many men and horses. They are at last taken, after they have been pierced with arrows and spears; for it is impossible to capture them alive. Their flesh is too bitter to eat, and they are only hunted for the sake of the horns and huckle-bones.

Source: Translated by J. H. Freese in *The Library of Photius,* vol. 1 (London: Society for Promoting Christian Knowledge, 1920), 117–118.

Commentary: *Many believe the physician and traveler Ctesias preserved a distorted account of the rhinoceros, which he learned secondhand from Persian travelers to India. How he observed their ankle bones (hucklebones) is anyone's guess, as is why Ctesias ranked ankles by beauty.*

The unicorn never walked the earth, but it nevertheless has existed in mythology from the time of Ctesias down to the present day, inspired perhaps by distorted accounts of the rhinoceros. In medieval Europe, unicorns attained great popularity due to their inclusion in the Latin Vulgate and later the King James Bible. Modern translations prefer to render "unicorn" as "wild ox" in keeping with the Hebrew and Aramaic originals (scanned from Joannes Jonstonus, *A description of the nature of four-footed beasts* [1678]).

113. The Earliest Loch Ness Monster Tale

St. Adamnan
Life of St. Columba 2.28
c. 700 CE
Latin
General

On another occasion also, when the blessed man [St. Columba] was living for some days in the province of the Picts, he was obliged to cross the river Nesa (the Ness); and when he reached the bank of the river, he saw some of the inhabitants burying an unfortunate man, who, according to the account of those who were burying him, was a short time before seized, as he was swimming, and bitten most severely by a monster that lived in the water; his wretched body was, though too late, taken out with a hook, by those who came to his assistance in a boat. The blessed man, on hearing this, was so far from being dismayed, that he directed one of his companions to swim over and row across the coble that was moored at the farther bank. And Lugne Mocumin hearing the command of the excellent man, obeyed without the least delay, taking off all his clothes, except his tunic, and leaping into the water. But the monster, which, so far from being satiated, was only roused for more prey, was lying at the bottom of the stream, and when it felt the water disturbed above by the man swimming, suddenly rushed out, and, giving an awful roar, darted after him, with its mouth wide open, as the man swam in the middle of the stream. Then the blessed man observing this, raised his holy hand, while all the rest, brethren as well as strangers, were stupefied with terror, and, invoking the name of God, formed the saving sign of the cross in the air, and commanded the ferocious monster, saying, "Thou shalt go no further, nor touch the man; go back with all speed." Then at the voice of the saint, the monster was terrified, and fled more quickly than if it had been pulled back with ropes, though it had just got so near to Lugne, as he swam, that there was not more than the length of a spear-staff between the man and the beast. Then the brethren seeing that the monster had gone back, and that their comrade Lugne returned to them in the boat safe and sound, were struck with admiration, and gave glory to God in the blessed man. And even the barbarous heathens, who were present, were forced by the greatness of this miracle, which they themselves had seen, to magnify the God of the Christians.

Source: Translated by the Bishop of Brechin et al. in Adaman, *Life of St. Columba, Founder of Hy,* ed. William Reeves (Historians of Scotland, vol. 6) (Edinburgh: Edmonston and Douglas, 1874), 55–56.

Commentary: *The motif of the saint who battles a dragon or sea-serpent is best known from the life of St. George but is otherwise found in a variety of medieval hagiographies, with obvious parallels in the Greek myth of Perseus and Andromeda, as well as other Indo-European serpent-slaying myths. This tale, clearly mythical, formed the nucleus of the Loch Ness monster legend, despite the original referring to the* river *Ness and not the lake.*

114. The Levitating King of Hungary

Hartvic
Vita Sancti Stephani Proto-Regis Hungariae 17
c. 1112–1116 CE
Latin
General
Discussion in WS

And when he [King Stephen I, d. 1038 CE] had persisted in prayer for a long time, the servants of his Lord, the eternal King, gathered together to take up his prayers; and the tent stretched out over him was lifted up from the earth so that it began to hang in the air for a long time, until the man of God, returning to himself from contemplation, relaxed his soul from prayer. This was known, although invisibly, only to those who have foreknowledge of things and to the angels who have knowledge of His secrets. However, to a certain man of great simplicity and innocence, who was at that time perhaps pursuing similar works, it was manifested visibly. The holy king became informed through the Holy Spirit that the man knew of his secret, so he called the man to himself and by pleasing conversation asked what he had seen; afterward, enriching him with royal gifts, he forbade him with threats from disclosing it to anyone so long as the king himself still lived.

Source: Translated by Jason Colavito from the Latin in Hartvicus de Ortenburg, *Vita S. Stephani Hungariae Proto-Regis,* ed. József Podhradczky (Buda: 1836), 77–78.

Commentary: *In WS, Jacques Vallée reports this based on a secondary source, Ebenezer Cobham Brewer's* Dictionary of Miracles *(1901), itself summarizing incorrectly material from François Giry's French-language* Lives of the Saints, *which in the 1863 edition of Paul Guérin had already misreported the above text thusly: "His soul was so moved by God that his body sometimes even followed: One day while he was praying in his tent, he was taken with it up into the air by angels until the prayer was finished" (my trans.). Brewer amplified the mistake by* *asserting that the king "frequently" levitated. In the original, only the tent levitated and only once. (Cf. the daily levitation of Mary Magdalene in **108**.) The story, attributed to a simpleton by the medieval author, does not appear in the text from which Hartvic copied the majority of his work, the* Legenda maior sancti regis Stephani, *which was contemporary with Stephen, and is instead believed to be a piece of royal propaganda invented by Hartvic a century after Stephen's reign, when the king had become a Catholic saint.*

115. Columbus Sees Mermaids
Christopher Columbus
Journal of the First Voyage
Entry for January 9, 1493
Spanish
General

On the previous day, when the Admiral went to the *Rio del Oro*, he saw three mermaids, which rose well out of the sea; but they are not so beautiful as they are painted, though to some extent they have the form of a human face. The Admiral says that he had seen some, at other times, in Guinea, on the coast of the Manequeta.

Source: Translated by Clements R. Markham in *The Journal of Christopher Columbus (During His First Voyage, 1492–1493)* (London: Hakluyt Society, 1893), 154.

Commentary: *It is widely believed that Columbus actually saw manatees. The above text is from Las Casas's abstract of Columbus's journal. A near-verbatim summary of the passage appears in his* Historia de las Indias *at 1.430, although there Las Casas says the African mermaids were seen "on the coast of Guinea, where is gathered the* manequeta," *referring to the spice called the Grain of Paradise (Aframomum melegueta).*

116. Nostradamus Predicts Hitler
Nostradamus
The Prophecies 2.24
1555
French
General

Beasts, wild from hunger, to cross rivers
The greater part of the field will be against Hister
In a cage of iron the Great One will be dragged
When the German child observes the Rhine.[1]

Source: Translated by Jason Colavito from *Propheties de Michel Nostradamus* (Avigno: Chez J.-A. Joly, 1815), 45.

Commentary: *Nostradamus' alleged prophecies were written in a mixture of Romance languages, purposely obscuring their content. His reference to "Hister," an ancient name for the Danube, prompted speculation in the twentieth century that the famed seer had predicted the rise of Hitler, who was born in Austria, through which the Danube runs. This quatrain is alleged to describe, in reverse order, Hitler's downfall (lines 1–2), Mussolini's capture (line 3), and the annexation of the Rhineland (line 4). More likely, Nostradamus was describing a historical incident related to the Habsburg Empire, as other so-called prophecies did. The Nazis, however, made propaganda use of Nostradamus. Propaganda minister Joseph Goebbels had false Nos-*

tradamus quatrains printed and dropped on France to demoralize the country. *The Allies countered with their own doctored Nostradamus prophecies, which they distributed in occupied countries.*[2]

Notes

1. Nostradamus uses *Rin*, which could either be taken to mean "Rhine" (*Rhin*) or "nothing" (*rien*) and probably puns on both. The whole sense of this line is uncertain since Nostradamus did not indicate the arrangement of "German," "child," and "Rhine" in terms of subject, object, and adjective.

2. Richard Smoley, *The Essential Nostradamus* (New York: Penguin, 2006), 37–38.

117. A Dinosaur in the Congo

Liévin-Bonaventure Proyart

Histoire de Loango, Kakongo, et autres royaumes d'Afrique, Chapter 6

1776

French

General

The Missionaries have observed, passing along a forest, the trail of an animal they have not seen but which must be monstrous: the marks of its claws were noted upon the earth, and these composed a footprint of about three feet in circumference. By observing the disposition of its footsteps, it was recognized that it was not running in its passage, and it carried its legs at the distance of seven to eight feet apart.

Source: Translated by Jason Colavito from the French in M. l'Abbé Proyart, *Histoire de Loango, Kakongo, et autres royaumes d'Afrique* (Paris: 1776), 38–39.

Commentary: *This passage is often cited as the first account of Mokèlé-mbèmbé, the alleged dinosaur of the Congo. However, based on the size of the footprint given in the text and Proyart's implication that this was one of many creatures of similar bulk, it appears that the Abbé Proyart, a French missionary in the Congo, was describing (secondhand) the footprints of a rhinoceros or a hippopotamus in their historic (but now much diminished) range.*

XII

Apocryphal Texts

Fringe history exists at the intersection of fact and fiction, where no idea, however old, wrong, or bizarre, is ever forgotten or rejected. Old ideas from past centuries are frequently recycled and reinterpreted, presented to new audiences as "suppressed" knowledge that some unknown "they"—usually academia or the government—doesn't want the public to know. It is therefore not surprising that when ancient texts fail to support some of fringe history's most outlandish ideas, its proponents turn to fiction, hoaxes, and fabrication to provide spurious support to unconventional ideas. Sadly, such efforts often include racist, nativist, imperialist, and colonialist texts and ideas, such as the anti–Semitic forgery, *The Protocols of the Elders of Zion*, considered by some ancient astronaut theorists and fringe historians such as David Icke to reveal the secret plans of the aliens or the Illuminati.

To some extent, of course, this has always been the case. Many genuinely ancient texts in the present volume are, in the most literal sense, forgeries. The *Book of Enoch* (**9**), for example, was most certainly not written by the prophet Enoch, though it claims to be a first-person account from his pen. The *Zeno Narrative* is similarly a hoax of more recent vintage. Modern fabricators follow in the footsteps of earlier authors who sought to create a history that would match their hopes and dreams.

This process continues today; in **62** I pointed to the creation of one such hoax from fragments of the *Mahabharata*. Another example comes from the pen of Peter Kolosimo, the Italian fringe history writer and journalist who in 1968 attributed to the Mayan books of *Chilam Balaam* this non-existent sentence: "Creatures arriving from the sky on flying ships ... white gods who fly above the spheres and reach the stars."[1] This chapter collects nineteenth and twentieth century texts—fiction and fabrication alike—that fringe historians have accepted as genuine ancient documents, or as genuine descriptions of prehistoric material.

Note

1. Peter Kolosimo, *Not of This World,* trans. A. D. Hills (New York: Bantam, 1973), 56.

118. The Stanzas of Dzyan

The Stanzas of Dzyan
Allegedly prehistoric
Allegedly "Senzar," or ancestral Sanskrit
Helena Blavatsky, *Secret Doctrine*, vols. 1 and 2
1888
English
Astro, Theo

Cosmic Evolution.

In Seven Stanzas translated from the Book of Dzyan.

STANZA I

[1] The Eternal Parent wrapped in her Ever-Invisible Robes, had slumbered once again for Seven Eternities.

[2] Time was not, for it lay asleep in the Infinite Bosom of Duration

[3] Universal Mind was not, for there were no Ah-hi to contain it.

[4] The Seven Ways to Bliss were not The Great Causes of Misery were not, for there was no one to produce and get ensnared by them.

[5] Darkness alone filled the Boundless All, for Father, Mother, and Son were once more one, and the Son had not yet awakened for the new Wheel and his Pilgrimage thereon.

[6] The Seven Sublime Lords and the Seven Truths had ceased to be, and the Universe, the Son of Necessity, was immersed in Paranishpanna, to be out breathed by that which is, and yet is not. Naught was.

[7] The Causes of Existence had been done away with; the Visible that was, and the Invisible that is, rested in Eternal Non-Being—the One Being.

[8] Alone, the One Form of Existence stretched boundless, infinite, causeless, in Dreamless Sleep; and Life pulsated unconscious in Universal Space, throughout that All-Presence, which is sensed by the Opened Eye of Dangma

[9] But where was Dangma when the Âlaya of the Universe was in Paramârtha, and the Great Wheel was Anupâdaka?

STANZA II

[1] ... Where were the Builders, the Luminous Sons of Manvantaric Dawn? ... In the Unknown Darkness in their Ah-hi Paranishpanna. The Producers of Form from No-Form—the Root of the World—the Devamâtri and Svabhâvat, rested in the Bliss of Non-Being.

[2] ... Where was Silence? Where the ears to sense it? No, there was neither Silence nor Sound; naught save Ceaseless Eternal Breath, which knows itself not.

[3] The Hour had not yet struck; the Ray had not yet flashed into the Germ; the Mâtripadma had not yet swollen.

[4] Her Heart had not yet opened for the One Ray to enter, thence to fall, as Three into Four, into the Lap of Mâyâ.

[5] The Seven were not yet born from the Web of Light. Darkness alone was Father-Mother, Svabhâvat; and Svabhâvat was in Darkness.

[6] These Two are the Germ, and the Germ is One. The Universe was still concealed in the Divine Thought and the Divine Bosom.

STANZA III

[1] ... The last Vibration of the Seventh Eternity thrills through Infinitude. The Mother swells, expanding from within without, like the Bud of the Lotus.

[2] The Vibration sweeps along, touching with its swift Wing the whole Universe and the Germ that dwelleth in Darkness, the Darkness that breathes over the slumbering Waters of Life.

[3] Darkness radiates Light, and Light drops one solitary Ray into the Waters, into the Mother-Deep. The Ray shoots through the Virgin Egg, the Ray causes the Eternal Egg to thrill, and drop the non-eternal Germ, which condenses into the World-Egg.

[4] The Three fall into the Four. The Radiant Essence becomes Seven inside, Seven outside. The Luminous Egg, which in itself is Three, curdles and spreads in milk-white Curds throughout the Depths of Mother, the root that grows in the Depths of the Ocean of Life.

[5] The Root remains, the Light remains, the Curds remain and Still Oeaohoo is One.

[6] The Root of Life was in every Drop of the Ocean of Immortality , and the Ocean was Radiant Light, which was Fire, and Heat, and Motion. Darkness vanished and was no more; it disappeared in its own Essence, the Body of Fire and Water, of Father and Mother.

[7] Behold, O Lanoo, the Radiant Child of the Two, the unparalleled refulgent Glory-Bright Space, Son of Dark Space, who emerges from the Depths of the great Dark Waters. It is Oeaohoo, the Younger, the ***. He shine forth as the Sun, he is the Blazing Divine Dragon of Wisdom; the Eka is Chatur, and Chatur, takes to itself Tri, and the Union produces the Sapta, in whom are the Seven, which become the Tridasha, the Hosts and the Multitudes. Behold him lifting the Veil, and unfurling it from East to West. He shuts out the Above, and leaves the Below to be seen as the Great Illusion. He marks the places for the Shining Ones, and turns the Upper into a shoreless Sea of Fire, and the One Manifested into the Great Waters.

[8] Where was the Germ, and where was now Darkness? Where is the Spirit of the Flame that burns in thy Lamp, O Lanoo? The Germ is That, and That is Light, the White Brilliant Son of the Dark Hidden Father.

[9] Light is Cold Flame, and Flame is Fire, and Fire produces Heat, which yields Water—The Water of Life in the Great Mother.

[10] Father-Mother spin a Web, whose upper end is fastened to Spirit, the Light of the One Darkness, and the lower one to its shadowy end, Matter; and this Web is the Universe, spun out of the Two Substances made in One, which is Svabhâvat.

[11] It expands when the Breath of Fire is upon it; it contracts when the Breath of the Mother touches it. Then the Sons dissociate and scatter, to return into their Mother's Bosom, at the end of the Great Day, and re-become one with her. When it is cooling, it becomes radiant. Its Sons expand and contract through their own Selves and Hearts; they embrace Infinitude.

[12] Then Svabhâvat send Fohat to harden the Atoms. Each is a part of the Web. Reflecting the "Self-Existent Lord," like a Mirror, each becomes in turn a World

Stanza IV

[1] ... Listen, ye Sons of the Earth, to your Instructors—the Sons of the Fire. Learn, there is neither first nor last; for all is One Number, issued from No-Number.

[2] Learn what we, who descend from the Primordial Seven, we, who are born from the Primordial Flame, have learnt from our Fathers...

[3] From the Effulgence of Light—the Ray of the Ever-Darkness—sprang in Space the reawakened Energies; the One from the Egg, the Six, and the Five. Then the Three, the One, the Four, the One, the Five—the Twice Seven, the Sum Total. And these are the Essences, the Flames, the Elements, the Builders, the Numbers, the Arûpa, the Rûpa, and the Force or Divine Man, the Sum Total. And from the Divine Man emanated the Forms, the Sparks, the Sacred Animals, and the Messengers of the Sacred Fathers within the Holy Four.

[4] This was the Army of the Voice, the Divine Mother of the Seven. The Sparks of the Seven are subject to, and the servants of, the First, the Second, the Third, the Fourth,

the Fifth, the Sixth, and the Seventh of the Seven. These are called Spheres, Triangles, Cubes, Lines and Modellers; for thus stands the Eternal Nidâna—the Oi-Ha-Hou.

[5] The Oi-Ha-Hou, which is Darkness, the Boundless, or the No-Number, Adi-Nidâna Svabhâvat, the ○;

i. The Adi-Sanat, the Number, for he is One.

ii. The Voice of the Word, Svabhâvat, the Numbers, for he is One and Nine.

iii. The "Formless Square."

And these Three, enclosed within the ○, are the Sacred Four; and the Ten are the Arûpa Universe. Then come the Sons, the Seven Fighters, the One, the Eight left out, and his Breath which is the Light-Maker.

[6] ... Then the Second Seven, who are the Lipika, produced by the Three. The Rejected Son is One. The "Son-Suns" are countless.

Stanza V

[1] The Primordial Seven, the First Seven Breaths of the Dragon of Wisdom, produce in their turn from their Holy Circumgyrating Breaths the Fiery Whirlwind.

[2] They make of him the Messenger of their Will. The Dzyu becomes Fohat: the swift Son of the Divine Sons, whose Sons are the Lipika, runs circular errands. Fohat is the Steed, and the Thought is the Rider. He passes like lightning through the fiery clouds; takes Three, and Five, and Seven Strides through the Seven Regions above, and Seven below. He lifts his Voice, and calls the innumerable Sparks, and joins them together.

[3] He is their guiding spirit and leader. When he commences work, he separates the Sparks of the Lower Kingdom, that float and thrill with joy in their radiant dwellings, and forms therewith the Germs of Wheels. He places them in the Six Directions of Space, and one in the Middle—the Central Wheel.

[4] Fohat traces spiral lines to unite the Sixth to the Seventh—the Crown. An Army of the Sons of Light stands at each angle; the Lipika, in the Middle Wheel. They say: "This is good." The first Divine World is ready; the First, the Second. Then the "Divine Arûpa" reflects itself in Chhâyâ Loka, the first Garment of Anupâdaka.

[5] Fohat takes five strides, and builds a winged wheel at each corner of the square for the Four Holy Ones.... and their Armies.

[6] The Lipika circumscribe the Triangle, the First One, the Cube, the Second One, and the Pentacle within the Egg. It is the Ring called "Pass not" for those who descend and ascend; who during the Kalpa are progressing towards the Great Day "Be With Us." ... Thus were formed the Arûpa and the Rûpa: from One Light, Seven Lights; from each of the Seven, seven times Seven Lights. The Wheels watch the Ring...

Stanza VI

[1] By the power of the Mother of Mercy and Knowledge, Kwan-Yin—the Triple of Kwan—Shai-Yin, residing in Kwan-Yin-Tien—Fohat, the Breath of their Progeny, the Son of the Sons, having called forth, from the Lower Abyss, the Illusive Form of Sien—Tchan and the Seven Elements.

[2] The Swift and the Radiant One produces the seven Laya Centers, against which none will prevail to the Great Day "Be With Us"; and seats the Universe on these Eternal Foundations, surrounding Sien-Tchan with the Elementary Germs.

[3] Of the Seven—first One manifested, Six concealed; Two manifested, Five concealed; Three manifested, Four concealed; Four produced, Three hidden; Four and One Tsan revealed, Two and One-Half concealed; Six to be manifested, One laid aside. Lastly, Seven Small Wheels revolving; one giving birth to the other.

[4] He builds them in the likeness of older Wheels, placing them on the Imperishable Centers.

How does Fohat build them? He collects the Fiery Dust. He makes Balls of Fire, runs through them, and round them, infusing life therein to, then sets them into motion; some one way, some the other way. They are cold, he makes them hot. They are dry, he makes them moist. They shine, he fans and cools them. Thus acts Fohat from one Twilight to the other, during Seven Eternities.

[5] At the Fourth, the Sons are told to create their Images, One-Third refuses. Two obey.

The Curse is pronounced. They will be born in the Fourth, suffer and cause suffering. This is the First War.

[6] The Older Wheels rotated downward and upward.... The Mother's Spawn filled the whole. There were Battles fought between the Creators and the Destroyers, and Battles fought for Space; the Seed appearing and reappearing continuously.

[7] Make thy calculations, O Lanoo, if thou wouldst learn the correct age of thy Small Wheel. Its Fourth Spoke is our Mother. Reach the Fourth Fruit of the Fourth Path of Knowledge that leads to Nirvana, and thou shalt comprehend, for thou shalt see....

Stanza VII

[1] Behold the beginning of sentient formless Life.

First, the Divine, the One from the Mother Spirit; then, the Spiritual; the Three from the One, the Four from the One, and the Five, from which the Three, the Five and the Seven. These are the Threefold and the Fourfold downward; the Mind-born Sons of the First Lord, the Shining Seven. It is they who are thou, I, he, O Lanoo; they who watch over thee and thy mother, Bhûmi

[2] The One Ray multiplies the smaller Rays. Life precedes Form, and Life survives, the last atom. Through the countless Rays the Life-Ray, the One, like a Thread through many Beads.

[3] When the One becomes Two, the Threefold appears, and the Three are One; and it is our Thread, O Lanoo, the Heart of the Man-Plant called Saptaparna

[4] It is the Root that never dies; the Three-tongued Flame of the Four Wicks. The Wicks are the Sparks, that draw from the Three-tongued Flame shot out by the Seven— their Flame—the Beams and Sparks of one Moon reflected in the running Waves of all the Rivers of Earth.

[5] The Spark hangs from the Flame by the finest thread of Fohat. It journeys through the Seven Worlds of Mâyâ. It stops in the First, and is a Metal and a Stone; it passes into the Second, and behold—a Plant; the Plant whirls through seven changes and becomes a Sacred Animal. From the combined attributes of these, Manu, the Thinker, is formed. Who forms him? The Seven Lives and the One Life. Who completes him? The Fivefold Lha. And who perfects the last Body? Fish, Sin, and Soma....

[6] From the First-born the Thread between the Silent Watcher and his Shadow

becomes more strong and radiant with every Change. The morning Sunlight has changed into noonday glory....

[7] "This thy present Wheel," said the Flame to the Spark. "Thou art myself, my image and my shadow. I have clothed myself in thee, and thou art my Vâhan to the Day "Be With Us," when thou shalt re-become myself and others, thyself and me." Then the Builders, having donned their first Clothing, descent on radiant Earth and reign over men—who are themselves....

Anthropogenesis in the Secret Volume
(verbatim extracts)

STANZA I

[1] The Lha which turns the Fourth is Servant to the Lha(s) of the Seven, they who revolve, driving their Chariots around their Lord, the One Eye of our World. His Breath gave Life to the Seven. It gave Life to the First.

[2] Said the Earth: "Lord of the Shining Face, my House is empty.... Send thy Sons to people this Wheel. Thou has sent thy Seven Sons to the Lord of Wisdom. Seven times doth he see thee nearer to himself, seven times more doth he feel thee. Thou hast forbidden thy Servants, the small Rings, to catch thy Light and Heat, thy great Bounty to intercept on its passage. Send now thy Servant the same."

[3] Said the Lord of the Shining Face: "I Shall send thee a Fire when thy work is commenced. Raise thy voice to other Lokas; apply to thy Father, the Lord of the Lotus, for his Sons.... Thy people shall be under the rule of the Fathers. Thy Men shall be mortals. The Men of the Lord of Wisdom, not the Sons of Soma, are immortal. Cease thy complaints. Thy Seven Skins are yet on thee.... Thou art not ready. Thy Men are not ready."

[4] After great throes she cast off her old Three and put on her new Seven Skins, and stood in her first one.

STANZA II

[5] The Wheel whirled for thirty crores more. It constructed Rûpas; soft Stones that hardened, hard Plants that softened. Visible from invisible Insects and small Lives. She shook them off her back whenever they overran the Mother.... After thirty crores, she turned round. She lay on her back; on her side.... She would call no Sons of Heaven, she would ask no Sons of Wisdom. She created from her own Bosom. She evolved Water-Men, terrible and bad.

[6] The Water-Men, terrible and bad, she herself created from the remains of others. From the dross and slime of her First, Second, and Third, she formed them. The Dhyâni came and looked.... The Dhyâni from the bright Father-Mother, from the White Regions they came, from the Abodes of the Immortal Mortals.

[7] Displeased they were. "Our Flesh is not there. No fit Rûpas for our Brothers of the Fifth. No dwellings for the Lives. Pure Waters, not turbid, they must drink. Let us dry them."

[8] The Flames came. The Fires with the Sparks; the night–Fires and the Day-Fires. They dried out the turbid dark Waters. With their heat they quenched them. The Lhas of the High, the Lha-mayin of Below, came. They slew the Forms which were two- and four-faced. They fought the Goat-Men, and the Dog-Headed Men, and the Men with fishes' bodies.

[9] Mother-Water, the Great Sea, wept. She arose, she disappeared in the Moon, which had lifted her, which had given her birth.

[10] When they were destroyed, Mother Earth remained bare. She asked to be dried.

Stanza III

[11] The Lord of the Lords came. From her Body he separated the Waters, and that was Heaven above, the First Heaven.

[12] The great Chohans called the Lords of the Moon, of the Airy Bodies: "Bring forth Men, Men of your nature. Give them their Forms within. She will build Coverings without. Males-Females will they be. Lords of the Flame also...."

[13] They went each on his allotted Land; Seven of them, each on his Lot. The Lords of the Flame remain behind. They would not go, they would not create.

Stanza IV

[14] The Seven Hosts, the Will-Born Lords, propelled by the Spirit of Life-giving, separate Men from themselves, each on his own Zone.

[15] Seven times seven Shadows of Future Men were born, each of his own Color and Kind. Each inferior to his Father. The Fathers, the Boneless, could give no Life to Beings with Bones. Their progeny were Bhuta, with neither Form nor Mind. Therefore they are called the Chhâyâ Race.

[16] How are the Manushya born? The Manus with minds, how are they made? The Fathers called to their help their own Fire, which is the Fire that burns in Earth. The Spirit of the Earth called to his help the Solar Fire. These Three produced in their joint efforts, a good Rûpa It could stand, walk, run, recline, or fly. Yet it was still but a Chhâyâ, a Shadow with no Sense...

[17] The Breath needed a Form; the Fathers gave it. The Breath needed a Gross Body; the Earth molded it. The Breath needed the Spirit of Life; the Solar Lhas breathed it into its Form. The Breath needed a Mirror of its Body: "We give it our own!"—said the Dhyanis. The Breath needed a Vehicle of Desires: "It has it!"—said the Drainer of Waters. But Breath needs a mind to embrace the Universe: "We cannot give that!"—said the Fathers. "I never had it!" said the Spirit of the Earth. "The Form would be consumed were I to give it mine!"—said the Great Fire.... Man remained an empty senseless Bhûta.... Thus have the Boneless given Life to those who became Men with Bones in the Third.

Stanza V

[18] The First were the Sons of Yoga. Their sons, the children of the Yellow Father and the White Mother.

[19] The Second Race was the product by budding and expansion, the Asexual from the Sexless. Thus was , O Lanoo, the Second Race produced.

[20] Their Fathers were the Self-born. The Self-born, the Chhâyâ from the brilliant bodies of the Lords, the Fathers, the Sons of Twilight.

[21] When the Race became old, the old Waters mixed with the fresher Waters. When its Drop became turbid, they vanished and disappeared in the new Stream, in the hot Stream of Life. The Outer of the First became the Inner of the Second. The Old wing became the new Shadow, and the Shadow of the Wing.

Stanza VI

[22] Then the Second evolved the Egg-born, the Third. The Sweat grew, its Drops grew, and the Drops became hard and round. The Sun warmed it; the Moon cooled and shaped it; the Wind fed it until its ripeness. The White Swan from the Starry Vault overshadowed the big Drop. The Egg of the Future Race, the Man-swan of the later Third. First male-female, then man and woman.

[23] The Self-born were the Chhâyâs, the Shadows from the bodies of the Sons of Twilight. Neither water nor fire could destroy them. Their sons were.

Stanza VII

[24] The Sons of Wisdom, the Sons of Night, ready for rebirth, came down. They saw the vile forms of the First Third. "We can choose," said the Lords; "we have wisdom." Some entered the Chhâyâs. Some projected a Spark. Some deferred till the Fourth. From their own Rûpa they filled the Kâma. Those who entered became Arhats. Those who received but a Spark, remained destitute of knowledge; the Spark burned low. The Third remained mindless. Their Jivas were not ready. These were set apart among the Seven. They became narrow-headed. The Third were ready. "In these shall we dwell," said the Lords of the Flame and of the Dark Wisdom.

[25] How did the Manas, the Sons of Wisdom, act? They rejected the Self-born. They are not ready. They spurned the Sweat-born. They are not quite ready. They would not enter the first Egg-born.

[26] When the Sweat-born produced the Egg-born, the twofold, the mighty, the powerful with bones, the Lords of Wisdom said: "Now shall we create."

[27] The Third Race became the Vâhan of the Lords of Wisdom. It created Sons of Will and Yoga, by Kriyâshakti it created them, the Holy Fathers, Ancestors of the Arhats....

Stanza VIII

[28] From the drops of sweat, from the residue of the substance, matter from dead bodies of men and animals of the Wheel before, and from cast-off dust, the first animals were produced.

[29] Animals with bones, dragons of the deep, and flying Sarpas were added to the creeping things. They that creep on the ground got wings. They of the long necks in the water became the progenitors of the fowls of the air.

[30] During the Third, the boneless animals grew and changed; they became animals with bones, their Chhâyâs became solid.

[31] The animals separated the first. They began to breed. The twofold man separated also. He said: "Let us as they; let us unite and make creatures." They did....

[32] And those which had Spark took huge she-animals unto them. They begat upon them dumb races. Dumb they were themselves. But their tongue untied. The tongues of their progeny remained still. Monsters they bred. A race of crooked red-hair covered monsters going on all fours. A dumb race to keep the shame untold.

Stanza IX

[33] Seeing which, the Lhas who had not built men, wept, saying:

[34] "The Amânasa have defiled our future abodes. This is Karma. Let us dwell in the others. Let us teach them better, lest worse should happen." They did....

[35] Then all men became endowed with Manas. They saw the sin of the mindless.

[36] The Fourth Race developed speech.

[37] The one became two; also all the living and creeping things that were still one, giant fish, birds and serpents with shell-heads.

Stanza X

[38] Thus, two by two, on the seven Zones, the Third Race gave birth to the Fourth; the Sura became A-sura.

[39] The First, on every Zone, was moon-colored; the Second yellow like gold; the Third red; the Fourth brown, which became black with sin. The first seven human shoots were all of one complexion. The next seven began mixing.

[40] Then the Third and Fourth became tall with pride. "We are the kings; we are the gods."

[41] They took wives fair to look upon. Wives from the mindless, the narrow-headed. They bred monsters, wicked demons, male and female, also Khado, with little minds.

[42] They built temples for the human body. Male and female they worshipped. Then the Third Eye acted no longer.

Stanza XI

[43] They build huge cities. Of rare earths and metals they built. Out of the fires vomited, out of the white stone of the mountains and of the black stone, they cut their own images, in their size and likeness, and worshipped them.

[44] They built great images nine yatis high, the size of their bodies. Inner fires had destroyed the land of their fathers. The water threatened the Fourth.

[45] The first great waters came. They swallowed the seven great islands.

[46] All holy saved, the unholy destroyed. With them most of the huge animals, produced from the seat of the earth.

Stanza XII

[47] Few remained. Some yellow, some brown and black, and some red remained. The moon-colored were gone for ever.

[48] The Fifth produced from the holy stock remained; it was ruled over by the first Divine-Kings.

[49] ... The Serpents who re-descended, who made peace with the Fifth, who taught and instructed it....

Source: H. P. Blavatsky, *The Secret Doctrine*, Vol. 1: Cosmogenesis (London: Theosophical Publishing Company, 1888), 27–34, and Vol. 2: Anthropogenesis (London: Theosophical Publishing Company, 1888), 15–21.

Commentary: *Helena Blavtasky concocted the* Stanzas of Dzyan *from a mixture of ancient and occult texts. The influence of Genesis 6:4 (8) on Anthropogenesis 10.41 is fairly obvious, and other passages reflect distorted and reworked sections of eastern and western mysticism, particularly the* Vishnu Purana, *the* Rig Veda *and various Gnostic texts. Its most original element was to suggest that the ancient gods were a sort of space alien, almost a birth certificate for the ancient astronaut theory. Blavatsky claimed to have traveled to Tibet where a secret* *brotherhood gave her access to the* Stanzas, *which she translated from an ancestral version of* Sanskrit; *it was an eastern reflection of Joseph Smith's claim to have translated the Book of Mormon from tablets in "reformed Egyptian" kept safe by angels in upstate New York and an anticipation of James Churchward's claim that a brotherhood in India gave him ancient Muvian tablets in the lost Naacal language, which he too could amazingly translate. Such lost books of prehistoric wisdom, a theme found as far back as the Babylonian flood myth (20), remain a staple of fringe history.*

The Stanzas of Dzyan *were highly influential in ancient astronaut circles. Erich von Däniken in his sequel to* CG, Gods from Outer Space *(1970), took them for a genuine account of ancient aliens and added that the texts were "older than the earth."[1] Perhaps the most interesting part of the* Stanzas *is the close connection between Anthropogenesis 11 and the Old Ones of H. P. Lovecraft's "The Call of Cthulhu" (1926) who similarly build huge cities, make their own images, and succumb to the rising waters. Lovecraft, who referenced Theosophy in that story, in private letters called the belief system behind the colorful mythology "crap." Interestingly, while Blavatsky made the* Stanzas *merely ancient human texts (and Desmond Leslie an Atlantean text), Lovecraft, in "The Diary of Alonzo Typer" (1935) fictionalized them to "antedate the earth"—the same wording Eric von Däniken used to refer to the texts, wording not typically applied to the* Stanzas *in fringe literature.*

Note

1. Erich von Däniken, *Gods from Outer Space,* trans. Michael Heron (New York: Bantam, 1972), 173.

119. Metallic Spacecraft Bombs Dwarkha

Allegedly from the *Mahabharata*
c. 400 BCE–400 CE
Sarath Kumar Ghosh
The Prince of Destiny, Chapter 5
1909
English
Discussion in TG

Krishna's enemies sought the aid of the demons, who built an aerial chariot with sides of iron and clad with wings (that is aeroplanes). The chariot was driven through the sky till it stood over Dwaraka, where Krishna's followers dwelt, and from there it hurled down upon the city missiles that destroyed everything on which they fell....

Source: Sarath Kumar Ghosh, *The Prince of Destiny: The New Krishna* (London: Rebman Limited, 1909), 58–59.

Commentary: *Presented as though it were a genuine passage from the* Mahabharata, *this quotation appears in a novel by the Indian writer Sarath Kumar Ghosh. Within a decade of publication, it was already being cited in works like E. Charles' Vivian's* A History of Aeronautics *(1921) and Charles Turner's* Aircraft of To-Day *(1917). From these sources fringe writers like David Childress picked it up verbatim, unaware that the original source was a novel. The incident in question is a paraphrase of material from* Mahabharata *8.34 (see 62), in which Siva drives a car the gods made from the heavens (its wings were night and day, its wheels the sun and moon) and uses it to destroy Dwarkha. Ghosh's paraphrase over-emphasizes (and, in the case of iron, interpolates) mechanical details.*

120. Frisian Migration from Atlantis
The Oera Linda Book
"How the Bad Times Came"
Allegedly after 800 CE
Old Frisian
Unknown hoaxer
c. 1867
Atlantis

During the whole summer the sun had been hid behind the clouds, as if unwilling to look upon the earth. There was perpetual calm, and the damp mist hung like a wet sail over the houses and the marshes. The air was heavy and oppressive, and in men's hearts was neither joy nor cheerfulness. In the midst of this stillness the earth began to tremble as if she was dying. The mountains opened to vomit forth fire and flames. Some sank into the bosom of the earth, and in other places mountains rose out of the plain. Aldland, called by the seafaring people, Atland, disappeared, and the wild waves rose so high over hill and dale that everything was buried in the sea. Many people were swallowed up by the earth, and others who had escaped the fire perished in the water.

It was not only in Finda's land that the earth vomited fire, but also in Twiskland (Germany). Whole forests were burned one after the other, and when the wind blew from that quarter our land was covered with ashes. Rivers changed their course, and at their mouths new islands were formed of sand and drift.

During three years this continued, but at length it ceased, and forests became visible. Many countries were submerged, and in other places land rose above the sea, and the wood was destroyed through the half of Twiskland (Germany). Troops of Finda's people came and settled in the empty places. Our dispersed people were exterminated or made slaves. Then watchfulness was doubly impressed upon us, and time taught us that union is force.

Source: Translation by William R. Sandbach, *The Oera Linda Book from A Manuscript of the Thirteenth Century* (London: Trübner & Co., 1876), 71.

Commentary: *Allegedly an ancient manuscript telling the story of the Frisians from 2194 BCE to 803 CE, the* Oera Linda Book *was revealed to be a hoax in 1879. Its brief reference to Atlantis (as Atland), however, earned it a notorious footnote in history when SS commander Heinrich Himmler accepted the text as genuine and as "proof" that the German race came from Atlantis. The text became known as "Himmler's Bible," but even many Nazi scholars refused to endorse the hoax.*

121. Jesus Studies in India during the "Lost Years"
Life of Saint Issa 4.1–5.27
Allegedly ancient
Allegedly Tibetan
Nicholas Notovitch
Uknown Life of Jesus Christ
1894
French
General, Theo
Discussion in AF

IV

[1] And now the time had come, which the Supreme Judge, in his boundless clemency, had chosen to incarnate himself in a human being.

[2] And the Eternal Spirit, which dwelt in a state of complete inertness and supreme beatitude, awakened and detached itself from the Eternal Being for an indefinite period,

[3] In order to indicate, in assuming the human form, the means of identifying ourselves with the Divinity and of attaining eternal felicity.

[4] And to teach us, by his example, how we may reach a state of moral purity and separate the soul from its gross envelope, that it may attain the perfection necessary to enter the Kingdom of Heaven which is immutable and where eternal happiness reigns.

[5] Soon after, a wonderful child was born in the land of Israel; God himself, through the mouth of this child, spoke of nothingness of the body and of the grandeur of the soul.

[6] The parents of this new-born child were poor people, belonging by birth to a family of exalted piety, which disregarded its former worldly greatness to magnify the name of the Creator and thank him for the misfortunes with which he was pleased to try them.

[7] To reward them for their perseverance in the path of truth, God blessed the first-born of this family; he chose him as his elect, and sent him forth to raise those that had fallen into evil, and to heal them that suffered.

[8] The divine child, to whom was given the name of Issa, commenced even in his most tender years to speak of the one and indivisible God, exhorting the people that had strayed from the path of righteousness to repent and purify themselves of the sins they had committed.

[9] People came from all parts to listen and marvel at the words of wisdom that fell from his infant lips; all the Israelites united in proclaiming that the Eternal Spirit dwelt within this child.

[10] When Issa had attained the age of thirteen, when an Israelite should take a wife,

[11] The house in which his parents dwelt and earned their livelihood in modest labor, became a meeting place for the rich and noble, who desired to gain for a son-in-law the young Issa, already celebrated for his edifying discourses in the name of the Almighty.

[12] It was then that Issa clandestinely left his father's house, went out of Jerusalem, and, in company with some merchants, traveled toward Sindh [i.e., India].

[13] That he might perfect himself in the divine word and study the laws of the great Buddhas.

V

[1] In the course of his fourteenth year, young Issa, blessed by God, journeyed beyond the Sindh and settled among the Aryas in the beloved country of God.

[2] The fame of his name spread along the Northern Sindh. When he passed through the country of the five rivers and the Radjipoutan, the worshipers of the god Djaïne begged him to remain in their midst.

[3] But he left the misguided admirers of Djaïne and visited Juggernaut, in the province of Orsis, where the remains of Viassa-Kriehna rest, and where he received a joyous welcome from the white priests of Brahma.

[4] They taught him to read and understand the Vedas, to heal by prayer, to teach and explain the Holy Scripture, to cast out evil spirits from the body of man and give him back human semblance.

[5] He spent six years in Juggernaut, Rajegriha, Benares, and the other holy cities; all loved him, for Issa lived in peace with the Vaisyas and the Soudras, to whom he taught the Holy Scripture.

[6] But the Brahmans and the Kshatriyas declared that the Great Para-Brahma forbade them to approach those whom he had created from his entrails and from his feet:

[7] That the Vaisyas were authorized to listen only to the reading of the Vedas, and that never save on feast days.

[8] That the Soudras were not only forbidden to attend the reading of the Vedas, but to gaze upon them even; for their condition was to perpetually serve and act as slaves to the Brahmans, the Kshatriyas, and even to the Vaisyas.

[9] "Death alone can free them from servitude," said Para-Brahma. "Leave them, therefore, and worship with us the gods who will show their anger against you if you disobey them."

[10] But Issa would not heed them; and going to the Soudras, preached against the Brahmans and the Kshatriyas.

[11] He strongly denounced the men who robbed their fellow-beings of their rights as men, saying: "God the Father establishes no difference between his children, who are all equally dear to him."

[12] Issa denied the divine origin of the Vedas and the Pouranas, declaring to his followers that one law had been given to men to guide them in their actions.

[13] "Fear thy God, bow down the knee before Him only, and to Him only must thy offerings be made."

[14] Issa denied the Trimourti and the incarnation of Para-Brahma in Vishnou, Siva, and other gods, saying:

[15] "The Eternal Judge, the Eternal Spirit, composes the one and indivisible soul of the universe, which alone creates, contains, and animates the whole."

[16] "He alone has willed and created, he alone has existed from eternity and will exist without end; he has no equal neither in the heavens nor on this earth."

[17] "The Great Creator shares his power with no one, still less with inanimate objects as you have been taught, for he alone possesses supreme power."

[18] "He willed it, and the world appeared; by one divine thought, he united the waters and separated them from the dry portion of the globe. He is the cause of the mysterious life of man, in whom he has breathed a part of his being."

[19] "And he has subordinated to man, the land, the waters, the animals, and all that he has created, and which he maintains in immutable order by fixing the duration of each."

[20] "The wrath of God shall soon be let loose on man, for he has forgotten his Creator and filled his temples with abominations, and he adores a host of creatures which God has subordinated to him."

[21] "For, to be pleasing to stones and metals, he sacrifices human beings in whom dwells a part of the spirit of the Most High."

[22] "For he humiliates them that labor by the sweat of their brow to gain the favor of an idler who is seated at a sumptuously spread table."

[23] "They that deprive their brothers of divine happiness shall themselves be deprived of it, and the Brahmans and the Kshatriyas shall become the Soudras of the Soudras with whom the Eternal shall dwell eternally."

[24] "For on the clay of the Last Judgment, the Soudras and the Vaisyas shall be forgiven because of their ignorance, while God shall visit his wrath on them that have arrogated his rights."

[25] The Vaisyas and the Soudras were struck with admiration, and demanded of Issa how they should pray to secure their happiness.

[26] "Do not worship idols, for they do not hear you; do not listen to the Vedas, where the truth is perverted; do not believe yourself first in all things, and do not humiliate your neighbor."

[27] "Help the poor, assist the weak, harm no one, do not covet what you have not and what you see in the possession of others."

Source: Translated by Alexina Loranger in Nicholas Notovitch, *The Unknown Life of Jesus Christ,* trans. Alexina Loranger (Chicago: Rand, McNally & Co., 1894), 105–112.

Commentary: *In 1894 Russian traveler Nicholas Notovitch announced his 1887 discovery of a manuscript describing the Indian adventures of Jesus, under his Arabic name Issa, in a Tibetan monastery (a fringe history theme indeed!), causing a sensation. After inconsistencies in his story emerged and the monastery denied knowing Notovitch or owning the document, Notovitch confessed it was a hoax. Nevertheless, it contributed to Islamic, Hindu, and esoteric claims of Jesus' tutelage in India that continue to be promoted down to the present.*

122. Arabs Discover the Americas in 999 CE

Ibn Umar al-Gutiyya (Ibn-el-Qouthia)
Allegedly medieval
Allegedly Arabic
Don Manuel Osuna Saviñón
Resumen de la jeografía física y política, y de la historia natural y civil de las islas Canarias
1844
Spanish
Hyper

Al-Jazir Al-Kaledat, that is, the Fortunate Isles, says Ibn-el-Qouthia,[1] were inhabited in the late tenth century, when the famous Ben-Farroukh[2] traveled to them with other Arabs, landing on the island of Canaria. This expedition, which took place in the reign of Abdelmehc[3] in the Arab year of 334, year 999 of Jesus Christ,[4] was the first of which we have certain knowledge. Ben-Farroukh, who at the time commanded one of the vessels defending the coasts of Spain against two Norman invasions, supposed there existed some islands beyond the Atlas Mountains, which because of their mild climate and fertility the ancients had rightly given the name of Fortunate.

Carried away by this implausible hope, he set out for the archipelago, and sighting the island of Gran Canaria, discovered the port of Gando, in which he landed in the month of February in the year 999. He entered at the head of 130 men that were with him, having to overcome all the difficulties that may hinder communications in a wild country, for the mountains were covered with thick forests, in which he could barely make his way through the trees.

A foreign presence was not a new spectacle for the Canaria natives, for they remembered several other expeditions of the Arabs, from which some of their companions had stayed among them so that the first relations of the captain with the islanders were very friendly.

He visited Guanariga, who was King or Guanarteme of Gáldar, and the Guayres or Counselors, and gave them to understand, through his interpreter, that he and his companions were sent by a powerful monarch to pay tribute to the goodness, courage, and generosity of this prince, and that they had braved the dangers of a long journey to establish friendly relations with him on behalf of their sovereign.

Guanariga was flattered with the embassy and intrigued by so much deference, believing himself to be even more powerful than in reality he was, since a monarch of some distant nation had come to ask his friendship; he sent to have the Arabs conducted to his palace, which they found adorned with flowers and palm branches, and well supplied with fruits and roasted barley flour, which is done in the Canaries to entertain new guests.

Ben-Farroukh, who wanted to visit the whole archipelago of the Fortunates, sailed to the west and surveyed four islands, designating them by the names of "Ningaria," rising to the clouds; "Junonia," a small island located to the south and very close to the first; and the islands "Aprositus" and "Hero," of which the last was the westernmost. Navigating then to the east of Canaria he found "Capraria" and next to it "Pluitana," which was near the African coast.[5]

Having surveyed the other islands of the archipelago and visited some of them on foot, Ben-Farroukh decided to return to Spain, not only because food was scarce but because they had to report to their monarch about the lands they had explored. So they returned in May of the year 999, after having remained in the islands about three months.

Source: Translated by Jason Colavito from the Spanish of Don Manuel Osuna Saviñón, *Resumen de la jeografía física y política, y de la historia natural y civil de las islas Canarias,* vol. 1 (Santa Cruz de Teneriff: V. Bonnett, 1844), 16–21. I have omitted the analysis Osuna Saviñón offered between paragraphs.

Commentary: *Islamic authors like Youssef Mroueh and other fringe historians claim this text as evidence of pre–Columbian Arab discovery of the Americas, suggesting that the last two islands visited were in the Caribbean rather than the Canaries.[6] The Spanish author of the text claimed that it was his own translation of an 1842 French translation of the Arabic original, made by a M. Étienne from Manuscript No. 13 in the non-existent "Biblioteca de París." Diligent work by Dr. Chil y Naranjo in the 1870s and Buenaventura Bonnet in the 1940s determined that the entire text was a hoax. The text adapts Classical material from Pliny's description of the Fortunate Islands in* Natural History *3.67 as well as material from the eighteenth century-historian José de Viera y Clavijo, author of a famous volume on the Canary Islands. Part of Viera y Clavijo's* Noticias *reads, in my translation, "that the Arabs, being owners of Spain and Portugal, embarked from Lisbon on a navigation to the west, and after long rough seas were forced to retreat to the Canaries...."[7] He further states that "you can rest assured that the Moors from the Peninsula had some knowledge of the Canary Islands, under the name of Al-Jazir Al-Kaledat, i.e., the* Fortunate Isles...."[8] *Many other direct plagiarisms occur, as well as a corruption of names from Viera y Clavijo's warrior Gariraygua to Osuna Saviñón's king Guanariga.*

Notes

1. A fictitious author of whom there is no trace before publication of the *Resumen.* The Francophone spelling reflects the author's claim to be translating from a French translation of the text.

2. The name is fictitious, derived apparently from the Andalusian use of the Arabic word *farrūǧ* as an epithet for valiant men. The word, which refers to young roosters, carried the meaning of "cocky."

3. The author is apparently referring to Abd al-Malik al-Muzaffar, Romanized in the nineteenth century

as Abdelmelic. He was the hajib (chamberlain) of Cordoba from 1002 to 1008 CE and the de facto ruler of Al-Andalus under the ineffective caliph of Cordoba, Hisham II. The author, or the typesetter, has obviously misread "*li*" as "*h*." The author likely confused Abd al-Malik's military title of *emir* (general), awarded after a battle in 987 CE by Hisham II, for its later use in Islamic history as a royal title for a prince.

4. The author has incorrectly correlated the Islamic and Western calendars, where, for the month of February, AH 389 = 999 CE, and AH 334 = 946 CE.

5. The names appear in Pliny's *Natural History* at 3.67, from which the author has crafted his description and applied it to the seven main Canary Islands.

6. Mroueh purposely ignores the easterly direction of these islands near Africa.

7. José de Viera y Clavijo, *Noticias de la historia general de las Islas de Canaria,* vol. 1 (Madrid: 1772), 264.

8. Ibid., 266–267.

123. Norse and Swedish Explorers in Minnesota

Kensington Rune Stone

Allegedly 1362

Old Swedish

Hyper, Holy

[8] Götalanders and 22 Northmen on an exploring (or acquisition) expedition from Vinland west. We camped by 2 skerries one day's journey north from this stone. We were a-fishing one day; after we came home we found 10 men red with blood and dead. A.V.M. (= Ave Maria) Save from evil.

(There) are 10 men by the sea (or lake) to look after our ships 14 days' journey from this island (or peninsula). Year 1362.

Source: Adapted from a translation by George T. Flom, *The Kensington Rune-stone: An Address* (Springfield: Author, 1910), 28, with corrections after the recent translation by Henrik Williams.

Commentary: *One of the most controversial of all artifacts documenting pre–Columbian European visitation to America, the Kensington Rune Stone, discovered in 1898 near Kensington, Minnesota, is widely believed to be a hoax,[1] one of many similar archaeological frauds created in the nineteenth century to support various diffusionist claims. In AF and elsewhere, Scott Wolter believes the text contains a hidden code from the successors to the Knights Templar, claiming the Mississippi watershed for the Holy Bloodline of Jesus.*

Note

1. George T. Flom made a famous early case for a hoax in *The Kensington Rune-Stone: An Address* (Springfield, 1910). Erik Wahlgren did the same in *The Kensington Stone: A Mystery Solved* (Madison: University of Wisconsin Press, 1958) and Theodore Christian Blegen in *The Kensington Rune Stone: New Light on an Old Riddle* (Minnesota Historical Society, 1968). Wahlgren updated his critique for *The Vikings in America* (London: Thames and Hudson, 1986). A more recent treatment that leans toward authenticity is Alice Beck Kehoe, *The Kensington Runestone: Approaching a Research Question Holistically* (Long Grove, IL: Waveland Press, 2005). But see also Kenneth Feder, *The Encyclopedia of Dubious Archaeology* (Greenwood, 2010), s.v. "Kensington Stone" for an opposing view.

124. George Washington Encounters an Angel or Alien

Allegedly by George Washington

Allegedly 1777 of 1778, recounted by "Anthony Sherman" in 1859

English

Charles Wesley Alexander

"Washington's Vision"

1861
Astro
Discussion in AA

I do not know whether it was owing to the anxiety of my mind, or what, but this after-noon, as I was sitting at this very table, engaged in preparing a dispatch, something in the apartment seemed to disturb me. Looking up, I beheld, standing directly opposite me, a sin-gularly beautiful female. So astonished was I—for I had given strict orders not to be dis-turbed—that it was some moments before I found language to inquire the cause of her presence. A second, third, and even a fourth time did I repeat the question, but received no answer from my mysterious visitor other than a slight raising of her eyes. By this time I felt a strange sensation spreading through me. I would have risen, but the riveted gaze of the being before me rendered volition impossible. I essayed once more to address her, but my tongue had become paralyzed. A new influence, mysterious, potent, irresistible, took pos-session of me. All I could do was to gaze steadily, vacantly, at my unknown visitant. Gradually, the surrounding atmosphere seemed as though becoming filled with sensations, and grew luminous. Everything about me appeared to rarify, the mysterious visitor herself becoming more airy and yet even more distinct to my sight than before. I now began to feel as one dying or rather to experience the sensations which I have some times imagined accompany dissolution. I did not think, I did not reason, I did not move; all were alike impossible. I was only conscious of gazing fixedly, vacantly, at my companion.

Presently I heard a voice, saying, "Son of the Republic, look and learn!" while at the same time, my visitor extended her arm and forefinger eastwardly. I now beheld a heavy white vapor at some distance, rising fold upon fold. This gradually dissipated, and I looked upon a strange scene. Before me lay stretched out in one vast plane, all the countries of the world—Europe, Asia, Africa and America. I saw rolling and tossing between Europe and America the billows of the Atlantic, and between Asia and America lay the Pacific. "Son of the Republic," said the same mysterious voice as before, "look and learn!"

At that moment I beheld a dark, shadowy being like an angel, standing, or rather floating in mid-air, between Europe and America. Dipping water out of the ocean in the hollow of each hand, he sprinkled some upon America with his right hand, whilst he cast upon Europe some with his left. Immediately a dark cloud arose from each of these countries, and joined in mid ocean. For a while it remained stationary and then moved slowly westward until it enveloped America in its murky folds. Sharp flashes of lightning now gleamed throughout it at intervals, and I heard the smothered groans and cries of the American people.

"A second time the angel dipped from the ocean and sprinkled it out as before. The dark cloud was then drawn back to the ocean, into whose heaving waves it sunk from view. A third time I heard the mysterious voice, saying, 'Son of the Republic look and learn.'"

I cast my eyes upon America, and beheld villages, towns, and cities springing up, one after another, until the whole land, from the Atlantic to the Pacific, was dotted with them. Again I heard the mysterious voice say, "Son of the Republic, the end of a century cometh—look and learn."

At this the dark, shadowy angel turned his face southward, and from Africa I saw an ill-omened spectre approaching our land. It flitted slowly and heavily over every village, town, and city of the latter, the inhabitants of which presently set themselves in battle array, one against the other. As I continued looking, I saw a bright angel, on whose brow rested a crown of light, on which was traced the word Union, bearing the American flag, which he placed between the divided nations, and said: "Remember, ye are brethren!"

Instantly, the inhabitants, casting from them their weapons, became friends once more, and united around the national standard. And again I heard the mysterious voice saying, "Son of the Republic, the second peril is passed—look and learn."

And I beheld the villages, towns, and cities of America increase in size and numbers, till at last they covered all the land from the Atlantic to the Pacific, and their inhabitants became as countless as the stars in Heaven, or as the sand on the sea shore. And again I heard the mysterious voice, saying, "Son of the Republic, the end of a century— look and learn."

At this, the dark, shadowy angel placed a trumpet to his mouth, and blew three distinct blasts, and taking water from the ocean, sprinkled it out upon Europe, Asia, and Africa.

Then my eyes looked upon a fearful scene. From each of those countries arose thick, black clouds, which soon joined into one; and throughout this mass gleamed a dark-red light, by which I saw hordes of armed men, who, moving with the cloud, marched by land and sailed by sea to America, which country was presently enveloped in the volume of the cloud. And I dimly saw these vast armies devastate the whole country, and pillage and burn villages, cities, and towns that I had beheld springing up. As my ears listened to the thundering of cannon, clashing of swords, and shouts and cries of millions in mortal combat, I again heard the mysterious voice saying, "Son of the Republic, look and learn."

When the voice had ceased, the dark, shadowy angel placed his trumpet once more to his mouth, and blew a long and fearful blast.

Instantly alight, as from a thousand suns, shone down from above me, and pierced and broke into fragments the dark cloud which enveloped America. At the same moment I saw the angel upon whose forehead still shone the word Union, and who bore our national flag in one hand and a sword in the other, descended from Heaven, attended by legions of bright spirits. These immediately joined the inhabitants of America, who I perceived were nigh overcome, but who, immediately taking courage again, closed up their broken ranks and renewed the battle. Again amid the fearful noise of the conflict, I heard the mysterious voice, paying, "Son of the Republic, look and learn."

As the voice ceased, the shadowy angel, for the last time, dipped water from the ocean and sprinkled it upon America. Instantly the dark cloud rolled back, together with the armies it had brought, leaving the inhabitants of the land victorious. Then once more I beheld the villages, towns and cities, springing up where they had been before, while the bright angel, planted the azure standard he had brought in the midst of them, cried in a loud voice to the inhabitants: "While the stars remain and the heavens send down dews upon the earth, so long shall the Republic last!"

And taking from his brow the crown, on which still blazed the word Union, he placed it upon the standard, while all the people kneeling down, said "Amen!"

The scene instantly began to fade and dissolve, and I saw nothing but the rising, curling white vapor I had first beheld. This also disappearing I found myself once more gazing upon my mysterious visitor, who in the same mysterious voice I had heard before, said: "Son of the Republic, what you have seen is thus interpreted: three perils will come upon the Republic. The most fearful is the second, passing which, the whole world united shall never be able to prevail against her. Let every child of the Republic learn to live for his God, his Land, and Union!"

With these words the figure vanished. I started from my seat, and felt that I had been shown the birth, progress, and destiny of the Republic of the United States. In Union she will have her strength, in Disunion her destruction.

Source: Wesley Bradshaw, "Washington's Vision," *The Guardian*, July 1861, 198–200.

Commentary: *Ancient astronaut theorists interpret this hoax text as proof Washington encountered an alien disguised as an angel. In truth, Charles Wesley Alexander penned this piece, allegedly by a very old man who knew Washington, and published it under a fake name as an allegory for the triumph of the Union in the Civil War. Other fringe theorists accept the text as referring to a real angel, while ghost hunters suggest a communication from the spirit realm.*

125. An "Egyptian" Tomb in the Grand Canyon

Arizona Gazette
March 12, 1909
English
Prehistoric, Hyper

G. E. Kincaid Reaches Yuma

G. E. Kincaid of Lewiston, Idaho, arrived in Yuma after a trip from Green River, Wyoming, down the entire course of the Colorado River. He is the second man to make this journey and came alone in a small skiff, stopping at his pleasure to investigate the surrounding country. He left Green River in October having a small covered boat with oars, and carrying a fine camera, with which he secured over 700 views of the river and canyons which were unsurpassed. Mr. Kincaid says one of the most interesting features of the trip was passing through the sluiceways at Laguna dam. He made this perilous passage with only the loss of an oar.

Some interesting archaeological discoveries were unearthed and altogether the trip was of such interest that he will repeat it next winter in the company of friends.

Source: *Arizona Gazette*, March 12, 1909.

ARIZONA GAZETTE

April 5, 1909
English
Prehistoric, Hyper
Discussion in AA

Explorations in Grand Canyon
Mysteries of Immense High Cavern Being Brought to Light
Jordan Is Enthused
Remarkable Finds Indicate Ancient People Migrated from Orient

The latest news of the progress of the explorations of what is now regarded by scientists as not only the oldest archeological discovery in the United States, but one of the most valuable in the world, which was mentioned some time ago in the Gazette, was brought to the city yesterday by G.E. Kinkaid, the explorer who found the great underground citadel of the Grand Canyon during a trip from Green River, Wyoming, down the Colorado, in a wooden boat, to Yuma, several months ago.

According to the story related to the Gazette by Mr. Kinkaid, the archeologists of the Smithsonian Institute,[1] which is financing the expeditions, have made discoveries which almost conclusively prove that the race which inhabited this mysterious cavern, hewn in solid rock by human hands, was of oriental origin, possibly from Egypt, tracing back to Ramses. If their theories are borne out by the translation of the tablets engraved with hieroglyphics, the mystery of the prehistoric peoples of North America, their ancient arts, who they were and whence they came, will be solved. Egypt and the Nile, and Arizona and the Colorado will be linked by a historical chain running back to ages which staggers the wildest fancy of the fictionist.

A Thorough Examination

Under the direction of Prof. S. A. Jordan, the Smithsonian Institute is now prosecuting the most thorough explorations, which will be continued until the last link in the chain is forged. Nearly a mile underground, about 1480 feet below the surface, the long main passage has been delved into, to find another mammoth chamber from which radiates scores of passageways, like the spokes of a wheel.

Several hundred rooms have been discovered, reached by passageways running from the main passage, one of them having been explored for 854 feet and another 634 feet. The recent finds include articles which have never been known as native to this country, and doubtless they had their origin in the orient. War weapons, copper instruments, sharp-edged and hard as steel, indicate the high state of civilization reached by these strange people. So interested have the scientists become that preparations are being made to equip the camp for extensive studies, and the force will be increased to thirty or forty persons.

Mr. Kinkaid's Report

Mr. Kinkaid was the first white child born in Idaho and has been an explorer and hunter all his life, thirty years having been in the service of the Smithsonian Institute. Even briefly recounted, his history sounds fabulous, almost grotesque.

"First, I would impress that the cavern is nearly inaccessible. The entrance is 1,486 feet down the sheer canyon wall. It is located on government land and no visitor will be allowed there under penalty of trespass. The scientists wish to work unmolested, without fear of archeological discoveries being disturbed by curio or relic hunters.

"A trip there would be fruitless, and the visitor would be sent on his way. The story of how I found the cavern has been related, but in a paragraph: I was journeying down the Colorado river in a boat, alone, looking for mineral. Some forty-two miles up the river from the El Tovar Crystal canyon, I saw on the east wall, stains in the sedimentary formation about 2,000 feet above the river bed. There was no trail to this point, but I finally reached it with great difficulty.

"Above a shelf which hid it from view from the river, was the mouth of the cave. There are steps leading from this entrance some thirty yards to what was, at the time the cavern was inhabited, the level of the river. When I saw the chisel marks on the wall inside the entrance, I became interested, securing my gun and went in. During that trip I went back several hundred feet along the main passage till I came to the crypt in which I discovered the mummies. One of these I stood up and photographed by flashlight. I gathered a number of relics, which I carried down the Colorado to Yuma, from whence I shipped them to Washington with details of the discovery.[2] Following this, the explorations were undertaken."

In the nineteenth and early twentieth centuries, Tibet was seen as a mysterious land of ancient secrets. On multiple occasions fringe writers have proposed that Buddhists from Tibet colonized the Americas, citing alleged similarities between Buddhist religion and iconography and those of ancient American peoples. The 1909 *Arizona Gazette* hoax alleged that an ancient statue resembling Buddha, described much like this Buddha statue from Kamakura in Japan, was found in an underground cave (Library of Congress).

THE PASSAGES

"The main passageway is about 12 feet wide, narrowing to nine feet toward the farther end. About 57 feet from the entrance, the first side-passages branch off to the right and left, along which, on both sides, are a number of rooms about the size of ordinary living rooms of today, though some are 30 by 40 feet square. These are entered by oval-shaped doors and are ventilated by round air spaces through the walls into the passages. The walls are about three feet six inches in thickness.

"The passages are chiseled or hewn as straight as could be laid out by an engineer. The ceilings of many of the rooms converge to a center. The side-passages near the entrance run at a sharp angle from the main hall, but toward the rear they gradually reach a right angle in direction."

THE SHRINE

"Over a hundred feet from the entrance is the cross-hall, several hundred feet long, in which are found the idol, or image, of the people's god, sitting cross-legged, with a lotus flower or lily in each hand. The cast of the face is oriental, and the carving this cavern. The idol almost resembles Buddha,[3] though the scientists are not certain as to what religious worship it represents. Taking into consideration everything found thus far, it is possible that this worship most resembles the ancient people of Tibet.[4]

"Surrounding this idol are smaller images, some very beautiful in form; others crooked-necked and distorted shapes, symbolical, probably, of good and evil. There are two large cactus with protruding arms, one on each side of the dais on which the god squats. All this is carved out of hard rock resembling marble. In the opposite corner of this cross-hall were found tools of all descriptions, made of copper. These people undoubtedly knew the lost art of hardening this metal, which has been sought by chemicals for centuries without result. On a bench running around the workroom was some charcoal and other material probably used in the process. There is also slag and stuff similar to matte, showing that these ancients smelted ores, but so far no trace of where or how this was done has been discovered, nor the origin of the ore.

"Among the other finds are vases or urns and cups of copper and gold, made very artistic in design. The pottery work includes enameled ware and glazed vessels. Another passage-way leads to granaries such as are found in the oriental temples. They contain seeds of various kinds. One very large storehouse has not yet been entered, as it is twelve feet high and can be reached only from above. Two copper hooks extend on the edge, which indicates that some sort of ladder was attached. These granaries are rounded, as the materials of which they are constructed, I think, is a very hard cement. A gray metal is also found in this cavern, which puzzles the scientists, for its identity has not been established. It resembles platinum. Strewn promiscuously over the floor everywhere are what people call 'cats eyes,' a yellow stone of no great value. Each one is engraved with the head of the Malay type."

THE HIEROGLYPHICS

"On all the urns, or walls over doorways, and tablets of stone which were found by the image are the mysterious hieroglyphics, the key to which the Smithsonian Institute hopes yet to discover. The engraving on the tables probably has something to do with the religion of the people. Similar hieroglyphics have been found in southern Arizona. Among the pictorial writings, only two animals are found. One is of prehistoric type."

The Crypt

"The tomb or crypt in which the mummies were found is one of the largest of the chambers, the walls slanting back at an angle of about 35 degrees. On these are tiers of mummies, each one occupying a separate hewn shelf. At the head of each is a small bench, on which is found copper cups and pieces of broken swords. Some of the mummies are covered with clay, and all are wrapped in a bark fabric.

"The urns or cups on the lower tiers are crude, while as the higher shelves are reached, the urns are finer in design, showing a later stage of civilization.[5] It is worthy of note that all the mummies examined so far have proved to be male, no children or females being buried here. This leads to the belief that this exterior section was the warriors' barracks.

"Among the discoveries no bones of animals have been found, no skins, no clothing, no bedding. Many of the rooms are bare but for water vessels. One room, about 40 by 700 feet, was probably the main dining hall, for cooking utensils are found here. What these people lived on is a problem, though it is presumed that they came south in the winter and farmed in the valleys, going back north in the summer.

"Upwards of 50,000 people could have lived in the caverns comfortably. One theory is that the present Indian tribes found in Arizona are descendants of the serfs or slaves of the people which inhabited the cave.[6] Undoubtedly a good many thousands of years before the Christian era, a people lived here which reached a high stage of civilization. The chronology of human history is full of gaps. Professor Jordan is much enthused over the discoveries and believes that the find will prove of incalculable value in archeological work.

"One thing I have not spoken of, may be of interest. There is one chamber of the passageway to which is not ventilated, and when we approached it a deadly, snaky smell struck us. Our light would not penetrate the gloom, and until stronger ones are available we will not know what the chamber contains. Some say snakes, but other boo-hoo this idea and think it may contain a deadly gas or chemicals used by the ancients. No sounds are heard, but it smells snaky just the same. The whole underground installation gives one of shaky nerves the creeps. The gloom is like a weight on one's shoulders, and our flashlights and candles only make the darkness blacker. Imagination can revel in conjectures and ungodly daydreams back through the ages that have elapsed till the mind reels dizzily in space."

An Indian Legend

In connection with this story, it is notable that among the Hopi Indians the tradition[7] is told that their ancestors once lived in an underworld in the Grand Canyon till dissension arose between the good and the bad, the people of one heart and the people of two hearts. Machetto, who was their chief, counseled them to leave the underworld, but there was no way out. The chief then caused a tree to grow up and pierce the roof of the underworld, and then the people of one heart climbed out. They tarried by Paisisvai (Red River), which is the Colorado, and grew grain and corn.

They sent out a message to the Temple of the Sun, asking the blessing of peace, good will and rain for people of one heart. That messenger never returned, but today at the Hopi villages at sundown can be seen the old men of the tribe out on the housetops gazing toward the sun, looking for the messenger. When he returns, their lands and ancient dwelling place will be restored to them. That is the tradition.

Among the engravings of animals in the cave is seen the image of a heart over the spot where it is located. The legend was learned by W.E. Rollins,[8] the artist, during a year spent with the Hopi Indians.

There are two theories of the origin of the Egyptians. One is that they came from Asia; another that the racial cradle was in the upper Nile region. Heeren,[9] an Egyptologist, believed in the Indian origin of the Egyptians. The discoveries in the Grand Canyon may throw further light on human evolution and prehistoric ages.

Source: *Arizona Gazette*, April 5, 1909.

Commentary: *The above articles are an elaborate but fairly typical example of their era's newspaper hoaxes, a frequent occurrence before World War I and the subsequent rise of objective journalism and increased journalistic professionalism. Better known hoaxes on similar themes include the* New York Sun*'s infamous Great Moon Hoax of August 25–31, 1835, which fooled many into believing flying aliens had been found on the moon; the* New York American*'s October 12, 1912 Atlantis hoax, which tried to convince readers that the grandson of famed archaeological adventurer Heinrich Schliemann had uncovered proof of the existence of Atlantis; and Mark Twain's humorous October 4, 1862 Petrified Man hoax in the* Territorial Enterprise*, which claimed that an ancient man had turned to stone and had been recently uncovered, frozen while thumbing his nose. All three fooled many readers.*

The careful reader will note that the earlier of the two Arizona Gazette *articles, possibly based on a story represented to the paper as true, contradicts key elements of the second and more elaborate article, for it makes no suggestion that a civilization had been uncovered, or that the Smithsonian was involved; indeed, the first version makes "Kinkaid" claim that the Laguna dam was more interesting than the archaeological discoveries!*

This hoax was not taken seriously in its day and was forgotten until the 1990s, but thanks to promotion from David Hatcher Childress, David Icke, Ancient Aliens, *and Scott Wolter, the story is now firmly entrenched in fringe literature as part of a vast Smithsonian cover-up. There is no record of any Smithsonian expedition to the Grand Canyon in 1909, or of G. E. Kinkaid or S. A. Jordan, nor is there any known cave fitting the description given above.*

Notes

1. Note that the hoaxer has mistakenly labeled the Smithsonian an Institute instead of an Institution.

2. The fact that these fictitious mummies do not exist in Smithsonian vaults led to David Childress's allegations of a Smithsonian cover-up in "SmithsonianGate," *World Explorer* 1, no. 3 (1993), yielding an entire sub-genre of conspiracy theories.

3. Cf. the Buddhists of Fusang in **95**. At the time, Native peoples, particularly the Maya, were thought to have a Buddhist-like religion.

4. At the time, the ancient peple of Tibet were imagined to be the earliest Aryans. Heinrich Himmler, who connected Tibet to Atlantis (see **120**), would send an expedition there in search of these remnant Aryans in 1938.

5. Note that if taken literally, this implies a *development* of civilization from crude to complex, contradicting later claims that a technologically-advanced or extraterrestrial culture first settled here.

6. Note the implicit racism.

7. This is a genuine Hopi legend.

8. Warren Eliphalet Rollins (1861–1962), a regional artist specializing in painting southwestern life. He spent all of 1900 painting the Hopi and Navajo in Arizona.

9. Arnold Hermann Ludwig Heeren (1760–1846) was not an Egyptologist but a historian. He speculated on the Vedic origins of the Egyptians, believing that the Aryans of India were the oldest civilization on earth.

126. Jewish Romans Colonize Medieval Arizona

Tucson Lead Artifacts
Artifact #18
Allegedly c. 775–1000 CE
Latin
Hyper
Discussion in AF

We were carried (or sailed) by sea to Rome Calalus,[1] an unknown land. They[2] came in the Year of Our Lord 775, and the peoples' Theodorus reigned.[3]

Source: Translated by Jason Colavito from a lead sword discovered near Tucson in 1924.

Commentary: *The many lead artifacts with their Hebrew and Latin inscriptions are said to document the rise and fall of Calalus, a Jewish-Roman colony in Arizona that fought the Toltecs of Mexico, whose supposed king was Toltezus Sylvanus. Fringe writers' translations of the very poor Latin on the lead artifacts (which archaeologists determined to be a hoax[4]) routinely smooth out the serious problems with the Latin grammar. More damning is the fact several lead artifacts contain sample Latin sentences given in Albert Harkness's popular* Latin Grammar *(1881), including this line from Sallust's* Conspiracy of Catiline *60.4: "Catilina in prima acie versari, omnia providere, multum ipse pugnare, saepe hostum ferire" ("Catiline was active in the front line, he attended to everything, fought much in person, and often smote down the enemy," as Harkness translates). In AF, Scott Wolter simply declines to consider the translation issues (he uses only Google Translate) and instead claims the artifacts are "Proto-Templar."*

Notes

1. The phrase "from Rome to Calalus" is probably intended, but an incorrect preposition and the wrong case are used. The original reads: "*Provehimur pelago ad Romam Calalvs terra incognita. Venervnt Anno Domini DCCLXXV et regnavit popvlorvm Theodorus.*"
2. The text inexplicably changes from first person to third.
3. Translated literally. I think the intended meaning was supposed to be "Theodorus ruled over the people," but "people" is in the genitive rather than the accusative, and in the plural rather than singular.
4. See Don Burgess, "Romans in Tucson? The Story of an Archaeological Hoax," *Journal of the Southwest* 51, no. 1 (2009): 3–102.

Index

Page numbers in **bold italics** indicate pages with illustrations.